Early Education and
Psychological Development

Early Education and Psychological Development

BARBARA BIBER

Yale University Press
New Haven and London

Acknowledgment is here given for permission to use previously copyrighted material, which appears as the first article in chapters 3–12. 3: From EDUCATION AND THE IDEA OF MAN, edited by Robert Ulich, © 1964 by the Council for the Study of Mankind. Reprinted by permission of Harcourt Brace Jovanovich, Inc. 4 (with Edna Shapiro and David Wickens): Reprinted by permission from *Promoting Cognitive Growth: A Developmental-Interaction Point of View*. Copyright © 1971, National Association for the Education of Young Children, 1834 Connecticut Avenue N.W., Washington, D.C. 20009. 5: Reprinted by permission of Barbara Biber and the Association for Childhood Education International, 3615 Wisconsin Avenue, N.W., Washington, D.C. Copyright © 1967 by the Association. 6 (with Patricia Minuchin): In *Language Remediation for the Disadvantaged Preschool Child*, Marvin A. Brottman (Ed.). Reprinted from Monographs of the Society for Research in Child Development, Serial No. 124, *1968*, Vol. 33, No. 8. 7: Reprinted by permission from *Young Children*, Volume 24, no. 4 (March 1969), pp. 195–205. Copyright © 1969 by National Association for the Education of Young Children, 1834 Connecticut Ave., N.W., Washington, DC 20009. 8: Reprinted by permission of Bank Street College of Education, New York, New York. 9: Originally published in the *Vassar Alumnae Magazine*, Vol. XXXVII, no. 2, 1951. 10: Reprinted, with permission, from the AMERICAN JOURNAL OF ORTHOPSYCHIATRY: copyright 1959 by the American Orthopsychiatric Association, Inc. 11: In *The Preschool in Action: Exploring Early Childhood Programs* (2nd ed.) M. C. Day & R. K. Parker (Eds.) Boston, 1977. 12 (with Margery B. Franklin): In L. G. Katz (Ed.) Current Topics in Early Childhood Education (Vol. 1) Ablex Publishing Corporation, Norwood, N.J. 1977.

Published with assistance from the foundation established in memory of Philip Hamilton McMillan of the Class of 1894, Yale College.

Designed by James J. Johnson
and set in Aldus & Palatino types.
Printed in the United States of America by
Edwards Brothers, Inc., Ann Arbor, Michigan.

Library of Congress Cataloging in Publication Data

Biber, Barbara, 1903–
    Early education and psychological development.

    Bibliography: p.
    Includes index.
    1. Education, Preschool.   2. Child psychology.
3. Child development.   4. Interaction analysis in education.   5. Play. I. Title.
LB1140.2.B523   1984   372'.21   84–40190
ISBN 0–300–02802–4

The paper in this book meets the guidelines for permanence and durability of the Committee on Production Guidelines for Book Longevity of the Council on Library Resources.

10 9 8 7 6 5 4 3 2 1

Contents

Part 3   Inner Processes: Feelings, Play, and Creativity

Part 4   Integrating Theory and Practice

Foreword

In the early part of this century, when the educational philosophy of John Dewey was at its apogee, many educators focused their efforts on the social and emotional development of the child. Emphasis was placed on fostering each child's personal adjustment and sense of social responsibility in a democratic society. The popularity of this orientation eventually declined, however, in part because of the excesses of those who did not fully comprehend it but also because of the natural and inevitable evolution of academic trends.

Some decades later the gradual dissatisfaction with the whole-child approach turned into intense and immediate refutation of the concept. This was not a result of new knowledge about child development or better insights into what constitutes a good education, but was spurred by historical events which had little to do with the intrinsic nature of children. Specifically, American attitudes concerning education were seriously jolted by the launching of Sputnik. This feat was interpreted by many as embarrassing proof that Soviet education was more rigorous and effective than America's academic fare. After all, the Russians were training their children in mathematics, science, and engineering, while Americans were training theirs in finger painting. A return to and glorification of the three Rs became the nation's rallying cry. Concern with the overall adjustment of the child thus gave way to an intense concentration on cognitive development.

This cognitive emphasis was soon joined with a facile and overstated environmentalism which I have referred to as the "environmental mystique." This hopeful doctrine, which swept the country in the 1960s and 1970s, promised that rather minimal environmental interventions could result in robust improvements in intellectual functioning. Bookstands were flooded with titles such as "How to give your child a superior mind," and even leading experts were writing articles for popular consumption such as "How to raise your child's IQ by 20 points." These remedial efforts might not be necessary if we started early enough, so academic prescriptions for infants appeared. It is hard to believe that anyone took seriously the advice that hanging mobiles over infants' cribs was a meaningful catalyst to cognitive development. Yet the market for mobiles grew tremendously.

America's technological ethos also contributed to the educational philosophy of the post-Sputnik years. The attitude developed that there was something wrong with America's children. If something was wrong, it should be fixable with the right technology. It was a short step from this belief to the discovery of talking typewriters and a variety of "toys that teach." The real work of the child, namely, free play, became suspect. Instead, if we would only subject them to enough drill and educational gadgetry, our children could enter the intellectual promised land.

I am happy to report that the view of the child as only a cognitive system is now defunct. Now there is a more differentiated systems approach in which cognitive development is viewed as being in close interaction with other subsystems of development including the physical, the emotional, and the social. This awareness is solidified in the nation's Headstart program, where the goal was never how to build more intelligence into intellectually inadequate children but rather to help children optimally utilize the intelligence they possess. This is achieved not only by intellectual training but by fostering the development of a good self-image, positive attitudes about others, and motives to actualize oneself in life.

The whole-child approach was rediscovered because it was never really lost. Solid programs like Headstart and perceptive scholars like Barbara Biber who truly know and care about children were not swept up in the fads but kept a clear if quiet commitment to the child's overall well-being and performance. Biber never let us lose sight of the fact that the everyday behavior of the child includes but is not limited to intellectual behavior. Her steadfast efforts helped to negate the view that the child is a passive agent who could be endlessly shaped through the manipulation of external programs and the right reinforcement schedule. She helped refine our understanding of development by treating the child not as a passive entity into which learning is poured, but as an active, exploratory, assimilating partner in the learning process.

Early in her career, Biber bravely proposed a revolutionary change in the goals of education. The school, she stated, should be responsible for supporting, guiding, and stimulating the affective and social as well as cognitive developmental processes in the child. These broadened educational efforts could give the child the foundation to achieve self-fulfillment and self-extension—that is, to become involved in the social world of problems and ideas.

In this book, as throughout her career, Biber addresses a broad array of topics that relate to the development of the whole child: thought processes, language, feelings, play, creativity, the environment, self-worth, socialization, and public responsibility. These topics are threaded into a unified whole just as they are in the fabric of development in the child. In the practice of education, much of this integration is the task of the teacher. Biber sees the teacher's role as crucial and complex in bringing the child's potential to the greatest possible fulfillment.

In describing the developmental-interaction approach practiced at the Bank Street College of Education, an educational program which Biber pioneered and has continued to develop over the years, she demonstrates how research and theory can be translated into actual educational practice. She relates not only the possibility but the logistics of how the comprehensive goals of early childhood education can be achieved by educators who are knowledgeable about child development, are sensitive to the child's needs, and can synthesize creatively the elements required for the child's optimal development. Perhaps the most difficult task she requires of the teacher is to weigh each technique or intervention in terms of its effects on other areas of the child's functioning. For example, a learning experience designed to enhance cognitive development should be evaluated with regard to its simultaneous effects on the child's self-image, attitude toward others, values concerning work, and general behavioral patterns. Similarly, the ways in which classroom experiences are depicted or transformed by the child are valued for aesthetic qualities and expression of feelings as well as for evidence of social and cognitive mastery.

Biber not only views but treats the child as an active participant in the educational process. Where the developmental-interaction educational approach is practiced, the environment provides opportunities for varied and flexible interactions among the child, peers, and the teacher. Children are given the opportunity to select, initiate, plan, and make their own and group decisions. Thus they learn that the teacher and others are available as guides for exploring the world and as resources for dealing with problems. As a result, as Biber tells us so eloquently, "the child finds strength and pleasures in creating order through his expanding thought processes, from sharing depth of feeling with teachers and children, and from recreating symbolically the meanings— real and fantasied—that are of the greatest moment to him." Instead of ingesting knowledge, the child gains a sense of autonomy and competence to utilize knowledge.

In this marvelous book we have a record of the evolution of Barbara Biber's thinking on early childhood education and the personal, scientific, and intellectual forces which shaped her thought. It is at once a personal and a scholarly account. The whole person that *she* is emerges as she draws on and creatively intertwines her own observations, experiences, and feelings as well as experimental data and others' thinking. The result envelops us in a sense of warmth, vitality, and unity.

It will be obvious to all who read this book why Barbara Biber has long been regarded as the premier worker in the field of early childhood education. She is a respected model of educator and scholar, and has long been my personal mentor in the early intervention discipline. I am grateful to have this opportunity to note my intellectual indebtedness to her.

EDWARD ZIGLER

Preface

Let me begin by identifying myself as a psychologist-educator. As will become plain in reading these chapters, I write from a viewpoint built on a psychodynamic orientation in developmental psychology and identification with progressive experimental practice in education. It has been my extraordinary good fortune to have been actively engaged in the development of the Bank Street College of Education for over half a century.

Founded in 1916 as the Bureau of Educational Experiments, the institution has traveled a pioneer route in several directions. From its beginning to the present there has been a built-in program of research related to the study of innovative concepts and practices concerning growth and learning in childhood and the functioning of educational institutions. Since the period of creative innovative design for schooling for under-three-year-olds in the 1920s, Bank Street has become a multifunctional institution: educating children from postinfancy through the eighth grade, educating teachers on a graduate level with emphasis on field-based experience and a unique program of individual advisement (counseling), offering consultant services to other school systems, public and private, and developing teaching-related programs for social workers and librarians. These and other programs involving developmental and learning processes beyond the domain of the classroom represent varied functions, undertaken and enacted with an internally coherent system of values and preferred methodology.

These can be only briefly referred to: the school has responsibility for the development of the whole person—his affective and social as well as his intellectual proclivities; educational goals are inevitably value bound; there is a high value on the kind of effective autonomous individuality that, in maturity, evolves toward social commitment; the learning process builds on several sources—cognitive functions cannot be separated from personal and interpersonal processes; and an optimal educational program maximizes the child's interaction with the materials, ideas, and people of his environment. In general, the school is considered a life sphere of search and discovery, trial and solution, self-awareness and social interchange, conflict and resolution, resistance and adaptation—in all, an experience in depth and achievement.

I should make it clear that where I use the first person form *we* with reference to Bank Street, I do not speak for the institution in any official sense but rather from my own identification with the institution and the way it has tried to accentuate depth in learning and integrity in social interaction.

In my youth I chose education as the sphere of work best suited to my deep wish for a better world—with more opportunity to fulfill what is so potentially good and poorly served by institutions, schools for example, as we have known them. Looking back over the years, I find it quite remarkable that the basic image of a fulfilled individual with a developed sense of social responsibility has been sustained as an ideal in the expanded and matured reality of contemporary Bank Street, albeit in the face of the negative social forces that we have known over these years. So I am attracted to the idea of looking back, remembering, and comparing: what lasts, what changes, what is the same, what is new. From the perspective of continuity and change, I have found it interesting to trace which concepts and values that Bank Street identified remained central in the institutional ethos even while practice reflected change in response to advancing knowledge and an altered social milieu.

For this book, I have selected twelve of my papers which were originally published between 1934 and 1977 and, reflecting on what has remained continuous and what has changed, I have written a companion paper to each one. The book is composed of these twenty-four papers. The original papers are weighted toward the earlier years of childhood, while the newly written papers take a broader perspective. In the earlier papers, I tended to use masculine pronoun forms in a general sense, in accord with what was then customary usage. At the same time, I tended to refer to teachers of young children in the feminine, in accord with my sense that most such teachers were women. To the extent that such usage prevails in the later papers, it is simply a reflection of habits of speaking and writing and not a reflection of attitudes. The order of chapters in this book does not follow the chronology of the published papers. Instead, I have chosen to place the pairs of newly written and previously published papers in four sections, representing different aspects of past and contemporary interest in this field.

I am aware that this manuscript ranges over a wide area, encompassing past and contemporary accounts of practice and opinion. The content of the new chapters represents studies and views most relevant to my interest in tracing what has changed and what has remained constant in the educational perspective with which I am identified. From a broader view, I hope it mirrors my professional interest in furthering cross-fertilization of insights between the fields of developmental psychology and experimental forms of education. Short pieces of recollection introduce each chapter. Though such ruminations are ordinarily screened out of professional writing, I have included them in the hope of sharing some of the personally meaningful context within which ideas and points of view take shape.

In the course of writing from a historical perspective, I have had the opportunity to acknowledge the educators and psychologists whose perspectives and professional contributions have proved most enlightening in the formation of a point of view. More personally, I appreciate and value all that I have learned from the extraordinary day-by-day working relationship with the students and the teaching staff of the Bank Street College of Education. Most especially I express my appreciation beyond measure for the opportunity over the years to know and work with the other psychologists of the Research Division. In preparing this book, I have called on many colleagues for advice and criticism. I particularly want to thank Bertha Campbell, Bettye Caldwell, Itty Chan, Barrie Chi, Marjorie Janis, Jenni Klein, Patricia Minuchin, and Jeanette Stone. Other colleagues shared materials with me and offered helpful comments at many points, and I gratefully acknowledge their contribution: Dorothy Carter, Barbara Bowman, Dorothy Gross, Ethel Horn, Lilian Katz, Leah Levinger, Rochelle Mayer, Anne Mitchell, Irving Sigel, Edmund Sullivan, and Lillian Weber. Over the years, I have worked closely with a number of people. Here I want to express my very special appreciation to Edna Shapiro and Doris Wallace, not only for their long colleagueship but for the particular contribution they made in their critical reading of parts of the manuscript of this book. I have been in the unusual position of having two members of my family as professional colleagues. My late sister, Charlotte B. Winsor, was a colleague for many years. Here, I want to acknowledge the keen and helpful advice she offered in her reading of parts of the manuscript. To my daughter, Margery B. Franklin, goes my loving appreciation of her special kind of clearheaded criticism, her profound insight, and her generous, warmhearted support during the times when my spirit flagged. I want to thank Jessika Chuck for her willing assistance in typing the manuscript when the project was in its early stages. To Ruth Kolbe I am greatly indebted for her special skill and inexhaustible patience in transforming disheveled copy into finished manuscript. I thank Jane Churchman for typing the manuscript and assisting in tasks of organization. I want to thank Gladys Topkis, my editor at Yale University Press, who has provided sound advice as I have worked to bring the manuscript to the point of publication. I also want to thank Alexander Metro, manuscript editor at Yale University Press, whose work on the manuscript in its final stages has been extremely helpful.

I have the privilege of including in this book several previously published papers coauthored with colleagues: "A Child Development Approach to Language in the Preschool Disadvantaged Child" was written with Patricia Minuchin; "Promoting Cognitive Growth: A Developmental-Interaction Point of View," with Edna Shapiro and David Wickens; and "Psychological Perspectives and Early Childhood Education: Some Relations between Theory and Practice," with Margery B. Franklin.

I would like to think that this book will be useful to all those who are committed to understanding and serving the early years of childhood, whether their choice is to penetrate the roots of our knowledge base or to invest their energies in putting the best available knowledge in the service of applied practice.

PART 1

Preschool Education: Practice and Point of View

CHAPTER 1

The Early School Years:
New Perceptions

*The recall of papers one has written draws on all kinds of images—
particular people, places, and problems—but sometimes the memory has a
clear mood quality. This paper has two contrasting moods associated with it.
It was presented first as a talk at a meeting in the period when nursery
school education was making its way as a profession, organizing in national
and state associations, and launching publications. After the talk, several of
us walked along Bank Street in a glow of good feeling, compounded of a
kinship of ideas and ideals and the sweet feeling of relaxation at the end of
the work week. It was Saturday noon (the five-and-a-half-day work week
was normal then). I remember Cornelia Goldsmith (1972) commenting on
what I had presented. In her quiet way, she whispered, "I wish I had said
every word." My respect for her wisdom and experience made that praise
especially heartwarming—a lovely echo to draw against in later occasions of
discouraging performance.*

*The other mood was as far down as that one was high. I had been
writing up the notes from my talk for publication in the New York
University library, hurrying to finish before dark. The walk across
Washington Square was not familiar to me, and I started out, meaning to
follow a mental map of the quickest route. I found myself caught in a
sinister cloud-darkness, fighting high winds. Swaying like the bending trees
above me, growing more and more anxious about ever getting back to
shelter, I did not know until later that I was battling my way through a
hurricane, but the mood was set. The physical terror aroused thoughts of
other terrors—I could think only of the breakfast I had had with a neighbor
a short time earlier. We had sat together over coffee, the morning
newspaper spread between us, as she told me in tears of her family and her
life in Vienna. The headline reported Hitler's march into Austria. The storm
threatened near and far.*

*The late 1930s were like that: high hopes for a whole new way of life
to be lived in school, and deep despair over what man could do to man. It
was natural that what we put into words for publication came through as a
two-part credo, stating explicitly what we opposed and wished to undo as
well as depicting what we favored, wished for, and were committed to. It
was a credo that had matured through a decade of exploration and
definition.*

Nursery School as the Beginning of Education (1939)

The concept of school is changing. School once meant, and in practice still
largely means, the learning of skills which depend upon abstract symbols, the
acquisition of a great deal of information about faraway, half-real places, the
effort to understand such adult affairs as wars and chief industries and taxation
and tariffs, the mastering of the trickery of arithmetic and algebra, and the
ability to be interested in all of this for its own sake.

School has meant the acceptance of the teacher as an authority, one who
knows what there is to know and tells what there is to do. School has meant a
place to compete for supremacy at the blackboard or in the playground or a
readiness to be content with being an anonymous nonentity. School has meant
a lot of sitting still and listening and reading out of books and learning the rules.
The right way to behave, the right way to do a problem, the right way to spell,
the right way to reply to an adult's inquiry, the right way to keep the line during
a fire drill. This kind of schooling has been considered inappropriate for the
child under six years of age, who is so full of wanting to romp about, who cares
not at all for learning for learning's sake, to whom the letter A is a picture or a
pattern and not a symbol, to whom mother and father are gods enough, and
whose deepest thoughts and interests are well contained within the area of his
block, his family, and his dog. No one who knows and understands little children would wish to see them living out the early years of childhood under the
physical and psychological restraints of "school," not so long as we fill in our
mental picture of school from the memories of those of us who were children at
least a generation ago.

At the present time, it has become a matter of major importance that
everyone—parent, layman, legislator—realize that the nursery school is no
such place, and to become aware as well that, as soon as the plans and programs
of modern educators come to fulfillment, the "old" school will be a museum
piece to be set up beside the city's first fire engine.

The nursery school belongs to a new school, a new, revitalized concept of
education, a new ideal for the lives of children. According to the philosophy of
the newer education, the child lives one life. He does not shed his home self
when he enters the school door. It should not be possible for him to leave his

Adapted from Nursery school as the beginning of education. *The Young Child in Education*, 1939,
1, 2–5.

school self out on the front porch when he returns home. Schooling must be as real, as vivid as life itself; must become the tool by which the child meets the real problems of life more efficiently, with a greater yield of happiness to himself and a greater promise of service to the community in which he will live as an adult.

The task is not a simple one: to understand what are the basic needs and interests of children at different periods of their development; to understand the underlying problems of growing up, to plan a school life that will help children to develop and direct their interests, their feelings, and their abilities; to create a school atmosphere that grants each child his full psychological right to be himself and at the same time nurtures a growing willingness to be one among others, as a child and ultimately as a grown-up. It means new kinds of school buildings, a new kind of training for teachers, new ways of teaching, and new things to learn. The question becomes a practical one: What does the child need in his early years? How can we provide a foundation experience upon which he can build with security and beauty?

Children at all ages need an atmosphere of warmth in which to thrive, the warmth of close, honest human contacts. They need the feeling that adults, teachers, and parents like them, are interested in them, enjoy them, and feel ready to be responsible for them, to protect them even from themselves when occasion demands. They need free and full expression for the physical energies of childhood, space to run, heights to climb for the young, and games of skill and team play for the older ones.

What do children care about? First and foremost, themselves. Their earliest needs are associated with realizing themselves, becoming aware of their own names, feeling their psychological position in the family. These needs constitute the matrix of their earliest interests. Their first comprehensions are deeply personal: who they are, what they do, what they have, how they get it, where they live, where they go, what they like, what they don't like, what frightens them, what thrills them.

With skillful understanding, grown-ups can build a continuous bridge between these basic needs and interests of young children and the remote regions of history, geography, and social studies which, to so large an extent, have been banished to an exile of schoolish unreality and unimportance. This unreality can be broken down only when teachers and parents become sensitive to the relation between a child's interest in himself and his slowly maturing interest in other people, to the need for maintaining a delicate balance between self-fulfillment and self-extension, to the close kinship between the four-year-old's interest in starting and stopping the flow of water from the tap of a washbowl to the twelve-year-old's study of the city's reservoir system.

At this moment in the world's history, we are astounded and frightened by the indifference of most adults to the problems, the threats of each morning's newspaper. The new school is intent upon educating a generation of citizens for whom such indifference will be impossible. If people are ever to accept the complex problems of the world at large and give them a place of importance in their individual lives, the schools must do their jobs better than they have been doing them. The larger, more abstract human problems and concerns must emerge slowly, logically, and potently from the intimate, personal interests of young children. They must share the bedrock of feeling as well as under-standing.

These are end-purposes. While he is still young, the child needs help toward feeling the confidence of familiarity and power in his own world. He must be helped to make his own discoveries. His learning must be his own, accomplished through the intrinsically child-ways of doing, exploring, experi-menting. The teacher becomes his support and guide, the person who helps him clarify his confusion, introduces him to experiences that feed his interests, provides his next steps. No longer the mental monitor, no longer the arbiter of intellectual right and wrong, she becomes his ally, more experienced than he, to be sure, but above all his friend. Through methods that must be subtle as well as cognizant, the child, in his years of growth, should be helped toward feeling first that he belongs in the world and second that the world belongs to him, that it is his world, and that it is utterly appropriate that he approach it in a spirit of confident expectation and interest in making it over.

The growing child is nothing fixed. His feeling of belonging must be established and reestablished as he grows from the status of baby in the confines of home and family to the status of adolescent in a no-man's-land between childhood and adult life. Along the whole path of his growth he is an active, dynamic system of feelings, sensitivities, and conflicts. He has a family, he belongs to a family. He has friends and enemies. He is a boy or a girl, an athlete or a grind, short or tall, fat or thin, fast or slow, pretty or plain-faced, gawky or graceful. He has wishes and impulses that cannot be fulfilled. He is frightened of himself. He is proud of himself. He is ashamed. He is lonely or gay. He wins. He loses. He laughs. He cries.

Somehow, out of the years of quick tides of feeling, overwhelming surges of understanding, he must become a stable, effective human being. This cannot be accomplished by denying him his moods, his occasional impulses to fight, his sporadic resistance against order and routine, his right to fantasy and creative expression. He needs ample opportunity to use the creative materials of all the arts, in a genuinely creative situation, as an outlet for his struggles. He needs ease of expression as a tool for the child's major task in growing up: to keep re-creating the world of his childish experience, so freely, so truly, that, as he grows, his own child's world with its compound of fantasy and fact takes on the aspects, the truth, of objective reality, the real world of adult life. He needs love, space, time, opportunity, freedom, sympathy, appropriate experience, and rich expression in order to establish an active, creative, effective relation to life.

If this is indeed the air which the children in the new school breathe, when shall they take their first breath of it, when are they ready, when does education rightfully begin? It begins whenever a child is experiencing enough of life to be developing attitudes toward people, feelings about himself, ideas about the world; whenever he is beginning to acquire the basic tools by means of which individuals express what they feel and say what they think for the pure joy of expression or for the human delight of communication; whenever he begins to emerge as a distinct personality with his own individual patterns of wishes, frustrations, powers, fears, and interests.

Where on the age scale shall we place these beginnings? At six years? What of the life of the child before he attains his sixth birthday? In the course of everyday observation each of us has been aware, at one time or another, of a variegated profusion of two-year-olds' victories, three-year-olds' personalities, four-year-olds' jokes, five-year-olds' struggles, all of which bespeak the considerable variety and range of life experiences of the little child. Science contributes the now well-known conclusion that the life experience of the young child is not only rich and varied but all-important. In these early years the fundamental groundwork of a child's personality is laid down. He meets decisive problems. His ways of meeting his nursery-age problems, the residue of feelings, attitudes, inclinations laid down in the course of his childhood victories and defeats, will contribute a basic pattern to his later growth. At six, he is in no sense a finished human personality but he is, to an amazing degree, a formed human personality. Obviously the new school, dedicated as it is to education for effective living, cannot afford to neglect these years in which each child is building the basic structure of the person he is to be.

What happens to the child during these years? What problems does he solve or fail to solve or half-solve? What does he learn? How can he learn it? How does he express himself? How does he reveal himself? How much has he become a member of the world in which he lives?

Long before he is eligible for the youngest group in the nursery school, he has made biological adaptations that constitute the groundwork of his education: learned to take solid food, to wait for feeding times, to begin to inhibit the functions of elimination, to avoid the radiator, to spit out the foods he does not relish. There are variations among children in the degree to which these adaptations constitute problems and conflicts and in the kind of struggles attendant upon them. But through them every child gains a body of feelings about himself and his parents which become the axis of his future growth.

Long before he is six years old, the child will have initiated himself into the especially human needs for questioning and understanding the world in which he lives. His earliest relations to his environment have little to do with the kind of questioning and understanding that we associate with words and language and the ability to communicate. Given half a chance, the young healthy child will set up an endless stream of experiments. These will involve him in pushing and pulling, putting in and taking out, running, jumping, sliding, covering and uncovering, closing and opening, climbing up and climbing down, throwing and rolling; they will yield him a gratifying familiarity with what things are like, what can be done with them. In this area too he will be building a feeling of himself. Whether this feeling is one of confidence, of power, of delight, will depend on the grown-ups—when they helped, what they provided, what they encouraged, how aware they were of the educational by-products of the child's first games.

Questioning and understanding do not long remain a matter of things and the exploration of the world of things. Concurrently with these ventures, the child begins to speak. Speaking at first is another way of playing, and the poetry of the race attests to its importance. Children can play, can find expression, not only with words but with crayons, with wood, with twigs, with blocks—with anything, in short, that can be used to express, to describe, to tell. They will use everything available to fulfill the deep needs which they have during these early years to depict and thus relive, in their own ways, the real experiences they have. We all know and remember the endless hours of playing house or store or farm or school. Furthermore, they will use everything available to rid themselves of feelings of anger, of fears, of imagined enemies through picturing and playing and telling.

This is what they do, and those who observe carefully note that in the course of their doing the children have learned—even according to the conventional meaning of the word. They learn connections: what belongs with what, what comes from what. They learn processes: how paints are mixed, how seeds grow, how boats float. They learn people: how to fight, how not to fight, how to live together. What they learn matters only a little. What matters most is whether they are left with newer, broader feelings about themselves, feelings of power and strength on which to construct the basic feeling that the world is theirs to understand, to influence, to re-create.

This is a mere glimpse of the young child and is only intended as such. Yet it may serve to illustrate that the young child, no less than the older one, is a suitable candidate for the best that education can provide. Furthermore, it may support the premise that any educational scheme that does not take responsibility for the youngest children is passing by the years of fundamental growth and adaptability and, by so much, weakening the opportunity to make of all education something that lives of itself and contributes to the lives of all of us.

Images of School Influence: Social Change and Child Personality

Very Early Beginnings

Some of the earlier burgeoning of experimental ventures in preschool education is recorded in a book drawn from a series of publications sponsored by the Bureau of Educational Experiments (later to be called the Bank Street College of Education) between 1917 and 1924 (Winsor, 1973). A number of newly organized schools described their programs briefly with statements of their underlying rationale. They had in common a commitment to an experimental approach to early childhood education, rebelling against the "traditional" methods dominating education at that time; new concepts of childhood and the learning process; and a dedication to record and analyze their experimental ventures. Within this unanimity there was, however, great variation in underlying psychological theory and in the educational modes established to serve the learning ethic. For example, free creative expression for the young child was a central ideal, but enactment varied from the opportunity given the pupils in the Children's School (now the Walden School, New York City) to draw from their own impulses, often expressed in elaborate design products, to the way, by contrast, teachers in the Gregory School encouraged the children to move toward representation in their drawing activity.

A Confluent Pattern

It was not until several years later, in 1928, that Harriet Johnson's *Children in the Nursery School* spelled out the theory and practice that characterized the program for the under-three-year-olds, established as the youngest group in the City and Country School, under the aegis of the Bureau of Educational Experiments.

Both the theoretical premises and the implementation of this particular pattern of early education were shaped by the thinking of three people, each enriching the total conceptualization in distinctly individual ways. Harriet Johnson was committed to applying insights from her meticulous observational study of the children's behavior to continuous revision of the educational world she designed for them. Caroline Pratt applied her talents (Pratt & Wright, 1924) to creating a school ethos for the whole span of the elementary years that placed highest priority on sustaining autonomous individuality within a democratically organized school society. Lucy Mitchell (1934), with her finely tooled intellect, stretched in several directions in search of illuminating "relationships" (her favorite word). As an educator, Lucy Mitchell expected curriculum design to be shaped and related to developmental stages; as a geographer, she clarified how the interrelation of natural phenomena and political realities had determined the boundaries of European nations.

As I see it now, my 1939 paper was a kind of marker for the positions that were clarified in the decade of the 1940s—with respect to both theoretical orientation and social responsibility. It tried to stake down an image of the nursery school as an educational institution in contrast to the day-nursery setup, long established to give "custodial care" to children of families in need—usually families in which the mother worked full-time because of economic necessity. The concept of *custodial care* was the core of the controversy between education-oriented program planners and welfare-oriented funding agencies.

This was also a period when we selected and established our kinship groups within the wide-spreading preschool movement. That there was a selection to be made from among basically different perspectives was not always recognized. In their text on *Nursery School Education* (1939), Foster and Mattson stated that they had tried to give the reader "a feeling of the spirit and philosophy of the nursery school." A fair enough general statement, but misleading if one infers that the nursery school movement was a homogeneous body of principles, practices, and underlying goals across the country in the late 1930s—in private nursery schools, in the publicly funded Works Progress

Administration (WPA) nurseries, in the home economics departments of universities, and in the laboratories of child-development research centers. The differences were not codified or widely recognized but they were nevertheless significant for the future development of the movement. It was a long way from the present systematization of differences among the various models for Follow Through programs, but programs like ours differed early on from many of the others in several basic ways.

The Theoretical Perspective

We found ourselves affiliated in theory and cooperating in various ways with the work that Lois Murphy and her associates (Lerner et al., 1941) were doing at Sarah Lawrence College as the basis for studies of child personality, with the educational program for teachers and parents at Vassar College summer sessions headed by L. Joseph Stone and Mary Langmuir, and with the clinical orientation of Caroline Zachry (1940). It was in these programs that the psychodynamic theory of development and the influence of personality factors on learning experience were being brought to bear on experimentation in early childhood education (see Jahoda, 1977). Our shared theoretical orientation with these psychologist-educators did not mean identical educational designs. It never does, since more than theory determines what a school is. But we had in common a psychological foundation for educating young children that was basically and importantly different from the programs developed at university centers. It is only fair to say, first, that all the early centers, ours among them, leaned toward the advantages, in socializing children, of putting procedures and requirements on a reasoned rather than an arbitrarily authoritative basis, and of providing an expanded exposure to more varied experience. But, beyond that, insights from dynamic psychology raised more complicated questions and uncertainties about how impulse expression and the resolution of unconscious conflict in the early years should be understood or become part of the educator's responsibility (see Senn, 1975).

Though it had been quite a leap from John Dewey in 1916 to Susan Isaacs in the 1930s, the basic thinking was really on the same course: the behavioral surface is not an adequate guide for the educator's design. Underlying motivation and the inevitable conflicts of growth into the human family and society became central considerations. We did not expect to find simple, clear-cut techniques for integrating these insights with the Deweyan philosophy of education to which we were committed. In fact the integration of these perspectives remains an active pursuit, for practitioners and scholars alike (Morton, 1960).

So it was to be expected that Susan Isaacs's reports of the Malting House experimental schools in London were of great interest to Harriet Johnson, and that Isaacs's major works on intellectual and social development appeared on my reading lists for students in teacher-training programs during this period. Our interest in Isaacs's work did not involve explicit adherence to her particular school of psychoanalytic thinking; it did mean a communion of thinking about deeper sources of early childhood behavior and admiration for her accomplishment in creating a scheme of education bearing specific relevance to a theory of development.

Looking back to my own paper of this period, I regret the way I shortcut the relation of the children's experiences to the prevailing concept of learning. I did point out that

> in the course of their doing the children have learned. . . . they learn connections—what belongs with what—what comes from what. They learn processes—how paints are mixed, how seeds grow, how boats float. They learn people—how to fight, how not to fight, how to live together.

But I did not communicate the extent to which observing, inferring, differentiating, relating, and conceptualizing formed the firm substance of the children's experiences, continuously and consciously stimulated by the teachers, although not in the vernacular of developmental stages of cognition familiar to us now. I almost took all that for granted in my concern to articulate other goals for self-fulfillment and social-psychological resolution. "What they learn matters only a little," I said. Not true, and I argued that down later for many years. But I admit my error, and I regret the contribution this emphasis may have made to the erroneous impression, in the minds of some psychologists, that Bank Street and our ideological colleagues as educators were interested only in social-emotional development. A clear image asserts itself that contradicts that impression. I recall Jessie Stanton, as a teacher in the City and Country School, coming out of her morning with five-year-olds, waving her arms and saying, "They are the world's most wonderful." She could hardly contain the excitement of responding as a teacher to those probing, inventing, questioning young minds.

As founders and explorers in progressive education, we had an interest in and identity with a larger span than the nursery school movement. We saw the early years as foundation and, as soon as it became institutionally possible, added an elementary school to our program. We had no illusion that sound experience in the early years by itself could inoculate against the faults of subsequent educational experience.

The pioneer front had to be extended and sustained. We saw the nursery school movement as only one lever for changing the larger educational scheme of things. It was plain that, to be effective, educational reforms needed broader goals than just creating a more productive and satisfying experience for the early years. There was a vision—maybe, to be realistic, more an assumption— that positive attitudes and modes of functioning realized in the nursery school would serve as a template of what the experience of later schooling might be.

Instruments for Action

The wish to bring together forward-looking educators with a common voice had been manifested, to a small extent, in the bureau's effort to stimulate and publish the early position statements. That was in the 1920s. In the late 1930s, the Associated Experimental Schools was formed, composed of like-minded progressive schools, with a view to consolidating the group's position and finding ways to project it to the wider educational world. As an example of its agenda, I can refer to one issue of concern to the group that has come to have major importance today. Should nursery schools be attached to the existing school system? Foster and Mattson, like many others, had a clear answer: "It is now merely a matter of time until every school system will include a nursery school as its basic unit." That statement could be read, and was read by many of us, as a warning rather than as something to be hoped for. It might come to mean, in view of the reality of bureaucratic systems, that the entrenched practices of traditional elementary schooling would move down to the earlier years. Our thrust was up from nursery school into the later grades, a revolutionary movement to be built on awareness of developmental processes and stages as well as on a whole new approach to learning processes, teacher–child relationships, and socialization of the individual. There was much in-group difference of opinion on this score. Those who were "purely principled" argued that the preschool movement would be contaminated and defeated in its essence if it were attached to public education. The pragmatic-minded argued that it would never get a start unless it could be attached to the ongoing public system of education. These lines are now being drawn again. The early childhood professionals are holding out against a move to transfer Headstart from the special auspices under which it is now governed and make it part of the larger public school system. The position that continuity from preschool into the primary grades is necessary in connection with changing educational practice has been recognized and faced in our times. There had to be Follow Through to supplement Headstart. In its time, the Associated Experimental Schools was ideologically integrated and outwardly directed, but it was a small in-group with no influence on public affairs or even on public opinion to any large degree.

In the Public Arena

The maturing of the nursery school movement as a social force was stimulated from several sources. Two spokespeople for what we as a nation should provide for the care and education of young children—Ruth Andrus (Andrus, Nash, & Stanton [n.d.]) and Lawrence Frank (1938)—exerted major influence; both were actively concerned not only that we develop educational methods adapted to our growing insights into early childhood but also that we establish governmental structures to stimulate and protect this educational domain. Each, in a different way, found effective instruments to serve these purposes.

In the 1930s and 1940s it was possible for those who were so inclined to participate and contribute to advancing the professional sophistication of early education programs and, at the same time, to be protagonists for public and political recognition of the needs of young children. At Bank Street we were on both paths. Some momentum was circumstantial but progress was not accidental. Educators took an active part in the schools established under the WPA, and not only in order to be useful in the government's effort to undo the hardships of the depression. Beyond the immediate need, they saw this national emergency as an opportunity to require and establish higher standards for the care of young children than would ordinarily be mandated in a large government program. Bank Street staff members, along with others, offered their services to teach and prepare volunteer workers for their jobs, and gladly exploited the opportunity to communicate the concept that meeting the developmental and educational needs of young children was as essential as guarding their health in group care. We were building an elevated image of services in the care of young children.

World War II offered a similar opportunity on a far greater scale and was utilized for similar gains in disseminating understanding and offering practical images for enacting high purposes. It was during this period that New York City, in its Health Department, institutionalized its responsibility. The Day Care Division has been teacher and monitor to the city's programs for the young ever since, carrying the difficult load of translating high standards into legislative enactment. Its productive history reflects the long years of leadership of Cornelia Goldsmith (1972) and, I am pleased to add, the presence on the staff, year after year, of many Bank Street College graduates.

Maybe it would be fair to call the 1939 paper a credo in light of the extent to which it not only tried to forge an image of suitable schooling for young children but also implied the hope, really the assumption, of an impact on the future with a focus on social change. More than that, there was a rationale for how certain experiences and relationships in early childhood could lead to more socially responsible and committed adults, to the competence and motivation to undo social faults—to change a world that obviously needed making over. The rationale rested heavily on the assumption of basic personality formation in the early years and on the force of early immersion in a climate of positive values. Where does that assumption stand today?

We have come full circle. The 1939 paper was published in the first issue of a journal representing a local chapter of a national association which had been taking shape slowly over a period of 12 years. Its increase in size has been explosive since that time—evidence, at last, of the major importance of the early years of childhood. The catalogue of the upcoming national meeting of that association lies beside me on my desk—four days of intensive consideration of the practical and theoretical issues in the contemporary scene, to be attended by several thousand actively involved members of the profession.

The title of the 1939 paper tells only part of the story. Not only was nursery school defended as a suitable beginning of education; it was perceived as a lever for basic change in education in the large—a way of making a breakthrough toward a whole new philosophy of education. This conception of nursery school education was a built-in phase of the progressive education movement with a common body of basic principles and purposes. At another level, there is something tender in this loving, albeit somewhat romanticized, image of what transpires in nursery school and something sad in the naive faith that, "as soon as the plans and programs of modern educators come to fulfillment, the 'old' school will be a museum piece to be set up beside the city's first fire engine." "As soon as" is taking a long time.

CHAPTER 2

Preschool as a Public Responsibility

What made it plain that The School and Society *(John Dewey, 1899) was not just the title of a great book by a great mind? That there was no escape from a world in distress into a beautifully run school for well-cared-for children?*

There had been a depression. Next door to our school building the construction of a new apartment house had been abandoned, leaving a strange formation of apertures along the unfinished outside wall, roofed over with concrete, so that the whole resembled some ancient formation of caves. In the morning, on the way to school, we could see the men who had slept in these enclosures rousing themselves to face their dreary days.

"Why are they sleeping there? Why don't they sleep in their homes?"
"They are very poor, and maybe they don't have homes to go to."
"Then why don't they work and earn money and get homes?"
"They would like to work but they can't find jobs—maybe they'll have better luck today."

It was a little less painful to answer the questions about the people waiting on the breadline outside the neighboring hospital. For a preschool child, the fact that the men were being given food offered some immediate solace to the feelings of unease.

There was more to do than answer one child's heartbreaking questions. The nursery schools established by the Works Progress Administration in the 1930s were primarily job oriented, founded in part to create jobs for unemployed teachers and to free women to contribute to the livelihood of their families. It was up to the professional educators who took on the task to think of the children, to make of this emergency a great positive opportunity for the early years of childhood. Schools had to be established in makeshift places; teachers had to be trained quickly. New

15

adaptations had to be made: health needs were crucial; eating tastes were different; troubled, anxious parents needed understanding and support; when there was no other way, children had to be called for and brought to school by the teachers. To this work, Jessie Stanton, director of the Bank Street Nursery School after Harriet Johnson's death, committed her extraordinary energy and imagination, as well as her special talents and insights on how to make the nursery school a place of learning (1939).

There was Jessie, again in the forefront, a few years later, when the war emergency needed women in the labor force, enlisting us all in the task of turning volunteers into pros in a matter of weeks. The training course she designed for volunteers to work in the quickly established centers in New York was adopted in many states, but who could duplicate Jessie's way of screening applicants? It was described in the New York World Telegram *of June 27, 1942:*

> "Is there a well-balanced person in the audience?" [With these words] Jessie Stanton, whose 25 years as an educator have not dulled her zest for the job, bluntly started her search for volunteers as child-care aides. Then she showed off her bruised shins to discourage aspirants of the I-just-love-children school of thought, and to shock an auditorium of women out of their generalities about child care in wartime, Miss Stanton let fly a stream of bad language "the children taught me."

Experience with children under stress during the depression and again during the war years was not only painful but embarrassing. We expected more of our society. We felt we knew one kind of magic that would relieve the harsh reality of troubled, often beleaguered early childhood years. That was the image I called "A Dream for the Nursery Years."

A Dream for the Nursery Years (1942)

If we were to conceive freely the school of the future, what would we want for our youngest children? Would we want nursery schools as we know them today? Schools on the model of the best ones we now have but in every community where there are young children? Or would we want something new? Something we might have instead of nursery schools? What do America's youngest children need?

Fortunately we have concrete, well-worn experience to feed into our dreams for the future. We have experience of great satisfaction on the job, but also of occasional confusion, of impatience and frustration. There are problems we are aware of and cannot do anything about. There are problems some of us do not want to think about. There are problems we cannot imagine being able to solve. We can reduce all these to two groups: (1) those that reflect larger social problems and influence the nursery school indirectly; and (2) specific nursery

Adapted from A dream for the nursery years. *Progressive Education*, May 1942, *19*, 243–50.

school problems which need to be resolved through direct study and experimentation within the nursery school. But aside from all our problems now or in the future, we have an underlying goal for what good education in the nursery years should accomplish for the children. Let us begin with an attempt to state what this goal is.

Affect, sensation, wonder, thinking—the child's experience is a rich composite of all of them, and his education should be a rich response to all of them. For his fullest development as a person we must succor his feeling experience wisely, giving him strength through loving and understanding. As he grows he will need, gradually but steadily, to free himself from the infantile gratification of dependency and protection. He will need to feel strong in the ways of the world as it opens up to him. He will need the strength that comes of being able to do, to create, to solve, to understand. He needs experience, in his earliest years, suitable to his powers, that will heighten his natural sensitivity, support his curiosity, that will lessen confusion and pointless frustration, that will yield him pleasure through the growth of skills and interests.

This, then, is the goal for education in the nursery years: how to create a situation which will offer the child opportunity to develop a deep sense of belonging in the world of people and simultaneously initiate him into the important pleasures and powers associated with being able to sustain an effective creative relation to his environment; how to find, for each individual child, the best ratio between experience that will enhance his value of self and experience that will help him extend beyond himself; how, in the group situation of nursery school, to provide for differences among individual children with respect to these needs and yet to keep coherence for the children as a group.

Only a few nursery schools, only a handful of children, are now involved in a creative attempt to accomplish this goal. In these few places, there is a vast resource of information and experience, tried-out techniques, trained workers. We face a paradox that is familiar in the American scene: great understanding of childhood being applied to a pitifully small group in our population. Our asset is information and understanding. Our weakness is that what we know as scholars we do not know how to advance as citizens.

This is no paper paradox. No matter how developed the educational skill and insight of a small group of fine schools, these schools themselves cannot be free of the educational mores and, more important, of the social mores and conditions that surround them. Thus every nursery school teacher faces certain problems with her children which she can only hope to relieve. These are problems that can never be resolved until the community in which she works takes greater responsibility for the protection of all young children. The dilemmas involved would show plainly if we could catch a teacher's reverie:

. . . There is Peter. His mother feels proud that she has brought him up scientifically; never spoiled him, stuck to his feeding schedule, walked him conscientiously for his outdoor airings. Hard to convince her that Peter ought not to have his thumb in a splint to prevent sucking. "Why

let him get bad habits," she asks. "Won't it be hard to break them later?"
In fact, the doctor suggested the splint. Of course, this mother has just the
personality that would fall in with this advice. But still, the doctor is the
voice of authority, giving advice that would not at all tally with that of the
teacher who is, after all, another voice of authority. Why should Peter's
thumbsucking be shunted back and forth between us? It doesn't need to
be. There could be a way of getting doctor and teacher and everyone else
involved with children to work out common understandings and procedures on common problems. More than that, I ought to know what his
doctor can tell us about Peter physically. I could teach more successfully
then. That's what there should be for Peter—a pool of what everybody
knows about Peter and a plan for Peter that takes all of him into account.
That's what there should be for all the Peters. . . .

. . . There is Nancy, who was so quiet and restrained when she first
came to nursery school. The well-groomed look she came with that
morning lasted clear through the day. It is hard to believe this is the same
child, digging into the clay, rubbing the extra bits onto Jonathan's face,
shouting across to Tony to play in her game on the roof. Even her parents
seem to be freer and more spontaneous since Nancy has been in school.
Only this morning her mother reported how much easier things were at
home lately. She has given up expecting Nancy to be able to keep all her
toys put away or to say thank you at every appropriate occasion. She
could see how much happier Nancy was and she is really enjoying her
more every day. There is so much more laughing and so much less
scolding around the house. But it is getting harder for her to take Nancy
visiting, especially to her grandmother's. Grandma looks askance at Nancy's "rough" unladylike ways. Why can't Nancy be more like her cous-
ins? And Nancy doesn't want to visit grandma these days. A new problem, not serious, but hard on Nancy's mother, so obviously dependent on
grandma's approval. Will she be able to handle it for Nancy? And for
herself? What would it be like if we weren't a minority? If everyone,
really everyone, even grandma, understood how stultifying can be the
effect of making Nancy a "lady" prematurely? What would it be like if all
America's ideology for children were in tune with what we really know
about children? . . .

. . . There's the foundation down the street. They will be pouring
the concrete there any day. It would be wonderful to have the children see
it happen. That is, most of the children. They have been talking about
houses so much, telling what is underneath their own houses, even underneath the cellar. And yet John and Christopher explained to Mary
only last week that the house they built with blocks didn't need a cellar
because it was a skyscraper! Just the moment for a trip to see how far
down the roots of tall buildings go. But then there is June to consider.
Every night for a week she has been asking why they put Uncle Jim down
in the earth when he died. What would she think of the foundation? And

Andy never fails to go to pieces after a trip. Just too much stimulation for him. And Mary and Diana, just recovered from measles, seem too tired and listless to brave the December atmosphere. What I need is a good assistant, someone who could stay behind with June, Andy, Mary, and Diana while I take the others to see the foundation. But that's not what our budget needs. I wonder if we can ever run this school without having to make it self-supporting? I wonder if we can ever give these children just what they need. . . .

. . . There are the children in other nursery schools. Not those who have warm homes or enough food so that they can be choosy or new shoes as soon as they outgrow the old ones or birthday cakes and presents. These other children cannot take the security of food and warmth and shelter for granted. They sense their parents' anxiety that they may lack these essentials of life. They may already have felt want. There are many in America but there is only room for a few in the nursery schools set up by WPA. . . .

. . . There is Tony, who eats so much dinner in such absolute silence. Is he storing away food against the chance that his supper plate won't have very much on it? Or is he remembering his mother's warnings to be good and cause the teacher no trouble? And there is Emma, who begs to water the plants every day. What would she say if she saw a whole meadow full of daisies or could feel a hill rise under her feet? And there is Sam, whose mousy mother loves and adores him and hangs her head when she brings him because the neighbors know that she doesn't know where Sam's father is. And Teddy, whose father takes care of him in a loving, inept, masculine way because only Teddy's mother can find work. Underprivileged children? What a word! As though food and a home and parents not weighed down with worry about work and money were a privilege! . . .

Too much nursery school energy, looking at it in the large, is now being spent in meeting difficulties in children that have their origin far outside the walls of the nursery school room. For the moment, this is important work. For the future, we can foresee a plan for children that will try to meet these problems at their source.

We should have centers for young children established in every community, supported by public funds, responsible for the total welfare of children. Through a socialized plan, a medical staff would provide regular examinations. Guidance for child care would be handled as a joint medical and psychological function. Play groups would be flexibly organized with sufficient staff so that there could be groups of various sizes, some small and some large, according to the needs of individual children. Records of health, observations in the play group, accounts of home behavior and conditions—all would be pooled and digested periodically as a way of guiding each child's growth and securing his total health. This would require recorders, psychologists, psychiatrists, and case-study specialists so that indications from the study of a child could be followed through at the center where the child is thoroughly known. The needs of a child for individual therapy, for a change in play-group experience, for an altered diet could be handled through specialists within the organization of the center we propose.

Not the child alone but everything that affects the child will be the center's concern: the child at home, the parents' ways with the child, the pressures on parents that affect the child. For its program with parents it would need staff members skilled in every kind of adult education: to lead discussion groups on general questions, to give guidance through individual interviews, to make positive contacts with parents and children at home. From center to home, from home to center, the child would live one life, one set of mores. Parents, teachers, home workers, physicians would be co-workers in a single job. The psychological significance of how weaning is begun and carried through, how a home can be simultaneously comfortable for both children and grown-ups, how much hostility can be expected from a young child toward a parent, what shall be done when children fight—the answers to these questions do not need to be the exclusive possession of experts. A little imagination applied to parent education on a broad scale can make it possible to extend to every parent enough understanding of children and of human behavior in general so that he can become, in large measure, an expert in his own right.

But is this all a matter of information and education? No, certainly not. For the success of the center for children we will have to hope that there will be other cooperating centers where parents, who are also people, can find the guidance they need as people. Didactic parent education would be of little avail. Children are affected by what their parents are, by their basic personalities, far more than by what we or even the most expert teachers of the future can teach them to do. What their parents are, their values, their hopes, their fears, their anxieties will reflect the world they live in. Certainly even the centers of the future will not turn out streamlined personalities. It will take a "brave new world," with a thoroughly revamped set of social and economic mores, to create the kind of parent personality which, by our present level of imagination, we conceive to be ideal.

The center's work will have to have yet another arm—something of broader scope than its job with the children or with the parents. It will be the spearhead of the community's provision for parenthood. If we were given this ideal center tomorrow or even the day after, we could present it with an intricate problem in parenthood to work on at once: the problem of the working mother. Surely we can assume that women of the future will do part of the world's work in industry, in the arts, in the professions. It is justifiable to assume, too, that children will benefit from having mothers who have a satisfying relation to the world's work and whose gratifications do not come exclusively from the experiences of bearing and raising children. We know, too, that children need and should have close, intimate contact with their mothers during infancy and early childhood. The solution of this problem requires major social readjustments.

For mothers whose earnings are important to the family, there should be a subsidy during childbearing and -rearing years to help the family maintain its standard of living. For women whose work is professional, we need a change in psychology. Women are now trying to be accepted on men's terms; they feel the necessity to carry a load equal to a man's, to perform as men do, in order to feel adequate professionally. Often enough, their opportunity to continue to work depends on this kind of performance. The problem is both practical and psychological, not one to be solved in a day. This kind of problem would become part of the joint program of parents and staff of the child center.

It is essential that we envisage this center for young children as an extended health program. We understand now the value of a preventive medicine program for all children in the community. We must learn to understand how socially crucial it is that every young child in America should have experience out of which to build a strong personality as well as a diet on which a strong body can grow.

In this dream of ours, the community center for young children will represent the best advice, care, and guidance that anyone can get anywhere for children. This, in itself, can constitute a great democratizing influence. When the free schools are the best schools, when public child centers offer the best facilities for child health and guidance, it will no longer be possible to accentuate class lines by buying expensive doctoring and schooling for one's children. If children from all social groups come to these centers, so will their parents. Here, then, would be an important social locus for functioning democracy; parents from all groups brought together to learn, to plan, to act in the interests of what is of deep concern to all of them, their children. If this part of the nice dream seems dubious, spend an hour in any park in a conglomerate neighborhood where everybody's baby comes for an airing and everybody's youngster plays catch. Watch for the social ease that is created around children, the reticence that disappears, the community of feeling that supersedes class, culture, and color lines. The old cliché about how "the whole world loves a baby" is true. Moreover, it is probably true as well that in so doing we exhibit the most lovable sides of our adult natures. Democracy needs to make the most of potentials such as these to successfully further its own ends.

In a situation such as this, the job of the teacher in charge of the children's group experience will be substantially different from what it is now. She will have greater facilities for attacking the basic questions of education in early childhood. She will need to do less "compensatory" teaching, less making up to the child for what he misses because of his parents' helplessness or ignorance and because of his community's outdated mores concerning the woman and child. She will be freer to live through with the children the wonderful experiences of new-found sounds and sights and words and tricks, the slow dawning of hows and whys, the big moments of skill and power.

She will no longer need to be the paragon of all virtues which we now look for in a nursery school teacher. In her stead there will be a group of workers. But the prime requisite will still be her own personality as an adult. There will be no place in the play groups of tomorrow for young women seeking escape, by associating themselves with little children, from the demands of adult life. The play group will be part of the center which will take on the clearly adult aspects of life that have to do with children's home and family lives. The children then will need, as they need now, teachers who seek not a way out of life but a way into it; who will try to develop security for the children not as an end but as a foundation for happy, effective living.

It is not too much to hope that in the near future we will put aside the restricted notion that education of the young child for happiness in his early years and effectiveness in later life is solely dependent on the refinement of classroom techniques. The value of these techniques, the problems which they must be used to solve, have and will continue to have great importance. However, we look forward to the time when nursery school workers will have equally clear awareness of the influence of the entire social setting upon the education of young children.

The Dream Realized: Twenty-five Years Later

By the time the paper *A Dream for the Nursery Years* was published in 1942, an immediate crisis took the place of dreams for the future. Teachers had to help children deal with the threat of war. In reading a collection of past records I found it interesting to see how teachers in schools like the Oak Lane Country Day School[1] in Philadelphia and the Bank Street School for Children in New York spontaneously used their knowledge of developmental periods in childhood to inform the children and allay anxiety. It was a time in history when four-year-olds could be reassured by hearing how long it would take enemy craft to cross the distance between Europe and the United States. In our times, the potential immediacy of danger necessitates a changed perspective on what to tell children. At what age levels and with what balance of reassurance and knowledge of real danger can we now, as adults, continue to give support to children?

It is interesting to see how, unknown to each other, the adults in both schools were drawing on two common principles: there must be truth between adults and children, even when the truth is hard to take, and the help adults can give children under stress depends on understanding how differently experience is filtered by children at various stages of development. In both these accounts, neither fear nor danger was denied. In both, there was informed adaptation to developmental stage characteristics expressed in the efforts made to mitigate anxiety and to enlist understanding, gradually, as part of coping strength. For the youngest, the three-year-olds, it seemed best to build up

---

1. I note with interest that Betty Shuey, whom I came to know very well during another war, the war against poverty in the 1960s, was the teacher of the two-year-olds and the three-year-olds at Oak Lane Country Day School at that time (see The first week in a Pennsylvania school, *Progressive Education*, 19 (1).

familiarity with the physical particularities of the air-raid shelter, to extend a finger to hold onto while walking toward it through the street. The question "Are they going to a fire?" upon hearing the sirens was factual. "No, this is a practice air raid," or, more in the children's form of discourse, "a pretend air raid."

For fours and fives, who could no longer keep their interest in playing about shooting and killing and war as pure fantasy, the adults took the role of verifying what the children were hearing around them from people and on the radio. "Yes, there is a war," and "Yes, planes do drop bombs." But they defused the growing sense of danger by emphasizing distance, putting the distance in concrete terms: it would take until Monday, Tuesday, etc., for the planes to get here.[2] But we are reminded that no matter what we do, fear in childhood finds its own tunnel, as one four-year-old was overheard saying, "If you call Hitler bad names he will fight America."

The seven- or eight-year-old had new images with which to people his fears: "If Hitler gets us, we will all be slaves," and struggled to accept as true what did not seem to be immediately present: "I cannot believe we are in a war. It doesn't seem like it." At this stage, the paradigm of fighting and how winning and losing happen has high valence in the child world, so the teacher who talked about the line of planes on guard along the coast and recalled the great number of planes they saw lined up at the airport when they were there on a trip built a reassuring case for our being on the winning side.

At the Oak Lane School, where there were older children, the preadolescents gained strength by sorting out the facts, undertaking intensive map study of the war areas, issuing a paper of their own, and preparing mimeographed informational material from available sources. At the same time, they made decorations for their Christmas tree, and one boy asked the teacher plaintively: "Isn't it a shame that there is a war?" That even these older children needed more than usual support shows in the statement: "There was a marked tendency toward dependence upon the teacher shown in simple, subtle ways: overuse of her name, addressing the majority of remarks and conversations directly to her, asking how she felt about bombings and the possible danger to Philadelphia."

Taking a long look, one can say that the war, like the depression before it and the war against poverty after it, had, ironically, some positive side effects. Education in the early years of childhood became a visible phenomenon to thousands of Americans, valued by parents as bringing better health, more pleasure, and more signs of a better kind of growing up for their children. Scholars increasingly recognized this period of childhood as a rich field to be mined for extending scientific knowledge of the course of human development in the most salient early years. But the fact of being carried along on social-political tides inevitably forced the growth of the movement into spurious

---

2. This is a lost technique for today's teachers. The immediacy of threatening danger is one price we pay for advancing technology.

directions. In each of the three upheavals, it has been necessary to fight for primary educational values, to ensure that the development and education of children are soundly composed and adequately budgeted.

Dynamic Psychology as Foundation

What came of the "dream" projected in the 1942 paper, and who were we long before Headstart? As I have previously noted, the goals to which we were committed were not ours alone. Closest to us, geographically and ideologically, were the programs for the nursery years of the experimental progressive schools: City and Country School, Little Red Schoolhouse, and the Walden School in New York City, the Sarah Lawrence College Nursery School in Bronxville, New York, and the Vassar College Summer Euthenics Institute in Poughkeepsie, New York. The terms of our thinking were developmental processes—self-feeling, identity, socialization, thinking, effectiveness—conceptualized more as a tapestry of interacting phenomena than as a list of categories. To understand the ferment of the growth processes, we leaned toward dynamic psychological theory, comprehending behavior in its undersurfaces of drives, conflicts, regression, and primitivity, as well as the observable manifestations of growing skills, mastery, and adaptation. A humanist value system was the basis for the goals—individual fulfillment and social commitment—toward which we wanted educational experience to propel these processes.

We were a deeply committed group with a pathetically small voice. We were not on the same track as the great and influential institutions, like Columbia's Teachers College. Evelyn Weber (1970) pointed to the way Patty Smith Hill[3] "linked the social interactionism of Dewey to a concept of habit formation . . . that eventually led to an elevation of designated habits as goals for the education of young children"—for example, habits of cooperation, courtesy, promptness, orderliness. Weber is critical of this trend: "She [Miss Hill] failed to realize that a fixed set of habits used as objectives tended to negate the flexible pragmatism Dewey espoused." "We do not need," I said in 1942, "to go through the process of slaying straw men," referring to the dogma of early habit formation and the school of thought that advocated emotional toughening. We were confident that, while they lingered in practice, they were outdated as principles. This was the mood, even the expectation, that was reviewed in a presentation by Judith Schoellkopf on the occasion of the twentieth anniversary of the founding of the Sarah Lawrence College Nursery School, on April 25, 1959. Looking back, she referred to the Watsonian behaviorism that still reigned in nursery schools in the 1930s—the preoccupation with measuring maturity in terms of physical functions, the fostering of the earliest possible independence, and the aloof, neutralized role of the teacher—as "remnants" of an earlier period. She decried the misinterpretations of psychoanalytic theory

3. Patty Smith Hill established the kindergarten at Teachers College, Columbia University, at the time that John Dewey was an active member of the faculty.

that took place in reaction against Watsonianism. But she had enough confidence in the ultimate stability of psychodynamic theory and its educational implications to advocate, as realistically feasible, a cross-disciplinary training for teachers incorporating its postulates.

We saw ourselves as the wave of the future. We could not have imagined the important place that behavior modification as applied to preschool education would attain in the 1960s and thereafter as part of government planning in particular and in academic circles in general. We also could not imagine how much the past would be forgotten or misread, as though "thinking," because it was not called "cognition," had had no place in the earlier educational designs. We could not imagine that what to us was a steady course of experimentation directed toward basic change in the philosophy of early education would come to be designated as "traditional." The ideological fundamentals that we assumed would gradually gain general acceptance came upon hard times in the 1960s when a narrow scholasticism dominated experimental programs in search of single-track solutions to the pervasive damage of poverty in early childhood.

The second aspect of the "dream," the extended parameters of what schooling for young children could be, has not fared badly. In the intervening years there has been a steadily increasing awareness of the limited potency of the school, of the need for integrating the multiple factors that influence development in childhood and making them functionally related to the learning environment. The importance of reconstructing the role of parents in relation to the whole endeavor is recognized at last. Headstart, established in 1965, is the dream come true. I want to quote from the leading protagonist for government support of a comprehensive educational offering to young children, Edward Zigler:

> What, then, are we trying to accomplish for children through the Head Start program? As stated at its inception, Head Start attempts to influence a broad array of a child's personal attributes, including his physical well-being, his formal cognitive development, his more circumscribed academic achievements, and his social-emotional development. No one of these attributes should be judged as pre-eminent; all should be seen as interacting in order to enhance social competence. (Zigler, 1973a)

The Positive Score—Forty Years Later

I am tempted to draw up a later score sheet of the questions and problems posed in 1942. I will even dare to sort out the changes that are likely to be permanent from those that represent complex issues, both social-institutional and intra-educational, and are in a condition of dynamic uncertainty, with fair expectations for wide shifts of position in the future.

In the settled column I place acceptance of the idea that education is important for the preschool child, and that it behooves the society as much as the family to make provision for it. Those who remember the 1950 White

House Conference on Children and the fury of the argument against preschool education as the enemy of family life and influence will lend ready agreement. They may even remember that some of us learned a political lesson the hard way from the first few sessions. We decided to skip breakfast after we realized that the way to gain strength for our position was to arrive at the sessions early, get seats near the floor microphones, and be ready to jump up fast, grab the microphone, and argue.

The position for the future was becoming clear: society has the responsibility to develop the institutional wherewithal for education in the early years of childhood (Zigler & Valentine, 1979; Slaughter, 1982). While this is now a generally accepted position, there has been only slow progress in making preschool education available to the thousands of children who need it most. Nationally funded experimentation with "models" signifies genuine concern and stimulates professional and public interest, but the availability of service on the scale that is needed depends ultimately on priorities in the allocation of public funds at national and local levels.

To understand contemporary trends in the care and education of young children it is useful to think back and forward in time from that 1950 conference. Recognition of society's responsibility for care of young children whose mothers were drawn into the work force during World War II led to further development of the day care movement. In the course of time this service, caring for children from six to ten hours daily, has taken two different forms: daytime care of a few children in a private home and child care centers for groups of children. In many such centers the original custodial function has been replaced by the kind of experience that is part of preschool educational practice (Pemberton, 1977), but this is not an intrinsic feature of the licensing procedure. There are no nationally established requirements with respect to professional training of teachers or guidelines for meeting the intellectual, social, and emotional needs of children. While provisions of social services and involvement of parents in day care center life have become characteristic of many centers, these, too, are not incorporated as part of the national agenda and vary greatly from region to region.

A changing image of day care is documented in a review of ongoing research on the care of infants and under-three-year-olds away from home (Caldwell & Freyer, 1982). The authors suggest the kind of research—more process oriented and more ecologically focused—that would serve the primary social function of day care more suitably. They regret the continued separation of day care and early childhood education, expressed as it is in the neglect of research findings in one field by the other as, for example, lack of communication on curriculum research from early childhood education to the field of day care. They foresee day care as the modal childhood environment as mothers of young children enter the work force and day care becomes conceptually and operationally indistinguishable from early childhood education programs. (See also Fein & Clarke-Stewart, 1973.)

It was in 1965, fifteen years after that Washington conference, that

Headstart was launched with a clear focus on providing the kind of experience in the preschool years that would counteract the developmental disadvantages of growing up under conditions of poverty. There are advantages and disadvantages in its position as a nationally funded government program. One advantage lies in the opportunity to disseminate and put into practice, on a national level, advanced knowledge in child development and early education; a disadvantage appears in the need to convince legislators of the national importance of investing in this route toward ameliorating the damage of social ills such as poverty.

The evolution of the Headstart program can be looked upon as an instance of inevitable problems to be faced when there is government-supported movement involving basic change in a social institution. Headstart represented revolutionary change in the dominant concepts of learning in early childhood and in the relation of school to family and community—*revolutionary* meaning here that knowledge and principles that had been developed in a sector of society with a small voice were to be applied in the encompassing public sphere. There were conflicting ideal images. Was the Headstart experience to be the most efficient route for children of poverty toward adaptation to the expectation and ideology of the existing public educational system? Or, was Headstart, as it developed as a movement, to be a stimulant toward incorporating new concepts of learning and socializing experience into the public school system? The challenge was social as well as educational.

Evidence of the gradual maturing of the Headstart program came in the development, analysis, and documentation of the educational components, in the functionally realistic inclusion of parents, in its outreach to health and social services, and in the stimulation of evaluative research. It is not surprising that, while the image of the program for learning, built on a psychological as well as an educational view of development (Stone & Janis, 1974), was accepted as the foundation, other images of the teaching–learning scene developed and were accepted. While programs share the common basic objectives of responding to developmental needs and individual differences, the range of preferred educational practice varies widely, including both behavioristic and developmental-interaction curriculum designs (Wallace, 1977).

Enactment of a changed concept of what learning could and should be called for a new program for developing teacher competence, which had major attention even during the first years of the program. The outcome is a specially planned teacher-training program that has comprehensive developmental goals for children in contrast to a restricted focus on achievement and skills proficiency. The training program, leading to credentialing as a child development associate, has several distinct characteristics. The basic competencies for the role are articulated in broad terms; the training experience is planned to derive the benefits of combining theoretical study of child development with the direct experience of learning the teaching role with children in a center; qualification is based on functional competence for taking responsibility for a group or a class within a center, as judged by observation of performance; the course toward certification varies with individuals since functional competence cannot be achieved within a specified time line (Biber, 1973; Klein & Lombardi, 1982). By 1983, there were 10,000 credentialed child development associates, evidence of the importance of adapting professional training programs to the reality of field operations, with measure of functioning competence as the central criterion. For many, this accomplishment becomes a step toward further professional study and qualification.

It took fifteen years of research activities to produce evidence of long-lasting effects of Headstart experience (Palmer & Anderson, 1979; Darlington et al., 1980). Positive measures of later school functioning and achievement can be attributed to the influence of the preschool learning experience and supportive activities such as the special contribution of parent participation. Appreciation of the evidence of sustained positive effects of the program and associated increased funding needs to be placed in the discouraging background of the relation between need and available support. The program serves only 20 percent of the eligible population and restricted funds impede continued development of the high standards that have been established for this program (Headstart, 1980).

How shall advances in preschool programs influence the going practice of public elementary education? Not surprisingly, there are different answers concerning the nature of affiliation between new and existing programs. In a study of five day care programs affiliated with public schools, Levine (1978) neither excludes nor endorses public school alignment. In the communities studied there were differences in all aspects of this complex institutional arrangement. Analysis of the issues of parent involvement, the nature of the educational program, the range of school responsibility, and the location of administrative and financial authority revealed divergent opinions on the question of affiliation of preschool programs with the public school system. The author foresees most positive outcome when the adaptation to such divergent opinions takes place in local communities rather than on a national level and when it is expressed in the perspective of each community's preference for the degree and areas of affiliation.

From the viewpoint of Headstart, mergence of the program with going school programs and organization would be most inappropriate. The public school, as organized, could not support the multiple functions that have been developed as intrinsic to the Headstart program: emphasis on competency-based teacher training and delivery of health and social services (Bowman & Kemble, 1976). Distinct from the image of mergence, Headstart has been interested in building jointly planned programs with elementary schools both to facilitate transition for the children and to move toward continuity in educational theory and practice (Project Developmental Continuity, 1977).

Plans for a more extensive project to integrate Headstart philosophy with changes in elementary school curriculum design and operation have been formulated. This design, now being distributed throughout the country, combines a focus on learning outcomes in specific content areas with the importance of individualizing programs and supporting motivation, curiosity, and interest in learning as a lifelong attitude. The design builds on a "whole school" concept with the basic goal of establishing continuity between Headstart and elementary school and between parent and teacher (Klein, 1978).

Integrating preschool with public elementary school practice evolved gradually in the Headstart program. At the same time, another extensive national program designed to evaluate varied practice in the first three grades was given government support. Established in 1968, Follow Through was oriented toward study of educational practice planned to be continuous with Headstart preschool experience, including parents and community in the life of the schools (Rhine, 1983). It had a distinctive purpose: to study and evaluate a series of varied approaches to changing educational practice in the early school years. The selected program models differed widely—some enacting behavioristic theory in contrast to a developmental-interaction approach or, in other terms, differing between a highly structured and sequenced curriculum and an open classroom approach. Within the schools working within any one of the selected study sites the teachers had the option of partaking in the new project or continuing with their former patterns. This made operation of this project structurally and psychologically different from the "whole school" approach taken by Headstart when it began to establish projects in elementary schools.

The Follow Through Project was constructed as an extensive research undertaking with high priority given to the evaluation of outcomes in programs differing in central goals and applied educational practice. There is general agreement that the research core of the project stimulated important and often original self-study within each model but the comparative studies have raised questions. How closely can the programs enact and exemplify the practices and principles of the model designs, and are our methods of large-scale statistical analysis suitable for measurement of the subtler, less objectively definable elements of an educational design? Despite the complexities of interpretation there is an advantage in the heightened awareness that differences in educational practice are aligned with basically different theories of learning and, beyond, with differences in fundamental value systems.

In thinking of these three programs together (day care, Headstart, Follow Through) we see different ways of directing awakened social conscience. They represent greater awareness of the importance of enriching school experience in the years of early childhood, especially for the poor. They represent also concern for the nature of care to be provided for the younger and younger children of the increasing working mother population, who represent varied economic levels.

On the positive side we see also the recognition that we need more adults around schools, especially for young children, to enact more differentiated roles with the children if the "teaching" role is to be distributed among assistants, aides, paraprofessionals, and parents. The fact of difference from child to child is becoming built into organizational structure by the use of more flexible, differentiated programming and scheduling, new kinds of child grouping, and more opportunities for child-to-child interaction. The walls that surrounded the profession of education have come down. Social workers, health workers, pediatricians, and child psychiatrists are making their own important contributions to the scene in enough places to build toward the model of a comprehensive center of which we "dreamed."

Perhaps most important on the positive side is the change in the social-psychological position of being poor. The old assumption that the children would internalize a sense of shame and inevitable defeat in relation to "comfortable" society has been considerably eroded in the face of the gains in opportunity for education and a participant role in society's mainstream, as well as the mighty force of an aroused national conscience. But the road is still uphill, as becomes plain when changing political currents reverse commitments that seemed to have been established as priorities in our society.

The Issues in Ferment: Social

On other issues there seems to have been less progress. The best we can say for them is that increased awareness in itself represents promise for the future. There are more voices, each with its own rights and insights, on what education should be, at the preschool as well as other levels. From one prespective, this denotes more democratic functioning: from another, it is disturbingly like a Tower of Babel. There is agreement that sound education must be relevant to the social-cultural-situational particularities of children and their families. But *relevant* is not easily defined or exemplified. And what should be constant, if not immediately "relevant"? Are there common principles, derivatives of the available scientific knowledge of childhood, that can be the foundation of diversified practice? At what level? Knowledge alone, even in a more advanced condition than is now at hand, could not answer the problem of diversity of values. We educate toward an ideal image of man and of adult functioning or, to be realistic, toward different ideal images in our pluralistic society, in which success, happiness, and morality have varying, sometimes contradictory, components. Concern about how education can respect and take into account divergent values from social class to class and from one ethnic group to another is in the forefront.

This general issue becomes concrete when the culture of the school contradicts that of the family. For young children, contradictory behavioral expectations, sanctions, areas of permissiveness and denial, and modes of adult–child interaction can be confusing, even disorienting. The "two lives" formulations sometimes offered the children—at home one way, but at school another—has internal faults at a stage when the processes for differentiating the self and the world scene are barely formed. The imaginative teacher bridges the gap in every possible way—through language, through food, through familiarity with home situations and the subcultural milieu, through keeping an open door for family and neighborhood members. But the greater challenge is to bring about maximal congruence between the school's and the family's codes and goals for the child. Goodwill, easy communication, imaginative translation can go a long way. I have in mind an instance in which parents, understandably eager for their children to begin to learn early, asked for homework for the four-year-olds. The teacher (Kessler),[4] sensitive to the parents' concern, planned the kind of homework that suited and interested the children and subsequently was able to use the content as material for communicating to the parents how activities that do not seem to have anything to do with learning to read are really the important foundation experience. But this will not always work. There come times of impasse when what parents want violates the teacher's personal and professional ethic. What happens then depends on how power is aligned; that there are times when teachers may need to be the ones to yield to parental demands, individual or collective, is evidence of the basic shift that has taken place. The gains and losses from this shift are not easily assessed, at least not in the early stages of social change, when motivation is high for correcting past misalignments of authority and is less focused on thoughtful reevaluation of previously accepted criteria for the essential enterprise. Concretely, what kind of parent–educator joint decision-making will best serve the long-range goals of both parents and professionals?

The Open Questions: Psychological

In addition to these social-institutional issues, which are in an uneasy state, there are major areas—intraeducational in nature—that are no more settled now than they were 40 years ago, although perspective is vastly enlarged and we have far more theoretical understanding and empirical insight to bring to bear upon them. In the intervening years, theory and practice may have found a comfortable alliance between developmental psychology and the concepts that were the foundation of progressive education, but there is a clearer, sharper divergence between developmentalists and behaviorists and the educational implications of these theoretical positions than was true in the past. The question of socialization can be put in the context of developmental stages, but we are more aware now that this perspective cannot be insulated from goals. Children *can* conform to socializing demands in the early years without extreme duress in given cultural settings, as has been observed by visitors to the People's Republic of China. But when there is (looking at ourselves) a strong emphasis on individual identity and autonomy in these early years, what happens? Is there a lasting loss or only a postponement of the socializing process? When we think in these terms, taking a long view developmentally and socially, we must remember the opposing position geared to the immediate: namely, that young children, especially those with harder roads to follow, need the kind of early socializing experience that will make it easier for them to "fit" the later school years, as these are now envisaged and enacted in the public schools in this

4. Inge Kessler is now senior educational consultant to the Agency for Child Development in New York City.

country. That raises a large question. What happens to the children during a period of slow, agonizing change in primary and elementary education such as is under way in projects like Follow Through? Are we studying children's adaptation to basically different learning climates?

It is still worth asking such questions as how to deal with the expression of hostile feeling in school situations: whether and to what extent aggressive behavior, when it is permitted, will constitute release or, contrariwise, will be a source of guilt feelings when diverting the feeling from direct expression is the adult maneuver. But this intrapsychic focus is only part of the problem in the light of children's exposure to the expression of destructive anger in the adult world today. The episodes of violence that the inner-city child sees on the street and often at home resonate with his own aggressive impulses.

The saturation of TV presentations with violence of all kinds provides similar resonance for all children. What many of us conjectured about the impact of TV violence has now been substantiated in the review of studies (*Television and behavior*, 1982) conducted during the 1970s, which demonstrated a causal relation between televised violence and later aggressive behavior in children from the preschool years (Singer & Singer, 1981) into adolescence, for girls as well as for boys. It has been verified that hour after hour of watching violence portrayed on television led to an acceptance of violence as normal behavior. For some children it leads to an overestimation of the amount of violence to be expected in their own communities, engendering fear and mistrust (see also Cohen, 1979).

In a conversation with several Bank Street teachers I heard that preoccupation with replaying TV themes, violent and others, was diminishing the high level of creativity that had characterized the use of the play process to understand reality in the era before television. The concern of educators has generated opposition to highlighting violence on TV programs and has stimulated the development of newly designed programs to help children understand the medium in ways that will lead to critical viewing skill. The school as an institution is presented with a new challenge: to help children internalize a code of positive values that is antithetical to the images of adult mores presented to them impressively day after day through TV technique and programming.

On the question of freedom and permissiveness in school settings, it is more clearly understood now that there can be no fixed formula for how much relaxation of authority, how much opportunity for free choice, will bring about the desired autonomous behavior. Decisions have to be made in terms of how much the total life experience of the children has made it possible for them to use relaxed authority productively without reacting with either increased anxiety or boundless license. And then, when presumably temporary adaptation of what is preferred practice is made, there is always the danger that the adaptation, which should be a transitory phase, may become routinized and institutionalized, losing sight of the original, ultimate goal.

The question of play in relation to early childhood experience in general and to learning in particular has suddenly and happily come in for prime attention. It is moving in so many directions and filtering through such different conceptualizations that it is too soon to say what effect this resurgence will have on educational practice and also on theoretical reformulations. In a later chapter there will be an opportunity to look at the growing acceptance of play as curriculum in the early years of schooling.

The other most active development at present, infant group care, was not thought of at the time I wrote my earlier paper and now derives its strong impetus from opposite social poles. It is now considered socially imperative that the infants of poor families and the babies of adolescent mothers should have the benefits of good health and early stimulation that cannot be provided for them at home. Deprivation of these benefits in early infancy is now considered to cause almost irreparable damage. From another direction, professionally employed women are organizing facilities for the group care of their infants, in the tide and in the spirit of the women's liberation movement. Our memories seem short. Was our erstwhile concern over separation anxiety overexaggerated? Or was the presumed advantage to the infant of a one-to-one relation to the parent an unsubstantiated theory? How is the extensive work of Bowlby (1969) and others on the question of attachment and separation, or studies such as the one by Janis (1964) dealing with separation at entering nursery school at two years of age, being reconciled with this movement?

In the case of infants in families under distress, there is a ready rationale. Some form of group care or family day care is the better alternative. The rationale for middle-class mothers is more convoluted. Perhaps out of the experience with infants in group care will come greater knowledge of when and under what circumstances the child, developmentally, can optimally separate from the intimacy of the mother–child relation. We can be encouraged by the fact that, in some situations, both the knowledge of early childhood education and sophisticated research procedures are being built into ongoing investigations. In one multidimensional study with a sample of 400 infants (Golden & Rosenbluth, 1978), three conditions were the subject of investigation: infants in group care facilities, those in family day care homes, and those reared at home. From the measures employed, infants in group care showed more advance in intellectual development than did those in family day care or home-rearing situations, but there were no differences in measures of social competence, emotional functioning, or cognitive style.

But, as might be expected, in view of the complexity of the problem, the findings from ongoing research studies are not in agreement. In one study (Kagan, Kearsley, & Zelazo, 1978), infants up to the age of 2.5 years who were attending a group care center five days a week were compared with children of the same sex and family background who were being reared in a typical nuclear-family context. On the dimensions studied, the findings did not corroborate the general expectation of differences. The children in group care were neither more cooperative nor more aggressive than the home controls; there was no evidence of greater insecurity or of a weakened emotional bond between child and mother. The authors, somewhat surprised by their findings, recognize the possibility that available methods may not be sufficiently sensitive to find areas of difference, which may indeed exist. In another study of infants in day care (Provence, 1974), there are contrary findings: "If children are in full day care from the earliest months of life, there will be some interference and delay in the formation of a close attachment to the parent." The author comments that the separation experience (feelings of longing and anxiety) is a recurring one for these young children and needs special attention by the caretakers.

An incisive critique of the faults of many infant group care programs appears in Dorothy Gross's statement (1977). She points to the disadvantages of rigidly maintained groupings in six-month age intervals, to overadaptation of the children's program to the needs of mothers or of research projects, to the emphasis on stimulating cognitive development (especially language) as separate from social and emotional experience, to ineptness in integrating the needs of both parents and the babies, and, finally, to insufficient individualization of care in line with child-development principles. Furthermore, she notes, there is insufficient awareness of the financial investment necessary to provide good group care for children in infancy. In sum, she writes,

> research programs . . . tended to overly structure the child's day and environment and transmit a sense of unnaturalness, as if the child were in an antiseptic box, removed from the ebb and flow of everyday life. The [poverty programs] were often patronizingly prescriptive to the parents, taking into insufficient account the reality of the child's life at home.

She supplements her critique with an analysis of good programs she observed that can serve as desirable "models." She writes in a mood of being ready to serve a social need and, at the same time, keeping her thinking open. After outlining the basic need for healthy experience in infancy in terms of complex developmental concepts, she asks: "Can he receive all this in a group day care center? I don't know for sure."

The importance of the formation of the "love bond" between mother and child in human infancy and its determinant influence on subsequent ego development from the psychoanalytic perspective are fully expounded by Selma Fraiberg (1977), who indicts our society for its failure to provide for healthy development in childhood. Her standards for substitute mother care are as high as her criteria for what constitutes basically positive mothering in the home. And as an advocate, she applies these standards to her image of an adequate day care center, which she spells out practically, in terms of minimal acceptable conditions, such as the proportion of babies to each caregiver. Though from a different vantage point in theoretical terms, her image of what constitutes adequate care for infants in group care corresponds with the goals that Dorothy Gross has established for programs in progress. We can take some hope from this kind of correspondence. But the question of group care for infants deserves continued study as well as consideration of alternative plans that have been developed in other industrialized nations. A plan for part-paid leaves preceding

and following childbirth has been projected for the United States (Zigler &
Muenchow, 1983). (See also Cordes, 1983.)

In this brief attempt to take stock of what has come to be accepted over the
past 40 years and what is still in ferment, one general trend seems to have
emerged. While we continue to strive for more defined techniques in rearing
and educating children, we are now committed to far more conscientious efforts
to take account of the complex surrounding social factors that condition the
efficacy of these techniques. Furthermore, we have strengthened our institutional means for achieving our goals.

CHAPTER 3

Socialization in the Context of Culture

It seems strange that reading about schools in the People's Republic of China should remind one of Public School No. 79 on Kosciusko Street in Brooklyn in the second decade of the century. On the page facing page 115 in Childhood in China *(Kessen, 1975) there are two pictures of children in a schoolroom. They look like first graders. In one picture, the children sit in pairs at the familiar old-fashioned school desks with seats attached. Their right hands are raised, their left hands behind their backs. The caption says that the children raise their hands to be called on and that "when a name is called, the child will stand straight at the side of his desk and call out the answer."*

In the second picture, in a room similarly equipped, a child stands in each row, making contact with one of the children seated in the row. The caption explains that these are row monitors, carrying out morning inspection, checking to see that each child has a clean face, clean hands, a handkerchief, and a cup.

These could be pictures of my second-grade classroom in 1910. We sat at desks exactly like those, raised our right hands to be called on with left hands behind our backs, and had row monitors who, instead of checking cleanliness, had the privilege of dispensing supplies for tests. I especially liked the long, narrow, white, ruled pads from which the monitors would tear the pages to be used for spelling tests. Seating was assigned according to merit, not to facilitate social interaction, God forbid! And merit was graded regularly on the three categories of our report cards: Effort, Proficiency, and Conduct. The monitors in the front seats gained place according to how the teacher's value system weighted those categories. In Miss Windchester's class I had achieved the coveted first-row first seat, a conforming child, enjoying the experience of learning, thin as it was, and trying to live up to family expectations.

A visitor would not have seen the whole story of that classroom or known that my conforming had other reinforcement. Miss Windchester was the kind of teacher called a "murder" by a child I knew many years later in a Harlem school. She believed in punishment and, without benefit of a rod, kept us all scared. Her technique was to issue a loud scolding, synchronized with grabbing a child by the hair and banging his head on the desk behind him. As I think of it now, I cannot see how this could really be done physically, but the frightening image of the gesture is still clear.

What happened one day remains a lifelong mystery to me. In the back of the classroom there was a closed wardrobe where the teacher hung her coat. There was I, one day, before the bell had rung, up in front of the class, imitating Miss Windchester in one of her tantrums, with great histrionics. I cannot remember how I felt when, as I reached my highest pitch, Miss Windchester walked out of the wardrobe closet; the trauma has blotted out recall of the moment. But I remember the sequel: I was moved from the first-row first seat to the third-row first seat, just below her desk, where, she said, she could keep watch over me and my deviltry. Mild, shy, scared "me"! I suffered through the episode alone, lacking the courage to tell my mother or my older sisters of my disgrace. To ease my hurt feelings, I remember comforting myself with the knowledge that I was still a monitor.

Could some psychologist of personality have predicted that this was the seed of rebellion that led me to Bank Street and another image of education?

Preschool Education (1964)

To Strengthen the Self

The evolution of the socializing process of the individual can be seen as a sequence of breaking the boundaries of the self; it means extending the sphere of kinship from parents and family to school, to teachers, to sex, to neighborhood; to those who share one's skills, one's interests, one's religion, one's viewpoint; to profession, community, region; to ethnic group, to a nation, and now to mankind. This development optimally consists of a cumulative extension of self, not a bartering of one identification for another. In the process of growing up, therefore, the primordial self of the infant gradually becomes a multiplicity of selves acting in complementary ways in the integrated individual.

It appears that a concept of individuality in which self-realization comes to fruition, not through a survival by competition of multiple selves or through moral repudiation of baser selves, but through an integrated progression from a

Adapted from Preschool education. In R. Ulich (Ed.), *Education and the idea of mankind.* New York: Harcourt Brace, 1964.

personal to an extended self, is essential in order to give reality to any expectation that concern for mankind can become a potent social force.

The hope of our era, if there is time, lies in our new-found knowledge of the deep-lying motives of human behavior, in our ability to bring this knowledge to bear on this ideal for mankind through the social institutions of the family and the school. Progress in this direction will condition how far human nature can be cultivated so that ways of feeling, thinking, and being support ideals. The goals of education are thus clearly bound up with available knowledge of inner processes, with the transmission of values through experience rather than verbal precept, with consciousness that the educative process has a vital impact on the human spirit as well as on mind.

During the last few decades a philosophy of education, consonant with humanistic ideals, has emerged in which the concept of extended individuality is a primary value. In this philosophy, the principles and methods through which teaching and learning are enacted utilize psychodynamic theory concerning the nature of experiences and relationships presumed to be conducive to developing ego strength. The maturity of an extended self, by this theory, depends on the development of psychic strength at every stage of growth, incorporating basic affirmative attitudes and the capacity to resolve conflicts noncorrosively and to conduct adaptive and creative interactions with people, work, and ideas. This philosophy of education is young and difficult to enact. It has been an imaginative forefront in American education and has suffered from distortion and misinterpretation; it takes hold slowly because it demands fundamental departures from traditional concepts of education, as well as the development of a new kind of teacher. Its foothold is firmest in preschool education because there is less tradition to be put aside and because the interaction between the child's inner processes and his mode of relating to his life environment is more open to observation and understanding.

To understand and educate the preschool child it is necessary to take cognizance of certain elemental processes that inevitably involve conflict. The way in which these conflicts are resolved furnishes basic attitudinal material for the personality in formation.

The younger the child, the more dependent is his perception of reality on the particular configuration of each separate experience. Recognizing the lines of connection and constancy between experiences separate in time or differing in constellation is part of gradual maturing from infancy on. The faith that the mother, when gone, is not lost forever is part of learning; the absence of this faith easily becomes a generalized separation anxiety. For the preschool child the ultimately reassuring rhythm of separation and reunity has usually taken place within the familiarity and constancy of the home. When he enters school, he relives this experience in a new, unknown setting. Awareness and acceptance of the child's possible anxieties by school people become educationally fruitful when they supply for him the bridge between what is being left behind and what is being entered, by acts relevant to the child's emotionality: no stricture against crying or regressive behavior, bringing home toys to school, having parents stay in school during early phases, offering food, and supporting physical contact.

Yet, support for anxieties associated with the child's loss of familiarity of setting and separation from the closest figures in his life is only part of the educator's task; it is primarily her task also to offer the child a meaningful new phase of life in which to partake, rich in opportunity for finding gratification for the maturing powers of body and mind (Hartmann, 1958). Optimally, then, the goal is twofold: first, to reduce the possible trauma of experiencing separation as irretrievable loss, and, second, to make the experience of entering new orbits of life experience stimulating and satisfying to the forward drives of the individual.

The problem of possession represents another basic process in the emotional life of the preschool child, one that is rooted in the experiences of infancy and is relived and reshaped during these years. The infant's basic feeling of safety in belonging to the protective mother is inevitably threatened as the child encounters the reality of the mother's other ties—to husband, to siblings, to her own parents and friends.

The teacher who recognizes that a child who desperately clings to a favorite "thing" or pushes to sit right next to her in the story circle is involved in living out and working through deep, universal human conflicts of possession and rivalry is faced with more complex goals than the teacher who wheedles or forces children's behavior into pleasing social molds. Arbitrary demands on young children to give up, to give away, without a feeling of loss may exact a terrible price. It may be teaching them to avoid loss by giving up the disposition to care or to want deeply in any way. For the child to whom beloved things may be almost part of his psychic self, the demand may be felt as a deep violation. This does not mean that children do not need to learn to give, to yield, to wait. It does mean that the teacher's feelings, insight, and technique should make it possible for her to guide the child gradually to give up what may be dear to him without feeling destroyed as a person, to feel a deep tie to her while knowing she is similarly tied to others, to control his primitive ways of expressing his rivalry with other children without feeling overwhelming guilt for having had such feelings in the first place. In such an educational atmosphere the primitive self does not have to be castigated, thrown off, and replaced by the civilized self. Its vital energies and passions are needed for the ultimate capacity to live deeply and fully; they should be educated, not censored or denied.

Another basic transformation of the preschool years takes place in the sources of pleasure. The self, even after infancy, is in important ways still a body-self, and it is understandable that in a puritanical society such as ours, there is pressure, conscious and unconscious, to wean the child as fast as possible from the natural pleasures he can find in body sensations and in the active exercise of his physical powers. Thus shame, if not threat, and, in either case, the arousal of deep guilt are the means used to train the child in his habits of elimination and to stop his impulses toward thumbsucking or masturbatory activity. Once more, by these methods, part of the elemental self is chipped away and lost as a wellspring for full growth toward emotional maturity.

Education during the preschool years has a delicate task to perform in this area of development. It must create an atmosphere in which body functions and impulses are not associated with disgust or shame while at the same time it gradually initiates the children into socialized ways of handling these drives. A second task is to provide the opportunity and equipment for finding pleasure in discovering endless possibilities of engaging physically with the world of things and space, of experiencing mastery in the skills of the body. The goal is to help the child gradually outgrow the autistic sources of pleasure and instead find gratification of the body-self through an outward course into an extended environment. The image of a four-year-old who has not only reached the top of the jungle gym but has managed to suspend himself head down and explains excitedly for anyone to hear what an "upside-down world" looks like can suggest how fulfillment of the powers of the body-self is part of the educational task in the preschool years.

A few general principles emerge to serve as guidelines for the education of the young child: elemental impulses are to be accepted and rechanneled, not denied and stamped out; impulsivity in general is an irreplaceable source of vitality and depth, not to be sacrificed by premature socialization or taboo setting; to strengthen the self, education needs to provide appropriate encounters between the child and his world at every stage.

One of the significant confrontations for the young child is his experience of the strength and authority of the people in his world vis-à-vis his own weakness and social impotence. In the nature of this experience lie alternate possibilities. His natural drives to explore beyond possible bounds, to release aggressive impulses in dangerous ways, or to seek his own strength by resisting adult authority cannot be given free reign if he is to be physically or emotionally safe. If these drives are harshly, arbitrarily, or punitively curbed, the child's resulting good behavior will be accompanied by a sense of inner badness and the kind of repression of primary and retaliatory anger that is most likely to become a dangerous reservoir of latent hostility. There are alternative ways of exercising control over the young child that avoid the stamp of sin, which invite him to enter into the rationality of authoritative acts and which leave room for expression of negative feeling within limits. This is one of the most studied aspects of preschool education at the present time; it is worth noting that it is also one of the areas in which neophytes in the profession find themselves most troubled by the rearousal of feelings connected with their own childhood relations to and conflicts with authority figures.

It is not the intention of educators to spare the child the inevitable conflicts of growing up; this, if it were true, would be the most egregious error of all since it is through the meeting and resolution of conflict that the self gains and feels its deepest strength. The goal is to guide the child in his preschool years through the inevitable conflicts associated with the family drama and his induction into socialized living, in such a way that he emerges capable of accepting control but uncowed, capable of love without demanding exclusive right of possession, without a feeling of sin attached to his psychic or physical self, ready to move on to taste the pleasure of knowledge and mastery in an ever-widening world.

One elemental process during these years that can be the very hand-maiden to the educative process is the child's ambivalence and the ready accessibility of his opposite feelings. He has not much face to lose if the child he tried to pummel on Monday is his best friend on Tuesday; while he may join enthusiastically in a contagious outburst of stamping feet, he is happy and relieved when the teacher restores the collective calm he also wants; the lingering wish to stay young, to depend on adults for support, reassurance, and control lives alongside the deep wish to grow up, to strike out for independence and forgo the comforts of enveloping protection. The skillful teacher, dedicated to the growing rather than the training processes, can tune her response to the shifting behavior that bespeaks the child's ambivalent feelings. She can believe in his positive drives and wishes even when he is engaged in maneuvers that are destructive to himself and others, help him bring his positive self into dominance, and show him to himself in a warm, good light. Perhaps this can be considered the essence of healthy self-knowledge: to know and accept one's self as a source of good and evil and to trust that the positive self will provide the major drive for living.

The "Extensor" Processes

At this point, it is time to consider other growth processes that characterize the preschool years and the known possibilities for channeling these processes toward deepened and extended identification of the individual with his environment. If a single term could be at all adequate, the term *extensor* processes might be employed to refer to the burgeoning impulses of the healthy young to make contact with his world, from the earliest days when all he can do is taste and smell it, to the time, four or five years later, when it is an idea world as well as a thing world that he feels challenged to master through understanding. The stubbed toes and dirty knees of the two-year-old determined to explore every unknown corner, to achieve the top of the stairs at the cost of no matter how many bumps, are the forerunner of the wrinkled brow of the five-year-old trying to sort out his scrambled ideas about "olden days," when people had only candles for light, when his father was a little boy, and no airplane, not to speak of a jet, had flown across the sky.

The urge to get at and into the world beyond the self goes through miraculous transformations in the short span of the preschool years: they are characterized by accelerated maturing of the human apparatus in its physical and mental capacities, and the momentum generated by the powerful drives for mobility (Mittelmann, 1954) and curiosity (Murphy, 1958). What these transformations are is the resultant of native equipment and social impact. Every child enters the sphere of symbolic discourse, which leads eventually to a system of explanatory and interpretive thought, synchronous with the logos of his society; every child creates a pattern of coherence for his perceptual and ideational experience that has attitudinal as well as cognitive elements.

In relation to the issue of education and mankind, there are two intrinsic questions to be raised. What can early education do to lead the young, groping mind toward the kind of intellectual potency that is represented by the capacity to deal analytically and synthetically with the ever-widening world of objective knowledge and personal experience? How can the young child experience the deep, creative involvement in his early encounters with the world of things, problems, and ideas that will ensure against superficiality and indifference and lay the groundwork for an attitude of commitment to hopes and ideals for human progress?

Children themselves, under almost any circumstances, construct an era of discovery out of the span of the preschool years. Education for this period holds the possibility for helping the child build an image of himself as a discoverer of a way of life within which he expects to move from the unknown to the known, from the mystifying to the comprehensible. For such a possibility to be approximated, it is essential that teachers themselves be attuned to the ordinates of early childhood: sensory-perceptual-motor modes of relating to experience, establishment of meaning through self-reference and personal experience, rapidly shifting bases of idea structures from contextual simultaneity to cause–effect paradigms, and, most important of all, the preeminence of the subjective life, expressed in the child's satisfaction with fantasy as a mode of bringing coherence into the welter of fact and feeling that constitutes his experience.

On the simplest level there is the concrete, physical world, to be known through exploration and discovery. Every home has a chair to creep under and climb over, a dark corner to hide in, things hard to reach for, and in-between spaces to squeeze into, all of them opportunities for knowing the physical world. In school during these years another kind of setting is carefully created for this aspect of experience in "knowing": greatly increased opportunity, through the provision of equipment and space, to engage with the physical world in a varied round of maneuvers, including climbing, swinging, sliding, balancing, heaving, and stacking, and freedom to invent new variations of accomplished patterns of manipulation and coordination. In this setting, relatively free of the restrictions that must be made at home to keep life safe and enjoyable for all those who compose a family, the limits on courage and opportunity to try new feats can be set in terms of the child only: at what point will his drive to explore lead him toward physical injury or psychological damage in the form of excessive frustration? What kind of support can one child have for his bold, courageous adventuring? How can another be weaned from a tendency to hang back from the uncertainties of such new frontiers?

To the outside eye, they are busy, active children enjoying themselves. To the conscious educator, they are learning new skills; they are accruing new knowledge of themselves. Not only a child but a new self-feeling swishes down the slide with outstretched arms after the child has climbed to the top of the jungle gym for the first time and, standing alone, has scanned the endless vista of the neighboring roofs. Such children are gaining direct knowledge of the nature of the physical world, knowledge that, in a few years, will be transformed into abstract concepts of weight and pressure, of wheel and axle, of hoisting and leverage. The adults in this world echo the child's pleasure in the expanding sense of himself as he moves about in his physical world and they see in his playful elaboration of physical feats the evidence of his individuality, making over in his own shape the "world" he has been given.

In application, this principle guides preschool organization at all levels, from decisions on purchasing to criteria for selection of teachers. The "things" of the preschool world offer a wealth of sensory experience: the rough sand in the box, the smooth velvet covers for the doll bed, the red paint jar beside the black one, the hard blocks that cannot be squeezed into a small space, the too-soft clay that cannot be made to hold a shape, the tap on a triangle, the rush of water in a sink. The "things" alone are not adequate teachers, though, unfortunately, there are many schools even at more advanced levels where there is a false dependence on materials, equipment, and buildings as the carriers of learning. In this young world it is the sensitive teacher who supplies the accents for the child's experience, perhaps by standing quietly with a few children, so quietly that one can try to hear the sounds the fish make when they pass one another in the tank, or still for so long that there is time to see the last bit of the boat pass over the horizon; perhaps by clutching a pan of snow in her arms, after the excited tramp in the snow piles, for the children to watch as it melts inside the warm room and to touch its smooth, icy surface when it is brought in from the window sill the following morning. The teacher's sensitivity can sometimes be measured indirectly; it is almost as if it correlates negatively with the amount of verbalization that accompanies this aspect of her teaching capacity.

The young child's naturally high impressionability, his freedom from the need to act through a structure of systematic purposes and means to ends, the available energy of the extensor processes provide his teachers with limitless possibilities for deepening his powers of perception and response to an accented, differentiated life environment. Through these experiences he becomes an observer; through observation, he is being introduced to one of the basic processes of learning; by deepening his own capacity for observation he is strengthening one form of vital communication between the self and the environment.

It is during the preschool years that the human mind performs its greatest magic: the child is freed from dependence on sensory-perceptual-motor experience as the sole channel of communication with his environment (Solley & Murphy, 1960). The evolution of the capacity to deal with experience symbolically represents the key extensor process of the maturing organism. It manifests itself in every medium of expression known to man and runs the full course from the simplest gestural representations to advanced levels of abstraction. The string held to the ear is "telephoning" to the child who has nothing like a three-syllable word in his vocabulary; the spinning five-year-old who drops to the floor in delicious exhaustion is an astronaut in orbit; from the crayon lines of the three-year-old a "face" appears; the clay in the hands of the four-year-old walks like a dog; the leftover strips of lathe in the wood box are regenerated as a helicopter. Symbolizing through gesture, through two-dimensional and three-dimensional representation, is a natural child mode of reiterating the more meaningful aspects of experience, thereby strengthening the joining lines between the inner self and the outer world. Equally exciting to the child, and ultimately the keystone of his ability to deal effectively with the complexity of human living, is his gradual mastery of the word and the idea as tools for symbolically organizing experience. The very young child, intoxicated with the insight that everything has a name, stumps the adult with his unanswerable question: What is the name of yesterday? A very few years later, the six-year-old's unanswerable questions are of another magnitude: If settling arguments with words instead of fists is a sign of growing up, then why do we send soldiers to fight in wars?

The intermediate steps in this progression toward more complex, conditional, and comprehensive concepts are not random; patterns of increasing differentiation and integration follow a discernible sequence. Elements in experience are seen by the child as belonging together through acts of repetition, through similarities of projected affect as well as object attributes, through classification based on use and function. Differences in degree are added to absolute contrasts; time perceived at first through a sequence of familiar events matures into the syntax of seasons, days of the week, hours of the clock. The child's first universe of given things in an eternal state of the "present" gives way to a world of change over time; his fascination with the "how" processes of making, doing, and fixing is close to the generic meaning of *manufacturing;* the span between beginning and end, then and now, expands to a primordial sense of history.

The responsibilities of education for this period of growth become clearer when it is recognized that it is possible for the child not only to acquire knowledge of what constitutes his world and how it functions but also to learn an attitude toward himself as one who can gain mastery over ignorance, perplexity, and confusion; not only to enlarge his vocabulary and engage in traffic with ideas but also to learn how the process of thinking can be an exciting, gratifying form of exploration and discovery; not only to look to adults as the source of information and know-how but to learn how to transform what, in the last analysis, can only be borrowed from others into a self-absorbed and internalized understanding of one's own. To fulfill such possibilities requires highly specific attitudes and techniques on the part of teachers; these can be referred to only briefly in the context of this paper.

There is a concrete method for firsthand study of the environment, creatively conceived and skillfully developed by Lucy Sprague Mitchell (1950), which is adapted to the constant revision and revolutionary changes in the child's world of reality. The emergence of television and the space age, for example, requires basic rethinking of what a child's world of ideas is. Techniques of group discussion in school make thinking a socialized experience, in which a wide range of accepted relevance and a minimum of right–wrong orientation invite the child's mind to roam fully with the raw materials of thought and allow the teacher to guide by accenting connectives, by opening up new and richer fields for wonder and research, by leading thought processes to more advanced organization, as, for example, when children first engage in cause–effect reasoning.

There is a danger, of course, that the teacher may overdo her function as a guide toward mastery of reality in terms of increasingly clear and logical thinking and, in so doing, sacrifice the opportunity to nurture creativity at its source (Biber, 1959b). In the intellectual realm, this problem is analogous to the damage to creativity in the sphere of the emotions inherent in too early or too strict denial of impulse expression. There are manifold ways in which the young child's creativity in assimilating and organizing experience can be kept vital and gratifying. One of these is to provide the materials, the setting, the atmosphere for full and free activity in the nonverbal modes of symbolizing and reorganizing experience, to give psychological space to physiognomic as well as representative symbolizing activity.

Another way is to understand and accept the young child's need to use the self as the nucleus around which meanings and concepts are developed. To develop the mind, the teacher needs to be in close touch with the self. Concepts of time are threaded around the emotions of birthdays. When a five-year-old, watching a group of three-year-olds with his teacher, turns to her and asks, "Do you remember what we looked like then?" he is comprehending growth. The boundless curiosity about all origins, about where things come from, is rooted in the great mystery of one's own birth. The skillful teacher constructs a continuous bridge from the central self to the extended realities of the nonself, thus presumably preventing a system of dichotomous affect between the personal and nonpersonal, between the individual and the outer world. Unless such processes as these are rooted in the early years of personality development, is there much reason to hope that self-transcendence can be psychologically healthy in mature life?

The most significant opportunity for supporting creative processes in young children lies in the way in which their life of pretending is understood, responded to, and provided for. A first principle is to recognize the dynamic aspects of the play life of children and perceive it as a complex counterpoint of active selection and transformation of experience, in which material from the deepest levels of affect can be merged with recently acquired factual knowledge. There are transformations of self-roles: the child turns himself into a baby, a tiger, an engineer, a cyclone. The interpersonal and mechanical relationships of everyday life are relived and reinstituted; meals are cooked, babies lovingly tended; windows and elevators appear in block buildings; planes crash and cows escape from the pasture. The complex of relations among the children within which the play sequence develops is characterized by its fluidity but is never random with respect to individual personality. Some children project relatively fixed roles: the baby, the victim, the captain, the pessimist, the idea man. Some move in and out of a variety of roles as varied qualities of interaction take shape: dominating, supporting, joining, aggressing, manipulating, distracting, and so on. There are no mandates for what the things in the real world shall be; a rusty muffin tin is a beautiful cake; a small wooden cube is a traffic light; a sawhorse is a bridge or a tunnel or a mountain; an enclosure is a house or an airport or a jail or a field of wildflowers.

When the educational setting and atmosphere offer guidance without imposing direction on the play life, the children are the masters of selection, sequence, and timing; for future development, it is important that the child counteract his feelings of powerlessness by being given the chance to experience autonomy in such creative, constructive activities, not through his natural resistance to an adult-ordered world alone. By reliving the most meaningful aspects of their experience through self-initiated play, children actually master the realities of life experience. Thereby, they intensify their insights and, at the same time, create situations that lead them on to new and deeper levels of wondering and questioning; how great the gain depends on the quality of teaching available to them.

The play of young children, however, serves a far more intricate function than to advance and extend their mastery of reality: it is the child's natural vehicle to bring about a dynamic fusion of mastery of reality with subjective expression. Emotional responses—positive and negative—are projected and relived as actively as cognitive responses. The freedom to symbolize experience through play, away from objective, logical modes, gives the child emotional safety. This, in turn, makes it possible for his play to become a catharsis for living through defeats, frustrations, and pain and thus has value, in general, for working out inner conflicts in an external field.

For play to serve these multiple functions, it is necessary that teachers be able to read the language of play and be aware of the extent to which coherence can be achieved on a symbolic level while play roles and relationships may deny the simplest facts of reality. Only then will teachers be able to provide the balance between the child's dual impulse toward fantasy and reality while at the same time respecting the integration of the two, which the child is accomplishing at a deep level, in his own idiom.

In this paper I have attempted to illustrate how preschool education is related to the nurturing of individuality, conceived in terms of self-knowledge, self-realization, and self-transcendence. Two major propositions have been developed. First, the socialization of the young child need not, should not, mechanize the impulses associated with the elemental processes of development lest it sacrifice creativity, spontaneity, and a positive self-image at the source. Second, the intellectual development of the child, identified as the extensor process, can be guided so as to enhance his powers of establishing a pattern of deep, personal involvement with the world around him, by protecting his modes of integrating experience through fantasy as well as reality, by fostering an image of self-strength and an expectation that it is the individual who, through his own potentialities for being impressed and making an impact, continually makes and remakes his world, as a child and in maturity.

Self-worth and Socialization

The preceding paper on preschool education was first published in a book called *Education and the Idea of Mankind* (Ulich, 1964), a social-philosophical work that gave me the opportunity to place a philosophy of preschool education in the context of the complex process of the socialization of the individual. I took the position, as I still do, that generative social commitment is built on a foundation of appropriate fulfillment of individual needs and propensities adapted to shifting perspectives and problems in successive life stages.

From this position, socialization had best be a slow evolutionary process through which the young child first internalizes a positive sense of identity and self-worth as an individual. Gradually, he is helped to establish a network of interpersonal relations in which others are sensed, accepted, and enjoyed as individuals with wishes, troubles, and styles of responding that are particularly their own. Learning the conventional, positive forms of social behavior among people is kept subordinate to sustaining the quality of interchange on a genuine feeling basis of mutual interest and concern. Otherwise there is the danger that forms, verbally learned and expressed, may be mistakenly taken to represent underlying psychological reality. Because the socializing process is so complex and the child, in his early years, must weather a period of emotional conflict which tries his sense of safety, it is to be expected that the capacity, the willingness, even the pleasure in responding to others' needs will be wavering and will need sympathetic guidance. Of course, there is an underlying assumption, from the long view, that this socializing process of youth will mature and ultimately take the shape of commitment to a humanist, democratic society. The potential validity of this assumption depends on how much the social mores of the external world the child encounters as he grows up support or, at least, do not violate the way of life he has internalized in early childhood.

A Socializing Classroom

It is possible to create in classrooms a climate of human relations—adult-to-adult and adult-to-child—that exemplifies benign, supportive, mutually beneficial and enjoyable interaction. We think we know how to do this between teachers and children in our classrooms. In fact, this kind of experience of a way of life in which the boundary lines of age, authority, and status are muted is an essential complement to the nurturing of individuality in our paradigm for socialization. There is a dynamic point of view that understands behavior not only in its acted-out components but also in terms of underlying motivation. Or, to put it in another way, the socializing impulses and the course they will take are to be trusted when the motivation is inner generated, not when the behavioral components are didactically learned. It would be naive to think that an idyllic taste of life in the few preschool years would be so powerful as to overcome the pressures toward competition, aggrandizement, and power that our children encounter in adult life. Rather, this paradigm for early childhood has been conceived as a beginning: a mode of learning and living in school to be incorporated in the social enterprise of education at all levels and thus in itself to become a force for social change. I must admit that, as out-of-school forces such as television gain influence, my confidence in the power of the school to effect social change *by itself*, even if we could have it in our own image, falters.

Another Image: The Soviet Union

I have not visited the People's Republic of China or the Soviet Union, but I am greatly interested in the reports by other Americans and their views on how their observations stir up new thinking about our own educational scene. Our pluralism shows through. American visitors taking an identical trip together have drawn somewhat contradictory inferences from their common experience. As a reader, I find myself saying "yes" to some of my colleagues' reactions and "no" to those of others. I realize that my comparative image is drawn from my own experience in a mode of education that does not represent dominant practice in our country, no matter how much I may wish to believe that there are signs that it is the wave of the future.

On the other hand, I see little to be gained by taking the old P.S. No. 79 image as typical of contemporary education, on the whole, in comparing U.S. and Soviet education. The truth about American schools today lies somewhere between schools that implement progressive trends, like the Bank Street School for Children, and the old closed-in world of rote learning, teacher–pupil distance, and pressures for behavioral and ideational conformity that characterized the public schools of the beginning of the century. It is to this midway reality that we need to address our thinking.

Drawing on his study of Soviet education, Bronfenbrenner (1970) asked that our school system take greater responsibility for the social and moral development of the child, especially in light of the fact that the American family has been defaulting on its child-rearing responsibility. He sees the rebellious, antisocial, rising aggressiveness of the youth peer group in our society as the product of the inadequate performance of the school and the family in guiding youth into the ways of a cooperative and mutually supportive style of life. As a possible corrective to our faults, he saw certain values in the Soviet methods: in the central use made of collective social forms and mandates in "socialist" competition of group with group, and in the continuity between the values inherent in school life (specifically, the elevation of the values of work and service to others) and the value priorities underlying the adult communist society. But from the viewpoint of some of our own preferred values, he raises questions. To what extent is what, from a logical perspective, can be called continuity actually accomplished through a variety of pressures to conform? Further, will not disciplinary methods such as withdrawal of parental love in response to misbehavior in early childhood and the customary mode of public self-criticism in later childhood seriously diminish the potential for autonomous functioning?

Drawing on his Soviet analysis and contemporary social-psychological studies, he asked for a new style of socialization, one in which there would be more intensive relationships with adults—parents at home and teachers in school—whose adult models of positive human interaction, combined with deeply meaningful involvement with the children, would counteract the drift of adolescents and youth away from the moral foundations of a democratic society.

It is easy to endorse many of the specific directions in which he wishes to move. But it would be useful to take account of how far we are already moving in these directions and ask what impedes further progress. In the case of schools, for example, the methods for establishing a socializing climate are not only known as theoretical deductions to research psychologists. They have had many years of sophisticated trial in progressive, experimental schools. There is an articulated philosophy and a seasoned methodology for teacher training and cooperative living. There is continuous analysis and assessment of the optimal balance between nurturing individuality and educating for social commitment—the challenge that is crucial to a democratic society as it is not in an authoritarian system.

Why Don't We Do Better with the Socializing Process?

The problem for us is why, since we have available experience and considerable inclination, we do not make greater progress. There are, of course, a number of conjectural answers: Movement in a pluralistic society is slow; individualism can be and often is construed in its "rugged" embodiment as indifference to social components; dreaming of a better life stays more on a personal than a social stage; the realistic possibility of going under in a capitalist economy is conducive to a self-protective drive for competitive success and power; and so on.

Thinking of education as a social force stimulates other lines of thought. In a paper on the contributions of developmental psychology, Ginsburg and Knitzer (1976; see also Keniston, 1977) argue for recognition of the major role that nonpsychological factors—poverty, value conflict, and so forth—play with regard to problems that academic psychologists mistakenly try to solve with the tools of their own discipline. To make progress in implementing the knowledge we have of the components of positive child development, these authors ask psychologists to become interested, knowledgeable, and skillful in social-change strategies and to move closer to the mechanisms of government. The same applies to educators who see a direction in which they wish education to move. In the field of early childhood education, because it is a relatively young field, the governmental agencies have been most open to forward movement and have established productive liaison with professionals.

That gets me back to the position I stated earlier—namely, that for social commitment to be solidly grounded in personality structure, it should be a gradual emergent from an early childhood period of individual fulfillment. It should be sustained as a reciprocal process in which the individual gains strength and pleasure from merging with the group at the same time that he establishes his identity by feeling free to assert his independence of the group, as occasion and mood dictate. This view influences the choice that we make, as educators, among different socializing influences. It leads, for example, to a positive view toward facilitating cooperation as a group process in tasks and activities that are necessary and serve to smooth the life of the classroom. It takes exception, on the other hand, to the suggestion that "such 'customs' as group applause for correct answers or selection and honoring by classmates of members showing greatest individual progress" are desirable methods of group reinforcement. Should we not be wary of developing other-directed personalities, with shifting dependence on external approval?

Early Education in China

The American observers who visited China in the early 1970s came back with mixed feelings of admiration, doubt, envy, and puzzled surprise. Reading their reports without having had their experience, I found myself sharing some, though not all, of their reactions—with less envy than some and less surprise than others.

In the broadest sense, we Americans share the goals of the Chinese people, their dreams for a just society, different as are the means toward that goal taken by a capitalist democracy and a socialist society. The Chinese travel a different road from ours toward commitment to the social good. They are direct, less troubled by conflicting images of the ideal and by differing theories about the means. The primary goal that the individual should serve society—conceived as it is in the image of a just and strong instrument for the protection of a good life for all its members—is expressed with emphasis and constant repetition in the mores, the content, and the methodology of the educational experience, at all stages of development, from the earliest beginnings.

I have read three accounts of education in the 1970s, during the Mao Zedong era—two by visiting Americans, one by a native Chinese educator who is now a member of the American educational community—and have found it interesting to see how differently they sort out their impressions, especially with reference to the question of individuality and socialization.

In brief, this is what we get descriptively from the book-length report of one group (Kessen, 1975). I find myself juxtaposing their practices with ours at Bank Street, which I have placed in parentheses. The pressure of an ideological image is everywhere—in school and out. Images of socialist heroes protecting the people, morality lessons about good and evil permeate the settings and the content of the learning environment—songs, drama, arithmetic lessons. The ethic of "serve the people" is expressed and portrayed at different levels—general themes of social merit such as working to make the earth produce food as well as the more intimate interpersonal selflessness of adults or children in helping, giving, or supporting roles. These are the images on the walls of classrooms (not the first images of the children's efforts at using paint on paper that we see in our classrooms). The moral lessons are clear portrayals of the evil actions that should be censured, and the phrase *speak bitterness* is a reminder that children should be kept aware of the evils of the past from which this new life will protect them. (During World War II, we did not stop our children from inventing fantasy tortures against Hitler and the Nazis; he was the bitter enemy, and we considered their play a way of dealing with their anxiety and their fears that we might not overcome him. But the images seeking relief from anxiety were child initiated.)

The calm of the social atmosphere sustained with these young children surprised the American visitors. They saw minimal assertion, resistance, or aggression; the teachers expected the children to conform and they did. They were neither criticized nor disciplined. Specific approval techniques took the place of direct expression of disapproval by the teacher. The teacher was likely to make her approval public, thereby formulating and codifying the generally accepted patterns of good behavior. The children gradually took on the monitoring role with respect to one another and gained teacher approval for doing so at the same time that they were encouraged to love and care for one another. Within a general atmosphere of warmth and devotion, it was the teacher's function to encourage self-reliance and not to indulge dependence.

Whether by temperament, cultural mode, or conditioning, these were young children who could watch with fascination without trying to touch a mechanical toy before them on the table. Any individual impulses toward behavior that might be disruptive to the group were well controlled by the children (assuming that they were incipiently present). Yet, these same children were spontaneous, outgoing, and spirited in other appropriate situations. Where there were infringements—the teachers reported only minor "naughty" episodes to the visitors—the children were talked to about who was right and who wrong, not punished, and gradually "persuaded" to desist from anti-social behavior. Gradually, the children were expected to become self-critical and to place themselves within the collective authority of the peer group as the source of both support and censure.

The ethic of work has high priority and does not have the figurative meaning for these young children that is implied when we say: play is child's work. The children carried out genuine work tasks, perhaps a simple assembly task for a neighboring factory, suited to their level of ability, as part of their socializing experience—contributing productive labor to society. (We, too, place especial importance on valuing work and workmanlike attitudes but find ways to use the children's self-directed play and activities as the vehicle for nourishing an attitude of productiveness). The children relate to the world of work in other ways: in their songs, in the roles they take in dramatic performances, in visits to sites where work is going on. (Here we are on familiar ground: our curriculum for the early years is built on direct experience with the work in the world around the school and with the people who fill the work roles.) Part of the preparation for adult functioning is the combination of work and study. The "productive labor" of the young children within the school setting is presumably the grounding for this life attitude. (This is where our psychological theory leads us in a different direction. We look upon the sequence of development epigenetically: An underlying attitude to be sustained over the whole developmental period need not be expressed in the specific behavioral form that it will ultimately take in mature life; in fact, it will go through metamorphoses in response to changes in successive developmental stages.)

The teaching strategies of this period were highly traditional—at the opposite pole from our preference for discovery learning and open classroom climates. The day is highly structured, with few opportunities for choice. Methods are didactic: children are taught the right answers and learn skills for preset tasks. Emphasis is on skills, not on self-initiated problem solving on the part of the children. It is the teachers who initiate, maintain, and terminate activities, often changing frequently from one to another. Group recitation and chanting in unison are patterns for the children's response. Artwork consists of copying teachers' forms. There are few books or materials for play. Play activities follow established group patterns for collective games. Within the context of didactic teaching and collective responding, questions put to the teachers by visiting educators about how individual differences were dealt with did not seem to lead anywhere. The frequent answer, "Children are all the same," sounded as though the question had touched a sensitive nerve, as though thinking in terms of the individual would have a deviationist quality.

The children showed phenomenal skill in singing and dancing. They performed for the visitors, presenting complex, elaborately costumed and choreographed dramatic plays which required skills of memory and technique far beyond what we would expect of American children of this age. It was not only in these performances that they showed spirited exuberance. They could shift readily from quiet, controlled, focused attention to expressive, happy, gracious engagement with one another or the visitors.

Reflections about What Was Perplexing

The observers came away with questions to which they offered varied conjectural answers. It might be expected that the positive control techniques, the emphasis on collective responding, the repetitious exposure to a clear code for which values are to be accepted and which rejected, and the structured environment offering few alternatives would result in conforming behavior on the part of most children. (Our traditional schools and their relatively benign teachers over the years have also produced conforming children.) But why such complete absence of disruptive behavior and, more significantly, how to explain that these children, though conforming, sustained their spontaneity and exuberance without becoming docile, apathetic, or inhibited?

Projecting the question of child behavior in school against the background of social revolution (from correspondence with Lilian Katz) calls for recognition of the dominant optimistic mood for the future transmitted from teachers to children. The adult positivism (parents and teachers) can be seen as having an energizing effect upon the children, contributing to expression of alertness and spontaneity in tandem with the passivity and acceptance of regimentation characterizing the teaching–learning experience. The teacher's adherence to didactic, routinized methods is related to the society's dominant value of collective participation in contrast to appreciation of individual variation and a society's potential gain from its recognition and sponsoring.

Either as visitors or as readers we come away thinking and rethinking old assumptions. If the early years are understood as periods of conflict over separation, possession, authority, where is it expressed in this child society? Can it be that there is no rivalry in this atmosphere even though the teacher is so actively a praising figure and therefore implicitly discriminating? No envy of someone's superior athletic prowess? Is it all so different because the children grow up with wider affiliations in extended families? Because there are so few things (toys) that private ownership is not part of reality? Or are conflicts repressed by the young and denied by the adults? Are the beautiful performances by the older children, with the frequent themes of victim and conqueror, another means for resolving conflict? Dramatically, they are more distant, projected, and symbolized than our children's free dramatic play, but they may be psychologically useful in the way fairy tales have been, according to Bettelheim's interpretation (1976). One could even conjecture that the investment in such dramatic performances is evidence of their psychodynamic function—whether it is recognized or not.

It is hard for us to accept the reply that "children are all the same," and I am inclined not to take it in its literal meaning. I hear it as an expression of the opprobrium against assuming differences associated with social class and of the anxiety that recognition of difference in any plane is a trap that may lead to better-and-worse-than or stronger-and-weaker-than delineations that in themselves seem to be contradictory to egalitarian, socialist living. Nevertheless, the emphasis on group patterning of the learning experience must surely diminish awareness of and response to individual differences.

From these observations it seems that, although we share the development of social consciousness and competence as a primary goal, we have questions about the educational course toward that objective—specifically, the expectation of conforming behavior, the didactic teaching methods, and the indoctrination of the social values of adult society in the years of early childhood. And in the primary years, are there questions to ask about the custom of public self-criticism in school and the monitoring of peers by one another as a means of elevating social consciousness?

From Another Perspective

Among another group of visitors (Cohen, Lerner, & Weissbourd, 1976) during this same period (the early 1970s) we see the question of individuality and socialization considered from the new perspective of a socialist society within the context of centuries-old attitudes toward children. Where, the authors ask, do we see a supportive network for children as individuals within the momentum of socialization? How will the culture's old values for childhood—correct behavior, filial piety, self-denial, reverence for authority—be transformed into images of self-reliance, independent thinking, and problem-solving proficiency within the context of bringing realized individuality into service for society?

These authors take a broad view of the experience of young children from infancy through primary school years, including the experience of the child in family and in community as well as in school. Within the structured rote-learning experience of the school they visited, they saw instances of encouragement toward independent thinking and problem solving. When the seeds the kindergarten children had planted did not grow, the problem of "why" was opened up with the children, who made the discovery that the soil had been packed too tightly in that plot. The heterogeneous grouping of children in these classes did not mean that all children, as individuals, are the same. It meant that differences must not be allowed to be structured institutionally in ways that might interfere with each one's identity as a member of a classless society (exemplified in the classroom) and with the way the children feel about one another and become related as people. Provision is made to give support to those who are slow to learn as well as to recognize those with special abilities—but all in a spirit of maximum fulfillment, not competitive satisfaction. We are familiar with this ethic in our Bank Street culture, but in a socialist society it is expected that maximum fulfillment of individual capacity will be put to the service of the state. There may be games of winning and losing, but individuals do not emerge as stars. This is epitomized in the slogan "friendship first, competition second."

These authors place the goal of progress toward a socialist ethic within the framework of the intensive support that is provided for the individual, especially in childhood, from the society. At the same time, in schools and centers from infancy on, the nurturing of mutual helpfulness in social interaction is a major development goal. The morality of helping one another and the assumption that one will thereby attain a stronger inner self influence the structure of school experience in the early years. They influence the practical assistance the children expect to give one another, the support they can count on from adults, the theme of the dramatic presentations, the turning to social interaction in contrast to our emphasis on the discovery of self in the creative play life with materials we provide for the early years.

From these authors we see a role of protective nurturing from adult to child. "We never saw a baby cry it out." A crying infant was picked up, held, talked to, cared for, and soothed. Children are expected to be toilet-trained by 18 months. To the question "And if a child isn't toilet trained by then," the reply was "Then he is not ready yet and we wait." These are instances of what is described as a supportive, "totally nonpunitive attitude" of the adult toward the young child. It is consistent with the attitude toward older children described in the previous report, where children were talked to about who was right and who wrong, were not punished, and were gradually persuaded to desist from anti-social behavior.

Turning to society outside the school, the authors describe another source of the "sense of wholeness about themselves" that these children seem to have. They see the children as part of a caring world of adults. Rooted in the Chinese tradition of identification with an enlarged family beyond the parents, the children today extend the sphere of belonging to the community and the society. The socialist society in which they live places highest priority on caring for and developing the children, and in this society there is "consistency in message and values between parent and teacher." The entire society, with its strong traditions and new commitment, is a support system "for the children." For the individual, the social ethos and the contemporary society's concern for the child as a person build toward a *social coping self* in contrast to the personal, *individual coping self* which is a major component of growing up in our society.

The comparison of these two accounts of the same period reminds us, first, that for those who enact official policy there are different ways of carrying through mandates in education even in a controlled society and, second, that for those who come from the outside, the perspectives of individual observers puts a distinct meaning on what is described.

A Historical View

Then the time comes to take a somewhat broader perspective, to look beyond the particular influence of the school and take into account the long history of how social customs and mores influence the course of what happens to education in revolutionary times—an analysis available to us in the work of Itty Chan (1977). The construction of socialism in China builds on the humanistic philosophy that has been basic in that society for centuries and, with it, the basic belief that human nature is positive at base and "can be shaped, educated, and enlightened by the human environment." The belief that all people are educable challenges a society to reconceive the role of education and redistribute opportunity in order to undo the effects of class-determined discrimination and inequities of former eras.

The basic sense of self in the individual is influenced by the way the culture establishes the roots of belonging. In China, the historically established tradition of belonging to an extended family, in contrast to our nuclear family, offers a psychological base for an expanded identity. Within this established cultural system, socialism has a base from which to move toward a broader individual identity, from membership in an extended family to a "sense of self in society." This extended belonging has a two-way social-psychological meaning in childhood: the child's growing identity and intimate contact with an enlarging universe of people, places, and values, and the adults' expanded interest and responsibility to the children beyond the intrafamily membership. Obviously, what happens to children and how they feel—which added problems, which added sources of strength—is qualitatively different from the child-in-the-family structure that we know.

There seems to be continuity between past and present in China's history for the care of children up to the age of three. Perceived as "seedlings," they are protected, indulged, and enjoyed, accepted as belonging naturally in social situations. After that age the growing child is educated to become an active, responsive, cooperative member of society. For the primary years up to age seven, the central interest in developing the social self is expressed in the extent to which group activities—song and dance, stage and dramatic play—take a major place in the curriculum; learning materials and playthings have secondary importance. Since social activities are, by the nature of things, cognition bound, they serve broad developmental needs. Education reflects the basic values of the socialist ideology: to relate learning to life, develop people-to-people interaction, learn from firsthand experience related to real-life experience, and learn by doing. Being part of a productive society can be expressed for young children by planting a vegetable garden as part of school experience or assembling flashlight bulbs for use in the outside world. It is not hard to place this design for learning within a Piagetian framework, but beyond Piaget, in this system, the theoretical base emphasizes also the role of the social environment in acquiring experience and forming ideas.

When I read the sentence "The human environment is varied and less emotionally intensive than in the West," I seem to find a possible answer to some of my quandaries—for example, about the low incidence of aggressive behavior and the effectiveness of reasoning about it. The creation of an atmosphere in which children help and support one another does not surprise me, but the image of children persuading one another to change unacceptable attitudes and, further, reflecting upon and confronting conflicts within themselves and with others seems to be based on an unrealistic level of inner peace. Still, perhaps here, too, there is a major cultural distance to bridge when I read a description of how articles by contemporary psychologists in China are frequently presented to a group of professional peers. "Many writers," it reads, "display an unexpected frankness, which appears in criticism of their own procedures and suggestions for alternate interpretations of the data (Stevenson et al., 1981).

A Changing Social Perspective

The visitors who traveled to China five years later, after the death of Mao Zedong, came into a changed social situation. In becoming familiar with two accounts[1] of observation of early childhood education at that time, I have found it interesting to see where there seems to be change, and perhaps, to come closer to understanding what does not seem to change in response to social-political upheaval. The pictures on the schoolroom walls alongside Mao's portrait still carry the socialist message of work and workers but are chosen to be more likely to communicate with young children. The beginning of a drawing period is handled didactically by the teacher, but there follows a free period in which the girls choose to draw ballerinas and the boys bombadiers. There are materials available now—pegboards, nesting cones, table blocks, picture books—but these seem to serve an almost recreational function. Instead, major energies and time were invested in the creation of dramatic presentations, elaborately produced and costumed, with teachers and children working together—the children articulate, exhibiting extraordinary abilities to remember and respond to cues and enjoying the pleasure of it all with teachers and visitors. When one hears that the theme of one of these plays was ridding the nation of flies, not a reproduction of a classic story, it is easy to think that there is a new investment in this medium for learning that we recognize as well as fulfillment in dramatizing. And a changed emphasis on understanding contemporary reality.

I seem to see more clearly in these accounts than in the previous ones the workings of an extended support system in these early years that includes the individual child, the teacher, and all the other children. When an embarrassed child is persuaded to speak his piece, the teacher hugs him and the children applaud. When the child finds a correct answer after a few failures, with the teacher waiting patiently beside him, the children applaud. And, how is this socialized support related to the child who, when in a position of choice, takes the smaller apple for himself and leaves the larger one for someone else? And how is it related to the experience of one of the visitors? Having lost the address toward which she was headed, she found herself on a bus where neither driver nor passengers could speak English. After a few verbal twists, the driver understood. The passengers on the bus applauded. Are these stylized, learned gestures or expressions of socialized empathic feeling? Is this an internalized mode of interaction—people-to-people feeling—that is related to the observation of how effectively persuasion seems to displace punishment? And how does one place this image of childhood into the complex, sometimes conflicting realities of the encompassing adult culture, historical and contemporary?

I have been fortunate in the opportunity to put my questions about what has changed to two colleagues who have had ongoing professional contact with Chinese education over the years before and after the death of Mao. From Itty Chan I have heard about the radical change signified in the swing of the educational pendulum to the reestablishment of key (model) schools for selected

1. This material is from interviews with Bertha Campbell, director, Bureau of Child Development and Parent Education, New York State Education Department, Albany, N.Y., and with Selma Knobler, adviser and member of graduate division faculty, Bank Street College of Education, New York City.

students and teachers and the return to a system of entrance examinations, signifying a selective course of educational opportunity.[2] Though these particular changes do not directly affect the earlier levels of schooling, there is a changed focus in the early years that also reflects the general direction.

In the previous period, when China was in an era of postrevolution, the curriculum was directed toward strengthening the fundamental qualities—self-reliance, independent thinking, and the ethic of serve-the-people—considered essential to unifying a people involved in reconstructing a new society. In the more recent years of the decade, education reflects the social change involved in moving toward a new era. The contemporary educational emphasis is on conscientious and disciplined study, toward higher aspirations and a spirit of reaching out to a wider world. These changes do not alter the importance of developing the social self, the central value long established in Chinese culture, taking its changed shape in response to the challenge of a changing social structure. Returning to the question we have been pursuing—the balance of individual self and social self—Itty Chan looks forward to finding a little more emphasis on the social self in the United States and more on the development of the individual in China.

My image of the school experience of the young child after 1977 has been amplified in conversation with Barrie Chi.[3] As background, I learned that the change in the general direction toward a more individualistic outlook is represented in the reinstitution of the university to its former modes of functioning. Nor is the image of the ideal society as unambiguous as pictured, although it does not resemble the diversity to which we are accustomed. There are instances resembling our preschool situations, with more opportunity for activity and less complete acceptance of regulations, but there are fewer materials available and the children are inclined to be more contained in their behavior than the children we know in the United States. In general, the variety of school settings we are accustomed to find in our society is a reality in China as well. Barrie Chi also describes a kindergarten where children had little to do, sat with hands behind their backs, in the charge of a teacher obviously in a caretaker role.

The plays the children create are not so political as they were previously; there is more likely to be a dance based on Chinese history or customs. The earlier concept of productive work for the society as part of school activity is phasing out. Methods are not universally didactic, and there are modifications of rote learning. The prominence of copying in art activities was explained as essential to learning how to use the Chinese characters. The teachers are sensitive and responsive to individual differences. There is a trend toward supporting the personal self—perhaps a by-product of the examination challenge—which diminishes somewhat the socialized-person image.

2. This material is from an interview with Itty Chan, a member of the bilingual staff, Boston public schools.

3. This material is from an interview with Barrie Chi, instructor, College of Staten Island, Staten Island, N.Y.

The schools the visitors see show signs of change.

> The polished performances of the kindergarten children that impressed so many foreign visitors . . . are less highly esteemed in 1980. . . . "Mao Zedong" thought no longer guides teachers and parents. . . . They look instead to new sources of information and guidance, including the work of experts on child development. (Stevenson et al., 1981)

There are questions that arise in the framework of our own value systems, while keeping open the reminder: this is another culture, in both its old and its new forms. What is the loss in variation, creativity, and autonomous functioning in this kind of social system? If we look ahead, beyond early childhood, can this society forgo the productivity and self-realization we assume to be related to those qualities of life experience? From a less practical view, is there a viable supranational argument speaking for variation, internalized ethic, and autonomous individuality integrated with social commitment that is a great promise for man?

In the end, we come out humble—or should. There are two kinds of errors, at least, in moving into another culture with the conceptual tools and values of our own framework (whichever ones we have chosen from our own society). For example, we may tend to treat the concepts of psychodynamic theory, as exemplified in developmental stage differences, as universal instead of having grown out of our own particular social reality. Recent research findings bring that error to the foreground. In short, our theories and therefore our deductions may not be applicable (Kagan & Klein, 1973). This could be called the error of irrelevance, seeing others not only through our own eyes but from the perspective of our less-than-universal theories. The other kind of error may involve us in perceiving differences in enactment as ideologically unimportant, leading us to argue that the basic goals are fundamentally the same as ours, even though the means of realizing them may seem to move in contrary directions. This might be called the error of the wish to unite, to find that other cultures through different means can fulfill the goals we hold beneficial to humankind. What may be somewhat "softheaded" in the first error has the quality of "goodwill" in the second.

The Individual in a "Relaxing" Revolution

It would be interesting to compare what observers have recently learned about China to studies of the Soviet Union, which has outlived its early revolutionary period, and to compare these forms of collective upbringing with the Israeli kibbutzim, where dynamic psychology has been an underpinning of theory and practice during all the years of their development. The major issue of the individual and socialization is central to all of them, and there is reason to think that the resolution of this issue changes as a society moves from early to later stages of revolution.

In this connection, it is interesting to read Bronfenbrenner's citation of an official Soviet document (Novikova, 1967) that deals with changing opinion concerning the relation between the collective and the individual, and the social-historical reasons for that change:

> The function of the collective in relation to the individual in socialist society was expressed differently at different periods of socialist development. In the early years, in connection with the revolutionary reorganization of society, the upbringing functions of the collective were connected mainly with the development of revolutionary self-consciousness among its members, with the formation of the civic outlook. Having just mobilized all of its internal resources, the society could direct all the will and consciousness of its members to overcoming the difficulties connected with the war and the destruction of the economy. . . .
>
> At the present time the solution of problems confronting the society depends in significant measure on the effectiveness of the process of forming personalities, personalities that are not only active socially and politically but also developed in all respects . . . permitting them to realize with maximal effectiveness the individual abilities, talents, and gifts. *If earlier we were confronted with the problem of creating that type of collective which could insure the necessary conditions for the existence of all its members, then today we have to discover how to create the kind of collective which will insure the most full and most many-sided development of each person.* (italics mine)

For those of us who find the constructs of developmental stage theory an essential tool in our efforts to understand the complexity of the individual growth process, it ought to be relatively easy to take a developmental view of the course of social change. After periods of revolutionary paroxysms, societies undergo developmental processes in which the course of change is a function of the basic challenges particular to each stage of the society's evolution. As is clearly illustrated in the excerpt on changing Soviet education, we should not expect the beginnings to be prototypes of later phases. We can expect that current fundamental changes in leadership and revolutionary ideology in China will be reflected in education, though more radically, perhaps, in the later phases of schooling than in the early years.

CHAPTER 4

Cognitive Functioning as a Developmental Goal

The answers change but the basic questions are perennial: What difference can education make? Is there a far-out vista beyond our present image? In my college years the question was crucial to our image of the future in the large and to the choice each of us would make of a path in which to invest our life energies.

We read; we talked; we worried. Does each individual have a basic intellectual capacity that is constant in relation to that of others in our culture? If yes, and if it can be measured in quantitative terms, does this imply the possibility of predicting the rate and power of learning and, beyond that, the suitable vocational and social position for the individual in maturity? I had encountered the question and the implicit social issue before I was aware that the intelligence quotient and its application would become the center of controversy for years to come.

On many a spring day in the early 1920s, a small group of Barnard College undergraduates carried their lunch-hour sandwiches to a grassy slope in Riverside Park. Our appetites were keen, and for more than food. Two classes of the morning session, again and again, nourished the hunger for the life of the mind. First we heard the biologist Henry Crampton teaching the inexorable mechanisms of the hereditary process.[1] Following him, Franz Boas presented the weight of evidence from his anthropological studies.[2] From him we heard that the races of mankind show equally the human capacity to develop cultural forms, that all surviving human groups have evolved equally but in different ways, and that differences are to be attributed to historic cultural, rather than genetic, factors. That was a radical view in the early decades of the twentieth century.

Boas won in our arguments under the trees along the Hudson, for

1. As I recall, Dr. Crampton was professor of biology, Columbia University.
2. Dr. Franz Boas was professor of anthropology, Columbia University.

mixed reasons. He easily became a hero figure. We learned that he liked to play Beethoven's piano music, and three of us[3] had the courage to present him with a bound volume of the sonatas. We were entranced by his thoughtful, German-accented, repeated use of the phrase in-so-far-as, which we mimicked at first and then adopted as a formula when we thought the subject called for a mood of deliberate consideration. For me it has lasted as a lifelong echo, a protection against careless generalization.

The continuously tearing eye and the scar on his cheek we were sure were part of a courageous field-study venture. But, more importantly, we loved what he was telling us—that man can change with his environment. To idealistic college students, this was a go-ahead sign. Find the way to be part of a better world in the making; hold to the assumption that human nature is modifiable. The assumption of the modifiability of intellectual functioning for individuals and for the different subgroups of the human family is no longer debated. The question has become not whether one can but how one can best stimulate and elevate the universal potential.

Years later, my youthful sense of affiliation with Franz Boas strengthened in two different ways. His scholarly insight moved into the scene of social action. In the 1920s, a decade after its publication, The Mind of Primitive Man (Boas, 1911) became a support for the opposition to U.S. immigration restrictions based on presumed racial differences. In the 1930s until his death in 1943, Boas worked energetically in the front of the crucial issues of those years—with organizations fighting racist hatred, discrimination, and limitations of freedom of speech and of the press. With the situation intensified by the continued existence of the Nazi threat, he devoted himself to public activity and to programs in behalf of displaced Germans. In Germany in the 1930s the Nazis burned The Mind of Primitive Man. But, revised in 1937, the book had an influence in the civil rights struggle of the 1950s.

In a second stream of association I remembered clearly the way Boas pronounced Kwakiutl when we listened, fascinated, to his description of a whole different way of life in a strange and faraway place, and of the thinking and imagining in which it was embedded. So when, in 1980, I found an essay entitled "Boas on the Kwakiutl: The Ethnographic Tradition" (Goldman, 1980), I read it for old times' sake. To my surprise, I found that it dealt with an important contemporary issue in method in psychology as much as in anthropology. The author defends the importance of the ethnographic method, in which the data consist, first, of detailed records of every aspect of the functioning society, as the base for subsequent theoretical analysis. It is interesting to relate this argument by a contemporary anthropologist to the current trend within psychology to invest in direct observational studies as basic ground material for subsequent conceptual formulations. And I wondered to what extent

3. These were myself, Natalie Jaros, and Isabel London.

anthropologists were taking Goldman's reminder of Boas's approach as a way of rethinking contemporary research fashion.

On the Broadway bus on which I ride to work, I meet students on the way to their Columbia classes. One day the young woman sitting next to me was reading a book on anthropology, so I opened a conversation with recall of when I had studied anthropology with Franz Boas all those years ago. "But I don't suppose you hear much about his approach to studying primitive societies nowadays." "Oh, yes, we do—we have been talking about his contribution for days."

.　　.　　.

As I look back on those early twentieth-century decades, it is interesting to recall how a quality of youth—a faith in undoing the errors of their elders—covered a much wider social terrain than the image of those few students working their way through the contradictory views of their professors while eating lunch on the grass in Riverside Park. It was an initiation into my lifelong experience with contradictory interpretations of the course of psychological development and diverse inferences for educational practice drawn therefrom.

Promoting Cognitive Growth: A Developmental-Interaction Point of View (1977) with Edna Shapiro and David Wickens

The educational program and philosophy described here derive from what we call the developmental-interaction point of view. The term *developmental interaction* denotes its distinctive features. "Developmental refers to the emphasis on identifiable patterns of growth and modes of perceiving and responding which are characterized by increasing differentiation and progressive integration as a function of chronological age. Interaction refers, first, to the emphasis on the child's interaction with the environment—adults, other children, and the material world—and, second, to the interaction between cognitive and affective spheres of development. The developmental-interaction formulation stresses the nature of the environment as much as it does the patterns of the responding child" (Shapiro & Biber, 1972, pp. 59–60).

Guidelines for the Development of Cognitive Proficiency

It is assumed that some aspects of experience may be primarily cognitive and some primarily affective but that these domains interpenetrate each other.

Adapted from *Promoting cognitive growth: A developmental-interaction point of view* (2d ed.). Washington, D.C.: National Association for the Education of Young Children, 1977 (coauthored with Edna Shapiro and David Wickens).

Thus the goal of furthering cognitive power must necessarily be viewed and implemented in connection with other program goals. The most highly regarded method for achieving these developmental goals, in this program, is to advance the functional use of language and the thinking processes in the context of the child's own activities and play (Minuchin & Biber, 1968).

This requires on the teacher's part sensitive awareness of the children's thinking processes—where the confusions are, where the openings for new insights are—as well as specific skill in using the moment-by-moment interchange.

It cannot be assumed that because a child has had a particular experience—seen a bulldozer at work, observed the transformation of water to ice, or even correctly performed an act such as placing the triangle in the triangle slot or selecting the correct block to complete a structure—that he understands and has mastered the processes involved. The teacher's role is not only to find ways to assess the nature of the thinking that is going on—how particularized to a given act or how generalized and transferable—but to gauge the appropriate stimulation that will lead the child, or the children as a group, to new levels of conceptual mastery, or will broaden the scope of content they can bring under control in the already attained level of mastery. Cognitive strength is distinguished by breadth and richness of repertoire as well as by position on a ladder of complexity.

The stimulation to be supplied by the teacher is drawn from several sources. How the material of the children's activities and play is utilized as a primary source of language development and cognitive stimulation is illustrated in the analysis of the items (see "Analysis of Teaching Techniques" below). There is, in addition, a pervasive aura of *think-it-through, think-ahead, why did this happen?* that governs the quality of interchange between teachers and children.

Another pervasive interaction pattern appears in the orientation of the teacher toward posing problems that allow for inductive thinking. She emphasizes hypothesis-making by differentiating experience into "if-then" formulations. For example, social functioning within a peer group is developed through constant reiteration of the "if-then" relationship between individual children: "If you hit Johnny, then what do you think he will do?" or, in other realms of experience: "If you mix blue and red, then what color will you have?"

The teacher also needs to remember that not all thinking is logical, that intuition and association are also forms of thinking. Intuitive thought is not necessarily a precursor of logical thought, although in many instances intuitive solutions are replaced by logic as the child acquires information and can meet greater demands for precision and accuracy. Associative and intuitive thinking remain part of the adult's repertoire and are especially important for the generation of ideas and for creative thought. For the young child, intuition and the association of ideas seem to be natural, untaught modes of thinking.

The essential purpose of this paper is to describe the potential for cognitive stimulation implicit in ongoing school experience and to illustrate teaching techniques which are presumed to *promote the potential for ordering experience through cognitive strategies.* This goal has been selected from a comprehensive series of eight goals considered significant for the preschool period. The attempt to break down the many facets of a program into its components may seem overly complex. It is essential, however, in order to be specific about the kinds of learning the teacher is stimulating and the ways in which her actions and attitudes support a particular goal as defined.

Another purpose is to illustrate how a technique directed toward a particular goal selected as a target is likely simultaneously to affect one or more of the other goals of the same system. There is a general principle involved in this second purpose: the choice and evaluation of any given technique should be based on consideration of the interdependence of response systems—cognitive and affective, behavioral and internalized, individual and socialized.

"Analysis of the Learning Environment: Cognitive Categories" is followed by a roster of eight "Educational Goals for the Preschool Years." Indicators for what the school should provide are included only for goal 2 in this series, namely, "To promote the potential for ordering experience through cognitive strategies." (Amplification of the other seven goals related to the school's functioning appears in Chapter 11.) In the section "Analysis of Teaching Techniques" samples of experiential records are annotated with reference both to cognitive categories and to educational goals.

Analysis of the Learning Environment: Cognitive Categories

The following categories are used for analyzing a series of teaching–learning events occurring in preschool classrooms. Under A, below, are listed five kinds of experience considered fundamental to the development of cognition. Under B are listed seven categories used to classify cognitive functioning.

A. Experiences which support the instrumentalities for cognitive functioning:
   1. Direct experience with the qualities and relationships of the physical world: sensory experience, large body action.
   2. Nonsymbolic, constructive, manipulative activities with things.
   3. Experience with a variety of modes of nonverbal representation.
   4. Learning the symbol systems: spoken and written language.
   5. Integrating nonpresent experience conceptually.
B. Aspects of the conceptual organization of experience and information:
   1. Identity of objects and persons: e.g., through spoken and written signs, variation in perspective.
   2. Classification and differentiation: e.g., based on perceptual attributes, functions, roles, feelings, processes.
   3. Quantifying by different criteria: e.g., size, amount, degree.
   4. Orientation in space and time: e.g., near–far, past–present–future, map thinking.

5. Awareness of transformation processes: e.g., combinations, growth, decay, origins, manufacture.
6. Causality: e.g., based on sequence, prediction, and outcome, both in physical and interpersonal realm.
7. Formulation of uncertainty and confusion: e.g., by means of informational questions, expression of puzzlement.

Educational Goals for the Preschool Years (3–5)
1. To serve the child's need to make an impact on the environment through direct physical contact and maneuver.
2. To promote the potential for ordering experience through cognitive strategies.

The school therefore should provide for:
- Extending receptiveness and responsiveness: e.g., variety of sensory-motor-perceptual experiences, focus on observation and discrimination.
- Extending modes of symbolizing: e.g., gestural representation; two-dimensional representation with pencil, crayons, paints; three-dimensional representation with clay, blocks, wood.
- Developing facility with language: e.g., word meanings and usage, scope of vocabulary, mastery of syntax; playful and communicative verbal expression.
- Stimulating verbal-conceptual organization of experience and information: e.g., verbal formulation; integration of present and nonpresent; accent on classification, ordering, relationship, and transformation concepts in varied experiential contexts.
3. To advance the child's functioning knowledge of the environment.
4. To support the play mode of incorporating experience.
5. To help the child internalize impulse control.
6. To meet the child's need to cope with conflicts intrinsic to this stage of development.
7. To facilitate the development of an image of self as a unique and competent person.
8. To help the child establish mutually supporting patterns of interaction.

Analysis of Teaching Techniques

In this section we present a small sample of teaching–learning events. These have been taken from observational records and interviews with teachers of preschool children. Each has been annotated in terms of the teaching techniques which are congruent with the principles of an optimal learning environment, classified in terms of the aspects of cognition and fundamental experiences noted above, and cross-referenced in accordance with its relevance to other educational goals for the preschool years.

In selecting these events, we have tried to use experiences likely to occur and recur in preschool classrooms. Rather than search for the unusual, we have looked for the everyday in order to point up the ways in which teachers can use ordinary transactions in the classroom to promote cognitive growth.

The first entry in each item is a brief description of the behavioral event. In each case a note is appended which explicates the analysis and/or teaching technique. The notation that follows refers to the system of analysis of cognitive categories which appears on pages 67–68. Finally, the probably simultaneous influence on other goals is noted in order to point out the interdependence of the cognitive goal with the seven other goals.

Item 1   The teacher establishes the custom of having the children call out the names of the objects they see when approaching the play area. One day she introduces a variation: "Let's go a different way this time," choosing an alternative path to approach the play equipment. This stimulates the children to appreciate the sameness of objects seen from different perspectives.

Note   The teacher's lead-in to the lesson has basic appeal to children. "Going a different way" has the quality of fun and adventure when young.

Categories   A4.   Learning the symbol systems

B1.   Identity of objects and persons: constant identity from different perspectives

Relevance to Other Goals

Goal 3   *Knowledge.* The children are learning to learn from their own observations. They will have the opportunity to rehearse these observations spontaneously individually every day.

Goal 8   *Interaction.* The children are involved as a group in this thinking activity. Thinking together becomes important for child-group cohesiveness.

Item 2   In each of the rooms, the paintings done by the children are displayed with a large, clear name label underneath each painting. Often the children watch as the teacher writes their names.

Note   The stimulus to recognize one's own name in writing from among the others is present in the environment, to be responded to according to the child's interest. Watching the teacher write one's name is a focused stimulation.

Categories   A3.   Nonverbal representation

A4.   Learning the symbol systems

B1.   Identity of objects and persons: recognition of a written symbol

Relevance to Other Goals

Goal 7   *Self-image.* The child's sense of self as a "maker" is being accented.

Item 3   The teacher tells a boy who is set to rush into the elevator ahead of the others that he can be first to go in when he has learned to know the numbers on the buttons so that he can tell which must be pushed to make the elevator go to the right floor.

Note   Instead of restraint, the teacher is offering the child an alternative response pattern which is conditional upon his mastery of a cognitive task.

Categories   A4.   Learning the symbol systems

B1.   Identity of objects and persons: discriminating signs for numbers

Relevance to Other Goals

Goal 5   *Impulse control.* In being offered behavioral alternatives instead of restraint, the child is helped to internalize control and to perceive the teacher's authority as rational.

Goal 7   *Self-image.* If the child can control the impulse and master the task, the experience should contribute to his autonomy; he will have become the decision-maker for the elevator's route.

Item 4   The teacher asks the children if they know any place on the street where they can get wet. They describe the fire hydrants, which in some streets are opened on hot days for children's water play. The teacher starts a discussion about how firemen put out fires. The children are thrilled by the realization that the firemen come to the same place they themselves do to get water.

Note   The teacher presents a relatively complicated object–function problem by presenting a function and asking for the object to match it. There is warm affect associated with this particular cognitive task.

Categories   A5.   Nonpresent experience

B2.   Classification and differentiation: selection of nonpresent object that suits a named function

Relevance to Other Goals

Goal 3   *Knowledge.* The children learn that water from a hydrant is a means for the important job of putting out fires, as well as a source of fun for children.

Goal 8   *Interaction.* The "thrill" may bespeak the sense of a bond between adult and child. They, the little children and the big firemen, come to the same hydrant.

Item 5   While reading a story about firemen, the teacher recalls the children's confusion about the different roles people perform. She asks, "Is a fireman a daddy?" The children answer, "No." The teacher does not correct them but waits for the girl whose father she knows is a fireman to enlighten the children, which the girl does.

Note   The teacher uses the content of the story as the vehicle for putting a question to the children that is just ahead of their level of cognitive mastery. Reading to children is an important part of the program of language mastery and increasing the children's knowledge.

Categories A4. Learning the symbol systems
　　　　　　A5. Nonpresent experience
　　　　　　B2. Classification and differentiation: multiple roles
　　　　　　Relevance to Other Goals

Goal 8 *Interaction.* The children are learning from one another and come to regard one another as well as the teacher as sources of information.

Item 6 The teacher stands with the children in the outdoor play space and watches with them to see how long one can see the plane that is flying away into the clouds.

Note The teacher is stimulating the children to become focused observers and to pay attention to a designated perceptual phenomenon, and thus, to increase sensitivity to the world around.

Categories A1. Direct experience
　　　　　　B4. Orientation in space and time: experience with space as indeterminate—not made explicit
　　　　　　Relevance to Other Goals

Goal 3 *Knowledge.* Skill and disposition to observe the "passing scene" in detail can became a significant tool for acquiring knowledge; the teacher takes responsibility for stimulating the children to be observers of their natural environment

Goal 8 *Interaction.* A shared, unusual experience, with few or no words spoken, no directions given by one to the other, and no expectation of compliance can create a bond between teacher and child.

Item 7 Jerry comes to visit his three-year-old brother in another classroom in the center. He says to the teacher, "Look, I can turn the light out!" The teacher asks him not to, but quickly adds, "I remember that when you were in this room you were too short to turn it off." Jerry smiles and says, "I won't make it dark. These kids are still babies."

Note The teacher recognizes the child's pride in growth and his sense of increased competence; at the same time she expects him to accept her restraint and understand the reason for it.

Categories A5. Nonpresent experience
　　　　　　B5. Awareness of transformation processes
　　　　　　Relevance to Other Goals

Goal 7 *Self-image.* The child experiences the pleasure of his competence vis-à-vis the memory of himself when younger.

Goal 8 *Interaction.* The child takes on the teacher's role of protecting the younger children. He also enjoys the teacher's recall of him as a little child.

Item 8   The children are troubled and call the teacher's attention to the fact that the story of Mary and her little lamb is different in two books. The teacher points out that the basic story is the same though the telling is different. She then suggests that they look at the houses they have built with blocks—each different from the other, yet each admittedly a house.

Note   The children are able to communicate a perceived inconsistency. The teacher is able to cue into their annoyance and use it for further learning growth—moving them toward the concept of variations around a common theme.

Categories   A5.   Nonpresent experience
         B7.   Formulation of uncertainty and confusion: expression of puzzlement
         Relevance to Other Goals

Goal 8   *Interaction.* In perceiving the teacher's way of dealing with the discrepancy they had observed, the children are building an image of a teacher who finds ways of resolving contradictory elements of experience and making things come out right.

Summary

There is a central thesis governing the choice of techniques for advancing cognitive proficiency within the developmental-interaction point of view. As stated earlier, this thesis maintains, first, that in a coherent system, techniques selected in the interest of a particular educational target should be justified in terms of a comprehensive concept of an optimal learning environment. Second, there needs to be constant weighing of the impact of any given technique on any other established goals for the development of the child.

In support of that thesis, each item, incident, and episode has been analyzed according to categories of cognitive functioning, and has also been annotated to explicate the teacher technique and qualities of the interaction established by the teacher. In the notes on relevance to other goals, the focus is on the child and the impact on developmental processes. The material presented is, obviously, a selection—a very small sample, indeed, from myriad illustrative possibilities. Although the sample is small, the notations offer concrete illustrations of the principles postulated, in general terms, in the early pages. By way of summary, it may be helpful to refer to a few of the specific instances in the context of some general postulates.

The body of material, in toto, demonstrates how the method of advancing "the functional use of language and thinking processes in the context of the child's own activities and play" is implemented. The teacher who has a weather eye out for each opportunity that will help children bring their experience under greater cognitive control develops a repertoire of skills that she can call on spontaneously as occasions arise.

We wish to counteract any erroneous impression that the teacher takes a passive role—quite the contrary. She is, in actuality, teaching all the time. She makes the management aspects of classroom responsibilities serve as thinking stimuli. She initiates a thinking, let's-see-what's happening approach, not a reading of the law, in the case of social dilemmas. She puts questions to the children that stimulate perceptual and conceptual search maneuvers.

Whether she is making use of opportunities as they arise or preplanning specific activities in the interest of cognitive advance, the teacher's ways of talking, responding, and acting reflect both her interest in the child and her belief that the content of learning experience should be in tune with what is meaningful, important, and pleasurable to young children.

We have tried to point out, also, how the developmental-interaction approach affects priorities in the classroom. There are underlying processes to be nurtured and protected. Symbolizing experience in many media is fundamental to the mastery of language. On this basis, considerable importance is placed on using crayons, paints, clay, and blocks to depict and reproduce experience, and on child-initiated dramatic play as a way of restating and reworking cognitive and affective elements of experience representatively. Competence in the use of language has intrinsic value, but it is also viewed as a medium for deepening interpersonal communication.

What the teacher does not do or correct sharpens our understanding of her priorities. She does not cut off the child's wrong name for a fruit (the child's initiative in wanting to "name" is not to be blunted) but finds a moment soon thereafter to give the correct name. She does not correct wrong pronouns at four; this use of syntax will become self-corrective as the child hears grammatical English spoken. What matters to her is that the child shall feel free to explore the world of words. She will not intrude on the moment of pleasure in solving a problem by correcting a tense form; she will find a more neutral moment to deal with tenses.

Both the records and the notations reflect adherence to the principle that optimal learning is active learning. The word and the idea *hydrant* gain meaning from the experience of actually going out on the street to look for it; if there are questions about firemen, there are firemen in the firehouse to whom they can be put directly, after the children have been encouraged to do the kind of active thinking that is involved in trying to guess. There is active learning also in the way problems are put to the children that call upon them to probe for an answer—are firemen daddies?—beyond their immediate mastery, or to bring recall of past solutions to bear on present problems.

The implementation of the principles on which these cognitive strategies are based—keeping learning active, tuned into childlike interests and pleasures, and interwoven with the stream of ongoing activities—contributes specifically to the images of themselves the children construct.

The teacher's choices and priorities in connection with cognitive process were bounded by the kind of relation she wished to establish as an adult and as a teacher, by the nature of the adult image she wanted to project. In these records, the children perceived the teacher as an adult who was a source for resolving dilemmas—intellectual and social; who was not remote from childlike interests and pleasure; who could guide the way through complex thinking and acting operations; who would understand and keep faith.

This presentation has dealt with only one of eight goals for a developmentally based educational program. These eight goals are necessarily interrelated, and we have emphasized the fact that teaching techniques must be assessed in terms of the total system of goals, not in terms of any one goal considered in isolation.

Perspectives on Cognitive Development

There is a sense in which educational systems have to serve two gods. There is a primary responsibility to prepare individuals to prosper in the given mode of a society's functioning, or, at least, within the context of anticipated social change. Serving the second god asks, expects, education to position its practices within an integrated theory of how people mature and learn within a preferred image of individual realization. Conscientious educators in the path of John Dewey strive to serve both gods. That means constructing and reconstructing education to keep it grounded in advancing developmental theory and, at the same time, related to an image of positive functioning for the individual within the complex social forces of an era. The 1960s and 1970s were a challenge to educators in both domains, and it is interesting to note that there has been renewed interest in Dewey's way of meeting a similar challenge in another era.

Since the course of development of cognitive functions has become such a central area in recent years, it is interesting to consider the different ways in which new insight has stimulated educational change—sometimes through revising existing practice, sometimes through developing radically different innovative programs. Great interest in change was stimulated by Piaget's original and challenging contribution to our understanding of thinking processes and the implications for rethinking existing educational paradigms. From its earliest dissemination in the United States (as far back as the 1930s), Piagetian developmental concepts were incorporated into existing Bank Street ideology. In fact, Piagetian theory, or rather its implications, strengthened principles and practices that had been developed from the applied progressivism of John Dewey.

Dewey and Piaget

From both perspectives the image of a positive learning environment was radically different from traditional educational practice. The child was perceived as an active organism at all stages of development, so, although Piaget's conception of underlying psychological process is different from Dewey's, we were provided with a common image of a new order of learning experience. In the Piagetian framework, knowledge is not absorbed in its established form; it is constructed individually, when school makes it possible for children to initiate the search to know and understand. The principle of action as foundation is fulfilled when the school is designed as an opportunity for exploring, questioning, experimenting, searching, and problem-solving. Closure comes as insight, not verification or approval by the teacher, whose role it is to create an environment that stimulates and supports the inquiring mind. The course of development is conceived as a succession of stages characterized by qualitatively different modes of thinking to which curriculum content and method are to be adapted (Piaget, 1950).

Beyond this area of commonality, the programs, based on Piaget, have a dominant interest in applying the newly gained insights to cognitive processes. The programs designed experimentally to build on the application of Piagetian insights into development involved a challenge that has confronted educator-pioneers repeatedly: how and to what extent can educational practice be aligned with a preferred theory of psychological development and the learning process?[4] Accounts of the application of Piagetian theory to teaching modes in the elementary schools from Schwebel and Raph (1973) and Wadsworth (1978) offer realistic images of the enactment of basic principles, such as increasing motivation by raising questions that match the child's developmental level and broadening children's direct experience in their world as the stimulus for having "wonderful" ideas and pursuing them. Concentration on stimulating cognitive functioning has generated some fresh teaching techniques, supplementing those long familiar to established nontraditional schools with progressive ideology. But the total conspectus of curriculum innovation is planned to be consonant with Piagetian genetic epistemology, reflecting the centrality and sequential order of cognitive processes in the total design.

It is not surprising that this highly developed theory in the important area of cognition and its application to school practice have raised questions from the viewpoint of both theory and application. How can we justify the distinction that is made between stimulating an inquiry approach in the areas of physical and logical-mathematical knowledge but proceeding by custom in relation to social knowledge? Does the theory of irreversible sequence of stages of development have the universality that is claimed? Does the application of stage-succession theory to curriculum design obscure the wide range of individual differences within any stage and the particularity of the course of each child's maturing?

Skepticism about basing educational programs on Piagetian theory has varying origins. For some, though the Piagetian insights and findings are major ways to understanding the thinking processes, their application to educational practice is premature. This position is expressed from different viewpoints.

In one view (Victor, 1978; see also Lawton & Cooper, 1978), the basic equilibrium theory of cognitive maturing, which posits stable structures in

4. See "Psychological Perspectives and Early Childhood Education: Some Relations between Theory and Practice," in chap. 12.

successive epigenetic stages, distorts the reality of what may be perceived alternatively as an ongoing dialectic process of change. Victor points critically to the relatively insignificant role attributed to varied experience in relation to cognitive development and to the extent to which the child is seen predominantly as reacting to external input, without sufficient recognition of the extent to which he himself is making an impact on the environment. Victor decries what he considers to be literalistic application of Piagetian theory and findings to education. Piaget, with his philosophical orientation, constructed tasks to penetrate the nature of cognitive functioning, not to lay out a design for the educative process. There have been programs in which curriculum is much influenced by that theoretical sequence. In Victor's view, this represents a dual error: first, the use of Piaget's research tools as models for teaching method; and, second, the overweighting of curriculum design and activities in the direction of cognitive stimulation.

From a different perspective, Sullivan (1969) also decries attempts to align educational design and practice with Piagetian postulates as these have been developed so far. On the most general level, he sees a large measure of predeterminism in Piagetian theory, resembling though different from Gesell's position. While the theory of assimilation and accommodation and the emphasis on effects of social experience bespeak adherence to an interactionist position, there is a deterministic perspective in Piaget's concept of development as a "spontaneous process tied to embryogenesis concerning the nervous system and mental functions as well as bodily development."

Sullivan rejects what he considers to be a too rigidly conceived developmental stage theory. He disagrees with the way the concepts of readiness and sequencing are applied as guides to curriculum in what he considers an overzealous attempt to "match" educational input to potentialities as these are defined in successive Piagetian developmental stages.

He is critical of what he considers one-sided emphasis on self-discovery as the preferred, dominant mode of learning. Looking at it historically, he sees the priority given to experiential learning and self-discovery techniques as an important progressive reaction against the exclusively didactic modes of an earlier era, but in the contemporary scene he aligns himself with Kohnstamm (1966): "It is important for all of us to find the balance between these extreme views. For it is simply not true that children ought to discover all insights by experience."

Sullivan's image of the desirable teacher role takes a mid-position. The teacher should be a participant member of the learning experience, guiding without intruding; providing for self-learning through the child's own activity but also engaging in verbal teacher–child interchange; not expecting children to discover everything through their own experience; and conceiving directed learning experience as interacting with the child's inner developmental structures.

I doubt that the completely passive teacher role he conjures up as the image of applied Piagetian theory exists to any great extent in the reality of classrooms. In the Bank Street and Piagetian programs, for example, the teacher's input builds heavily on the preferred interrogatory mode of teacher–child discourse, which passes the cognitive search and adventure back to the child.

Sullivan's critique of certain postulates of Piagetian theory and of its premature application to educational design is counterbalanced by his appreciation of Piaget's exploration of the intricacies of conceptual processes, both through his clinical methods of interrogation and through his ingenious experiments. We have been provided with invaluable guides, he points out, for analyzing and assessing curriculum practices, for exploring these in depth with fresh perspectives. While it is premature to use currently available Piagetian theory to determine structure and sequence of curriculum, a new and exciting front for exploration and experimentation has been opened up; it needs thought, revision, and openmindedness (see Bruner, 1983; Gruber & Voneche, 1977).

Holistic Theory and "Distancing Behavior"

If we put aside the general question of constructing educational programs on the foundation of Piagetian theory and the emphasis on the cognitive processes that have characterized those designs, it is interesting to consider alternative practice where cognition is placed within a holistic view of development. Such a general concept does not, however, define the specifics of application. This is illustrated in the difference between the Bank Street and Sigel et al. (1977) modes of stimulating cognitive processes within the context of an educational program.

Between these two theoretical systems and educational enactment there is substantial common ground. Both systems take responsibility for providing a theoretical foundation for program design. Both rest on developmental stage theory as the base for the educational goal of what Sigel et al. call representational competence and what we have called cognitive growth. It is agreed that these functions develop in a sequence of predictable stages with observable outcomes; environmental quality, broadly conceived, is a factor of how fully those functions will be developed; the nature of the educational design influences the quality of utilization of given propensities. The capacity for representational competence develops as a constructive process in accord with how actively the child is involved, in contrast to concepts of passive absorption of external experience. There is common ground in the image of the whole learning environment and in the organization of activities. We are in familiar territory with Sigel in the suggestions made for arranging the physical environment for maximum independent accessibility, supplying materials with maximum potential variety in the way they can be used expressively, and creating an atmosphere of analyzing, reflecting, and thinking about experience in both its conflictual and creative manifestations. The general goals are equally familiar: to enhance problem-solving activity, to learn to think in symbolic terms, and to understand a variety of communication media, including language, art, gesture, and dance.

Taking into account both the quality of interpersonal relations and the opportunities for creative and re-creative activity provided for the children, it is comfortable to accept the authors' image of a positive preschool classroom as one in which the children interact independently, cooperatively, and thoughtfully.

The term *distancing behavior* is used by Sigel et al. to refer generally to those relations and experiences in an educational environment that are most likely to activate the child's thinking: to stimulate resolution of discrepancies, foster "conservation of meaning," and advance growth of the child's internal representational system. They recommend six basic classroom strategies to stimulate "distancing behavior" that are familiar as components in established "modern" educational programming. Among them we recognize the preference for presenting questions that are searching, giving opportunity for making choices and decisions, stimulating children to discover the consequences of action for themselves, and guiding children toward finding solutions to their problems.

As enacted with Sigel's program, the goal becomes not only to stimulate thinking about experience but almost to stimulate thinking about thinking or, at least, to make the child aware of the reasoning processes behind his decision-making. For example, the teacher brings reasons for the child's changing his choice of activity to consciousness: "Oh, I see you have left the puzzle and gone to the Magic Markers. What made you decide to do that? . . . Who were you working with at the puzzle? . . . Here you are at the art table now . . . What made you decide to come here?" Another instance is the questioning that is recommended to accompany the children's activity in making play-dough (combining wet and dry ingredients), where the children are asked to be specific about *what* will happen and *why* they think it will happen. The predominance of interest in stimulating the cognitive processes shows clearly in suggestions for guiding the children who have used poster paints and who are, for the first time, being offered watercolor paints. As an accompaniment to the children's exploration, it is suggested that the teacher ask questions about "attributes of these paints, such as color or texture, how these paints differ from the poster paints. . . . If children appear to be interested in reconstructing a certain item, the teacher may ask questions about that item, where the child has seen it, the parts of it, shapes, sizes, colors of parts, etc."

This "lesson plan" orientation toward the goal of stimulating representative thinking appears to be intrusive in different ways—at times by asking for explicit statements of reasons for behavior when something quite other than "a reason" may have been the activating force; at other times, by overfeeding ideas and overdirecting the child's course of action and play, albeit in the form of persistent questions.

In comparing the series of illustrative lesson plans described by Sigel et al. with the method of stimulating cognitive processes in the paper "Promoting Cognitive Growth," we find two basic differences in enactment of a generally common theory which influence the total gestalt of the learning experience. One revolves around the difference between an activity program in which the stimulation of cognitive processes has a central focus, formulated in a series of lesson plans (Sigel et al.), and, by contrast, another kind of activity program in which the children's constructive experience in a varied, stimulating environment is primary (Bank Street). In the latter program the course of events is utilized at propitious experiential moments as material for introducing a questioning, comparing, probing discourse and often a nonverbal search experience. The purpose is to add the dimension of wondering, comparing, generalizing, and hypothesizing to experience as a natural, integral concomitant of the doing, acting, and making components. Although the school situation described by Sigel et al. is similar so far as the available materials, the psychological atmosphere, and the openness of choice in a play program are concerned, the way the teacher utilizes the children's experience to activate cognitive processes moves toward a different psychological process.

The Bank Street approach is similar to that described in a modern (progressive) school, designated as the Conrad School, in a study of nine-year-olds attending four schools with differing educational orientations (Minuchin et al., 1969). For the Conrad School teachers, it was not the intent to "make [the child] consciously aware that he possesses a useful thinking tool" and there was "little tendency to point to the experience . . . or to extrapolate and make articulate the procedures and sequences" by which the ideas evolved (p. 403).

The second difference between the Sigel et al. formulation and suggestions for the teaching role and the Bank Street paradigm concerns what goes on in the teacher's mind. In our view, the teacher's role should be constructed with sensitive recognition of the thinking processes as one strand, admittedly of great importance, in a series of concurrent systems of sensing, feeling, and responding. Teaching behavior, therefore, whether it takes the shape of stimulating or responding, should percolate knowingly within the various psychological spheres of interaction. The brief exposition of method in "Promoting Cognitive Growth" is an effort to objectify what we favor; namely, that the teacher's behavior, even when cognitive responsiveness is at the center, should be attuned to consideration of the other simultaneous systems that are acting and being affected. Promoting the potential for ordering experience through cognitive strategies is placed, therefore, in the context of a series of concomitant goals toward each of which a comprehensive educational design has responsibility.

The episode described as item 1 is perhaps a clear example of the span of awareness we consider important in the way the teacher functions. The teacher changes a familiar action pattern—going to the play area—to bring to awareness the "sameness of objects seen from different perspectives"; the experience is not a lesson, it is part of the reality of school life and has the fun of adventure; the teacher, intentionally, is stimulating a cognitive leap—constant identity from different perspectives. At the same time, in the context of other, noncognitive developmental goals, we point to the fact that the knowledge gained has been more experientially than verbally stimulated, and that the thinking experience has been part of a social process.

The distinctive characteristics of the Bank Street design appear in the extent to which the Bank Street program is organized "to establish a thinking stance about experience *as it transpires*," in the teacher's awareness of and commitment to responding to the noncognitive (the fantastic, the factually distorted, the affect-invested) elements as projected in conversation or play as well as the realistic-representative, in the disinclination to pursue the roots of the children's thinking experience overtly and verbally, and in the preferred technique of holding some kinds of questions in abeyance until relevant experience within the school's environment or beyond it can yield answers or relieve confusion.

Although at Bank Street we share with Sigel et al. a common framework of developmental theory and the image of a positive learning environment, there is a difference in the enactment with respect to, first, the segmented attention they give to cognitive processes as though these can be insulated from coexisting affective, imaginative processes and, second, the direct instructional mode adopted for stimulating thinking. This program is only one among many specific instances of the different ways in which developmental theory, Piaget based, is applied educationally, ranging from literal adoption of the tasks Piaget used in his research procedures to reflective reexamination of old educational practices in the light of new psychological insights. There is little doubt that the exercise of positioning Piagetian theory in the sphere of educational theory has been stimulating and beneficial, regardless of what some have considered errors of interpretation and application for educational practice. It is not surprising that so comprehensive a theory should arouse diverse forms of questioning and dissent at the same time that it is recognized as a major invigorating contribution to our understanding of thinking processes and our reconsideration of our design for stimulating thinking in the context of the comprehensive program.

Piaget Plus for Infants

While we appreciate and utilize Piagetian insights into the evolution of cognitive powers, there has been an increasing number of voices asking that we continue to rear and educate children within the broader perspective of emotional processes and interaction with people. In one study of infants, the authors report (Birns & Golden, 1973) the ineffectiveness of efforts to directly stimulate cognitive processes during infancy. At the same time Birns and Golden describe the advantages in increasing adult awareness and sensitivity to how infants learn through their own exploration and self-initiated activity when provided with an appropriately stimulating environment: "Through such understanding perhaps they [the adults] can develop a respect for the infant as a scientist-explorer on his voyage of discovery through his new and uncharted world."

They speak as well for sensitivity to the infants' experience in growing up in a world of people, reminding us that it is the quality of relations with the adults who care for them—"attentiveness, affection, enthusiasm, and verbal and social interaction"—that provides the base for infants' learning about the world. They call to our attention, referring to Erikson's formulation, that the infant is building an image of what the world of feeling will hold for him: what equations between denial and fulfillment, safety and danger, failure and mastery will be forming in his earliest life experience. Taken as a whole, here is one more perspective, located in the study of infancy, which appreciates the expanded insight derived from Piaget's work on cognitive processes and simultaneously calls for recognition and response to coactive dynamic processes, as described by Erikson.

In their study, Birns and Golden present an image of a positive adult role in the care of infants that is based on understanding the particular qualities of the young child's maturing processes and an affectionate, natural kind of interaction with them. It is natural to ask what facilitates enacting such a role with infants and preschool children. In a study of student teachers who were working with children at three successive developmental levels, Rosen (1972) related competence at each level with the content and quality of the students' autobiographies. Her question was: Would there be autobiographical themes distinguishing each of the three student teacher groups that would suggest "special potential" for responsiveness to and effective work with the children of a given period?

Rosen's perception of the child needs and desirable teacher roles for the first developmental level, the two-to-five-year-olds, matches that of Birns and Golden. Her study of autobiographies describes a source in life experience, apart from professional training, for competence and gratification in teaching these very young children. In their life stories these student teachers saw themselves as having been given security and support as well as limitless opportunities to "move out and explore their worlds with a sense of sureness and safety." The use of colorful language, a general mood of optimism and openness suggests the potential for "sympathy and communication with young children." The relation between a teacher's life history and the psychological characteristics of the teaching role as it is enacted at different stages fulfills the promise of the title: "Matching Teachers With Children."

A voice for comprehensive theory, also leaning toward incorporation of insights from psychoanalytic sources, comes from Brewster Smith (1978):

> A radically and cumulative interactive—that is to say dialectical—approach to the development of selfhood, as we find in Piaget and Mead, seems appropriate to human phenomena. But, as we know, Piaget and Mead in their concrete theorizing were so preoccupied with the cognitive side of selfhood that they gave little attention to the life of impulse and affectivity. We must turn elsewhere, especially to the psychoanalytic tradition.

The image projected in Smith's statement is fully represented in Greenspan's (1979) comprehensive analysis, which provides an integration of psychoanalytic and Piagetian developmental psychology. The position he develops theoretically may provide a more extended foundation for educational design that is built on the basis of cognitive–affective interaction. This new level of analytical thinking may be a stimulus for new fronts of educational change in the best tradition of theory and practice interchange.

PART 2

An Enlarged Social Perspective

CHAPTER 5

Interpretations of Poverty in Childhood

We were a small group of members of the educational profession, sitting down to a discussion of the concept of deprivation, sharing our dissatisfaction with the theorizing and the educational practices that had evolved therefrom. But before tackling the impersonal issues of what constitutes a satisfying, productive learning environment for the children, we found ourselves asking questions and sharing experiences closer to personal life histories. Members of the group who had been poor in childhood and into their adult years offered a fresh perspective—a corrective to the idea that poverty is an unmitigated blight, a completely diminishing experience, and felt as such by people and children who are poor.

Looking back, for one person, having been poor was a positive and decisive force in the life pattern and professional work she had chosen. Qualities she values in herself and in her working role she attributes to having been poor: "I am the person I am because I was born poor."

From another we heard a different sentiment: "I too am a product of poverty. And I think sometimes as I lie in my bed at night, 'Well, I'll be damned, if my parents had had money to send me here and there and there, with the little bit of gifts I had—if they had been nurtured—if there had been more humus to add to the soil—maybe I would have been a more fantastic person and still have the values I gained from my life with my family.'" The gap between self-feeling and social perspective was also expressed: "What matters is how the family and the society feel about it. I lived on the GI bill with two children for four years, and that could be called a poverty income—but I didn't feel poor." And someone else: "I was superpoor, but I didn't find out I was poor until I got to Bank Street. We were poor, obviously. My father was at work three-fourths of the time in the mines. But I never knew how poor I was until I read Martin Deutsch's material" (1967).

Others' comments were further warnings about not projecting onto

children a sense of deprivation and poverty that they may not feel. They
create a world of adventure and pleasures for themselves. A disheveled
empty lot may turn up surprises that may have more attraction than the
spic and span climbing apparatus in the park, and in "making do" with
what they have, the children may uncover deep levels of inventiveness and
satisfaction. It is not their position as poor children that is central in their
awareness in the early years of childhood. Only later, when they begin to
seek a place in the beyond-the-family-and-neighborhood domain, do the
realistic disadvantages of being poor surface.

Because it communicates so poignantly the pleasures a child can find
under adversity, I am including excerpts from a document in which the
author recalls the inner feelings of a poor ten-year-old boy. He is describing
his shift at a newsstand from 4 A.M. to 10 A.M.:

> In the spring and summer, as I walked in the small, dark hours of the
> morning up Lexington Avenue to the newsstand at 129th Street, I felt
> beauty about me. The tenements may have seemed to lean over and
> hedge in the streets, and the streets themselves may have been dirty
> with the refuse of the day before, but I felt an unearthly peace and
> quiet that, in the balm of these spring and summer nights, comforted
> me and gently aroused dreams of future attainment. And as I stood at
> the newsstand, I watched the dark of the night fade, the colored light
> of the dawn arise and the last of the Saturday night drunks stagger
> home. I heard the clang of the garbage cans, the sounds of the horses
> drawing the milk wagons, and saw a city come awake. . . . These
> sights and sounds caused delight in me, the beholder.

> Winter was a different matter. The misery of the ever-present cold
> had darkness as an ally, for the sun did not rise until after seven
> o'clock during these deep winter months. But ten o'clock would finally
> come, and I was free to go. The walk home would not seem so long,
> however cold it was, and eagerly I would climb the five flights of stairs
> to our apartment. As I opened the door a pleasant ambience would
> envelop me. My mother had started the fire in the stove several hours
> before, and the kitchen was warm. The rolls she had purchased early
> that morning were on the table, and a freshly prepared pot of cocoa
> was on the stove. I would sit down at the table, with the newspaper
> spread before me, a buttered roll in one hand, and a cup of cocoa in
> the other. My gaze would occasionally turn to the stove where,
> through the small mica window, I could see the blue flames flicker and
> dance above the hot burning coals. The hot cocoa I drank seemed to
> enter my veins and drive the cold away, and I could conceive of no
> greater pleasure than sitting thus in my mother's kitchen.

> There are several episodes like this in my life as a child which, from
> one point of view, would be designated as the deprivation and misery

of utter poverty, but which have failed to impress me as such in my recollections. Is this because I, like others, have escaped from the rigors of poverty, and my feelings now permit me to recall those early incidents with a present sense of self-satisfaction? Is it because during the early years of this century, the truly deprived, ignorant of life's real ease, were happy at any scraps they could get, whether these were material or were the sensuous aspects of the world about them, such as could be perceived during a walk in the city on a bright, hot, sunny day in summer? Or is it because of other factors, such as the relationship of my mother to her children, which could have created happiness within the confines of poverty's prison?[1]

The Impact of Deprivation on Young Children (1967)

One of the serious things that may happen in bringing the four- and five-year-old children of disadvantaged families into school is that we may create stereotypes of the disadvantaged child or the disadvantaged as a group of people. We are not dealing with a *type* of people or a *type* of child. Children, like other members of the families from which they come, react differently to poverty and deprivation, or cruelty and misery. For most of them, the serious life deficits of living under poverty leave serious scars, but there are many children who will impress us by the way in which they have come out of unfortunate life circumstance and still are developing as effective, articulate, skillful children. Perhaps the basic issue is that we shall remain aware of each child for the separate person that he is.[2]

Our first task is to try to understand what really are the basic life deficits of most of these children and then, after that, to think about what adaptations of usual school procedures, or relationships, should be made to meet the children where they are. This kind of adaptation to the children is part of our general approach, in any case, to work with young children. The teacher of a young child perceives the child as a member of his family, coming from home into a strange school situation, needing and deserving to be understood as part of the life in which he has been growing up. It is possible to think of the life deficits of the disadvantaged child at different levels, some likely to be more seriously injurious to the child's whole development than others.

Briefly, three levels of deficit can be associated with the family life patterns in negative conditions of poverty.

Immature Language and Thinking

First, there is a pretty general observation that these children do not have the language skills expected at their stage of development; that it is not only the

1. This material is from the unpublished memoirs of Oscar Bodansky.

2. This article is adapted from The impact of deprivation on young children. *Childhood Education*, 1967, 44(2), 110–16.

language that is immature but the thought processes expressed in language: that they have not really advanced to being able to know the things in their world. Sometimes they do not discriminate one thing from another. Often they do not know the names of things. Their information is limited, and the usual expectation of an interested, curious, questioning, probing child is not fulfilled in the first days in which he comes into school.

Sometimes these deficits are explained by the fact that these children have had a restricted life experience, some never having been off the street on which they live: that they have not been in families where much conversation goes on or where the use of language is developed; that the family pattern is not one that includes reading or newspapers or books as a built-in part of home life; that many of these children have not had chances to play, have not had crayons and blocks or the kinds of things that middle-class families take for granted as part of their provision for their children. This restricted experience, in terms of both the use of language and the hearing of language, accompanied by the lack of experience with the objects and activities that other young children have at home, is the great hindrance in mastering language as a tool, since a child talks and thinks according to the model of talking and thinking he has before him in his home while young. The outcome of this deficit leads to difficulties in learning later on, learning to master the written language system, learning to read. The vicious circle intensifies when the child feels himself a failure in school in the first, second, or third grade and feels himself a relatively worthless human being. This is, of course, the great human waste that the antipoverty program is seeking to correct.

And even while we say all this, we have to correct ourselves and remember that there are some children who, in the clutter and the noise of city streets, have found wonderful ways of playing; have, in fact, exercised such imaginativeness in what can be done with a piece of wood or an old tire that one has to recognize that, for the children who can really overcome the barrenness and make something meaningful in their own independent play lives, there may be great power in their own resourcefulness to create and to overcome. We need to be aware that many of these children bring strengths as well as deficits into schoolrooms.

Lack of Close Relationships

There is another way—or maybe we could call it another level—of looking at the disadvantaged, of the life that's lived for most families and children in real poverty. Underneath the meagerness of language that the child experiences at home, there is perhaps a more serious barrenness. The people he lives with are not only not talking to each other, not using language freely in a richly developed way; it may well be that they are really not in close touch with each other as persons; that the child has not been noticed as the particular person he is; that adults have not played with him very much; that he has not been involved in the kinds of connections with others from the very beginning of his life that help a child know who are the familiar people, who are the strange people. Perhaps his relations have always been only the very practical, functional relations—life at its minimal essentials with little left of energy or resources for making life a little richer, more varied, more enjoyable.

In thinking of the earliest development of children, one wonders whether these children have had the experience that we have been familiar with. Before a baby can talk, in many families, there is a mother or a father or another adult who gurgles back to him his own nonsense syllables, who is there to respond to his earliest smiles, or, later on when he becomes a toddler and shows signs of playing, recognizes his play before he can say anything about it. Much joint understanding and communication go on among people without the use of language, and when a child is very young, this way of feeling related to other persons, especially those who are important to him in his life, is a significant part of his development. Is there someone who says "choo-choo" when he pulls his box along the floor? Is there someone who hands him a piece of cloth to cover up the doll that he begins to play with?

These are only the simplest examples of a way of life between children and adults, and a way of life among the adults themselves, that becomes part of a child's basic learning and development. It is a matter of connecting with people; being sensed as a person by others; being involved in many rich, important, and varied kinds of relationships with the human beings with whom a child lives; and of living in an atmosphere where the persons themselves are involved in such varied relationships. What the child misses here is not only a model of spoken language but, much more fundamentally, a lack of rich, meaningful communication beyond just the necessities of practical living. These lacks are deterrents for language use, indeed. Eventually they become deterrents for learning to read. But, more than that, more deeply, they are deterrents for being able to learn in general because it is through the active relationship with people, it is through being known and felt and understood as a person, that the child's basic curiosity and interest in the world begin to flower and develop.

Physical and Psychological Uncertainties

The third level of deficit is the most serious. Here we think of the children who live precariously on the edge of safety. This does not apply to many children, but those who come into a school group will be recognized as the children who will require understanding and skillful teaching.

These are the children who cannot be sure of the basic necessities. Will there be enough food? Is there someone to take care of you? There is uncertainty in their lives about whom they really belong to. Who is the father? And is the mother available to the child in important mothering ways? In fact, is there anybody who really cares about this child in a deep and important way?

The basic needs of the very young child to be sure that someone cares about him, wants him, and will take care of him are not fulfilled for these children. In the disturbed family lives in which they find themselves, the world is one of unpredictable threats; the parents, living under extreme conditions of stress and disturbance, do not represent consistent figures for the child. The child may be punished or deprived when there is no connection with something that he has done. He may simply be the innocent subject of the displaced panic of the parents. This means that the whole unpredictable world of the child carries a threat with it, and everyone who comes into his world is naturally suspect instead of trusted.

The psychological uncertainty of such a way of life is of course reinforced by the disorder of the physical environment, which is likely also to be characteristic of highly disturbed and deprived family situations. For children who come from these unusual but existing home situations, one expects deeply anxious forms of behavior. Here the deterrent to development is not only poverty of language and thought and experience; it is not only that the child has been living in a minimal world of human relationships and has not been realized as an individual; it is more that he is living in such a threatening, uncertain, unordered life environment that we do not expect him to be able to take his place in school or make use of what it offers without a great amount of guidance, support, and relearning in the kind of ordered situation that school represents. This kind of life deficit diminishes the development of personality at its very roots.

Adjusting Educational Practices

Just as there are different levels at which to understand the nature of developmental deficit for these children, so there are different ways of thinking about how we shall adjust our educational practices. Certainly we want to recognize the importance of bringing their language, ideas, understanding, and ways of gaining knowledge to higher and more developed levels than they have been able to accomplish thus far. One way of being sure that children become better talkers is to listen to them attentively and patiently, to try to understand them even when their words, accents, and pronunciation may be distant from what we expect. We need to recognize that they need to learn, too, how to be listeners and that they cannot be expected without preparatory experience just to sit in an orderly group and listen to a teacher reading a story.

Preparatory experience can be varied. The teacher may have many pictures on bulletin boards which she takes down and talks about to the children or asks them to talk about. It may be that when she finally tries to read a story to the children, she keeps to a minimum the amount of reading and chooses books with large, colorful pictures so that the children can respond to the pictures and not sit for an inordinately long time listening to a detailed story.

Experienced teachers, through use of a variety of games, involve the child not only in using words and learning the names of objects but direct him toward the discriminating and differentiating of his ideas that are basic to his thought processes. There are ways of developing songs in which the teacher mentions each child's name or some particular bit of each child's clothing and, in doing this, accomplishes two things: the child is made to feel that he is recognized as a person, as an individual, by the teacher; and the ideas and the words included in this kind of play and group life become the tools for further thinking.

Some specific techniques developed by teachers for this kind of learning experience have to do with recognition of written symbols: the teacher uses symbols that stand for each child before he can recognize his name; or, when children have become accustomed to school life, she puts labels on the buildings they make.

Free, spontaneous play and activities are especially conducive to the development of language and communication among the children themselves. Basic to the development of language and thought is that the children themselves shall have rich and extended experience, for which there are well-developed techniques. For example, planning is important in taking children on a trip outside school; the teacher needs to know how to prepare them, what to stimulate them to think about ahead of time, and how to encourage them to review and rehearse and play back the experience they have had.

In the early stages, the teacher's sensitivity is a vital factor; she is the one who recognizes how receptive she must be in order to communicate to the child—without saying so—that she wants to understand and hear what he has to say.

There are many opportunities for developing better cognitive skills in the course of children's activities. The teacher who is interested in having the children develop some skill in the number system puts questions to them. How many boys are sitting around the circle today? How many girls are sitting around? Do you want three more blocks or do you want two more blocks? In addition to using the daily life of children for developing their language skills and ideas there are other techniques definitely designed for this purpose. These may be useful to the teacher as long as she is mindful of the goal, which is that only the kind of experience that really supports the process of communication in these children is educationally important for them at this stage.

Emphasizing Order

To help these children, in still another way, make the best use of the opportunity for learning and development that we want them to have, it is essential to be aware that they are not accustomed to the kind of regulated, orderly life to which they have just been introduced. All children have to make some adjustment to the rules and regulations of life in a group situation, but these children come less ready, less prepared to take their places as individuals in a group situation. One of the most helpful things we can do for the children is to have things clear and well organized. There should be no higgledy-piggledy piling up of things; the daily schedule should be clear and children helped to understand and accept that now we do this, then we do that, then we do something else. Adults involved need to be alert for the moment when things are likely to become disorderly, such as times when children are changing from one activity or going from one place to another.

In presenting new materials, things, or activities, the teacher needs to be concrete, specific, simple, to demonstrate what she means rather than rely on verbal explanations. What she chooses for the children to do should be equal to what she thinks they can do rather easily, without frustration or likelihood of failure. For these children a negative experience can be a very inhibiting one. The goal is to build a world for them in the classroom that is a clear world, one in which they know where things are, what is going to happen next, and where they have a set of expectations that they can count on.

Teaching How To Play

Some teachers have been surprised to find that these children, far from taking to the toys and materials, seem indifferent to things—they pick them up and drop them, do nothing with them, perhaps allow them to break. There are different ways of trying to understand why the children behave this way with all these attractive objects. Perhaps they are just not accustomed to having things. It is certainly clear that they do not see these things as tools for play, since how to play is something that has not yet been realized by many of them. But there is another reason. Perhaps their indifference to these playthings is due to the fact that these children are not accustomed to really caring for things. In fact, if one has not been previously and deeply cared for oneself, perhaps one does not have a caring attitude toward other people or objects.

One teacher, confronted with such a situation, reacted by doing two things. First, she was practical. She tried to buy indestructible objects. Second, she tried to give some direct experience of caring. The teacher's aide was designated to sit at one end of the room and got the children to help her clean, mend, and rebuild things that had suffered from destructive use. This serves as an illustration of how, in working with these children, we try to see in their behavior the results of what their experience in life has been and to provide them with new experiences to replace the negative aspects of their early childhood lives.

There is another way in which the teacher of these children may carry out her role differently from the way she would if she were working with children with other life experience. One of her goals is to initiate these children into free play activity. She realizes that they need active guidance, that they need almost literally to be taken by the hand to be led to begin using things. Here the teacher has to do quite a lot of pump priming to get the child to be aware of what he can do. It may be necessary to spend an unusual amount of time playing with him and talking with him about what he could use this or that little object for or how he could make a building, talking with him about the ideas that he has of where he's going to take the doll, stimulating him to play, and leading him gradually to a more independent way of initiating ideas and thinking up play schemes that he can engage in with other children.

Relating to Teachers and Others

Basically, we cannot separate what these children will be able to learn—how much they can improve their language, how ready they can be for the next stages in school, how much they can begin to enjoy the healing and exciting experiences of play with things, toys, and one another—from the relations that the teacher and those who help the teacher come to have to the children as persons. This distinction requires an understanding on the part of all the adults that the children will not necessarily be expected in the beginning to trust and love those who give them all these good things. In fact, they may treat adults with suspicion, may be distant from them. They may need to be encouraged to learn how to share pleasures, excitement, and understanding. This will take place to the extent that teachers are sensitive, do not move in too fast for the children but build up around the life of the school such a way of living with the children that they have extended the safety zone; that the children realize and believe these are supporting, predictable grown-ups. They come to learn also that there will be controls, that this is not a place where they can run wild, upset, and destroy. But this is a place where adults do not threaten or punish the child; instead, they are ready to give him new ways of learning how to handle his hostile feelings, his anxiety, and his anger.

Much of the development of trust and understanding has to do with what happens within the child, how he comes to feel that he is a worthwhile human being. Of utmost importance is the child's awareness that he is known to the teacher and the other adults as an individual with distinct characteristics, that he will not be ostracized for his negative impulses. Further, trust deepens as he knows the adults around him understand impulses and will help him control them and keep them from having terrible effects on himself and other children.

Perhaps, as a conclusion, one instance will serve to illustrate some of these points about a teacher's relation to children: A consultant coming into a schoolroom noticed that a bird in a cage had been placed upon a top shelf. The teacher explained that, since it was impossible to keep the cage at the level of the children because all they wanted to do was to bang on the cage and keep the bird fluttering around, she had decided that the best way to cope with their excitement at the bird's disturbance was to put it up out of the way.

To the consultant, a bird in a cage on a high shelf was useless for a schoolroom. She gathered a small group of children around her, a few at a time—which is important to note, because in the beginning one cannot expect to communicate with a large group of children. She sat down with the bird cage in her lap, with four or five children around, and talked with them about the bird. "With what does the bird eat?" "How do you eat?" In this conversation they were thinking, figuring out. They eat with mouths; they have two lips. "A bird eats, too, but a bird eats with a beak and that's very different. That bird's beak is like someone's mouth." She went on with observations and comparisons. How little the bird is, how big by comparison the children are! They began to see greater detail, about how the bird was made, about its feathers, how it sits, how it stands. And in such a process of communication the children were being guided by the teacher to see something in life they had never seen before, to see this in terms of themselves—a comparison between a bird and a child— and in so doing to establish a meaningful relationship with ideas, with language, with an adult. The bird came down off the shelf; both it and the consultant had become friends to the children.

It is in such teaching episodes that one sees exemplified the basic goals for educating all children and perhaps the special goal of bringing these children into more meaningful relationships with people at the same time that one extends and stimulates their understanding of the world around them.

A Holistic View of a Growth-Inducing Environment

Since I wrote the paper "The Impact of Deprivation on Young Children" (published in 1967), the concept of deprivation has been analyzed, differentiated, criticized as misleading, and discarded by many investigators. The effects of deprivation cannot be assumed to be universal. They differ according to varied social contexts. Thus, in trying to understand the effects of deprivation as a step on the road to redressing inequities, it becomes essential to distinguish subgroups in the "deprived" population in certain broad terms: race, social class, inner city, rural area, subculture, ethnicity. But it is the immediate, psychologically defined environment, referred to as the "proximal" environment, that is usually the focus of the educator's attention. Here it is that the teacher sets out to "compensate" for the environmentally induced deficits that are attributed to living under deprived conditions, as defined.

The relations I posited between a poor home environment and the children's response to the school situation when they came into it were also conjectural, though some of the presumed relations appeared to have greater probability than others. That poverty would involve more restricted experience in early differentiation of the environment on a circumstantial basis seemed a safer assumption than that it would impair the depth of interpersonal relationships. Stated generally, the relation between poverty and the specific characteristics of the life environment is only probabilistic (National Institute of Health, 1968) and only by careful study of variations could we measure the validity of what are taken to be dominant central tendencies. In my 1967 paper I decried the tendency to "type" the poor family or the poor child and called attention to the children who were exceptions to the presumed effects of poverty: ". . . but there are many children who will impress us by the way in which they have come out of unfortunate life circumstance and still are developing as effective, articulate, skillful children." I have known too many such stalwart individuals in my own lifetime to have made the error of overgeneralizing.

A View of Deprivation and a Rationale for Education

Although there was correspondence, there was also significant difference between what we considered the components of a deprived environment and what was emphasized in most other analyses in the 1960s. Whereas most formulations were centered on locating the antecedents for school failure and concentrated on cognition variables, we took a more holistic view. We were more concerned with the affective correlates of experience and theoretically, as developmentalists, committed to the interaction of cognitive and affective factors. The children's changing subjective images in the course of their preschool experience was at least as important to us as their increasing behavioral adaptation and intellectual competence, interdependent as we consider these to be. The deprivation of their environments, over and above the aspects noted by those who were cognition focused, involved, in addition, important intrapersonal lacks.

Rightly or wrongly, we saw the children, most of them, as having missed the pleasures, the sense of a constructive, creative self that a young child gets from a well-nourished play life and the opportunity to act out his burgeoning understanding and troubled feelings. We saw them as missing also the deepened and clarified sense of individual identity that is the by-product of multiple instances of variegated interaction and modes of communication with adults on the child level, the sense of inner peace and safety from living in a world of dependable, expectable adult behavior. From this view, what the children lacked, what they were being deprived of, was seen as the fallout of what society had denied their parents. What matters educationally is the fact that a brief but comprehensive interpretation of the concept of deprivation such as was attempted in my 1967 paper leads to a very different remediation program from one that is based primarily on a theory of retardation of cognitive processes—as though cognition could be separated from other developmental processes.

Fortunately, we did not have to be lone adventurers of comprehensive programs. In the 1960s and 1970s this position was being put into practice impressively in the design and practice of the Headstart program. From its inception Headstart was based on supporting a comprehensive developmental image in which the complexity of interaction of social-emotional factors and intellectual competence was the foundation for program planning. In Headstart the "whole child" perspective was sustained during a period when it was almost eclipsed by Piaget-stimulated interest in cognitive processes and investment in experimental preschool programs concentrated on elevating cognitive functioning in the early years.

A comprehensive concept of what constitutes deprivation in the young child is the analogue of a comprehensive concept of what constitutes a positive, growth-inducing environment. Though envisioned in the context of a school situation it has sufficient generality to be applicable to home life. In each orbit—home and school—exploration, sensitized discrimination, action manipulation, symbolization, and verbal skills and conceptualization—the basic educational methods described—have a dual purpose. They are adapted not only to advance competence and conceptualization but also to deepen the child's inner sense of his own powers, of his intimate connectedness with the world in which he moves, and of trust and feeling of communion with the adults who stand in a position of authority.

In the paradigm I offered, the totality of this experience was expected to release the capacities of the deprived children, like those of all other children, to the measure of their full potential. The special techniques and adjustment of the stimulating environment were secondary means—efforts to undo the restraints and the self-defeating patterns that had been developed. These efforts were not random; they were tied to the hypothetical interpretation of which aspects of the "deprived" child's environment were deleterious to his full potential development. For example, the suggestion for keeping the stimulating environment more orderly than usual with respect to time, place, and sequence followed from the assumption of low discrimination in a hard-to-manage poverty environment; the suggestion that the teacher take a more active role in guiding the children into the symbolization of dramatic play was based on the assumption that the home environment had not been able to provide the physical or psychological setting in which the child can, on his own initiative, indulge and elaborate his fantasy life. The intently listening teacher was more concerned to understand, and communicate her understanding, than to correct formal verbal errors. Such a teacher is in a better position to reinforce the satisfaction of clear communication than the preoccupied adults in a poor household.

For and against Intervention Programs

It is not a simple task to place our early review of the problem in the mood, the arguments, and the expectations of the intervention programs of the 1960s. We were both aligned and opposed. The surge of professional recognition of the importance of the preschool years supported our commitment of fifty years' standing to develop an educational curriculum for nursery-age children in contrast to custodial, welfare-oriented day care programs. Significant research findings such as the study reported by Bloom in 1964 supported what had been largely an assumption, namely, that because of the rapid acceleration of growth in the first four to six years of life, this stage is a salient period for environmental stimulation of intellectual growth. Still, we could not accept the implied now-or-never position. Our own workshop programs for revising school programs in the elementary years assumed that locked-up potential could be released to a significant degree by a changed atmosphere of learning and radical revision of teacher–child interactions in the primary and elementary years. This position was also voiced by Lilian Katz (1970/71): "Development is not as irreversible as we had once believed. . . . I am suggesting that early education is very important, but it is not more important than all later education." Here, too, there was support in research findings, for example, in Kagan's work (1973) on Guatemalan children and his conclusion that intellectual deprivation in the early years of childhood is not decisive with respect to the quality of functioning in later stages. It would be clarifying and comforting if the general concept of malleability of the human organism could contain these presumably contrary findings: the greater impressionability of the early years need not gainsay the continued developmental openness of later childhood. What we do not know enough about is which experiential input at which stage under what sociocultural conditions can bring about maximum expression of basic powers. The development of life span studies is a major source of enlightenment on this question.

Support for an inclusive stimulating environment in early childhood was expressed in Fowler's general position, which governed his approach to cognitive-stimulation techniques: "On a broad plane our findings generally support the notion of the equal, indeed essential, value of both symbolic, guided cognitive orientations and self-propelled free play. . . . Far from being uneconomic, integrated, cognitive-interpersonal approaches to child rearing foster the development of competence, autonomy, and personality development in children from many social backgrounds" (1971). It is interesting to note that this passage is excerpted from a paper published in *Young Children*, a journal whose teacher-readers must have welcomed warmly this authoritative support for the position they held empirically.

We were opposed to the programs in which stimulation of cognitive processes, apart from consideration of the other interacting developmental processes, was the center—sometimes the whole content—of the compensatory programs. This emphasis characterized the programs originating in academic situations, designed usually by psychologists with relatively little direct experience with the total complexity of the early years of childhood: rapidly emerging powers, awakening identity, and the challenge to resolve social-psychological-instinctual conflicts. There were two wasteful errors in the 1960s: one was a restricted perspective on the learning process; the other was a misconstruing of one discipline by the other. The first error led to extracting cognition from the total developmental process and subsequently developing narrow training techniques where comprehensive experiential programs were called for. The second error was the misperception of the highly developed discipline of early childhood education as being a socialization-mental health model, seriously neglectful of cognitive stimulation, with more serious consequences for the disadvantaged than for the middle-class child. Actually, anyone willing to read *cognition* where *thinking* was written would have found a rich resource in the literature describing long-established preschool programs—in the built-in emphasis on why-thinking, in the stimulation of hypothetical thinking, in the experiential testing of assumptions, and in the rich, individual encounter with symbolic processes through autonomous, spontaneous play. Educators identified with these purposes and programs, at Bank Street and elsewhere, felt seriously misunderstood by the critics from academe. Subsequently, after the 1960s, there came a period when "the bloom was off the rose" for compensatory education. Partly this was true because the anticipated gains from cognitive-focused programs had not been realized, partly because continuous direct work with children in school had an impact on previously held theory.

In the position we took, we saw the condition of family life under poverty as per se a denying factor. The ever-present struggle for subsistence, the anxieties associated with economic uncertainty, present and future, the relative meagerness of material wherewithal to fulfill needs, not to speak of wishes, seemed to leave relatively little room, materially and psychologically, for most parents to be closely involved in the guidance of the subtler aspects of their children's experience.

Potential and Performance

Turning to the children and the way they functioned when they came into school, we saw inadequacies relative to the more advantaged preschool children's manner and performance in terms of verbal-conceptual development, expression of affect, mode of utilizing the experiential opportunities, and quality of interaction with adults and children. The comparisons were based on teachers' observations in ongoing situations, day by day, free of the errors associated with judgments based on brief testing episodes. The school vernacular (unfamiliar to the less advantaged children) that obscured meaning, and their understandable suspicion of a strange adult's purpose in an unfamiliar relation, yielded unreliable estimates of capacity. Here, too, it was the Headstart perspective that turned the tide against using measures of program effectiveness that were psychologically and sociologically irrelevant to the experience of the children whose capacities were being estimated. A new, broader concept of measurement had been formulated in terms of measures of social competence reflecting "first, the success of the human being in meeting societal expectancies. Second, these measures of social competence should reflect something about the self-actualization or personal development of the human being." Specifically, the proposed roster of measures includes physical health and well-being, a measure of formal cognitive ability, an achievement measure, and a measure of motivational and emotional variables (Zigler & Trickett, 1978).

The assertion that difference in performance must not be taken to imply difference in potential capacity between the children in the poverty group and others in our society was part of a broader premise about variation in human societies and in subcultures within a society. The universality of potential was stated by Kagan (1972): "The capacity for perceptual analysis, imitation, inference, language deduction, symbolism, and memory will eventually appear in sturdy form, for each is an inherent competence in the human program." I had learned the basic concept in those early Barnard days from Franz Boas: "There is no fundamental difference in the ways of thinking of primitive and civilized man" (1911). Analysis and trying-out of the conditions under which these universal capacities will appear in sturdy form is, or should be, the appointed life work of the educator while it is recognized that the school, by itself, is not the mighty instrument it is often taken to be.

I was interested to find I. E. Sigel in 1973 taking the same position. He wrote: "In essence, I am arguing that man as a universal species shares characteristics that are inherent in his very biological nature. Psychologists must accept this fact and then distinguish the environmental components which influence the functioning of these various capabilities." And it is interesting to me personally that he, too, traces his view back to his own early learning, quoting from his master's thesis in 1948: "Anthropology shows us that man shares universal characteristics as far as his cognitive capacity is concerned, but that the culture sets the limits of its expression." Since I share a developmentalist position as well as an early exposure to anthropological perspective with Sigel, it is not surprising that his approach to the education of the deprived child, as stated in his 1973 paper, coincides basically with my paper of 1967. He emphasized, as I did, the whole-organism approach, the misplaced overattention to cognition, the importance of supporting the child's active discovery relation through play and interaction and of providing an environment that offers opportunity for expanding experience with language, symbolism, and reasoning processes—in all, experiential nourishment for what might be dormant. This is just another instance of the influence of theory on practice.

A Corrected Perspective

The view of deprivation expressed thus far has been severely criticized, especially by contemporary anthropologists, and labeled the social pathology view. But first there is room for self-criticism. While we did not accept the narrow cognitive-instructional approach of most remedial programs, we failed to indicate how each remedial program could and should be adapted to the varying degrees and kinds of comparative deficit behavior associated with different levels of disturbed home-life environments. In that connection, Minuchin's pilot study (1971) of curiosity and exploration in preschool disadvantaged children made a valuable contribution. She invites and exercises differentiated thinking not only about the incidence and distribution of levels of deficit but also about the perception of the nature of the psychological content. Through observation and a variety of assessment techniques, she found significant variation in expression of curiosity and constructive exploration. Within the group of 18 children in two centers, she found two internally consistent groups of children functioning at clearly different qualitative levels, 6 children in one group and 5 in the other. In summary, she found that the children in one group were "not only more active in encounters with their surroundings but [more able] to see the environment with greater coherence, have more expectation that adults will be helpful and effective . . . have a more integrated sense of self and a more orderly way of grasping system in the physical environment (i.e., conceptual mastery)." She did not wish to imply that these children's performance in school is on a par with that of their middle-class counterparts in knowledge, language, emotional security, or level of exploratory behavior, but they seem basically "more able to take useful experience from their environment." This sounds like the group I conjectured about briefly in the beginning of my paper and put aside, mistakenly, in my general description of effects of deprivation, as though they represented only a small portion of the total population.

Minuchin's study indicates the need for a broader search of the distribution. She describes the second group of children as a "high risk population . . . who showed little curiosity or constructive exploratory behavior, whose image of themselves was diffuse, who projected an environment characterized by sustained crisis, little coherence and ineffective, poorly defined adults, and whose conceptual grasp of order and relationships in the physical environment was comparatively low." Once we recognize that there is this degree of variation in what different children can utilize, school programs need more differentiated planning. For example, as Minuchin points out, it is doubtful that the children who are on the lower end of the continuum can benefit from the remedial programs that focus on language training, labeling drill, and conceptual exercises; they may have prior needs for being helped to explore at simple sensorimotor levels, to observe, and to question, in a predictable framework of events with supportive adults. Obviously, this study represents an essential step in correcting the error of "typing" the disadvantaged child and points to the importance of taking into consideration the multiple modes of acting and feeling that comprise a child's relation to an environment.

If failure to adapt educational procedures to different levels of deprivation was an error of omission (one that has since received further clarification), there was another error, more an error of commission. There is good reason to think that our image of life under poverty was a selected one, far from generally true, and maybe basically inadequate with respect to the total reality of the children's experience. This takes me back to a talk by Ralph Ellison at a seminar in 1963. Though he was speaking from the viewpoint of poor black society, his position was a precursor of what came to be, quite a few years later, the orientation toward other ethnic people not in the mainstream of American society and overlapping in good measure with the culture of the poor.

In his description of the qualities of black society in the South, he breaks down, convincingly, the misnomer *culturally deprived*. He describes the strength of a people who have survived through ingenuity and deep motivation and who do not accept the feeling of being diminished. He sees impressive strength in the ability to screen out chaos, in the uses of imagination in a backwoods surrounding, in the poetry of words, in virtuosity and the rich oral culture. Despite the negatives and the harshness of life, he recalls a "most wonderful place" where toys were somehow handfashioned, people taught themselves to play the guitar, and children had ways of finding treasures in the city dump—a society where the strength and the imaginativeness of a people were much in evidence.

He sees much of this richness filtered out in the move to the North, where, dispossessed of familiar reality, in a hostile environment difficult to deal with because of the barriers of poverty and race, children and youth are maimed by the confrontation with a strange world. The problem is not cultural deprivation, in this view. The reality is a different cultural complex of codes, customs, attitudes, and expression. Life patterns become distorted because of the inability to relate the culture of the parents to the diversity of cultural forms in which the young person must live in a pluralistic society. What develops is a counterscheme for living, shutting out the faraway world of theaters and museums of a great city, for example, and a retreat to the security of the gang. The task, much of it falling to the teachers, is to help children feel that what they have learned in their world counts, that they do not have to give up their sense of identity in accepting and adapting to the verbal discourse and the modus vivendi for functioning in the larger surrounding society. In conclusion, he puts his message in the first person: "If you can show me how I can cling to that which is real to me, while teaching me a way into the larger society, then I will not only drop my defenses and my hostility, but I will sing your praises and I will help you to make the desert bear fruit."

The papers by Minuchin and Ellison, respectively, spell out two correctives to my 1967 paper. Minuchin deals with variation in *below par* functioning in disadvantaged children in preschool settings (not a single pattern of deficit), which requires that the modes of relationship and the levels of stimulation that are inaugurated in school be suited to these different levels and modes of functioning. Ellison makes it plain that many children grow up in a subculture which contains sources of pleasure and fulfillment as well as of pain and frustration. With empathic understanding, appreciation for diversity, and commitment to the benefits of pluralistic social forms, it should be possible to make education an open path to successful functioning in the larger culture without denial of the intimacy and special worth of identity with the subculture.

From Deficit to Difference

The radical change from the cultural deficit view to the cultural difference perspective that matured in the 1970s had broad scope. It was compounded of specific criticism of the deficit view underlying compensatory educational programs for an underprivileged population. It was also, for many, a far-reaching indictment of the values and underlying social philosophy of our educational system, in the large. Taking a cultural-anthropological view, Baratz and Baratz (1970) were highly suspicious of intervention programs even when they seemed to accept a difference rather than a deficit view. From their perspective, these programs were built on wrong assumptions anchored in middle-class goals, values, and life-styles. They attributed the failure of these programs to the way in which values of superior or inferior are built-in distinctions reflecting a narrow ethnocentric view.

The critique of the deficit view points first to the errors in the image of the deprived child's functioning that was based on testing and experimentation which did not take sufficiently into account unfamiliarity with verbal forms, with the specific experiential content in which the problems are embedded, and the child's reaction to the social situational elements. In the view of anthropologists and many others, estimates of performance adequacy are useful only when they are made in the context of "natural" situations as distinct from contrived test and experimental conditions.

Recognition of the importance of the situational factors has been strengthened in comparative culture studies where the evidence leads to the conclusion that "cultural differences in cognition reside more in the situations to which particular cognitive processes are applied than in the existence of a process in one cultural group and its absence in another" (Cole et al., 1971). When this principle is applied to the difference between a subculture and a main culture, it undercuts both the deficit position and the inference of superior vs. inferior capacity.

It is the concept of *linguistic deprivation* and the associated assumption of lessened cognitive capacity that have been attacked most vigorously in Labov's work (1970) with black children and youth. Rejecting the methods of standard interview and test situations as threatening to the slum child, he turned to the natural locales of home or club or street for his studies of language. In changing the situation, he found that the children who were quiet and restrained in the more formal situation conversed with him freely and openly in dialect when on "home" ground. He disputes the assumption of those psychologists who regard nonstandard English as a liability to the course of cognitive development. Analyzed linguistically, in terms of the rules of grammar and phonology that represent the underlying structure of language, black English, he finds, is on a par with standard English. He describes a rich verbal culture and facility in reasoning among gang members in which, however, the content of what is expressed violates middle-class values. Thus, in this view, it is not a deficit in language use or cognitive style that accounts for less adequate performance in school, and it is not only the problem of conflict between the spontaneous uses of black English and the uses of language that are to be learned in school. It is more basically a mismatch between the ideology of the school and the poor child's motivations, values, and identity within the subculture.

From this view, it is ignorance of and insensitivity to the nature of the subculture and the conflicts involved for the children in the school environment that lead to misperceptions; namely, the error of taking school performance to be an accurate measure of potentiality and the view of the children as culturally and verbally deprived, as "empty vessels, waiting to be filled with middle-class culture" (National Institute of Health, 1968).

Cultural deprivation thus comes to be seen from a broader perspective as a "special class of cultural difference which arises when an individual is faced with demands to perform in a manner inconsistent with his past (cultural) experience." It is interesting to consider this statement, from a paper by Cole and Bruner in 1972, with a parallel statement by Ellison in 1963: "When a child has no fruitful way of relating the cultural traditions and values of his parents to the diversity of cultural forces with which he must live in a pluralistic society, he is culturally deprived." The implications of taking the perspective of difference rather than deficit for the classroom teacher should, according to Cole and Bruner, have a dual influence. They should "change the students' status in the eyes of the teacher," and this change in attitude should provide change in performance. It should lead the teacher to learn how to "get the child to transfer skills he already possesses to the task at hand." Further, it is the psychologist's task to "analyze the source of cultural difference so that those of the minority, less powerful group may quickly acquire the intellectual instruments necessary for success in the dominant culture, should they so choose" (1972).

Voices against Compensatory Education

When I came upon a book entitled *The Myth of the Deprived Child* (Ginsburg, 1972), I regretted the ambiguity of the title because I value the book's contribution to this murky problem. The author integrates the "cultural difference" position with the Piagetian theory of learning, and developmental theory in general, and on that basis establishes a case in favor of the open education approach. He disputes the assumptions and techniques of the compensatory education movement from two perspectives—psychological and educational. First, the poor child's environment contains its own patterns of stimulation adequate for acquiring the cognitive universals; children are active learners, biologically geared to organizing their mental processes and adapting to the environment, not passively subject to environmental influences; the erroneous assumption of retardation of thought processes obscures recognition of certain unique intellectual abilities that are adaptive in their own environments. Second, the teaching techniques of the traditional school are maladapted to the needs and proclivities of all children, especially the deprived.

He sees the open classroom philosophy as built soundly on the assumption of the child as a storehouse of potentiality, not defect, and on construction of the teacher's role so as to support the child in developing in a self-directed way. Compensatory education, tied to traditional views, assumes that there are deficits to correct and that the process of remediation is in the hands of the adult. For the poor child, the open classroom has an advantage in that it recognizes and is sensitive to his potentialities and contribution, is innovative and flexible in adapting teaching modes to the special aspects of the children's receptivity.

At the same time that I welcome his movement of the problem into the elementary school level and his advocacy of the open school approach to learning in general and to the needs of the poor child in particular, I regret the extent to which the structure of his argument and the resolution of the problems deal with cognitive processes almost exclusively. Without more interest in the subjective aspects of affective experience, which he recognizes only parenthetically, this approach remains incomplete.

The ideology of open education represented a maturing phase of the progressive philosophy. In reviewing the history of progressive education as a social movement MacDonald (1975) analyzes the elements which have remained as the foundation for open education. He summarizes seven basic principles as a lasting legacy, among them individual right to freedom and choice, concern for individual differences, the method of intelligence (problem solving), the disciplines as potential endpoints rather than starting points for pedagogy. As is familiar in other pioneer movements, the shift from being a fringe movement in the 1920s and 1930s to being embraced by the large instrument of public education in succeeding decades altered the basic ideology. In this instance this was exemplified by a shift from social idealism to a leveling off concept of children's potential capacity and a trivializing of the educative process.

But this is a partial image. The basic ideology of the progressive movement, moving with new psychological insights into individual development and growing sensitivity to dynamic concepts of the social order, took new forms of expression in the open school movement, among them, a psychosocial orientation for the preschool movement, allegiance with other educational systems with similar values such as developed in England, involvement of the professions (psychology, sociology) in experimenting with changes in curriculum and the social organization of the life of the school. The fact that initial experimental methods needed rethinking and revision does not negate the importance of a change-oriented perspective which found support in the 1970s from foundations representing forward looking views for American education. Then what does Ravitch (1983) mean when she takes the subsequent conservative backlash against progressive education as evidence that the movement had died but then, in the end, summarizes: "The influence of its pioneers was present wherever projects, activities, and pupil experiences had been intelligently integrated into subject-matter teaching, wherever concern for health and vocation had gained a permanent place in the school program, and wherever awareness of the individual differences among children had replaced lockstep instruction and rote memorization" (p. 80). One reviewer (Lehmann-Haupt, 1983) of her book explains: "She trapped herself," meaning she did not find the path of deterioration which she expected to find (see also Cremin, 1964).

There is some encouragement to be found in the paper by Ginsburg and Knitzer (1976), taking the position that psychological approaches are valuable but, no matter how sophisticated, innovative, or theoretically grounded, are not sufficient in themselves. To the contribution of the developmental psychologist they would add the program of child advocacy in the social sphere first formulated by the Joint Commission on Mental Health of Children in 1969. It is a social change strategy drawing on political and legal skills and community organization to challenge injustices affecting the quality of life for children. The targets of child advocacy interventions are the social systems that adversely affect children: schooling, child mental health services, juvenile justice processes. Through joint activities there would be a gain in a broader perspective for psychologists—clearer understanding of what it takes to effect social change, in a school system for example, and awareness of the nonpsychological forces that have immediate impact on the lives of the children. Child advocates, in turn, would gain deeper understanding of children's natures and needs if the developmental psychologist's knowledge could be put in their service. In sum, psychological, educational, and social systems approaches, supportive of and related to one another, offer the best promise—maybe the only promise—for coping with the problem of social inequities.

CHAPTER 6

Language Use and Thought Processes: Perspectives on Remediation

Thinking back to my years as an avid adolescent reader I recall lifting my eyes from a book I was reading—it may well have been The Spirit of the Ghetto *by Hutchins Hapgood, published in 1902, which still stands on my bookshelf—to ask my mother a question: "What is a 'yeshibah bahu'?" pronounced literally from what I recall as the phonetic spelling. It took a little time and a little mother–daughter fun until she explained that this was the English spelling of a Hebrew word designating a man whose life was completely devoted to the house of prayer—a term sometimes used pejoratively to describe unworldliness.*

The children of Eastern European Jewish immigrants in the first decades of the century had two barriers to overcome.[1] *They lived in the foreign language of their families (Yiddish, Russian, or Polish) and learned English in a dialect form which was not acceptable in school. They attended special classes to learn English in its proper form until they were ready to join the regular classes. It was a coaching, not a bilingual approach. Parents accepted growing distance from their children, whose welfare depended on becoming Americanized in the mores of that era.*

But there are always people ahead of their time, and it is a pleasure to look back, from the present period of relative fulfillment of their views, to their precocious insight. Partly pleasure. Partly pain. Why do good ideas need such a long period of gestation? In the early years of the century, in the American scene, insights for the future came from social workers— Grace Abbott, Jane Addams, Sophinisba Breckenridge, Julia Richman. They were a common voice protesting the failure to appreciate the positive gains in sustaining a foreign culture. They wanted educators to make it possible for children to move out of their foreign enclaves but, beyond that, help them to understand the psychological and societal loss in rejecting

---

1. See *World of our fathers* by Irving Howe.

subcultural mores as well as the associated guilt of rejecting parents'
language and cultural identity.

In contrast to the earlier era, the 1960s and 1970s represented an era
of imagination and scholarly attention to the questions of dialect and
bilingualism. A new perspective has evolved. We look to the school as a
social instrument to help children gain the advantage not only of two-
language competence but also of broadened understanding of social diversity
and an enlarged sphere of interpersonal communication. It is not surprising
that the goal is more established than the method. Two languages? Until
what age and grade levels? A divided curriculum? At what cost in
communication and social interchange? The subtle differences of method fall
within the larger context of complex political issues as well as divided
educational thinking, which pertains to this question as it does to so many
others.

A Child Development Approach to Language in the Preschool Disadvantaged Child (1968) with Patricia Minuchin

The nature and extent of language deficit among the children of the disadvantaged are by now well known, increasingly documented, and specified by ongoing research (Bernstein, 1960; Cohn, 1959; Deutsch, 1967; John, 1963; Raph, 1965). Though some have pointed out that the language of the inner-city slums has its own vocabulary and richness (Riessman, 1962), it seems clear that children of this population are often less articulate than their more privileged peers and less able to use language effectively as a tool of thought, learning, and communication. Further, their deficits are noticeable at very young ages and tend to persist or become more apparent as the children move through the elementary grades.

There are a variety of ways in which the deficits of these children can be conceptualized, and the preschool programs based on such conceptualizations are correspondingly varied. The point of view represented in this paper sets language and language deficit into the context of the child's more general psychological development. In essence, this viewpoint considers the growth of language to be part of the development of human communication on the one hand and part of conceptual development on the other. Further, this viewpoint considers the purposes of preschool education to be developmental in the broadest sense. In this context, the advancement of measurable language skills is an important goal for disadvantaged children, but not the only goal or, in all instances, the primary one.

Adapted from A child development approach to language in the preschool disadvantaged child. In M. A. Brottman (Ed.), *Language remediation for the disadvantaged preschool child. Monographs of the Society for Research in Child Development*, 1968, *33* (8, serial no. 124) (coauthored with Patricia Minuchin).

The psychoeducational philosophy represented in this paper is not new. It is a philosophy with roots in theories of development and emotional growth, and it has been basic to the more vigorous preschool programs over a number of decades (Biber, 1964; Biber & Franklin, 1967). It has had a complex and conscious perception of the purposes of a preschool; it has involved theory and planning concerning the experiences and materials to be provided for children; and it has involved an active role for the teacher.

This kind of preschool program has stressed the expansion of the young child's world. It has been interested in sensitizing him to the sight and sound and feel of experience and in helping him to differentiate it. It has provided him with materials for expressing his fantasies and his understanding of reality and for making his impact on the world around him. It has helped him with crises in relation to people he wants to be with, problems he needs to solve, and frustrations he needs to bear. These programs have seen the child's emotional growth and his intellectual learning as proceeding together, and they have involved teachers, at their best, who fostered this growth in ways that took into account the general characteristics of the developmental stage and the particular characteristics of the individual child.

There has been no radical change of goals and philosophy, within this framework, in relation to slum children. Clearly, they have special characteristics and problems; within the established preschool movement there is a good deal of groping and search for new procedures, styles, and points of balance for use with these children. These adaptations are taking place, however, within a framework that continues to have broad goals for the development of the child as an individual. This is partly a matter of preference—a value judgment concerning the purposes and legitimate scope of the educational process. It is also based on the theoretical assumption, however, that these children cannot become effective learners in any meaningful way unless they are helped to build emotional strength along with specific skills.

When we consider language development and deficit, it seems fruitful, as noted above, to look at language in two ways: as a form of communication among human beings, and as part of the development of symbolization and thought. It has, in other words, both a relationship aspect and a cognitive aspect. When language emerges and develops in an optimal way, it seems likely that the child has already had a history of rich preliminary experience. This includes exposure to verbal models and direct reinforcement of verbal behavior, but it also includes experiences that are not in themselves verbal. Primary among these are experiences with people who set up a pleasurable and satisfying interchange with the child. There is body contact, laughter and games, a reaction to gestures and babbling, and an attentive response to the moods, wishes, and needs that the child conveys nonverbally. Long before he can talk, if all goes well, the child is a communicator, with a set of experiences and expectations concerning the fate of his efforts to convey something to other people.

The growth of language and logical thought has other precursors, if we are to take seriously the developmental theories of Piaget, Werner, and others.

It is at a sensorimotor level that the child has his basic experiences with space and direction, sequences in time, the nature of contrasts and similarities in the way things feel and function. It is in active interaction with the physical environment, in other words, that he begins to develop rudimentary and intuitive knowledge of the world and how it works. And these early nonverbal schemata make possible the later growth of logical concepts and meaningful language.

It seems likely that primitive symbolic play is another relevant precursor. When the young child pretends he is a dog, barking and crawling on all fours, or when he pushes two cereal boxes as if they formed a train, he is involved in a primitive experience with things that stand for other things—as letters, numbers, and sounds will later stand, at a more abstract level, for facts, objects, and ideas.

We have tended to take these early experiences and precursors for granted. The evidence accumulating now about disadvantaged children, however, suggests that deficits may occur in any or all of these areas. For some of these children, human relationships have been tenuous, inconstant, or even traumatic. Life circumstances and family style, increasingly documented by current research (Bernstein, 1960; Minuchin et al., 1967; Pavenstadt, 1967), tend to militate against any elaborate, playful, or attentive interchange between adults and children. This is partly a verbal matter but partly a much more comprehensive matter of models for relationship and communication. Many of these children do have active physical contact with their environment. Yet, in the fact of its pressured, chaotic, insufficiently varied quality, they do not find the constancy or order from which to form stable and differentiated impressions of reality, especially if there is no one to help them specifically in finding their way through it. Further, some of these children exhibit little sustained contact with the objects around them; they do not engage much in the symbolic "as if" play that tries out roles and transforms objects (Mattick, 1965; Smilansky, 1965). Under these circumstances, the frequently perceived deficits in language and concept formation may have many roots. They are probably different from child to child and can include any of these areas, along with specific deficits in language training and exposure.

Given this constellation, what are the implications for language remediation and for the fostering of the capacity for logical thought? What kind of approach should be used in the preschool setting?

In the remainder of this paper, we shall consider five points relevant to language deficit and development, as expressed in preschool programs which follow the basic developmental theory and model described briefly above. Of these points, the third will be elaborated most fully since it distinguishes this approach most clearly from other programs and is, in addition, least generally understood.

a. Teachers in this kind of program do not always emphasize language and verbalization with these children. There are specific children, times, and situations where a stress on words seems to run the danger of defeating basic purposes.

There are times when teachers deliberately use few words. There are also times when teachers talk actively with children but are not basically interested in accurate labeling or the learning of concepts. Some of the children in this population are difficult to reach, afraid, and unrelated. Even if we are interested only in their formal learning progress, it is unlikely that these children will learn much from adults unless this lack of relationship changes (Lustman, 1966).[2] Teachers, thus, use any means they can to establish contact with these children. They give, they gesture, they smile, they touch—if the child allows it. They establish contact through offering the kinds of large, motor, climbing, and riding experiences that many of these children gravitate toward. Teachers may minimize words at first and talk more later, but they work basically on bringing the child into communication with other people, particularly the teaching adult.

With these children, teachers often listen and accept, rather than correct, and they try to mirror what the child is saying, in essence if not grammar. This is not the idiom of later academic success in any direct way, but it sets up an experience with language, sometimes for the first time, as a source of pleasure and a useful tool. Teachers in one center intervene in a pitched battle by saying, "Fix it with words," and help the children to resolve the crisis verbally. They are offering language as a problem-solving tool in a situation that has great emotional meaning for small children. It is sometimes said that disadvantaged children lack a conceptual language but have adequate language for "social" and "expressive" needs. Others have observed, however, that these children have particular difficulty in expressing their wishes and differentiating their feelings. Teachers in these programs work toward increasing the child's differentiated perception and expression of his own emotional states.

b. In these programs, there is considerable emphasis on extending the child's direct experience with a wide and differentiated physical environment. This direct contact, even if primarily nonverbal, is considered basic experiential underpinning for meaningful use of language and the grasp of logical concepts and relationships. There is also a fostering of the child's symbolic play—again because this is a probable precursor of language and symbolization. (These aspects of the preschool program have other and multiple purposes, of course, but they are not immediately relevant here.)

This point requires little elaboration. Preschool programs have always been very active in fostering and guiding the child's exposure to many kinds of materials and experiences. They are selected and offered, at least in part, so that the child can learn firsthand about the properties and functions of objects in the physical world.

c. The teacher often consolidates language and understanding in the context of the child's own play and activities. She has a variety of techniques for bringing direct experience to a more symbolic and conceptual level. As noted, this feature of the teaching most clearly distinguishes this approach from more

---

2. Psychodynamic theorists such as Lustman consider the deficit in object relations to be the basic and pivotal "disadvantage" in these children.

formal, programmed approaches. It is also least generally understood and therefore bears more elaboration.

In part, the teacher works through activities and events that occur regularly or that she introduces. The children in one of the centers go up and down the stairs to their playground. The teacher uses this repeated experience to accent the meaning of *up* and *down* while the child is involved in the sensation. "We're going up," she says, as they climb the stairs. She helps them develop a song about it; they play a game of raising their hands high up as they go; the children who reach the top call "hello, down there" to the children still on the bottom steps. And the teacher returns to this idea in various ways in this context and others.

There are many instances like this. They take place around mealtimes, while the children are dressing to go out, in connection with the hamster they feed and care for. Or they take place around particular experiences that the teacher introduces. For example, she brings fabrics of different textures that the children can feel and describe and compare. There is much structure in the sequence of the school day, and the teacher has considerable opportunity to plan and introduce this kind of teaching and translation.

What is more difficult to describe and more unique in these programs is the teacher's use of events that arise spontaneously. Here she cannot plan specifically. It is predictable that such events will occur but not exactly when, how, or with what content. Following are several examples of how such events are handled:

Example 1: The teacher comes out of the room with a few of the children. There is a door with a broken hinge leaning against the wall. A child asks, confused, "Is that a door?" The teacher stops; she tells them it is broken and needs to be fixed. She lifts each child in turn to see and touch the hinge and shows each one where it is broken. Later she may follow this in various ways— to check the process of fixing and to see a door that is functioning properly on its hinges.

Here the teacher uses a chance event. It is a good event to work with because, for one thing, it involves damage and repair, which are important psychological events. But for another, it is a live experience in object constancy. The door is still a door, despite transformation of its appearance, location, and function. The teacher helps the children establish constancy in the object world.

Though the teacher of any preschool group might react to this event, there are some features here that may be specific to the teaching of disadvantaged children. More often than middle-class children, these children do not notice or comment on the events around them (Minuchin, 1968). If the children themselves do not react, the teacher stops and brings it to their attention. (This focusing of attention may be one of the most important aspects of teaching disadvantaged children.) She is very concrete and relates to each child separately, giving him the words and ideas as she picks him up and puts him into contact with the door and the hinge. Among these children there seems to be little learning by proxy. The teacher cannot assume that the children in the background will get the general idea.

Example 2: Melissa is seated at a table painting with a sponge. She is applying orange paint to orange paper and she looks increasingly distressed. She calls to the teacher, almost in tears, "You can't *see* it." The teacher says to her, "Do you know why?" She stops a moment and searches; then she says suddenly, "They're the same," and points first to the paper and then to the paint. The teacher says, "Yes, they're the same. They're both orange. Let's take a different one." Melissa says, "This," and points to another color. The teacher says, "Fine. That would be beautiful," and helps to set it up with a clean sponge. Then the teacher says, "Do you know what color it is?" and helps the child to establish the fact that this different and more satisfactory color is green.

The teacher has caught an important moment for the child. The child has tried to create an effect and has failed. The teacher helps her resolve this, and she teaches her same, different, and color at a moment when these cognitive ideas solve a problem that has personal meaning for the child. We tend to think that this has staying power, though not necessarily as an isolated instance.

Example 3: Jennifer has been playing in grown-up clothing and is now putting things away. She moves methodically from place to place. She puts the high-heeled shoes on a shelf with other shoes, the long skirt in the box with other clothing. She searches the room for the box with colored beads, dumps the beads from her pocketbook into the box, then takes the pocketbook itself to a shelf with other pocketbooks. The teacher comments that she is putting everything with the things that are just like it: all the pocketbooks together, and the beads together, and the shoes.

What is Jennifer doing? Aside from being a "good, cooperative girl" and cleaning up, she is involved in several cognitive operations. She is dealing with what things are, what they go with, and where they belong—that is, sorting, classification, and orientation of self and objects in space. The teacher, with her comment, helps her to capture what she is doing and translates the experience to a more abstract level. She moves the child from the level of perceptual dependency to an idea of "commonness" that is not perceptually dependent (things that are alike go together). It is not certain how well disadvantaged children capture or generalize their learning by themselves; specific articulation by the teacher at such times may be of special importance for them.

Example 4: Keith is playing with plastic forms. He piles circles and squares separately, then concentrates on the circles. He begins an intricate game, trying to roll the circles into narrow spaces across the room. The teacher hands him a square to try. He tries it, smiles when it doesn't roll and hands it back. He continues to explore what he can do with the round forms. The teacher says, "What else is round like that?" He points to the wheels on a toy truck and begins to roll it along the ground. The teacher and the child talk about the wheels. "The wheels are round. Wheels roll. Round things can roll." The child tries several trucks, then picks out one with caterpillar treads and tries to roll it.

The teacher says it can't roll by itself because it has no wheels. The child says, "Oh yes, it has," and shows her wheels under the tread. Teacher and child decide why it doesn't roll freely the way other trucks do. Keith then rolls himself over and over along the floor and returns to play with the cars.

Again, the teacher has moved with the child's play. She feeds in contrasts to sharpen a principle (attempting to make the square block roll). She stimulates an ideational process by asking the child what else is round: he needs to discriminate the essential quality of roundness, whether in pure or representational form, before he can select and respond. She consolidates his experience with language and helps him to abstract a principle (round things roll). The child is an active part of this. With the teacher's help he moves back and forth between direct experience—even as primitive as his own body rolling—and the more abstract level of language and ideas.

To make the learning firm, the teacher returns to experiences and ideas, extending and varying the experience around any given idea. This kind of teaching reaches the child in his own world at a moment when experience has meaning for him, and it comes through an adult who has recognized his purposes and interacted with them. For some disadvantaged children, such an experience is rare and has particular importance as a paradigm for learning.

There are two additional points to note, at least briefly: (d) More formal materials for language and concept development play a definite and important part in the program.

Prestructured materials have long been part of preschool equipment, and recent developments have brought new and extremely useful materials into the field. Teachers who work within the framework described here are apt to use them selectively, employing them differentially for different children. They are seen as vehicles to accent and exercise the concepts a child is ready for or involved with: a table lotto game for Jennifer, form boards and discrimination equipment for Keith, and so forth. With these tools the child rehearses, consolidates, or extends what he is learning about contrast, color, or shape.

e. The purposes and methods of this orientation require a complex system of assessment, with multiple criteria for progress and a concern for evaluating the process of thinking as well as the accuracy of performance. Such techniques are not readily available, and they are difficult to develop (Zimiles, 1968a). The immediate goals of a preschool program conceived in these terms are not the same for all children, and the long-range goals are multiple. Such goals are not very adequately measured by IQ, vocabulary, or most concept formation tests, or even by first-grade achievement, though these afford a useful spot check on performance progress.

There seems to be no ready answer for assessment procedures. They pose a challenge to this field. An article in the *Saturday Review* informs us that "a typical Eskimo family consists of a father, a mother, two children and an anthropologist" (Culkin, 1967). Perhaps the typical preschool needs to consist of children, a teacher, a program, and a research psychologist. If the psychologist concentrates on language, he may want to assess not only the adequacy of language performance but the process by which language becomes useful to the child—serviceable as a vehicle for communication and as a tool for processing experience at levels that can become increasingly abstract and generalized without losing personal meaning.

Contrasting Views on "Developmental Lag"

It is interesting to take a reflective look at the interest aroused in the question of language within the disadvantaged child population during the 1960s and early 1970s. There were contradictory voices as to both interpretation and program. There are basic issues that still remain unresolved, stimulating new theory and changing practice in the course of trying out alternatives in two-language learning and mixed social group planning in school. It became increasingly awkward to draw clear lines between language usage and cognitive competence, between deficit and difference positions, or between the relative influence of poverty and ethnic background.

Pared to its essentials, the problem was the fact that poor children, black and white, did not do well by the standards of achievement in school. Why? Since language is central to the individual's grasp of reality and has a mediating role in the development of higher level thinking, could learning problems be attributed to some form of inadequacy in the way the verbal-cognitive processes were being experienced? From observation in preschool and school situations, there was general agreement that many children from poor backgrounds were not using language skills involved in verbal resourcefulness, expression, and communication of meaning and dealing symbolically with experience at a level comparable to middle-class children.

The inadequacy was usually conceived by psychologists as a developmental lag that could be corrected by supplying educationally the essential developmental nutrients which are lacking in children growing up under conditions of poverty. But within this general position, there were significant differences on where to locate the educational emphasis, what its content and contexts should be, and how much could be expected from educational procedures in the light of the pervasive impact of poverty on the child, the family, and his total life milieu. I will begin by reviewing briefly four programs, each true to a developmental lag position, which nevertheless represented basically different experiences for children.

Four "Developmental Lag" Positions: Bereiter and Engelmann, Blank, Bank Street, Sigel

The children in the Bereiter–Engelmann program (1966) were put through what has been called a "pressure cooker" model. (The preschool design has been adapted to elementary school, known as the Distar program [Engelmann et al., 1972]. For a good portion of the school day, the children, in small groups, are given direct instruction in language and conceptual patterning. The method employs high-tension question–answer exchange between teacher and children; the learning objectives are translated into small, specific tasks; sentence forms and concepts are presented one at a time in a preformulated and tightly organized program of instruction. Verbal responses are demanded of the children, regardless of interest, in a nonpermissive atmosphere. There is no interest in the cognitive processes that determine how material is incorporated. It is expected that the children will learn first through rote drill and later, through learned language structures, will move to higher level thinking.

In Blank's approach (1970), there was similar distrust of an overall enrichment program as the means to meet the problem.[3] Blank diagnosed the poor child's problem as a limitation in using language for higher level abstract thinking: namely, poor use of causal thinking and conditional statements, of achieving deductions and retrieving past events, and so forth. The poor child's disadvantage was seen not as lack of stimulation but, rather, as failure to develop a symbolic system by which available stimulation is perceived as existing in a coherent, logical, predictable framework. To compensate for this developmental disadvantage, Blank's method called for a one-to-one exchange with the child for a given period out of the school day when there was emphasis on organizing and reorganizing the experiential input in ways that helped the child achieve thinking strategies: selective attention, inner verbalization, ability to delay, imagery of future events, and so on. Without this foundation, it was presumed, the child would encounter difficulty with more complex learning situations to be confronted later. This is the kind of teaching, in Blank's view, for which insight into verbal-conceptual processes is needed; techniques of programmed instruction would not serve.

In the Bank Street developmental approach described in the 1968 paper that precedes this one, language and thinking are not separate or separable functions. They are part of the whole experience complex—evolving and maturing through communication and symbolizing. To understand poor children's less developed verbal-conceptual functioning (which was also assumed in this view), it is necessary to consider the possibility that the child has been at a disadvantage in the communicative and expressive interactions with people that precede verbalization, in the variety of experience that comes from exploring the physical universe, in the opportunity for symbolization through maneuvers with objects in an idea context in playful activity.

In this approach, words and language forms are not the initial focus. First there is opportunity for symbolic play—working with ideas without words— then language becomes the tool for expressing ideas, for representing actions and referring to objects. The teacher sifts the concept potential out of the child's

3. For an analysis of different levels of thinking which characterize teacher–child interchange in the preschool years as studied in and out of the classroom situation, see Blank, Rose, and Berlin (1976).

own experience and stimulates cognitive grasp of comparative or relational elements.

The same basic principles of learning apply for the children of the poor population, with adjustments to be made for their special needs. In the 1968 paper on language, for example, one can infer that it is important for a teacher to sustain close observing and talking contact with the children from a disadvantaged background. This is in line with Blank's emphasis on the importance of one-to-one contact, but there is an important difference. In the Bank Street approach, the teacher moves into the situation as it is established by the child and moves along with it to the next stage. It is not an adult-planned lesson in thinking; it is a way, natural to the social situation, for amplifying the object-relational maneuvers that the child has initiated and for opening up a new order of understanding of the perceptions that are implicit in his actions.

The "developmental lag" position is stated clearly by Sigel (Sigel, Secrist, & Forman, 1973) in introducing his experimentally designed program for two-year-olds. He writes: "The course of development of poverty children untouched by remedial programs is predicted to become socially pathological and dysfunctional. The remedial program we suggest emphasizes the acquisition of basic cognitive and social competencies whose interaction within the individual might be expected to extend the options a child has in his adaptation to environmental demands." The problem is not that of recognition; it is rather the knowledge that an object can be represented in several modes and still be a member of the same conceptual class. He established a broad-base educational program as an experimental approach with a clearly stated rationale. He chose the two-year-old stage since it is at this period that children begin to engage in activities that create distance (psychological, spatial, or temporal) between person and object, and it is these distancing behaviors that are the foundation of representational skills.

In this view, efforts to stimulate "representing" behavior, to be successful, depend on motivating the child to interact with a significant person or event in the context of a group setting, and on providing varied experience and a program with specific social and emotional as well as cognitive objectives. To satisfy this condition, it is necessary to create an environment in which significant adults are warm, accepting, and sensitive to the child's status and perspective, and tuned in to his comprehension level.

Sigel gives examples of his approach to raising the level of socialization (verbalize feeling rather than actually hit, fight, or pinch), and to acquiring concepts that are central to representational competence, such as stimulating the child "to consider things that are not present" (e.g., asking the child, "What would happen if an oversized block were placed on an already unsteady tower?"). Basically, it is a program in which the children are learning by "self-discovery and self-initiated actions," but the design calls for incorporating minilessons, with specific objectives, flexibly adapted to the children's interest. The group experience is supplemented with tutorial sessions in which the teacher takes the cue from the child's exploratory use of the materials, elaborating on what the child has started (e.g., the child may roll a large and a small ring, one in each hand; the teacher might show him that the smaller ring fits inside the larger and both can be rolled together). The authors' report of positive outcome is based on the tentative nature of findings and the almost insuperable problems involved in using traditional assessment measures.[4]

To sum up thus far: These four programs represent a common developmental lag position, but their differences are at least as important as their common basis. The Bereiter–Engelmann and Blank programs deal with language and thinking as a separate domain of learning; the Bank Street and Sigel programs treat language and thinking, and their remediation, as intrinsic parts of the complex interactions of a comprehensive educational design. It is important to differentiate these developmental lag positions, to perceive them in terms of their contrasting learning theories and program implementation, which call for distinctly different curricular and relationship approaches to the problems of poor children in school. Yet there may be a more educationally productive way to slice the pie.

Explanations and Doubts about the Developmental Lag Position

Intervention programs in the 1960s, concerned with ways to help the children catch up in their language and thinking proficiency with the performance level of white, middle-class preschool children, were following the "deficit" orientation for which I have preferred the term *developmental lag*. From this view, continued use of dialect would slow up the children's communication with others in mixed ethnic groups and/or with white adults in the school environment, especially important in their interchange with teachers, where mutual understanding is essential if there is to be positive socialization and productive learning. Beyond these personal interactional disadvantages, it was assumed that the black English dialect, regarded as an inferior language system, would interfere with progress in the thinking processes. It was expected that correction of pronunciation and grammatical forms would have a positive effect on thinking—representatively and symbolically. Even allowing for the fact that preschool teachers, more than those in the later grades, would be likely to proceed gradually and sensitively in trying to get the children to shift from their home speech to school speech, this view registers for the children the impression that the school way is the better way and the home way the lesser. Even in the best atmosphere, the child is being moved suddenly into a speech world of unfamiliar syntax and pronunciation—not a reassuring foundation for "falling in love" with school. But it was the basically incorrect understanding of the nature of dialect as a language and of its place in mediating thought processes that has been most challenged.

4. A description of this program at a later stage of development appears in Sigel, Saunders, and Moore (1977) and is discussed in "Perspectives on Cognitive Development" (chap. 4).

A much more codified explanation for poor children's less adequate performance in school was offered by Bernstein (1972). He put language into the context of social use and related two basically different modes of usage to internalized communication patterns associated with family structure. His phrase, the "bearer of social genes," captures his thesis that using an idiosyncratic mode of communication may lock a person into his own cultural group without having any significance concerning his potential capacity for using other language patterns under other circumstances. Bernstein distinguishes two codes—"restricted" and "elaborated"—restricted characterizing the use of language among the poor, in contrast to the elaborated code, which is predominant in middle-class usage. The differences are not a matter of grammatical components or use of dialect. They have to do, instead, with the kind of meanings that are expressed or communicated—or, put another way, with a different selection of which aspects of experience to draw on for verbal interchange with people. The use of language of the restricted code keeps meanings closer to the actual experiential context and is therefore more specific and particularistic. At the same time, it is more open to the projection of personally meaningful and imaginative processes. The use of language in the elaborated code, predominant in middle-class usage, makes it possible to communicate more universalistic meanings, relatively free of particular contexts, but is intrinsically less open to personalized projections.

Because the school as an educating institution stimulates the learning process to move toward more universalistic meanings, the working-class child finds himself in an unfamiliar communication system in which the symbolic system and associated values do not provide links with his life outside, and where the teacher's values, vested in proficiency in the elaborated code, put him at an initial disadvantage.

If I were to try to make a complex issue simple, I would say that Bernstein was asking us to accept these two codes as important for different ways of seeing and communicating meanings in human experience. He saw greater power for those who have the ability to deal with both codes, and would like educators to value both and adapt attitudes as well as techniques accordingly. However, mastery of the elaborated code at the adult level has special importance for the poor since it contains the means for analyzing the forces—in school and in society as a whole—which contribute to inequality of opportunity. It is a necessary tool for initiating and advancing social change. It is, therefore, the school's responsibility to help the poor child master the elaborated code, thereby giving him broader social flexibility as an individual and the means for greater social clout.

It is a little difficult to place Bernstein in the deficit-difference categorization. Actually, he has had to defend himself against misinterpretations. If we take the view that to master both codes has social importance beyond the mastery of the restricted code alone, and that the conditions of poverty tend to limit people to the use of the restricted code only, it seems fair to consider that the restricted code represents a social developmental lag, comparable to, but distinct from, linguistic-conceptual developmental lag. We have encountered this problem of how to conceptualize developmental sequence before. What Bernstein is saying is interestingly parallel to what Heinz Werner (1957a) has described as hierarchical integration. Development is conceived, optimally, not as displacement of earlier forms of cognitive processes by later ones, but by the capacity to sustain the earlier forms for appropriate enactment within the larger repertoire of different modes of organizing and expressing experience.

Criticism of Developmental Lag

Both the facts and the presumed explanations that we have identified as the developmental lag position have been disputed. The facts concerning the children's inadequate performance are not as pictured, it is claimed, especially since the findings are derived from testing procedures which are unreliable because of distorted situational and motivational conditions (Silverstein & Krate, 1975). In addition, the image of family life under poverty is also considered to be distorted or uninformed. In the last analysis, I see these criticisms as significant correctives to partial vision and premature inferences.

How much the picture of impoverished family life has been overgeneralized and overdrawn has become clearer through studies such as Minuchin's (1971), mentioned earlier. We need to differentiate, among the conditions of poverty, which ones cut back certain opportunities for the kind of childhood experience that we currently consider most propitious for the realization of individual potential. Some families are surely more vulnerable than others, both because of the wide range of the conditions of poverty and the denials involved, and because of different personality patterns, strengths, and weaknesses that adults bring to the challenge of sustaining a family under adversity, great or small. It is this kind of healthy correction that has been going on. It leaves me, still, willing to hold to the position that poverty has sufficient developmental disadvantages for many children and for the quality of family life, that its eradication should have priority in the agenda for social change.

An Opposing View: "Cultural Difference"

The relatively disappointing outcomes of many intervention programs stimulated a rash of second thought analysis—some of it directed at procedural errors, some at theoretical shortsightedness. In response to the input from other disciplines, the *developmental lag* concept was superseded by the *cultural difference* viewpoint, which takes the perspectives of anthropologist, linguist, and sociologist into account. In the formulation of this viewpoint, accompanied by the elevation of diversity in contrast to uniformity as a social value, a radically changed understanding of language dialect, in particular, was an important factor. In terms of linguistic analysis, black English is a well-ordered, highly structured language system, as every language is; one language is not developmentally different from or more primitive than any other. Differences that exist, important as they may be in the dynamics of the social system of the classroom, are superficial alternatives for the same meanings. There is nothing intrinsic in the use of vernacular that interferes with logical thought and no basis for assuming that dialect change would directly affect intellectual functioning. Although they differ on other issues, Bernstein (1972) and Labov (1973) are in agreement that the structure of language, for example, a dialect, does not interfere with cognitive functioning. For the sake of both teaching procedures and attitudes it becomes crucial from this position for teachers to see black English as an alternative, not inferior, language system. They need to recognize that the path toward stimulating and advancing cognitive processes needs varied strategies, among which sanctions against the use of black English in school is contraindicated.

Once we bring the problem of dialect into the general sphere of language, there comes the confrontation with the complex issue of language in relation to thought. The determinant role of language in the development of thought and how social factors condition its development have been expounded by Vygotsky (1962). We became familiar with the work that Vygotsky had been carrying out in the Soviet Union in the 1930s when translation became available some years later. His basic position was clear: "Thought and development is determined by language, i.e., by the linguistic tools of thought and by the sociocultural experiences of the child." It is through verbal interaction with mature speakers that the child learns how to process, directly and representatively, the information he shall attend to, and to test out tentative meanings of his experience. Language is perceived as the social means of thought; the child's intellectual growth is contingent upon its mastery.

This view brings Bernstein (1972) to mind. His contrast of the restrictive and elaborate codes, distinct linguistic forms that arise within a common language, also has a social influence orientation. He sees language as a set of rules to which all speech codes must comply, but which codes are generated, which ways of looking, thinking, sorting, and communicating dominate, is a function of the system of social relations. If, as he holds, the language code of a specific social structure conditions how and what a child learns (the particularistic vs. the universalistic), it is not hard to see why Bernstein wants the school to be a more inclusive milieu for giving all children, most importantly, the poor, the tools of language and thinking that make it possible to use both codes.

Four Cultural Difference Positions: Baratz, Labov, Hymes, Cazden

When we look into the educational programs that are favored or recommended from the cultural difference point of view, and the language dialect question in particular, we find once more that a theoretical position can supply a basic orientation but does not define a program for the black child's school problem. Under the same general premises, quite different programs develop and have strong advocates. This is the inevitable by-product of the fact that every educational program is the product of positions on a number of variables. Some program designs (projected or realized) seem to treat the dialect question as the crucial issue for the black child and concentrate on the most optimal technique for moving toward mastery of standard English from a black English foundation. (By this time, in this presentation, we are assuming that the teacher and the school establishment have accepted black English as a comparable lingual form and are seeking the best methods to help the child become bidialectical, with the option to use either form.) Baratz (1970) analyzes the black child's problems in learning to read: he must not only decode written words, he must "translate" them into his own language. His difficulty with a language that has a new syntax and the problem of learning the meaning of graphic symbols is magnified by the sense that there is something wrong with his language when his teacher thinks that saying "hep" for "help" means that he cannot read. She advocates teaching inner-city black children to read by providing them with texts in the vernacular as first readers, to be followed by transition readers before going on to standard English reading texts. The method, in her view, has additional advantages beyond reading competence, for example, ego support in the use of his own language and the experience of success in school. Gradually, the child can be helped to perceive where the two systems are similar and where different. There have been other efforts of this kind about which Cazden (1972) raises several questions, among them, "Does it matter that the use of such readers will increase racial segregation during reading instruction?"

Without being so specific as to technique as Baratz (1970), Labov (1973) also argues for teaching the standard through knowledge of the child's system, for not displacing the vernacular, and for adapting methods used in teaching English as a foreign language. Speakers of nonstandard English, if they are to succeed in test situations, need practice "in paying attention to the explicit form of an utterance rather than its meaning."

Still within the cultural difference orientation, Hymes (1972) takes quite a different viewpoint that moves away from the interests and concerns of the linguists. Language, in his view, should be studied in its social context, taking into account the variations that are associated with the communication of meaning in different relationships among persons, in group or larger community associations. The issue is one of how language is used and those qualities of communication—intonation, tone of voice, gesture, and so forth—that express different meanings in different subgroups. When we turn to the use of language in the classroom, it is essential to shift concern to social and stylistic rather than referential meanings. In Hymes's words: "When one teaches a variety of language to children for whom it is not a normal variety, one is engaged, not in logic, or reasoning, or cognitive growth, but in social change."

Whether or not the teacher in the classroom can overcome the resistance of children to accept a change to a new variety of language usage, with all its social implications, depends not only on the teacher's knowledge but also on attitude—on the ability to shape the environment surrounding language and its use in the classroom. Rejecting a child's speech may estrange the child and reduce the opportunity to effect change; acceptance of what the child's language means to him maximizes possibility for change. We cannot deal with linguistic and communicative competence apart from social role.

In Cazden's work (1971, 1972) we find not only an integrated presentation on the theoretical level (the cultural difference view and Hymes's modification of the linguistic approach) but also an explicitly defined position on school practices. About dialect as language, she takes the linguists' position that black English is a highly structured, grammatical system wherein vocabulary can be increased, and is as adequate as standard English for abstract thinking—not, in any sense, to be confused with lingual underdevelopment. But, like Hymes, she points to the error of focusing on the form of language instead of the nature of the use of language under varying situations, which results in failure to recognize the range of meanings conveyed. The way children speak reflects where and with whom they live; their models are their parents, or other home adults, where the affective factors—identification processes—are stronger than exposure to another dialect, through television, for example. Fairly early, they can learn more than one way to speak but there is no basis for assuming that to change the dialect, the form, will affect the intellectually more significant questions of vocabulary and modes of language usage. It is more important to work on which are the essential "verbal skills" for success in schools as distinct from the "verbal habits" of middle-class speakers. And it is equally important to take account of the situational variables—a concept that has been so forcefully expounded by Labov (1973). Cazden (1972) reviews studies of young children which appear to show that topics in which the children had personally significant investment stimulated longer and more complex verbal responses; that conversation with an adult was more likely to include a greater number of exchanges when it was initiated by the child rather than by the adult.

Taking motivation and situational variation into account leads Cazden to advocate an open classroom situation, in contrast to the traditional schoolroom, as being especially valuable for the young child whose home language is black English. He needs the kind of school experience that offers rich opportunity for using language: open, active verbal exchange among children and between teacher and child, children interacting as they assume responsibility for planning activities, materials, and setting for dramatic play and group discussion. Both native dialect, or a foreign language, and standard English should appear in the course of spontaneous verbal exchange among the children and with the teacher.

I saw this working out very naturally with three-year-olds in a day care center where the Spanish-speaking teacher made most contact with the Spanish-speaking children (the other teacher spoke only English) and in her conversation with the children often translated her Spanish response to the child in English, just as part of the conversational stream, not as a didactic interchange. While emphasizing language use rather than form, Cazden is interested in searching the ways, educationally, especially as related to reading skills, for helping children gain proficiency in using standard English. Educators have responsibility, she feels, to help children move into the larger society equipped with the necessary tools of which standard English is one. "To reject attempts to teach a single, socially prestigious language form," she writes, "is not to reject all attempts at change." In the larger contexts, she argues for "coordinate education for cultural pluralism, in which patterns of language form and use (and beliefs and values as well) in the child's home community are maintained and valued alongside the introduction of forms of behavior acquired in a technological society" (Cazden et al., 1971).

A Different Alignment

In this second go-around of language programs, I have used Baratz, Labov, Hymes, and Cazden as representatives of the cultural difference orientation in contrast to Bereiter and Engelmann, Blank, Bank Street, and Sigel as representing a developmental lag orientation. These classifications represent a dichotomy that has dominated the literature on this subject. My study of the question leads me to question the usefulness of that dichotomy as far as educational practice is concerned, while I value its importance on the level of interpretation and its importance in undoing the basic superior–inferior fallacy.

The differences *within* each of these two orientations (developmental lag and cultural difference) are more significant for educational planning than is the coherence of the general sociological viewpoint which each group represents.

Breaking up the classification as it has been drawn, I place Bereiter and Engelmann, Blank, Baratz, and Labov in one group, representing an approach in which language is sharply in focus, a particularistic viewpoint of verbal functioning in which ideas of how to meet the problem are restricted to one or another means for changing language experience per se. By contrast, Bank Street, Sigel, Hymes, and Cazden take a holistic view, are interested in dealing with the language problem in a wider functional context, paying as much attention to motivational and social factors as to specific lingual factors and looking to ways of meeting the problem by finding ways to help the child move toward a changed language system within the context of the whole stream of experience.

If I were to diagram the difference in alignment from both viewpoints, it would look like this:

Focus on methods specific to change in language usage and conceptual patterning — Bereiter and Engelmann, Blank; Bank Street, Sigel → Developmental lag

Utilize total stream of experience, verbal and social, for changing language and conceptual usage — Baratz, Labov; Hymes, Cazden (Bernstein) → Cultural Difference

I am inclined to think that there is a salient difference between the concept of language as a separable function and the view of language as embedded in a comprehensive experiential learning complex. Furthermore, it is the latter view rather than the sociocultural perspective that is most relevant to making educational decisions about what to do about language problems related to dialect or about stimulation of conceptual processes to compensate for presumed experiential lacks under poverty.

CHAPTER 7

Problems in Measuring Complex Educational Change

In talking about the contemporary challenge to bring home and school, parent and teacher, into some form of genuine interaction, I once said: "Distance is one of the mechanisms by which status-invested authority maintains itself—between school and parents as well as between teachers and children. Lessening the distance diminishes 'divine right.' " For me there are images of "divine right"—still clear after almost 70 years—behind those depersonalized words.

I could not reach to the top of the librarian's desk where I stood beside my older sister in the Tompkins Square branch library in the Williamsburg section of Brooklyn, scared and thrilled. Since I had learned to read before going to school, I was ready for that passport to the delicious world of books—a public library card.

"How old are you?" "Five years old." Fine. "Where do you live?" "302 Hart Street." Fine. "What is your father's first name?" "Wilhelm." Not fine at all. "You go home and learn how to say your father's name in English and maybe then I will give you a library card." Bang. I was not especially subject to obvious discrimination in later years, but that moment in childhood registered. It came through to me at some inner level that I belonged to an out-group and it wasn't a good place to be. It diminished me and never completely left me, despite my tremendous admiration for the Jewish people from whom I come and their valiant contribution to the highest dreams of man through the centuries.

I must have gotten the library card soon after that incident since I remember, in the years between five and sixteen, reading through the shelves of that small library and chafing at the restrictions, especially in the summertime, of only one fiction and one nonfiction book per day. Recently, I went back to find the old library. It was gone, replaced by a large recreational center and a spacious outdoor stadium.

The sentimental journey took me back to the brownstone where we had lived on the block that had endured through successive ethnic waves for half a century but had changed only a little in external appearance. In our house there were cut-out niches in the walls along the stairways that must have once held holy figures for a Catholic family. In our time the neighborhood had a mixed Jewish and non-Jewish family population. Now it was a black community. The delicately chased glass panes in the front door at the top of the outside stairway were gone, but not the memories of sitting on the top step in the dusk and waiting for the lamplighter to come down the street. For constancy, there were the same privet bushes that my mother had planted, still alive outside the front dining-room windows.

Home was home and school was school. Only the parents of the misbehaving were summoned to the teacher's or principal's presence. For the rest, parents, as far as their own backgrounds permitted, added to the awakening of their children—mind and spirit. Though cheated by circumstance out of a full measure of education for themselves, my parents communicated the promise of pride and joy in our pursuit of the life of learning. There are moments of salient recall of mind-stretching outside the school walls. I remember, as an adolescent, hearing my mother's criticism of a young mother in the circle of the Russian intelligentsia who was traumatized by the new knowledge of the dangers of "bacillen." She wore a white coat, kept her infant screened in and isolated, safe from the dangers of human contact. "A child," my mother said in criticism, "has a mind" and needed playing with and talking to even before it could respond. The importance of stimulation in infancy that rings through the child-development literature so many years later rings old bells for me. To mark my graduation from elementary school, my father took me to the top of the Woolworth Building (the highest New York City skyscraper at the time) and pointed out the wondrous crisscross of streets below, of bridges carrying cars and streetcars and ferries riding back and forth from the marvelous isle. Could I have guessed that here were the seeds for falling in love with Lucy Mitchell's brand of human geography and the community patterns the students created under her guidance?

But those parents and those teachers remained miles apart. Not so today.

Challenges Ahead for Early Childhood Education (1969)

How can I possibly reduce the world of churned-up experience in which we are now living as school people to a few controlled statements that can help make us feel more the masters than the pawns of accelerated social change? What kind of changes, what new directions emerge in the long run, depend on many forces.

Adapted from Challenges ahead for early childhood education. *Young Children*, 1969, 24 (4), 196–205.

Among them should be the voice of the educators, which will be strong and convincing, in the long run, if it is addressed as much to a lasting ideology of sound concepts for the education of young children as it is to the crisis realities of our times.

My assignment was to pinpoint the major challenges. It would have been easier to draw up a long list of problems to be solved, ranging from the distress elements of practical classroom management to the heady heights of infusion of research findings into the educational mainstream. I have settled for three major areas of challenge which I will discuss briefly, in succession.

Perhaps it would be useful to list these three areas at this point before proceeding to further discussion:

   I. To come to terms with the problem of goals.
  II. To have a basic rationale for choosing, altering, or instituting new methods.
 III. To deal with the bombardment of research, theoretical and evaluative.

I. To Come to Terms with the Problem of Goals

We face first the basic challenge of coming to terms with the problem of goals for the educative process and for the school as an institution in the service of educational goals. By coming to terms, I mean recognizing that among us there are contradictory points of view as to what constitutes optimal development for the individual and what our priorities are for the world in the making.

I have named as the first challenge to early childhood education the need to come to terms with goals—goals that are suitable to the concept of the school as a force in developing the total person and, thereby, influencing the processes of social change. The old goals have lost their "fit" with this expanded concept of the school's role. Yet little of the fervor for making schools over is expended on digging away at the level of basic purposes.

Developmental Processes as Goals for Education

I am suggesting a revolutionary change in how we think about the purposes of education, not just a shift in priorities in the old familiar list. I am asking that we change the dimensions by which we think of goals, that we shift our focus to the complex developmental processes of childhood and hold the school responsible for supporting, stimulating, and guiding these processes. This does not discard the old primary purpose of schooling: to impart knowledge and to advance achievement in skills and techniques. On the contrary, I give it a new position within a larger perspective of basic processes of development in childhood and a system of values as to the directions in which to guide them.

What, then, are these developmental processes? Of the many possible formulations, I am presenting a highly condensed version, in three parts, put into homespun language.

1. There is the process of becoming competent as a body and a mind, to make and do and think, registering in the inner self the feelings of being able to overcome obstacles, master confusion, solve problems, and feel oneself a doer and a maker in the world of objects and ideas. This involves the complex process of systematizing experience through mastery of the symbol systems, to have such use of language as makes it possible to work with concepts as the tools for organizing experience, to acquire knowledge and attain increasing cognitive power to judge, to reason, to infer within the logos of our society.

2. There is the process of building personal and interpersonal strength, the course by which a child can become, as he matures from stage to stage, a person capable of acting autonomously: making choices, developing preferences, taking initiative, setting his own course for problem-solving, evolving a code of ethics. This involves a growing sensitivity to and awareness of each individual's uniqueness, his ability to extend himself in nonpredatory relations of mutuality because of a solid sense and knowledge of himself, and his involvement with his world as part of an internalized momentum for knowing and doing. The task for education is to define those experiences and relationships at successive stages that will encourage progressive development from the impulse-ridden stage of infancy to the approximation of the integrated stage of maturity in which individual differences are not only tolerated but cherished and a sense of integrated identity can be achieved.

3. There is also quite a different kind of developmental process that I consider basic to any system of educational goals. It is not easy to find a denotative term for this process. I could lean on *creativity* and not be too far off-center. I have in mind the development of an open, expanding system of sensitivity and responsiveness that makes it possible to perceive and react to a wide range of phenomena. Maturity in this developmental process probably can be characterized as having available multiple modes—logical and alogical, reasoned and intuitive—for interacting as a self with the environment.

Obviously, implementation of these developmental processes as goals for education in the years of early childhood is no simple task. It taxes intellect and imagination; it calls for depth and commitment. It is infinitely more complicated when the children we work with have been living under such marginal conditions that some degree of corrosion of these developmental processes has already taken place from infancy on. We have to be more inventive and more daring at the same time that we need to spark investigations of our assumptions as to which method in reality supports our purported goals.

The Error of the Part for the Whole

But some of the problems we encounter are still of another order: they have to do with the part being taken for the whole. I refer to the priority given to stimulation of cognitive processes, beginning at the preschool level and earlier.

There are several explanations for the fervor of interest in cognition which pervades research studies, innovative techniques, and criteria for evaluating programs. One is the assumption that early training in the cognitive area is the key to avoiding failure in school. Another is the rise of interest in testing, by experimental design, Piaget's system for plotting the regularity of growth of the mind. A third is the growing weight of evidence that stimulation of emerging powers in the earliest months and years of life has a determining influence on later development.

It is a gain to know more about thinking from whatever source, to become aware of how the child enjoys and gains control and strength through creating conceptual order out of the diverse, disparate fragments of his experience; how he builds schemata of what goes with what, what comes before and after, what used to be, is, and will be, what lives and dies, and what never lives at all, what changes and what stays the same. All this is gain theoretically; furthermore, its differentiation provides much-needed leads for educational practice.

But this is where we need to be clear about the dangers and the shortcomings. Appropriate stimulation of cognitive processes is indeed an important responsibility of schooling at all stages; the challenge is to place this educational function in relation to the other developmental processes for which the school is equally responsible. We need to recognize that cognition cannot be isolated from other processes and conditions of human functioning; it affects and is affected by the state of feeling, the degree of trust, the pattern of attention, and the surge of curiosity. It is involved in a child's silently solving the problem of how to add a ramp to a block building; it is working in the play corner when someone hands down the dictum that only boys can be fire fighters; and it becomes a dilemma to the four-year-old who disputes the reality of his five-year-old friend's birthday because he, the four-year-old, is so plainly the taller one.

This issue of the centrality of cognition in the preschool field and how it crosses the problem of developmental goals had an interesting workout in a conference of leading research workers in the field of early childhood. The considerations of the conference are reported in a book entitled *Early Education* (Hess & Bear, 1968). The focus of the conference was "the environmental conditions facilitating *mental* growth—as opposed to social or emotional growth, intertwined though they may be." But the question of educational goals—particularly what kind of mental growth to foster—intruded itself at the very beginning and lasted to the end. There was a shift from mental growth conceived as increased facility at specific skills to a concept of creative, adaptive intelligence, not measurable by standard intelligence tests, as the preferred goal for education. Once interest in intelligence appears with adjectives such as *creative, adaptive,* or *effective,* any attempt to isolate cognition falls down. So it is not surprising that the educational goals related to effective intelligence included among others "intrinsic rather than extrinsic motivation for learning" and "self-knowledge and self-expression rather than rote-learning and a regurgitative intellect."

What I am here proposing as fundamental to all programs sounds to many like a luxurious kind of idealism not suited to the immediate crisis or to the children in greatest need. By their view, the crying need is to help children of poverty adjust to school as it is, to help them achieve what they have to achieve in order to succeed in the going school system. Not that this point of view can be too readily dismissed. It is, understandably, the perspective of the parent in this population whose child has one life to live and who is anxious that he shall "make it" by existing criteria of success. Granted that we are not going to change the basic faults of our elementary school system in a day or a year, can we, in good conscience, perpetuate its faults by accepting its highly questionable criteria of educational success as the standard-setters for early childhood education?

Problems with the Frontal Attack on Cognition

Programs are built on interpretations. In many preventive and compensatory programs, failure of the disadvantaged to keep up with middle-class achievement in the elementary school has been attributed to a deficit in language skills and verbal-reasoning development, with the accompanying inference that concentrated training in this area is the most direct remedial course. Practically, this leads to a curriculum that is a training program, geared to focus on the specific skills in which the disadvantaged child shows weakness, to engage him in this training experience as early and as intensively as possible, to use and invent methods intended to advance these particular skills, relying on varieties of drill, programmed learning techniques, and external reward systems. The coexistent developmental processes of the preschool child are either neglected or given cursory attention, and the side effects of the chosen methods are not evaluated systematically or even sensitively observed. Much that has been done in the interest of ameliorating early developmental damage has followed this course, involving tremendous investment of human energies and public monies. The Bereiter–Engelmann program is the archetype of this theory and practice.

Yet, this approach has not been altogether successful, as measured by IQ and scholastic achievement, in terms of its own *specific* goals, quite apart from the question of neglect of the broader developmental goals to which every program, in my view, owes responsibility. Where there have been gains, they have not been as great as hoped; more disappointingly, the gains made in early stages do not last through subsequent years of schooling.

Even if we take account of justified skepticism of the methods employed in gauging effects, the general drift seems to be that concentrated teaching of specific skills in the preschool years may, with the most liberal interpretation, raise the rate of academic achievement mastery for underprivileged children for a while, but there is little evidence that the rate of gain will be sustained and much less evidence, if any, that this approach will have an appreciable effect on fundamental cognitive capacity.

Well, why? One possible answer goes back to how one interprets what the basic deficit was in the first place. Some, looking back, see a far more complex problem than was envisaged originally. The interpretation of deficits was too restricted, too narrowly based on specific behavioral outcomes, whereas the loss the children had suffered was more pervasive, to be understood and approached in terms of building up fundamental psychological processes of impulse control, interpersonal trust, curiosity, and a positive tropism toward constructive mastery—all this as the foundation, not the substitute, for special training in special areas.

From one psychologist's view, there is no theoretical or empirical basis for expecting that specific training in language or arithmetic at the preschool stage will affect fundamental cognitive development or compensate for what the disadvantaged child has missed (Kohlberg, 1968). In his view, the limited exposure to varied experience of all kinds and to opportunity for interaction—physical and social as well as verbal—is the most serious deprivation. If a variety of experience is seen as the prime stuff of cognitive progression, only compensation along these lines, in Kohlberg's view, can be expected to support emerging intellectual capacities in any lasting way. One can place both Piaget and Dewey in such a formulation.

We come to another interpretation of why the gains of the preschool programs as they have been measured do not seem to have staying power—namely, that the programs initiated in the preschool years must be continued into the primary years in order to be effective. The plausibility of this position is apparent. How convincing it was to those who are deciding on the steps to be taken in the educational phase of the antipoverty program is apparent in the establishment of Follow Through. Apart from considerations of how successful this latest program may or may not prove to be, I find it impossible to be unequivocally enthusiastic about its underlying approach.

In fact, I feel challenged to discriminate among the widely contrasting models that have been included as eligible candidates for upgrading education in the primary years. Some, fortunately, are basically consistent with sound developmental goals such as those I briefly defined earlier, or those presented in the report of the Joint Commission on Mental Health of Children (1969). These programs may differ among themselves in the way children are grouped, in the relative importance of having parents active in the program, in how much the children are the choosers or the teachers are the assigners of activities, in the distribution of time between lessons and play, in their criteria of competence, or in the centrality of the teacher–child relationship, but they fit within a common ethic that puts a ceiling on imposition or manipulation of the child by the adult—at any age. In these programs, Follow Through represents a fine opportunity to work on clarification of ideas, invent new methods, and, most of all, gain insights on how any given model is shaped or changed, inevitably and necessarily, as part of being taken over by particular teachers for particular children and families in particular situations. There is everything to gain from this kind of activity, including the negative lessons of what does *not* work where or with whom.

But the roster of models included in the program does not reflect screening by any framework of accepted developmental goals or any such ethics as I have just named.

II. To Have a Basic Rationale for Choosing, Altering, or Instituting New Methods

A teaching strategy may zero in on a given goal but there is no escaping the fact that it has impact over a much wider zone than the eye of the target. The success of a method or its choice in the first place needs to be considered in terms of the total orbit of its psychological influence. Learning to read by the second grade, a desirable achievement by anyone's theory, is a ready illustration. Suppose second-grade children became efficient readers at the end of a training experience which, as a by-product of method, had minimized the tendency to raise questions, or had made them extremely dependent on the approval of the teacher. Suppose second-grade children became efficient readers at the end of a training experience which, as a by-product of method, had made books seem like a forced excursion into a foreign world with minimal relevance to one's own interests and meanings. Would we consider their education successful when our sights include a life in school that will nourish the curious, questioning mind, that will support the maturing of independence and people engaged autonomously with one another, that will make the world's literature—old and new— a sweet, rich source of deepening one's own small, private life?

Once we accept an expanded roster of developmental goals for education, we are responsible for protecting it whenever a new method or technique, directed toward some specific level of achievement, comes on the horizon. We must maintain a purview of the whole learning milieu of the child. Everything that happens—between the child and the teacher, between the child and the other children, between him and the things and experiences prepared for him— is a force of influence, informing him of the nature of the world and the people in it, giving him images of expectation around which he is developing styles of responding.

I think it is just because those who work day in and day out with young children are deeply aware of the complexity of growing up that they are disturbed by the contemporary stress on the cognitive processes and the extent to which techniques aimed to increase cognitive capacity seem to be taking over the preschool curriculum. This trend is seen by many as overspecialization that will lead to neglect of other major claims on the composition of an optimal learning environment—again, in the words I have used earlier, a part being taken for the whole. What is wrong? And how can it be set right?

It behooves the professionals to point to the preschool movement as a major forward thrust in aerating education in the twentieth century. It has been the proving ground for what has come to be known as the "open" school, referring to the kind of education that admits the life of feeling into the classroom, highlights the importance of the child as an active figure in the learning process, favors discovery experience, places high value on originality and initiative. The significance of play as a learning activity in the early years, for example, has only recently been recognized in the American research world as a rich resource for penetrating mental growth. But the preschool educators' defense of play as a natural idiom for learning and therefore an essential component of a preschool environment can be documented as far back as the 1920s, when Harriet Johnson wrote about a learning environment for two-year-olds.

Still it is important not to overdefend what has been but rather to assess the general scene. It must be conceded that only in some preschool situations was there as much invested in stimulating intellectual processes as in developing autonomous, expressive capacities and sustaining a climate of interpersonal equilibrium.

What is perceived as learning is highly variable, and it is undoubtedly true that preschool educators have not been as clear as they needed to be in interpreting their works to the uninitiated. It is still true that many a scholastic-minded visitor needs to be helped to perceive serious thinking in the lively images of children exploring the meanings of pictures in a book or learning the route from the classroom to the school kitchen; dragging the large building blocks to make an airplane or molding the clay to look like a bear; striding out of the play corner with a hat on backward and a low-voiced good-bye to be, impressively, the "father." In recent years, these basic concepts of how children learn in their interaction with their environment have been developed and analyzed by numerous scholars, among them Jean Piaget, Robert White, Jerome Bruner, Heinz Werner, and Lois Murphy. This congruence of the insight of the educator and the findings of the researchers is not only reassuring in the present; it holds tremendous promise for progress in the future.

Basic Principles and New Conditions

If the school feels responsible for multiple developmental processes, if the basic learning idioms of early childhood are understood and honored, and if, in addition, it is accepted that one cannot insulate the cognitive from the affective domain, thinking from feeling, or mind from personality, a major base for selection of method, certainly for elimination, is established.

There is no formula for a good learning environment that suits all children. Teachers are now facing the challenge of how to adapt the methods that can be defended theoretically and from prior experience to the needs of special child populations, specifically the children we know in antipoverty programs. The basic learning modes may be assumed to be general, but the sparse and self-diminishing experience of disadvantaged children in their early years confronts the teacher with a new baseline of responsiveness and motivation on which to proceed. She will have to find new ways according to old principles in order to bring about learning and growth: new ways of teaching the use of language and advancing the thinking processes within the context of the child's own activities and play, of introducing written symbols functionally in relation to the child's activities. She will change the balance within the program between structured activities with clear directions and more open-ended child-initiated activities; she will judge differently how much the child needs to be primed and where he can be left to his own initiative, how much to demonstrate and instruct, and when and with which children to depend on self-initiated exploration; she will listen harder and repeat more often.

She does not expect these methods, no matter how ingenious or well-grounded in theory, to work unless she can succeed in bringing the child to want for himself what she wants for him. To do this, she must become a trusted person in his image, involving often a complete psychological turnabout for children who have already become fearful, distrustful, and inhibited in their relations to adults, to authority figures, and to strangers. It requires energy and imagination to find ways of making contact and building up an image of an adult (a strange one) as a giving, supporting, caring person—giving not only affection and support in the face of trouble, but also the prime gift of the teacher: greater use of one's own powers to do, to make, to speak, to think, and the sense of self-worth that grows with becoming competent in one's world.

New Techniques and Other Climates

There are, in reality, two very different sources open to educators who are interested in finding and adapting new techniques and new approaches for education in early childhood. The first is referred to as *intervention,* a word that has recently become part of the educator's as well as the researcher's vocabulary. It usually designates a specific aim toward specific achievement. It may be the use of the electronic responsive-environment technology for teaching reading; or it may be programmed exercises in finding similarities and differences in pictured objects or geometric figures in the interest of sharpening perceptual discrimination. But the word *intervention,* or really the concept, seems unfortunate because of a common misconception and errors of inference that derive from it. There are, to be sure, need and room for new teaching devices, techniques, and materials. Prestructured exercises designed to stimulate cognitive processes have an important place alongside the methods which use incidental events and the ongoing experiences of classroom life toward the same ends.

But no technique can have a complete life of its own in a classroom situation. Each becomes part of the design and atmosphere of the whole curriculum, assigned varying degrees of priority, regarded with varying degrees of enthusiasm, and administered with varying degrees of exactness. A new method is a way of altering the balance of an existing program; it may very well affect the rest of the program while it is, in turn, being affected by what surrounds it. In any case, it cannot be an island of impact such as the word *intervention* implies.

The second source is a highly inviting one, namely, accounts of comprehensive designs for early education that have been developed in other parts of the world where goals and problems have much in common with our own. There are three such accounts that one hears about frequently these days: the British Infant School pattern (Featherstone, 1967); the kibbutzim of Israel (Bettelheim, 1969); and preschool and kindergarten education in the Soviet Union (Chauncey, 1969). I know no better way to raise the fundamental question of methods in relation to goals. Is self-reliance our goal, too, as it is in England and in the Soviet Union? Is the self-reliance of the Soviet scheme psychologically the same as the self-reliance of the British system? Are we dangerously individualistic? Is the collectivism of the kibbutzim the same psychologically as that of the Soviet? Are these cultures clear on how to educate the individual for his world? Are we? Do we have so clear a social system to educate toward?

III. To Deal with the Bombardment of Research,
Theoretical and Evaluative

The last and third challenge is quite different; it takes us back to academe. In pursuit of their expanding interests in developmental sequences and the emergence and early maturing of cognitive processes, research psychologists have turned a great deal of energy to early childhood and to the study of learning processes as these can be observed and experimented with in the situation of school. In another sense, they have been drafted. Federal support of new programs has required evaluation of effects, and psychology was turned to as the discipline with the most relevant techniques of assessment. I do not mean that psychologists, in general, resisted this call from the applied field, but many were far from satisfied with preestablished conditions for the evaluations, such as the stipulation for pre- and post-testing of program effects, with relatively short intervals between the pre- and post-phases.

The researcher asked to evaluate the effects of educational programs has problems of method to face. There are conventions that can be followed, such as measuring change in IQ points (the psychometrician's preference), adhering to the control-group design, or comparing pre- and post-test performance. There is the bugaboo of the Hawthorne effect: that the effect may be caused by the heightened motivation aroused by trying something new rather than by the new method or program per se. While it has been necessary, for practical reasons, to employ conventional methods, discontent with these conventions on the part of some psychologists who are now in more direct contact with children and schools has already stimulated a great deal of original, probing thinking about the problems of measurement.

In a brief paper that goes to the heart of the matter, Zimiles outlines the shortcomings of evaluations which are based only on the outcomes of the programs being studied (Zimiles, 1968b). He discusses some of the crucial points at which errors enter: the restricted number and kind of measuring instruments often selected for research convenience rather than program relevance; the few aspects of the program's influence that can be assessed from among the multitudinous and complex total; the impossibility of "learning about 'incubation' effects which first begin to manifest themselves at later points in time." For these reasons and others, Zimiles is willing to say that "negative evaluation findings may be attributed more to the procedures employed to assess a preschool program than to the preschool program itself." Alternatively, he advocates evaluation procedures that involve "intensive study of the influence process itself . . . an assessment of the goals of the program and its design of operation" and recognizes that this "requires the evaluation worker to become saturated with the life of the program he is studying."

To be sure, in some cases, implications for education have been prematurely and fallaciously drawn by psychologists from research findings. The clearest example of this is Jensen's conclusion that compensatory education has failed. What is more, he assumes that he has sufficient knowledge of educational alternatives to describe what a proper compensatory program should be (Jensen, 1969). Here it behooves the educator to be receptive to new knowledge made available but, at the same time, to bring one's own expertise to bear on the soundness of the inferences for practice being promulgated. It is at this point that a comprehensive image of developmental goals and a clear rationale concerning method are necessary tools for the educator in order to make the best, deliberate use of new knowledge.

It is possible that educators, instead of being either overimpressed or overwhelmed by the flood of interesting and relevant findings that are presented in print or at conferences, might gain new security and competence if they could adopt, in part, the attitudes of the researcher involved in the search for knowledge. There is no special mystique about the essential elements of the scientific method, especially when one recognizes that it is an approach to experience, a way of thinking in which one can share without being party to its special techniques. For the teacher, acquaintance with research findings can open up new ways of perceiving children—more focused listening and watching, more differentiated observing. A clearer focus on "exactly what" is happening almost inevitably generates its own "why" questions. Here, there are alternatives. Thinking can come to a dead end, passed over by some attractive conjecture of the moment, without building up any momentum for further analysis. But this does not have to happen. The teacher, like the researcher, can engage in hypothesis-thinking and pursuit. The answer to "why" questions can lead to a rationally chosen change in procedure which, in turn, is observed and assessed. Actually, teachers are doing this all the time, from a practical point of view, especially in situations where the teacher's role is not overstandardized and the educative process is flexibly adjusted to individual differences.

There is a gap, however, between the tremendous reservoir of knowledge and understanding that exists in the minds of teachers and the extent to which this information has been generalized or organized so as to come closer to the systematization of thought upon which new knowledge builds. This indeed *is* the special talent of the researcher, and it was heartening to me, recently, to hear Sheldon White, an outstanding psychologist in this field, ask teachers to supply material from their experience to psychologists and express his confidence about how much could be gained thereby. What I am saying is that there is a challenge for teachers to see themselves more in the research image, engaging in the analysis of their experience while serving a teaching function.

Evaluation: Responsibility and Problems

The problems of evaluation of school programs which I brushed over so lightly as one of the "Challenges Ahead" in my 1969 paper began to claim central attention in the years that followed. Evaluation procedure represents a spectrum of possible methods, and there are no certain guidelines as to the suitability of a particular method to a particular situation. Some issues regarding the design of an evaluation procedure are of a theoretical nature: Shall the elements to be considered be product or process designated? Some have a more practical base: To what extent should the involvement of public funds influence the course and design of a program evaluation? As was to be expected, these questions claimed primary attention during the years of high government subsidies of educational projects, stimulating the development of new, sophisticated techniques and the refinement of old ones. Evaluation, like educational ideology, in the 1960s and 1970s, became an active new forefront for a question that had been part of conscientious educational thinking for a long time.

The Responsibility to Evaluate

In a general sense, evaluation is part of an attitude, part of responsibility, part of an ethic. Is what I am doing worthwhile? The confusion begins with specifying *who* I am. The teacher in the classroom? The community school board? The state department of education? The federal government? The issue of *what* is worthwhile does not simplify matters in a pluralistic society with varied and often contradictory values. The controversial issues about which preferred values shall be exemplified in educational goals and what shall constitute evidence of realization in programs have had a long history. They are represented in overtly dissident educational movements over the years, as well as in slower, long-term transformation of the educational enterprise from a skill-focused curriculum to a comprehensive, developmental progressivism. Looked at historically, the open-classroom movement represented a steady, progressive reorientation of values despite the intermittent regressive back-to-basic phases (Spodek & Walberg, 1975).

There are multiple explanations for the shifting orientation: the disparate images in an increasingly mixed population as to where a society should be moving and associated conflicting educational ideologies; a new educational frontier without adequately skilled practitioners; and a retreat to a simplistic

solution when the challenges of changing social reality and deepened understanding of learning processes could not be faced. Here again it is an error to
assume that the retreat is universal and to fail to recognize the growing contribution of ongoing change movements within the orbit of public education.

Among these the evolution of fifteen years of pioneering in the Open
Corridor program and the Workshop Center at the City College in New York
City, headed by Lillian Weber (1981), represents how complicated, both trying
and exhilarating, is the process of stimulating change in an established social
institution. The analysis of the program in its later stages, when negative
criticism had gained a strong public voice (Weber, 1981), offers a well-docu-
mented account, in realistic school terms, of how attitudes and educational
practices could be altered gradually. For the teachers there was both imaginative
illustration, directly experienced, of what could be new and why in the learning
process and sensitive, patient understanding of what is involved personally
when teaching becomes an unexpectedly broader, deeper life experience with
new rewards, new challenges, and unending questioning. It is ongoing programs such as these, engaging also in more theoretical analysis (Alberty, Neujahr, and Weber, 1981), that contradict the image of open education as another
failed adventure. It was not the basic concept and image of open education or
progressive education that failed. What was missing was adequate understanding of the depth of change, ideological more than operational, that is involved in
calling upon education to liberate and enrich the thinking and feeling processes
and freeing the teacher–student relation from an arbitrary bind in authority to
move toward a humanizing, democratizing experience. The title of Weber's
paper, "Moral Issues for Teachers," indicates the depth underlying what should
not be taken superficially as changes in techniques. The emergence and continuous development of programs such as this one is evidence of important basic
trends that outlive the confusion and disillusion of application of inadequately
understood theory and the recurrent regressive periods when education bears
the burden of faults which should be attributed to more complex social processes. But it was the national government's activity in trying to wage the war
against poverty through equalizing educational opportunity and supporting
preschool education that necessarily spotlighted the issue of evaluation. To
which programs, on the basis of what outcomes, should government subsidies
flow? And the answers, in terms of selective appropriations, could not wait on a
gradual transformational historical process.

Overall, wherever there has been conscience, there was always evaluation, self-examination by the educator, in one form or another. When educators
like Harriet Johnson and Susan Isaacs in the 1920s established the importance of
carefully planned record-taking as the basic material for studying developmental change and pursuing theoretical inquiry, they were clearly on an evaluation
course. Now, so many years and so many standardized tests later, there is
revived confidence in documented classroom observation as essential data for
the analysis of educational input. It is interesting to have Harriet Johnson's
work and method (1928 [1972]) esteemed by a contemporary Bank Street

colleague who has had experience with current evaluation techniques and is discouraged with contradictory outcomes. Referring to the need to return to direct study of the classroom, Shapiro writes: "Such suggestions are, of course, a sad reflection of the state of the art of evaluation today. It may seem like advocating hand tools in a machine age, and perhaps their renascence is akin to that of home-baked bread and quilting. Indeed, the teachers in at least some of the nursery schools of the twenties always carried a notebook and a pencil to set down a telling observation" (1977).

Those early days were, by comparison, a privileged era. At Bank Street, for example, we could keep our assessment of what we were doing within the confines of our own selected purposes. We were thinking about the different effects of a defined educational experience on individual children, not comparing the effects of widely different systems on assorted groups of children in contrasting social environments. We supplemented continuous use of observational data with an unorthodox use of standardized intelligence tests for the preschool years (Biber, 1934) as a way of gaining additional insight into a child's total pattern of behavior. From the interpretations changes were made accordingly—for example, in the way the teacher guided the particular child's interaction with other children or stimulated opportunities for play in the classroom. The child's response to these changes appeared in the continuous recording. There was no name for it then but, obviously, it belonged in the category of formative evaluation in the context of the individual.

Phases in the National Evaluation Program

With the initiation of a national antipoverty educational program in the 1960s, formal evaluation was and had to be built in. No one foresaw that the procedures would go through a turbulent course of adaptation to successive disappointments and doubts about methods. But, more positively, it is clear that a maturing perception of the complexity of the problem evolved. It is possible to distinguish several phases of a changing approach during the 1960s and 1970s.

In the early stages of the program there was a positive mood about the perceptible gains associated with the Headstart programs and optimism about their potency in counteracting the problems associated with retardation in elementary grades. The studies undertaken in this period have been described as a "cottage industry" in the sense that they were not geared to the distinctive and comprehensive goals of the program and depended upon inappropriately conventional standardized methods (I.Q. and achievement tests) as indices of change.

But the challenge of evaluation, theory, and practice took a major leap in connection with the critical response to the comprehensive Westinghouse Study report (1969). The pressure for an evaluative study came, as could be expected, from government sources. Were there gains associated with Headstart experience that would be sustained in the primary years? In recognition of the criticism of earlier studies and the incompatibility between their standardized measures and the multiple program goals, the Westinghouse instrument included more varied measures of intellectual aptitude and achievement and a few measures of affective and social processes. Those who had conceived and guided the Headstart project would have preferred a longer proving time for the program, including more varied measures weighted toward social skills, changing self-image, and family-life factors, in clearer recognition of the program objectives. Their preferred alternative design for measurement was rejected. The most publicized outcome of the Westinghouse study—that the cognitive gains made by the children with Headstart experience were lost after the children had been in elementary school for a few years—had a serious effect, called the "blackest day" in the history of the program, from which it took many years, in the practical terms of financial support, for the program to recover. Criticism of the Westinghouse study from professional voices laid the ground for improved design for subsequent studies of this complex problem. Among the criticisms were the failure of the sampling to take into adequate account the differences in program content and total learning environment from center to center, the lack of continuity in learning style and interpersonal relationships between Headstart programs and the primary grades of most of the schools children enter, as well as the inadequate measures of affect and other social relations variables in the test agenda.

Another voice of protest against the acceptance of these findings led to a call for extended program strategy beyond changes in school experience and relationships. From this perspective the experience of school needs to be related to the extended ecology of multiple simultaneous influences. These range from the school's relation to home and family realities to the complex influences of basic cultural patterns on the educational system's ethos and choice of prerogatives (Bronfenbrenner, 1979). The subsequent inclusion of family role and neighborhood activity for Headstart programming represented movement in this direction. A carefully designed program of intervention studies, which had been initiated early in the program (Palmer, 1976), was extended into the early elementary years, focusing on possible gains, "sleeper effects," at third-grade level or thereabouts, which may not have appeared immediately following an intervention program. Palmer's adversary position was expressed in the statement: "Compensatory education has not failed. In mid-passage it appears to be a healthy child. Can we afford not to let it mature so that we can examine its conditions as an adult?"

In the major evaluation program, Follow Through (Rhine, 1983), there was recognition of two weaknesses in the previous approach. The reality of extensive variation in philosophy and practice had to be recognized, so the Follow Through program included a series of models, each representing its own educational credo. The importance of continuity in the learning environment from stage to stage should be recognized, so each program took responsibility for establishing basic continuity between the preschool and the first three grades. The range of educational designs in the different models varied from interest in behavioral basic skills to comprehensive programs such as the Bank

Street developmental-interaction approach, recognizing the reality of quite contradictory educational designs as part of the national scene. In addition, there was growing awareness of differences in the extent to which theoretical formulations of models are implemented in the programs for which they are the presumed foundation. It becomes a three-way inquiry: definition of the idealistic theoretical model, actual implementation of a theory in a program, and the methods for measuring the effects, intermittently and at the termination of a given period.

In these trial years, recognition of basic program differences was a forward step. Programs were aligned with contrasting aims as to what developmental proficiency should be given priority; contrasting values as to what interpersonal relationships an educational enterprise should be sponsoring; and contradictory psychological theories about the interaction of experience and the maturing processes. Such pluralism may be a recognized virtue in a democratic society but, from the perspective of government, which criteria of adequacy or excellence shall determine eligibility for subsidy? In reviewing the problems involved in the national evaluation before final completion, Rivlin and Timpane (1975) gave the subtitle of their book a plaintive tone: *Should We Give Up or Try Harder?* While these authors credit their work as valuable eye-opening education for evaluators and policy analysts like themselves, they communicate a more personal mood when they describe it as "trial by sword." There was not enough time or sufficient control of the conditions to make it possible for evaluators to adhere to the requirements of an experimental evaluation design. Many of the programs were not sufficiently tooled up to be ready for evaluation. To abide by scientific canons it would be necessary to develop a program with new and improved techniques, which would take years. This is where we meet Alice-in-Wonderland. Will not the shifting, complex social issues and changing perceptions of learning and teaching have outrun such a prolonged procedure? This skepticism by government spokesmen themselves was at least matched by psychologists, educators, and parent-consumer groups who did not take a dispassionate view of the problem or of the consequences involved for future educational planning and funding.

Criticism of Measurement Techniques and Methods of Analysis

The successive changes in evaluation designs and self-criticism by the evaluators, in addition to skepticism about findings within the profession, did not satisfy the psychologists and educators who peppered the literature with negative criticism of the evaluation program as a whole and of its use with the disadvantaged population in particular. Their extensive criticism can be summarized around three basic issues.

First, the formal testing situation is, per se, an inadequate and distorting method for gauging the relative success of substantially different programs. Children in the more structured, directive programs which follow behaviorist theory or more traditional practices, in general, are prepared for a formal test-taking situation by the very pattern of their daily learning experience. They are accustomed to decisive question–answer interchange and the challenge of knowing the answer promptly, in contrast to the children in the more open-ended programs, where search, consideration of possibilities, and reflection have prime value. The testing climate may be a special constraint for the child whose life-style may not fit the "produce on demand" paradigm.

Shapiro (1973) tried to assess an intermediate level of functioning: "neither the factual, informational, problem-centered, nor the dynamic interpersonal, but attitudes and expressions of feeling about the self, about school, about learning and aspects of cognitive functioning that do not depend on information or problem-solving ability but on the disposition to respond, measures of divergent rather than convergent thinking." The children's responses were analyzed qualitatively and quantitatively; the data included systematic classroom observations and interviews. From the observational data there were striking differences between the Bank Street Follow Through and comparison classes but no differences of any consequence in response to the testing situation.

Analysis of the factors involved led Shapiro to take a "second thought" position on the relative pureness of test findings. She saw them as situation-bound, affected by a variety of conditions that influence performance and may obscure the pattern of competence. She was impressed by the finding that the children's actions and interactions in the classroom represented markedly different levels and modes of functioning between the Follow Through and the non-Follow Through programs, to the advantage of the Follow Through classrooms as judged by the Bank Street program's criteria of progress. From a similar point of view, Sigel, Secrist, and Forman (1973) name evaluation as a major problem in their study of an intervention program for two- and three-year-olds. Children failed in test items which they understood clearly in the classroom context.

A standardized test is presumably a controlled way of sampling the powers available to the child in relation to his educational experience, assuming that these powers are so well established that they are situation-proof. By that logic, the merit of an intervention program can be judged by how the children handle the problems presented by standardized tests before and after specific educational exposure. But is it in the test results that we should expect to find the true index of what the children have gained? This long-standing assumption has been seriously questioned by investigators who require more than IQ and achievement tests as suitable measures of gain.

A second controversial issue concerns what the standardized tests test and, more significantly, what they do not test. The primary goals for some of the Follow Through models include hard-to-measure capacities and qualities of functioning: an analytic thinking style, curiosity, creativity, emotional strength, positive interpersonal attitudes, and self-concept. There is every reason to question whether the varied influence of different educational programs on these attributes can be measured by formal testing procedures.

It has been emphasized, also, that the use of restricted measures represents an indirect danger to the educational enterprise per se. This is especially true where program planners do not have clear goals and a worked-through rationale for the relation among goals, values, and program. There is room for an inverted process—what is measurable is taken to be the guide of what curriculum emphasis should be. In this turn-around, the content of IQ and achievement tests can begin to coopt educational programs and goals. Minuchin (1976) puts it plainly: "Measurement should be servant, not master."

The increased understanding of variations in programs and their widely differing underlying values had a healthy effect on the evaluation problem: it challenged individual program sponsors to create measures suited to their particular goals. The challenge was greatest to the developmentalists, who needed measures that would tap cognitive processes rather than achievement products, be sensitive to change in affective and social relations dimensions, and have a higher degree of relevance between the roster of selected measures and psychological functions in the reality of the classroom. Hard as it is to serve the whole child educationally, it is infinitely more complicated to take his measure through formal procedures, especially where comparison of outcome data requires quantitative analysis. In 1973, in a paper entitled "Project Head Start: Success or Failure?" (1973a), Zigler explained and disputed the use of IQ and the later use of measures of cognition as sole criteria for judging the value of programs. This segmented, limited approach was not suited to the comprehensive goals envisaged under his leadership.

A third issue concerns the monumental task and numerous pitfalls associated with the analysis of data. I found a comprehensive analysis of broad-scope evaluation problems in a paper by Selma Mushkin (1973). She reviews the unresolved technical problems associated with various methods as they have been applied to a whole roster of social programs—methods that follow an experimental approach using contrasting control groups or single-year surveys and longitudinal studies or multiple-regression studies. "In sum," she says, "evaluation studies are having a larger and larger impact on policy at a time when the methodology of evaluation is still inadequate to serve as an overall guide." She would like to see evaluation as an ongoing instrument of government in an atmosphere where evaluation studies will not be sought as a base for immediate action. To safeguard against the damage done by the use of faulty evaluation findings, such as premature cessation of valuable social programs, she envisages, a little idealistically, a new organization that would review evaluation studies and issue seals of approval.

Among psychologists it is not hard to find echoes of many of the critical points made by Mushkin. Thus, Sigel et al. (1973), after recounting the faults of the control-group, pre-post design used to evaluate intervention programs, conclude that the experimental research model is not appropriate for this kind of study and that we need to search for a method that is tuned into social realities. Zimiles (1977) points to errors in evaluation technique that may be attributed to the fact that, traditionally, the evaluator is a psychometrician following a standard technique and, by decision, an outsider to the program.

Not being equipped to deal with the content relevance of the instrument leads to more investment in testing for only a few of the possible outcomes that are best suited to available techniques; the differential receptivity of individual children found by averaging gains over all the children in a study is likely to be missed. Like Mushkin, Zimiles argues that the life of a program should not depend on the present less than reliable outcomes of large evaluation studies.

A Changed View

Out of the criticisms a few common principles have been crystallized. In any ongoing educational setting there is continuous, value-based decision-making that affects the pervasive quality as well as the specific content of the learning environment. In our times there are value factors implicit in choice of allegiance to contrasting theories of human behavior and learning—for example, the behaviorist and psychodynamic systems. Curriculum, interpersonal relationships, and social codes in the classroom are influenced by the values underlying contrasting educational designs. These remain a matter of choice. Evaluation is a handmaiden to assist in answering the question: Are we performing effectively in the interest of our selected goals?

Out of the criticisms of evaluation designs for large public projects there has developed a fresh image for preferred evaluation procedure. The standardized measures of intellectual functioning are inadequate and misleading. There needs to be broad-based, comprehensive assessment encompassing affective and social as well as cognitive processes. The focus of analysis needs to be on the processes involved—a far more complicated goal than the estimation of end products of achievement. We need to know and respond to the course of change (the formative process), not only to the final outcome (the summative measure). We need to find new terms of definition, more conceptual than behavioral, to serve as rubrics of analysis. We need to be working from the base of constructs, more open and abstract, instead of limited, concrete behavioral images, as guides for judging progress (Bussis, Chittenden, & Amarel, 1975).

This critical thinking stimulated a new way of working on evaluation. Actually, the new ways are new–old ways, in a sense, since the primary data in many studies are derived from the familiar source of classroom interaction. But the greater investment in analysis, new study techniques, and theoretical formulation promises to give observational data new potency in clarifying decision-making. In research vernacular, the first obligation is to study the antecedent condition in detail—to discard superficial short-paragraph designations and labels for different "models" that obscure the complexity of what transpires even on the surface and give no hint of the underlying dynamics. There are many different statements of this point of view but the meaning is the same. There has arisen almost a litany of voices speaking for return to study of the classroom.

What transpires in the classroom offers basic data, but how to record the complex phenomena in a way that lends itself to analysis and theoretical formulation is a challenge to the development of new methods. Two approaches, developed as part of the Bank Street College research activity, represent different methods of analysis that adhere to a common educational philosophy. In one of these studies (Stern, 1974) the basic data are derived from a preplanned method of diary recording in the classroom. The dimensions for the analysis of the records carry the conceptual system and predetermine what will be learned in the final analysis. By reviewing a sample of the scale headings one reads how a method reflects the philosophical base: for example: richness and weighting of curriculum content; interest in thinking process vs. correct answers; formality/informality of conduct of class; encouragement of curiosity, exploration, experimentation; and so on. By coding and frequency tallies it is possible to characterize the dominant teaching mode in a given classroom and compare educational environments. The basic data in this kind of study have advantages: the record is the reality that can be reread, reconsidered, and recoded. It has disadvantages: it is a time-consuming method because observer-recorders need special training and the data analysis has no shortcuts.

Another method based on classroom observation and developed as part of the Bank Street Follow Through program is the Brace system of interaction analysis (Bowman & Mayer, 1974). This system does not involve direct diary recording. The observer begins by mastering a complex coding system as the tool for observing one individual's behavior and interaction for a given period. The role, direction, content, and quality of action or interaction, as perceived by the observer, are conceptualized and subsumed under a comprehensive system of preorganized categories. Here, again, the list of categories for first-level analysis, embracing the range of interaction and expression of feeling, reflects the underlying perspective. For example: there is room for coding an act of a teacher as *extending and clarifying* if she carries a child further along on a line of thought he has initiated or as *calm, rational control of behavior* if she reminds a disruptive child of agreed-upon limits of behavior. Such rendering of teacher functioning, in detail and in depth, becomes another kind of material to be used for evaluation, either as self-examination or comparative study, leading toward projections of change in curriculum and teaching role.

A distinctive approach to systematizing observational data as the base for formal analysis of the teaching–learning process appears in the program developed by Carini (1975a) in a demonstration school for the state of Vermont. The teachers' records constitute the basic data for a research staff who have developed hypotheses for longitudinal assessments of processes in language, thinking, and problem-solving. Several qualities distinguish this project. It is a long-term, continuous, cooperative teacher and psychologist project; the goal is to develop an analytic schema that deals with complex functions such as "What level of differentiation is reflected in the child's resolution of the tasks?" The work is grounded in a developmental view: "Both our records and testing can be addressed to process and description," with interest in the kind of assessment that may provide a definition of both the limits and the plasticity of a developmental stage.

These are a sampling of evolving techniques that are needed to meet the standards of comprehensive evaluation and to embody broad-gauged understanding of children and the learning process. There is, further, the responsibility for reexamining the theoretical substructure of an educational design. Evaluation is most useful when it includes systematic study of outcomes in relation to what has been theoretically presumed. Analysis should include reconsideration of goals when new insights into the psychology of learning and development or the changing social scene demand rethinking of the purposes of the educational scheme as first conceived. This involves not only "if-then" thinking generally but also provision for the formulation and testing of hypotheses concerning the impact of the educational experience, in small or large parts. In the new view, the "outsider" evaluator is to be replaced by a process-oriented evaluator with research skills *and* a probing teacher-educator who generates problem-formulation and takes part in the pursuit for understanding. This view of the educator's role, briefly indicated at the end of the "Challenges" paper in 1969, has been fully developed by Minuchin (1976) and is an integral part of Carini's (1975b) approach to longitudinal evaluation.

Beyond Preschool

About ten years after the controversial Westinghouse study of the Headstart program an extensive analysis of the Follow Through program became available. The report of that analysis by the Abt Associates, "Education as Experimentation: A Planned Variation Model" (Bock, Stebbins, & Proper, 1977), concludes that "models that emphasize basic skills succeed better" and are superior to "affective approaches." These findings are seriously questioned in a reanalysis of the same data by House et al. (1978) under the auspices of the Ford Foundation. This study, which represents a comprehensive critique of the methodology and conceptualization of the original study, concludes that no reliable differences between the Follow Through and non-Follow Through students were found, and that the conclusion favoring basic-skills curricula is not justified by the data on which the analysis was based. The criticism of the Abt study deserves recounting in part because it coincides in many respects with the earlier criticism of the prior Westinghouse study. Though it is dismal to find evidence of a repetition of incorrect procedures in such a staggeringly expensive project, perhaps it takes twice around to learn.

Much of House's criticism is familiar: for example, the outcome measures that were used assess only a few of the models' goals and are inadequate for assessing the major goals of some of the models. They favored models that concentrate on teaching mechanical skills, giving poor coverage of the comprehensive systems that some of the programs were expected to enact. House's proposed recommendations go beyond the critique of this particular study. Programs should be described so as to include important qualitative components; field experiments should be randomized and smaller in scope. Further, the larger question is raised as to how sound it is for government, rather than a more localized authority, to be conducting evaluation programs. In a pluralistic society, embracing such a variety of ethnic and economic conditions, should any particular model be advocated as superior to others? Finally, evaluations under any auspices should be carried out in depth. House's systematic critique of the Abt Associates' study reinforced other critical voices on the question of evaluation—professional opinions from research and education that have been available to us for some years.

The problem of choice of method of evaluation remains a complex and uncertain issue. This is due partly to the essentially different functions of evaluation programs, especially between those that are responsible to answer for government subsidy and those whose analysis and/or justification is concerned with more localized inquiry, focused on situation-specific assessment. In general, contemporary thinking appears to favor approaches to evaluation that include the interaction factors of home and school experience and allow for study of the potential long-term effects of changed school experience, especially in a multipurpose program such as Headstart. This direction may encourage further development of qualitative methods of evaluation. From the sum of multiple, varied evaluation studies of Headstart it appears sound to attribute the magnitude of durable gains to "(1) whether parents extended the remedial program to the home through their own efforts, and (2) whether the preschool program was followed by a further special educational effort once the child reached elementary school" (Zigler & Valentine, 1979).

A major decision affecting the future of the Headstart program came in 1980 (Headstart Bureau), when it was given presidential recognition and increased financial subsidy. That this represented initiation of a new era was expressed in the *New York Times*, August 7, 1982:

> Judging by the success of Head Start, the toddler who's getting a jump on the alphabet and 2×2 is getting a jump on the future. So whether good day care centers and pre-kindergartens can benefit children is no longer the issue. . . . How to establish and fund more of them is.

Decisions involving national social policy will determine the future development of programs such as Headstart and Follow Through in their present forms or in accord with some future adaptation (Zigler & Berman, 1983).

Evaluation at the Crossroads

Objection to application of Westinghouse and Abt study findings was paralleled by active rethinking of evaluation method. The dividing line between complete reliance on standardized tests as distinguished from recognition and acceptance of factors less susceptible to concrete measurement is a debated issue that is plaguing other fields as well. As an illustration, Hein (1975; see also Hein, 1976) refers to the controversial "reductionist" and "holistic" positions in biology and quotes an eminent biologist who "characterized his approach, in accepting the 1973 Nobel prize for physiology and medicine, as 'watching and wondering.' " Hein himself takes a considered, carefully weighed position. The task in educational evaluation, he says, is to develop broader methodological approaches, blending the best of the reductionist and holistic views while remembering that the broader holistic approach is relatively new and needs to be validated through energetic research and disciplined as an alternative scientific approach. In his critique, from both a theoretical and a social point of view, of the evaluation methods that have been generally accepted, Hein looks favorably on alternative approaches. Among them he includes tests that are located closer to the processes being measured, as well as those measures in which the observations to be made and the questions asked are open-ended and responsive to the quality of performance that has been stimulated. Valuable evaluation findings can be derived from flexibly used achievement tests at one level and, by more elaborate procedures, from systematic, comprehensive record-keeping designed for long-term study of program development and the course of individual children's changing responsiveness.

Another approach to evaluation, known as the *"goal-free"* approach (Scriven, 1976), creates a different line of relationship among program developer, evaluator, and consumer. In order to avoid the bias or perspective of the program developer, the evaluator rejects prior background information and staff discussions about program goals, moving directly to study the effects of the program, how it is meeting the consumers' needs, and simultaneously taking note of side effects not envisaged in the original planning. The perspective in studying the situation is not narrowed to preformulated goals; the evaluator is in direct contact with the consumer, and the program in action and criteria for evaluation are based on analysis of consumers' needs. Questions have been raised concerning the use of this method, especially as to how this enlarged perspective of consumers' needs can be communicated to program developers and can influence the action to be taken. Scriven's position is based on the need for more objectivity and consideration of broader social-need priorities than can be expected of the program developer who is invested in and committed to his own purposes and ways of fulfilling them.

Another critique of the exclusive use of the method that uses the independent variable and controlled comparison group as the method for program evaluation has a sociological rationale. Guttentag (1977) argued that we are becoming a postindustrial society distinct from industrial societies in that we are centered on services—human, professional, technical. Modalities of scientific knowledge, higher education, community organization, and so forth involve cooperation and reciprocity. The movement is toward a communal society of collective negotiations and away from the industrial society in which men, materials, and markets are dovetailed for the production and distribution of goods.

For this altered social condition, we need a basically changed paradigm for evaluation and subsequent decision-making. In support of her position Guttentag cites changes in the philosophy of science: for example, the increasing perception of science as a social enterprise in which consensus changes over time; the retreat from prediction and control toward greater concern for understanding; readiness to legitimate a diversity of perspectives, each with its distinctive interpretation of social realities. When she applies this view to concrete aspects of traditional evaluative methods that she considers inadequate in a postindustrial society, we find ourselves on familiar ground. Human service programs are too variable to be treated as independent variables; diverse perspectives of different groups need to be included in the very definition of the program; the starting point of evaluation should be multiple perspectives; information provided by researchers should be attuned to the important objectives of each decision-making group.

We have been provided with an exhaustive analysis of variations in evaluation procedures (House, 1980) encompassing differences in philosophical orientation, special purposes to be served, and methods of analysis and communication. If we take a broad perspective, we can distinguish two basically different approaches to evaluation procedure: objectivist and subjectivist. Within each of these comprehensive categories there are differences in method and goal. For example, a systems-analysis approach such as the Abt study of Follow Through differs from a behavioral-objective approach in which outcomes are more specifically related to prespecified goals, but both are considered conceptually to be within an objectivist perspective. To name some of the methodological features they share: replication of findings as a key criterion; a value-neutral role for the investigator as the discoverer of facts separate from implications for practice; rigorous methods such as reliability of measurement representing adherence to standards. These procedural features, encompassed in the objective approach, are seen as derived from the assimilation of methods previously established in the social sciences. The suitability of this approach is being questioned empirically on the basis that the population being served did not find the outcomes of such studies functionally useful, and methodologically on the basis that the presumed value-free perspective of the investigator may represent lack of awareness of the influence of actually existing values. Previously mentioned accounts of method adaptations by Hein, Scriven, and Guttentag and reevaluation of the theoretical base illustrate ongoing modification of the objectivist approach and its base in social science techniques.

Alternatively, the subjective approach is based on a close linkage between a full measure of direct participant experience and implications for evaluating and altering educational practice. The basis for validity becomes the extent to which experience, in a variety of forms in actual situations, is fully explored, probed, and communicated. Methods are adapted to focusing on people, modes of behavior, and interaction with the vicissitudes of experience. This method also takes alternative forms. Its use in relation to art criticism, for example, is perhaps the most exploratory (Eisner, 1977). This perspective rests on the art of appreciation, "connoisseurship," exemplified in discerning subtleties, recognizing skill in use of form, appreciating imaginativeness, and discerning representative qualities. Transmuted to the sphere of education this view asks for sensitive observation: perception not only of events but also of quality of surround in which they are embedded, not only the context of verbal interchange but also the qualitative overtones of what is being transmitted. In this view, the skill and art of recording should employ "linguistic artistry replete with metaphor, contrast, redundancy and emphasis," called "thick" in contrast to "thin" description in order to be sensitive to what is subtle and covert beyond what is superficial and apparent. This approach has been called "a bold idea worthy of exploration" for which the issue of validity, especially in relation to public educational programs, needs further development (House & Mayer, 1981).

Of the techniques categorized as subjective, the case study is becoming increasingly popular though it may not have credibility in the scientific community. Several characteristics distinguish this method from the pattern of objective, evaluative techniques. To fulfill the basic criterion of usefulness the data are drawn directly from the program operation in several forms and developed and analyzed by techniques that are communicable to those who are "audience." Although the data may allow for representation of diverse points of view, the resolution is not intrinsic to the method but depends on the particular circumstance of the evaluation. In general, the method is considered more useful than others in understanding the inner workings of a program, but it is not easily carried through. It requires special talent and takes more time than other methods.

In a study of the Bank Street Follow Through model (Zimiles & Mayer, 1980), we find preference for the case-study approach carried through in a complex program, yielding data on 100 comprehensive interviews with teachers and other program participants as well as brief observations of 69 classrooms. Analysis is based on firsthand experience of personnel with varied kinds of participation in the program as relayed to the interviewers, whose method was more relaxed than formalized. There were, however, two basic questions: one concerning characteristics of child behavior which seemed attributable to participation in the Follow Through program and another about others' opinions about the principal impact of the program. Thus the interviewee was respected both in terms of individual experience as a program participant and as a source of opinion concerning the underlying problems of this complex program. The data, when analyzed, showed great diversity of reaction and opinion in response to these questions, but certain main lines of influence of the program as a whole emerged: "Classrooms have become more humane, children are treated with greater respect and more as individuals, a more functional and integrated attitude is adopted toward the teaching of subject matter, and teachers feel more accountable to the children—they begin to view their role not from the standpoint of training a child, but in terms of meeting his developmental needs" (p. 195).

Evaluation in Depth

Another subjective approach to evaluation has been identified by its adherence to the new forms of qualitative analysis of experience in contrast to quantitative evaluation, which had been the established method. The extent of the departure from the former perspective has been stated succinctly: "qualitative research: the importance of understanding people and programs in context; a commitment to studying naturally occurring phenomena without introducing external controls or manipulation: and the assumption that understanding emerges most meaningfully from an inductive analysis of open-ended, detailed descriptive and quantitative data gathered through direct contact with the program and its participants" (Patton, 1980).

In practice this approach creates a more complex role for the evaluator, requiring a new roster of skills. Gathering data calls for a delicate, complex role of being both participant and observer while also trying to understand the participant's perceptions of events and processes; for observing and recording a situation in detail as a social environment with its particular qualities of communication as well as the specifics of its operation.

From this approach there can be no preestablished format for recording observation since the content and form of a record reflect and express the relative sensitivity and breadth underlying the observer's experience, and these qualities change in response to increasing depth and differentiation in the observer's relation to the experience. The recording experience intensifies the sense of participation in the observed event, stimulating further reflection. "Observing and recording inform each other." Similarly, in the next stage of analysis, called "documenting," the account takes its shape through the interpretive thought of the documenter, which builds on perceiving the varied multiple patterns of relationships among the components of the observations. This holistic perspective becomes somewhat clearer when it is described as akin to historical analysis or biography.

This approach to evaluation is in clear opposition to the long-accepted methodology of the social sciences—psychometric techniques and statistical experimental designs—as the primary source of knowledge. By contrast, qualitative evaluative methods are based on a phenomenological view in which focusing on persons and their behavior and an everyday view of the world is central (see Carini, 1975a).

Perhaps all this adds up to a few trends that move in a common direction. The specific problems of evaluation are now better understood and errors more openly admitted; the methods being tried are more varied and exploratory; when alternatives to traditional kinds of evaluation become more acceptable in the research world, educators and psychologists will move toward a more common perspective; the classroom will be the important location for joint studies. And, beyond all this, we see the evaluation question in the context of probing issues associated with basic social change and revisionist views in the philosophy of science.

PART 3

Inner Processes: Feelings, Play, and Creativity

CHAPTER 8

Drawing as Expression of Thinking and Feeling

If you doubt that there was uniformity in the curriculum for the secondary school in the 1920s, just say "strawberry baskets" to anyone who attended high school in New York City at that time. You will get a burst of laughter, most of it in recall of frustrated effort and embarrassed failure in the long ago. I remember trying to draw a copy of a strawberry basket, set up on the teacher's desk, which was the standard task for the whole class. I remember nothing of instruction or criticism—though there may well have been some—only an inner bewilderment about how to translate the three-dimensional object into an image on a two-dimensional surface—how to begin, which way to go, how to make a line bespeak a direction or a space tell about a plane.

I remember a small retreat from the experience of failure. I could copy almost exactly the line drawings of decorative figures that were placed at the opening lines of the articles in our high school paper. In fact, this copying was very satisfying and I often indulged in a bit of copying here and there to relieve the irksome tasks of translating Virgil or solving quadratic equations. Many years later, I could be found at the Art Institute of Chicago in a drawing class in which our first exercise consisted of making a copy of a classic sculpture of a head. I was much improved over the "strawberry basket," but the two-dimensional statement never became an important way of expressing or reinterpreting experience. If I had had a deeper drive, Maddi (1975) would say, nothing would have stopped me—not even the "strawberry baskets." But if I had been a child at the City and Country School when William Zorach was the art teacher, or at the Walden School in the days of Florence Cane, maybe their ways of guiding expressive potential through an evolutionary course from open experimentation to the technical mastery of line, space, and form would have provided me with another language with which to speak. As it was, whatever drive was there

155

ran underground until it surfaced again, years later, when Children's Drawings *was the subject of my first research attempt. In the intervening years, I had found a more congenial medium for myself—the free expressive style of the Isadora Duncan school of modern dance. There was no fixed model or image to follow. There was wide open latitude for translating thought and feeling into the sphere of movement in a spirit of communion with music. Technique was a means, not an end, and, besides, there was the pleasure of being in rebellion against the strictures and preestablished patterns of the orthodox forms of the ballet.*

It was a happy circumstance that led me, in 1928, to those who were in rebellion against the strictures and preestablished patterns of traditional education. The "fit" was so good that it has lasted ever since.

Children's Drawings: From Lines to Pictures (1934)

The first drawings a child makes which he regards as pictures are not casual events. They are part of his widening experience, in which certain high spots stand out, of especial importance to him and definitely interesting to the adults who know and watch him. First pictures are a discovery as are first smiles, first reachings, first steps, first words. They impress the child. He is unprepared, in a certain sense, for what he finds he can do and seems pleasantly taken unawares, behaving as though something striking and exciting had happened to him.

When we look through a series of children's early pictures, the question arises as to what they reveal that is common to most children. Does the way in which young children begin to draw likenesses reflect their previous experience, the facility of their coordinations, or the level of their expanding intelligence? Do the stages preceding representation, the stages often referred to as those of childish scribbling, affect the characteristics of these first pictures? If so, how? The answers to such questions as these require not only the study of large numbers of drawings but also extended observation of children in the act of drawing. Before describing the whole sequence of drawing development, it will help to outline briefly the salient features of early representative drawing.

From a series of collections of early drawings in two nursery school situations, a group of first picture drawings has been selected as typical. They show primarily the characteristics common to early pictures and, incidentally, the variety of methods by means of which these pictures are drawn. Naturally, they do not illustrate the most successful attempts at representation or the qualities most appealing to adults. It is their common characteristics that make it possible to look upon early representation as a stage in a regular developmental sequence. Among these children it was found that the average age for making a drawing recognizable by an adult as a picture is about 195 weeks, about three months before the fourth birthday. This age varies considerably for

Adapted from Children's drawings: From lines to pictures. *69 Bank Street Publications.* New York: Bank Street College of Education, 1934.

individual children. It depends both on their previous experience with drawing and on extraneous influences which, in some cases, may prompt an earlier interest in representation than would otherwise appear.

These children of these schools were probably less influenced to make a start toward representation than might generally be true. They attended the Nursery School of the Bureau of Educational Experiments and the City and Country School, both in New York City, where a definite policy concerning drawing has been maintained for several years. In both these schools strong emphasis was placed upon safeguarding the child's independent attack on materials and in giving him every opportunity to experiment on his own level. Obvious forms of direction such as "Now we will make a house" were naturally outlawed. Furthermore, the teacher controlled both her own impulses and those of others to ask such leading questions as "What is that?" or "What are you drawing?" The purpose was to allow the child's interests to develop apace with his needs. This attitude was assured only to the children's school drawing experience. Home attitudes were outside the range of control and may have varied considerably from home to home.

In general, a child's accomplishments depend on the succession of controls he acquires during his infancy and very early childhood. We may read this succession from a series of events: his reaching for an object, his grasp on a rattle with his thumb opposed to his palm, his dependence on his eyes for directing the actions of his hands, his general strength of body expressed in muscular vigor, his ability to maintain an erect posture, his interest and pleasure in the records of his own actions, in the creative products of his behavior, his learning to deal with absent items of his experience, specific or abstract. These general lines of growth influence the skills he acquires, the techniques which come to serve his purposes. With this principle as a guide, it becomes an interesting and illuminating task to look at the child's pictures chronologically in order to discover, as far as is possible, how he came to acquire the control they display and how the history of this skill keeps step with the rest of his growth, conceived *in terms of both expanding muscular coordination and conceptual maturity.*

With the material at hand and the cases available for study, it was not possible to carry this line of inquiry as far back as might be most desirable. The youngest children observed were between the ages of eighteen months and two years. Each six-month period from this age up to that of four years has been characterized in terms of the sequence of developmental factors. The locating of these factors at a certain age is based upon what was found to be the course of development for most of the children studied and observed. As is to be expected, some children are likely to be somewhat advanced in this line of growth just as others are likely to be somewhat retarded. The individual child, whether he be slower or faster than most others, passes through the fundamental stages in regular order. The drawing development here outlined is of the spontaneous kind. The stimulation toward drawing was not laboratory controlled. The children drew when they were so inclined, and when no routines such as washing or eating interfered. Materials and drawing space were always available and their rights to uninterrupted periods of play were protected in this activity as in others.

Drawing before the Age of Two: Exploration

The illustrations in Figures 1–3 show that before the age of two years children can grasp a crayon with sufficient firmness to make marks on a paper. A well-sustained oscillating line, often drawn as an arc, appears in a variety of colors. This refers to the original drawings, made in color, which have been reproduced here in black and white. Dots and a repetitive circling are occasional. The paper is not entirely covered and, more often than not, the markings cluster toward one of the corners. Observation of the children as they draw bears out deductions which can be made from these drawings as to what constitutes drawing activity at this stage.

The muscular action involved is a large arm action evidenced in the arc form of the oscillating lines. The child's arm acts as a whole, usually from the shoulder, occasionally from the elbow. The child clutches his crayon firmly with four fingers and thumb opposed, the palm of his hand either at right angles to the paper or parallel to it. This latter position becomes more persistent as he grows older and, gradually, he liberates his index finger from the grasp on the crayon, extending it over the length of the crayon so that it becomes more prominent in controlling the drawing action. The action in his arm reverberates, to some extent, throughout his whole body. His head may bob vigorously or his legs wag synchronously under the table. If this drawing is especially vigorous, his whole upper body may reinforce his arm action, and it is not uncommon to hear a rhythmic vocal accompaniment.

Though the child has usually begun to favor one hand over the other for such functions as reaching and eating before his second birthday, his hand preference is not carried over to drawing until he has reached a later stage. At two, he still frequently alternates the use of his hands for marking, not yet having established definite functions for each hand. The hand that is not engaged in drawing is not necessarily put to holding the paper steady. In fact, the paper often slips from the table and is laboriously retrieved each time without the lesson learned. Or, at other times, he may work his crayons hard with both hands simultaneously. Obviously he is responding to crayons as tools for making marks although during most of the time he is not following with his eyes what his hand is doing. Once started, the hand action persists automatically while his gaze may be attracted by any one of a number of passing events. Consequently, his markings are not always confined to the boundaries of the paper though the disregard of boundaries is not so frequent in this stage as it is in the next, when the general vigor of the drawing attack is increased and more commonly expressed.

The child does not limit his contact with crayons to their use as a drawing tool. They answer the requirements for a toy too suitably to be neglected as

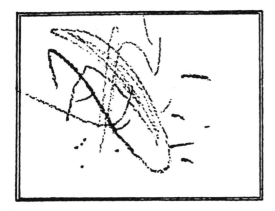

Fig. 1

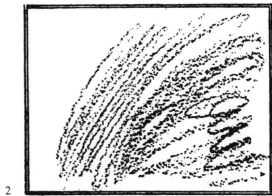

Fig. 2

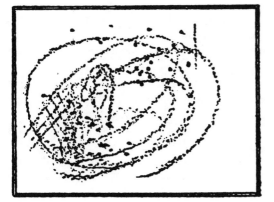

Fig. 3

such. The paper covering can be torn off bit by bit, itself an engaging occupation, not to speak of the pleasure of rubbing fingers along the smooth outer surface of the wax crayon. The crayons can be rolled across the table, studiously placed in their little box and just as studiously dumped out again. The child's interest in noises inspires him to the game of tapping the crayon on any accessible hard object. Occasionally, he puts his crayon in his mouth or marks his face and neck with it. The drawings produced are generally weak, only slightly varied, formless, and unorganized. They are more the incidental records of an exploratory kind of action than the coordinated products of a given type of activity.

Drawing between the Ages of Two and Two-and-a-Half: Control

With the passing of the second birthday the generally exploratory nature of the earlier drawings recedes in prominence and the children's products show various signs of increasing control (Figures 4–7). The repetitive circling line appears in more sustained and more definite form (Figure 4), showing the child's growing skill in both keeping an action going and locating it on a given spot on the paper. The markings are no longer clustered in the corners. The whole sheet is employed as a field, and, though in the more spirited drawings the lines still tend to spill over the edges, there are many instances in which the paper edge is regarded as the restricting boundary for the drawing.

During this period, the child not only exercises greater control of what he has previously learned how to do but also adds to the interest of his drawings by continuous experimentation with a variety of lines. The circled form now appears in a progressive looping which moves across the paper and is also varied to form more or less regular spirals. The use of a variety of lines on a single sheet is common (Figure 5), giving the impression of a child trying out his whole range of possible action with a crayon in hand. The resultant drawing shows no sign of organization of the markings within the field. The use of the smoothly flowing, muscularly controlled line in these various forms coincides, at this stage, with the first use of a line that is essentially different, in both appearance and manner of production. It is illustrated most clearly in Figure 6. Repetition is lacking; the smoothness is replaced by a jerked appearance. It is no longer merely the record of a rhythmic muscular action; it is produced deliberately through the coordinated control of hand and eye. The child watches this line as he makes it and, with increasing experience, he begins to use it predominantly. For this reason it is referred to here as the drawing line.

In general, it is true that the child at this time begins to depend less and less on automatic modes of response in his drawing. Repeated action passes its fullest point of development and the child learns to stop an action though it has been well started. An incidental result of this increased control is the appearance of spaced forms in contrast to masses of line. The circling action, cut short, leaves a clearly enclosed space. The child is not yet sufficiently in control to make a space deliberately but this does not preclude his being influenced by its

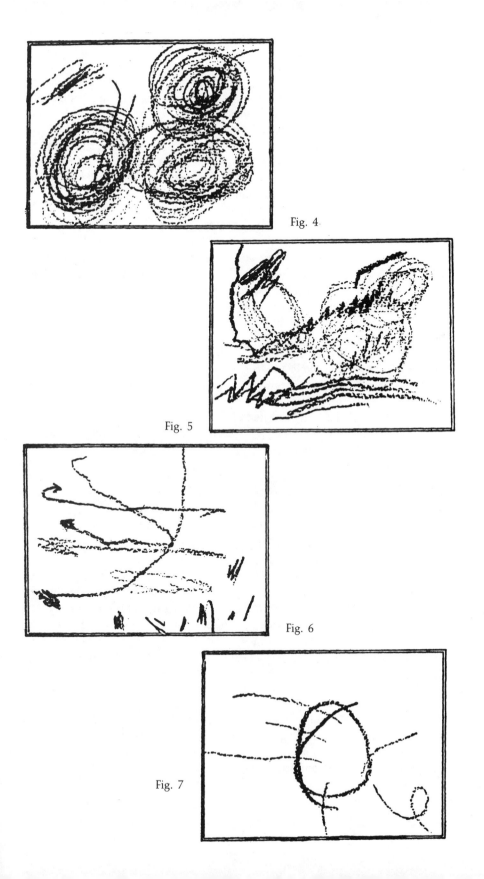

Fig. 4

Fig. 5

Fig. 6

Fig. 7

occurrence, incidental though it may be. The child's drawing development seems to proceed not only on the basis of the motions he feels himself making but also by the impressions he gets, visually, from the products of his actions. This is similar to his early speech development. The child makes a sound; he gets the feeling of making a sound and, at the same time, hears the sound he has made. Both these elements in his experience then contribute to his next steps in learning to talk. In much the same way, the consistency with which he watches his drawing contributes to his growing control.

Observation of the child at this stage shows changes that parallel those noticed in his finished drawings. He uses less of his body. The range of his motions is becoming restricted. There appears to be a shift of control in his arm from the upper to the lower portions. The spring of his drawing actions is moving toward the wrist. He still grasps his crayon between his four fingers and thumb but now seldom uses his wrist in a position of right angles to the table. The back of his hand is uppermost as he moves it parallel to the table. This overhand control resembles closely his technique for holding a spoon as he carries it, loaded, to his mouth.

Since his paper, at this stage, is more distinctly a field for locating his markings, the child is likely to clear it before he begins. The crayon box is pushed aside and the paper kept free of random objects as he proceeds. Crayons and paper are becoming more definitely materials for drawing, and drawing is now a special kind of activity. His use of the materials as toys is now about half what it was in the preceding stage. They serve a more definite function and his interest in their use is less subject to the influence of passing distraction.

Drawing between the Ages of Two-and-a-Half and Three: Technique

These next six months of the child's drawing are distinguished by the emergence of shape and form. It is obviously unsuitable to look upon these products any longer as incidental records of a few kinds of action. The single drawing line, involving coordination of eye and hand, is often found repeated across the page, giving the impression of parallel lines (Figure 8). The child gradually acquires the skill of enclosing a space by starting a line at one point, slowly and deliberately drawing it around until it is brought to a stop at approximately the spot at which it was begun (Figure 9). Roughly circular or oval shapes appear first but are followed shortly by a variety of shapes, some of which are angular.

At the same time that the child experiments with his newly found ability to block out these unit spaces, he puts the drawing line to another use (Figure 10). A single line is trailed over the paper, changing its direction, crossing back over itself at several points, thus making a more complex pattern. The line, as he uses it now, is not the end product of his efforts but becomes a means to another purpose, namely, the drawing of a shape or a form. Occasionally, the child responds to the oblong shape of his paper by drawing straight lines along the edges and outlining it completely. These uses, in a simple way, constitute an early technique.

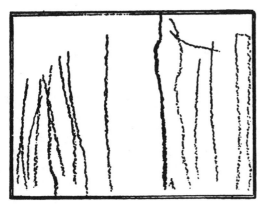

Fig. 8

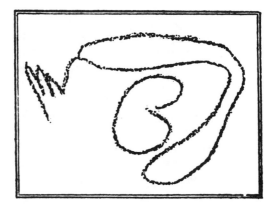

Fig. 9

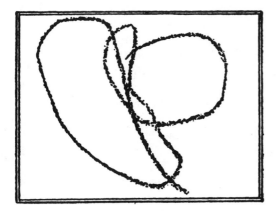

Fig. 10

Attitudes toward Drawing: Three-Year-Old versus Two-Year-Old

It is well to note the distinct difference between the drawing activity of the three-year-old child just described and that of the two-year-old. In the course of little more than a year his behavior with drawing material has altered from a diffuse, unspecialized attack to a controlled, directed use. Drawing has become a circumscribed activity. It has a place, a position, a posture. Its materials are tools, not toys.

The older child, feeling he would like to draw, asks for materials or gets them himself. He proceeds directly to a table, seats himself, arranges his paper and crayons, and begins to draw. His body, as a whole, is only posturally active, not overtly responsive. He watches his drawing as he makes it, uses one hand or the other consistently, holds his paper steady with the hand that is free. After applying himself for several minutes, he may look up, engage in conversation, draw again, stop, hold up his drawing and look at it carefully, turn to the blank side, draw again, and finally place his drawing on the allotted pile on the shelf. His interest in what he is doing is sufficiently fixed so that intervening distractions are not likely to disengage him from it completely.

The reaction of the child to his own drawing also undergoes a marked change during the interval between the second and third birthdays. The phases of the activity which interest him change, with succeeding stages, just as his skill does. This is due, in part, to the nature of his drawing materials. Crayons and papers are not toys to be discarded, outworn in function, at definite ages, such as rattles, mechanically operated animals, and peg boards. In other words, let the child be given the same drawing materials at successive ages and his use of them will reflect his gradual maturing along several lines.

At about the third birthday, the child shows a clearly personal relation to what he draws. "Look what I made!" is heard on all sides when a group of three-year-olds are engaged in drawing, addressed to children and adults alike. They scrutinize their drawings intently when they are finished, hold them up from the table to look at them in various positions, and show considerable concern to have their names written upon them by a nearby adult. A year earlier, this writing of names on the drawings was entirely neglected; the interest of the child, at that time, was in the act of drawing rather than in what was produced.

It is also at the age of three that, as has been mentioned before, the child makes a connection between his crayon drawings and pictures he has seen in books. This is evidenced by his suggestion of names and seems to indicate that the child feels that his drawings and pictures he has seen belong, somehow, in the same class.

The Place of Drawing in the Scheme of General Growth

What has happened to the child between his second and third birthdays in his drawing development is closely related to what we know to be true of his general growth. During this period he shows progressive control in the elimination of random motions. His motor responses become more successfully directed. By the time he is three, he can steer his way around objects while running, he can climb ladders without help, he can build delicately balanced structures with blocks, and he can eat with little spilling. His motor behavior, in addition to being more controlled, is also more differentiated. Certain parts of his body serve more specialized functions. He runs more with his legs and less with a general thrusting forward motion. What he does with one hand is less frequently duplicated in automatic motions of the other.

Within each activity in which he takes part there are increasing signs of advancing organization or, in other words, more patterning of the responses involved. In his block building, for instance, throwing, dragging, and pushing single blocks decline in prominence. Instead, he uses blocks constructively, placing them beside, above, across one another in a variety of ways. He is not only doing something. He is working out ways of doing things, and in so doing, is becoming less distractible, less susceptible to extraneous influences. When he starts an activity there is a stronger potential of "carrying through" than at his second birthday. The two-year-old, by contrast, gave the impression of passing amiably from one thing to another, responding with about the same amount of interest to the varying stimulations surrounding him.

His behavior, as a whole, is less repetitive at three than it was at two. This is true for speech and constructive activities quite as much as for drawing. The use of double words such as *car-car*, the simple piling of blocks one on the other or their horizontal arrangement in a row, have all become things of the past. Repetition does not entirely disappear, to be sure. The units of behavior which are repeated, however, are more complicated ones and the total result reveals considerable patterning in consequence.

As was stated previously, by the age of three the child gives evidence in the naming of his drawings that he sees a connection between his crayoning and pictures of objects seen in books. Here again, this step in drawing is only one manifestation of a more general growth process. He is passing from a manipulative attack on materials to an expressive use of them. He is no longer content merely to handle, carry, place, or move his materials. He is developing a gradual but persistent interest in getting a symbolic value out of what he does with them, as, for example, when he prefers to treat his block structures as boats, as trains. The three-year-old has entered upon the stage of seeing his materials in relation to the meaningful events of his daily life.

Drawing between the Ages of Three and Three-and-a-Half: Design

The next steps taken by the child in his drawing development tend toward more organization and greater skill in patterning. From Figures 11–13, illustrating the characteristic products of children between three and three-and-a-half years of age, we see that the child is working entirely with the spaces delineated by his lines rather than with the lines themselves. He is still using the relatively simple spaces evolved earlier, in the preceding stage, but is now finding various ways of relating these spaces to one another, giving an effect of more sustained design. One favorite method is the attaching of subordinate spaces, making a row extending out from some initial independent unit space (Figure 11). Or the spaces may be placed concentrically, intersected, or grouped loosely by a single surrounding outline enclosing several separate shapes (Figure 12). Sectioning lines cut off spaces within a space, and the attachment of subordinate spaces is varied to make not only a row formation but another type of figure (Figure 13) in which there appears a suspicion of symmetry and balance.

In all these drawings we note a consistent regard for the paper as a field. It is a far cry from the time when the child's first markings were scattered anywhere on the surface of the paper or indiscriminately laid over one another. The whole surface now serves as a unified background for the drawing, which is usually sufficiently sustained to extend over most of it. Each line drawn contributes to the total effect of the drawing. The child has progressed to the point where his interest lies not alone in enclosing spaces but in locating them on a field in organized fashion.

A striking elaboration in design was noted as a stage in development in some children in the next age group, that is, between three-and-a-half and four. It is at this age that most children begin representative drawing, as will be discussed later. The child who interests himself in the elaboration of design develops his use of paper as background and his grouping of spaces until his drawings show a degree of sustained control and a general composition effect which are very impressive. Figures 14–15 are samples of this elaboration of design: spaces emanating from a focal region; unit spaces attached to a long, single, spiraled line (Figure 14); paralleled, curved lines closed into spaced forms; angular forms combined in great variety (Figure 15); and combined use of long line spacing with short line spacing.

Attitude toward Drawing: Four-Year-Old versus Three-Year-Old

The year between the third and fourth birthdays sees not a new attitude but rather a strengthening of the one that arose at three. At three, drawing emerged from an amorphous stream of activity. At four, the child has come to regard it as one of several definite activities, open to his choice. The fact that drawing has become a technique with a variety of possibilities at his command affects his attitude. He can start with an assurance that he will have something when he is through, something that has a great deal of value in his eyes. His repeated request to take his drawings home to his parents or his occasional generosity when he offers them to another child or to a favored adult is ample evidence of this personal value.

Most of the motor coordinations involved in the drawing activity have become increasingly refined and, consequently, changes in them are less apparent. The handling of the crayon, however, undergoes a definite change at this time. By the time the child reached his third birthday, his hold on the crayon had shifted from a fist grasp to an overhand position in which the index finger

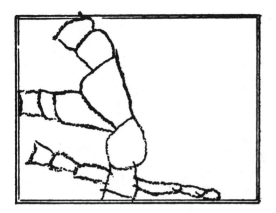

Fig. 11

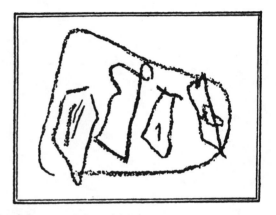

Fig. 12

Fig. 13

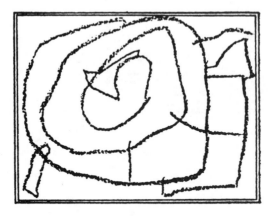

Fig. 14

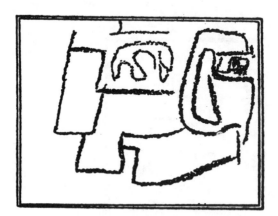

Fig. 15

guided the action of the crayon. By the time he reaches his fourth birthday, this method of guiding the crayon becomes less common; in its place, the child substitutes one which is substantially the same as that used by the adult in ordinary writing. His preference for using one hand or the other is clearly established and not likely to change except under adult pressure. His drawing materials are exclusively tools, now. Occasions on which he may play with them are rare and definitely inspired by some special stimulation such as a sudden impulse to glide a crayon along the crack between two adjoining tables.

At this stage a greater variation appears among the individual children. They show varying degrees of skill and marked differences in the extent to which they elaborate this skill. Just as they are not all equally adept at the handling of the crayon, so not all exhibit equivalent amounts of interest in its use. Preferences or disinclinations with regard to drawing show up clearly at this stage. There is no basis for assuming, however, that these feelings are lasting in all children. In some, a sudden realization of some new possibility in graphic expression has been seen to revive their interest.

Transition to Representative Drawing

At the beginning of this discussion the salient characteristics of early representative drawing were briefly described. It was pointed out that, on the basis of these characteristics, many writers hold the view that children's first pictures are essentially schematic, that is, the relations of space and proportion, for example, are not made consistent with those of the object being drawn. They have also held that this early schematic stage may be explained by the fact that the child draws mentally, portraying not what the object looks like but what he knows about it. According to this viewpoint, the child's greater attention to details and their placement, his more correct portrayals of factors such as proportion and perspective, and his attainment of successfully realistic drawing, constitute his progress.

In studying early pictures here, I have made an attempt to see them from two somewhat different viewpoints. First, they have been looked at in the more usual way, in the way described above, keeping in mind the characteristics of the drawing in relation to the characteristics of what is being depicted. Second, they have been considered in terms of the technical outlay involved, of the degree of line–space elaboration incorporated, as it has been described for the earlier stages. A group of pictures made during the first few weeks of the representative stage was divided into three classes, which corresponded to three recognizably different ways of drawing pictures. None of these methods is used exclusively in the drawing of an individual child; in fact, a single drawing may embody more than one method. As might be expected, certain children are more adept with one method than with another.

Pictures Depending upon Placement of Detail

In the first class, there are two pictures of people. The clue to the fact that they represent people is found in the face features present in all of them. Eyes, a nose, and a mouth are indicated. It is these details that carry the burden of the representation. The large enclosure within which these features are placed can be considered head, or head and body. Only the child can tell which is intended and he may not be certain. Figures 16 and 17 have radiating lines. These, as one may gather from the children, are intended as limbs. The head end, marked with an eye feature in Figure 18, legitimizes the naming of the picture after a whale and its fish-like qualities.

Figure 19, called "ladders" by the child, is an example of an uncommon tendency among these children to turn out representative drawings without altering, in any way, their previous technique. They utilize their experience to find appropriate names for a simple drawing design. Usually, this is found among those children who show little facility in drawing as a form of expression but whose idea content is high and whose verbal expression is free. Frequently, one encounters temporary epidemics of this kind of picture drawing.

The drawings of this class display, on the whole, a meagerness of line–space technique. They appear with the other classes of representative drawings, in the work of a given child, regardless of the skill he has attained during the stage of design. The spaces used are of the simplest kind, single line enclosures, round or square in form. The compositions achieved are also of a simple kind. Proportions in the total mass are commonly neglected. The principal contours are rigid and fixed; it is the markings inside the contour which carry the meaning of the picture.

The child displays other immaturities in his mode of expression, such as are often said to exist for a young child when he meets a new situation. In drawing at this stage, his new situation is using crayons to make, not a drawing, but a picture. Some of his pictures (see Figure 17) show a repetitive tendency associated with the early pre-representative stages. The radiating lines, with circles at their ends, probably representative of fingers, are repeated. On the left side, the repetitive factor runs riot as compared to the right. These lines start at what would correspond to the ear level. It is an open question here as to whether the child is revealing that he does not know where hands arise, and how many fingers there are on each, or whether the drawing that we see is a crude composite of his interest in depicting and of the habits he has previously acquired in using crayons as tools for making lines and spaces. Are these repeated lines with circles an evidence of his ignorance or are they a regression to his earlier habit of repetition, called out by the strangeness of the situation?

Pictures Depending upon Total Mass Resemblance

In the kind of representation illustrated in Figures 16 and 17, the child uses a minimal amount of line–space technique; his lines and shapes are simple and rigid and unadapted to the requirements of his representation. A few details carry the meaning. By contrast, there is a different kind of representation (Figures 20–23) in which part images, persons or objects, are inter-connected by the whole contour of the drawing. In the case of the human being, the

Fig. 16

Fig. 17

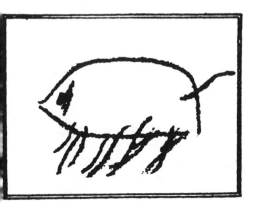

Fig. 18

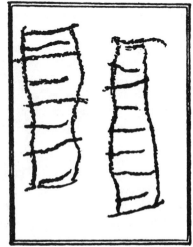

Fig. 19

drawing is faithful, at least, to the advantage of height over width in the human body. Head, trunk, and legs are likely to be differentiated in some simple way. The child's picture does not depend upon inserted face features for recognition (Figures 20, 21). It is a fairly true picture of certain mass relations in the human body.

This dependence of representation upon general outlines and mass relations holds true for the other pictures in this group as well. Baby carriages and cars (Figures 22, 23) have more width than height and are drawn accordingly. Certain other general characteristics have been successfully caught by the child. Both baby carriage and car are wheeled and bodied. These pictures, then, are pictures of whole objects whose outstanding general proportions, though not the proportions of subordinate masses, have been observed.

This class of pictures may be contrasted with the previous class in that line–space technique is used less rigidly and is more adapted to the purposes of the child at the moment. Spaces are more varied in shape—oval, triangular, circular, squared, and irregular—and the child uses greater skill in putting them together. It is of decided interest to observe also that, whereas the processes involved in the first class may be described as additive, those of the second may be regarded as constructive. That is, in the first class the child usually starts with one main space, to which he adds, inside it or around its edges, characterizing details as they occur to him. But, in the second class, there is a composition of spaces which from the beginning to the end of the drawing is kept within the compass of his representative idea. The parts of his drawing are here relatively more dependent upon their relation to the whole drawing for their representative significance. The picture is less likely to be a loose conglomeration of conventionalized symbols. Psychologically, this involves the ability to control a series of steps in the interest of a definite final product.

Pictures Depending upon Contour Resemblance

Figures 24–26 illustrate a third class of pictures, which is distinguished by the fact that representation is attained by enclosing a space with a line which itself incorporates a resemblance to the partial silhouette of the object. Attempts at profiled human drawings (Figure 24) and characteristic animal head forms (Figures 25, 26) are illustrative. This more flexible use of line to represent outlined contours is occasionally carried through the whole drawing; more often, in these first pictures, it is sustained only part way, the rest of the drawing being completed by a simple line–space method (Figure 24). In this class, the child is not depending chiefly upon placement of details though he may include them, nor does he get his resemblance by grouping spaces. He is relying on adapting his use of line directly to represent his object.

The division into the three classes just discussed is not to be construed as meaning that a given child uses only one of these methods, or that an individual drawing embodies one method exclusively, or that there is, necessarily, a developmental sequence from one to the other. The child is at work on several ways

Fig. 20

Fig. 21

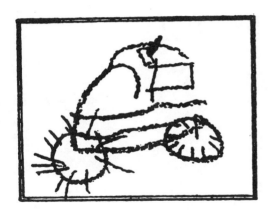

Fig. 22

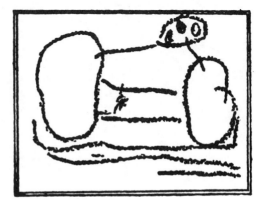

Fig. 23

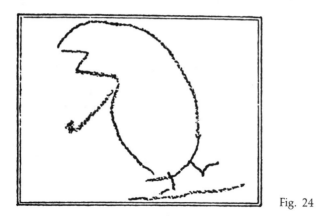

Fig. 24

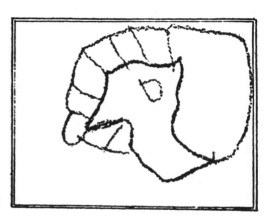

Fig. 25

Fig. 26

of approaching the representative problem in employing, at different times, varying degrees of drawing skill and of organization and in attaining varying degrees of resemblance. He appears to plunge into the use of all these different methods during his early weeks of representative drawing.

Reconsideration of a Child's First Pictures

In considering the history of the child's drawing development previous to his first pictures, it may be seen that his progress is regular, that there is a steady incorporation of first achievements into later ones so that there is an integrated developmental sequence. His first pictures, when they appear, constitute a next step in this sequence. Like the previous stages, representative drawings incorporate the experience that has gone before.

Before he starts out on his picture career, the child has attained a considerable familiarity in drawing lines and spaces, in placing them interestingly, and in accomplishing design effects. He has this much to work with when he comes to drawing pictures. He uses this, though, under a new and added strain. Before, his drawings were relatively free. Now they fall within the control of his representative idea. We need not be surprised if, under the strain of adapting his old technique, the child's product seems, at first, a little disheveled.

In the light of these observations it seems unwarranted to state that a child's first representations are completely mental, that they are inadequate, or that he progresses regularly from the schematic to the realistic picture. Rather, it seems that for a more complete interpretation of early representation, it is necessary to consider the resources the child has developed during his pre-representative drawing experience. A child's first pictures, then, should be regarded as the resultant not only of his unfolding mental concepts but also of his direct experience with a technique.

Drawing Experience in Relation to Developmental Theory

The title of that fifty-year-old paper stated a problem that has had increasing attention in the intervening years: How do we proceed to understand that quintessential human capacity to use symbols for referring to experience and thereby encompass meanings beyond the bounds of time and space? Although the research perspective varies, there appears to be a constant paradigm to follow. Materials are needed to serve the symbolic process; begin at the beginning and study how the materials are used. Watch where, when, and how a given way of using tools passes out of the stage of performing elaborate exercises, satisfying in and of themselves, and begins to serve as means for a qualitatively different purpose: to refer to some remembered elements of experience. Then watch the complex ways in which, at first, the tool technique exercises a certain mandate over the symbolization process, and how later the requirements of the symbol act to reshape the way the technique is used.

I went only part way in that early study of drawing—up to the appearance of symbolization. But I engaged in an argument, nevertheless. I disagreed with the thesis, predominant at that time, that a child draws what he knows, not what he sees, and that, therefore, drawings are indicators of intelligence quotient. I learned from this early study that presymbolic activities have a developmental life history and that symbolization, when it appears, is continuous with it. I learned that becoming aware that children use a variety of techniques in the presymbolic stages made one more sensitive to variation in modes of symbolizing, when they emerge. I enjoyed trying to find congruence among the developmental changes in the drawings, the children's changing attitudes toward the drawing experience, and other concurrent developmental phenomena. It was a small attempt and I never studied drawing again, but the roots of a developmental approach that took process as well as product into account were firmly planted.

Drawing and Thinking

In the intervening years there have been analytical studies of the young child's drawing experience that interpret the sequence of changes in terms of contemporary developmental theory and which deal with drawing or painting as an integral phase of basic learning experience. The perspective of the researcher has changed; I started with observation and study of the activity and arrived at a few simple insights into the developmental process by the route of "molecular observation" in a natural situation. The contemporary analyst brings systematic theory to bear on a body of material and, in a sense, it is the usefulness of the theory that is being studied in the context of an activity analysis.

In the case of children's drawings, different theoretical perspectives have been applied that seem to complement one another, each needed as part of the whole when it comes time to draw implications for educational procedure. A study of early painting by Nancy Smith (1972; see also 1983) analyzes the sequences and the processes in terms of developmental cognitive theory, illustrating how, up to adolescence, painting, like other modes of symbolization, is linked to basic processes of thought. We recognize the sequence she depicts from presymbolic to symbolic painting: the beginning of visual control and differentiation of line and space that follow the first rhythmic-motor painting activity. Smith draws on Piagetian and Wernerian theory to explain transitions to later stages in which the child's integration of line and surface space begins to generate interaction of shapes with one another. She traces the changes in this course as a succession of integration and differentiation processes, emphasizing the salience of the stage in which early drawing activity is removed and distanced from the self, so that the patterns delineated become less and less automatic. The further evolution takes a well-developed course until, in Smith's description, "During his exploration of shape interactions Marc stumbles onto discovery of a symbol." Thus, it is the pattern that is prior; at first the object concept is gradually fitted to it until, with new developing schema of symbolization, the old modes are adapted to new purposes, the lines and shapes begin to correspond more with the spatial arrangement of the object. For a considerable time, the symbol is tied to a dynamic, holistic object concept; gradually, the identifying and ordering processes that are part of the emerging logic of classification begin to exert influence over the earlier physiognomic processes.

From this theoretical perspective, one sees the early person drawings (the circle with the marks for limbs and a few circles for facial features) as holistic thinking; this is a person, not yet either boy or girl, small or large, using a holistic schema for depiction. The depiction on the paper is not the measure of what the child *knows* about people; it is rather as much as he can say in line and space within the limits of his available symbolizing techniques, not a translation of visual recall. His painting is a composite of what he knows and what he can do with his knowledge through the graphic skills and patterns available to him from his presymbolic experience. The experience is a form of symbolization that is a mediator between action and thinking by means of which he internalizes the natural world. Smith sees this process as a solution by the child, within his powers, for what is necessary to serve as a *functional substitute* for experience, not a translation of visual recall.

Two children's paintings placed alongside each other are never exactly alike. The qualitative differences are surprising, refreshing, and informative. And it is no surprise to come up against, once more, the need to interweave within any developmental sequence—be it drawing, block building, language, or posture—the way each individual's mode shapes and gives particular character to what is common to all. The old formula about knowing and seeing was too simple. We see first pictures as results of mental concepts mediated through the level of experience with techniques and the child's expressive preferences. His graphic skills are a limiting factor; he may know that there is a discrepancy between his image and realistic details of the object. His expressionistic-stylistic preference may exercise control over inclusion of detail. His purpose in drawing and painting is different from the adult's. While Smith recognizes and describes the way affect contributes to qualitative differences in the children's products and, in fact, calls almost wishfully for a synthesis of cognitive and affective interpretation, her contribution stands out as an explanation, primarily in terms of cognitive theory, of a developmental sequence that others have only described.

In Shapiro (1975) we find a presentation of that wished-for synthesis. She writes: "The impulses that give rise to, and the emotions that are expressed in, creative work are mediated by cognitive processes which determine their form and the possibilities for their expression in a given medium" (p. 17). This perspective is expressed in her description of successive developmental stages. Not until the age of about one-and-a-half to two years does the child's use of crayons show emergence of symbolization and the course is uncertain while the child is not yet clear about the distinction between reality and representation. Looking at a picture in a book may be as frightening as the reality it represents. While he becomes randomly active with pencil, brush, or paper, the activity, lacking direction and intentionality, is not yet a creative experience. The change, psychologically, comes when shapes, parts, patterns are used so as to fulfill intended representations. At this stage there is no longer the earlier confusion between self feelings and outside reality; elements and reality are fused and represented symbolically. What children produce in representative form cannot be taken as being parallel to the level of their conceptual differentiation or realistically expressive of their emotional quandaries.

It is interesting to turn to a brief analysis of pre-representative drawing that contributes directly also to the synthesis of cognitive and affective factors. In a study of a group of middle-class two-year-old children in a research nursery, Drucker and Shapiro (1979) relate the sequence of changing use of line and space to the ongoing stages of psychological maturing.

For each of four stages, spanning development prior to the second birthday, through the second year and just beyond, the authors point to congruity between the use of the drawing medium and the underlying maturing processes. The progression in drawing mirrors basic changes.

Early random scribbling, a motor process, is related to lack of awareness of boundaries that distinguish self from others. A later stage of the sequence, when the drawing paper is recognized as having boundaries and drawing of parallel lines appears, is seen as representing the more general "organized intentionality of the older toddler." In a later stage the two-year-old has achieved sufficient mastery of the medium to engage in considerable freedom and experimentation. He draws diagonals and angles in addition to circular forms and has new ideas of where a line should go. The authors relate this progression to a new psychological period in which children have acquired pleasure in autonomous functioning, are comfortable with being "separate," and have begun to trust their own self-controls.

Increased complexity of drawings and qualitatively differing styles at a later stage, involving various combinations and use of color, are seen as related to changing developmental processes such as the ability to consider different ideas at the same time and experience ambivalent feelings toward the same object. (Teachers tell about rescuing a drawing before a child demolishes what he has drawn by masking it over with scribbling.) The stage of Put My Name On It and assigning representative labels to the drawings represents pride and pleasure in feeling one's self as creator and in the advance toward a new mode of potential communication.

The Differentiation–Integration Sequence

While the developmental sequence in the evolution of drawing skills described by Arnheim (1974) corresponds to other descriptions as far as the nature of the product is concerned, his analysis also relates the sequence of changing forms of expression in a two-dimensional medium to changing psychological experience. In the early years, the quality of markings on the paper can be seen as expressive of individual personality qualities; early markings can also be seen as descriptive, in the sense that the lines on the paper may be the product of the reenactment of a given motion experience. The emergence of the circle is the crucial event in the sequence, a "miracle of nature," controlled by the eye in contrast to appearing as the product of motor rotation, ushering in recognition that shapes on paper can stand for objects in the world. At first, the circle drawn by the child has general meaning, representing "thingness," as it does universally in models of the earth or molecular models of chemists. This signifier of "thingness" of a solid object as distinct from nondescript ground does not yet stand for the quality of "roundness." Various combinations of circular forms serve a variety of representative functions: "hair, fingers and legs are made to sprout from all around the central base in order to preserve the centric symmetry of the whole." The circle begins to signify the specific quality of roundness only when other forms—squares and triangles—appear in the child's repertory as part of the developmental process that moves from early holism to greater differentiation.

The use of the straight line leads to new possibilities for depicting. It makes possible the notion of direction and the use of the right angle, which is the basis for the vertical and the horizontal on which rests our entire conception of space. The straight outstretched arms of the human figure in early figure drawings clarify, in simplest form, the functional distinction between body and arms. These figures are to be seen as schematic, representative concepts, not straightjacket images, but indispensable forms of early conceptions, not to be interpreted, out of context, for example, as expressive gestures of despair. In the succession of stages which then lead to moving toward oblique relations of parts and to fusing into contour forms, the drawing images change in quality from stiff angularity to richer, more alive, more lifelike representation. Further development involves more differentiation of parts, which then leads to greater integration at a higher level—an ongoing process in which subdivision and fusion alternate dialectically. Arnheim parallels this interpretation of the developmental sequence to the transition in the conception of science and philosophy which moved from atomistic "thinking, interpreting natural phenomena through interrelations between constant elements, to the gestalt conception of integrated field processes."

His conception of the circle as a generalized form leads Arnheim to reject the "tadpole" concept, which interprets the child's drawing of the human figure as omitting the trunk and erroneously attaching arms to the head. At this stage in the drawing sequence the circle has broader significance than symbolizing the head. This interpretation of what the child is depicting is in alignment with the gestalt perspective that characterizes Arnheim's analysis and interpretation.

Adding the Psychodynamic Dimension

In two comprehensive studies of children's drawings, DiLeo (1970, 1977) also sees changes in symbolization as moving parallel with advancing intelligence, and he, like Smith and Arnheim, takes exception to the position that what the child draws gives the full measure of what he knows. In his terms, the child makes a representation, not a copy, a concept that seems quite close to Smith's "functional substitute." He also regards the old formula as a half-truth. The child knows more than what he draws; his drawings are a graphic expression of what his technique permits him to tell of what he knows. But, more than that, DiLeo demonstrates, his drawing is influenced by his feelings expressed in the way he varies line quality, proportion, shape, and decides about inclusion and omission of parts and characters.

The early sequence in scribbling, in the use of line and space, and the discovery of the symbol are correlated with cognitive development. Early drawing, like child thought, is subjective, depicting what is known, not seen, but it is also unconsciously expressionistic. DiLeo sees portrayal as expression of inner realism: not only what is present in awareness at a given time so far as content is concerned but also as unconscious expression of underlying emotional elements, and it is qualitatively consistent with basic personality traits. He sees the drawing that is made with firm pressure and a continuous stroke as belonging to a secure child in contrasted to the restricted, lightly drawn product of an insecure child. More specifically, he takes a clinical perspective and sees the children's drawings in terms of projected meanings: the figure without arms taken to indicate timidity, excessive shading as an indicator of anxiety, the windowless house with people drawn by a child who lives in a residential center, the active, sociable four-year-old whose figure has many fingers and nine legs.

DiLeo not only maintains a dual perspective in his analysis—both developmental and psychodynamic—he deals directly with the problems and the possible errors of interpretation in attempting to work from this complex perspective. His commentary on the illustrations of the children's drawings offers concrete guidelines on how to distinguish what is developmental from what is pathognomonic. For example:

> In this drawing by a bright, well-adjusted girl of four years, seven months, we see the long spiky fingers that are typically seen in drawings by preschool children. After all, representing fingers by sticks is by far the simplest way of handling a very difficult problem. Spiky fingers at this age level may not be symbolic of emotional disorder. (DiLeo, 1970)

He recommends caution in attaching symbolic value to items that may be of developmental rather than pathognomonic significance—the large head and conspicuous eyes, the disproportionately small trunk are typical features of young drawing to be taken as expression of the primacy of the head in the child's concept of body image. Excellence of diagnosis in other domains as well as in drawing depends, of course, on knowledgeable insight into the developmental substructure within which deviations have significance.

In DiLeo's formulation, child art is nonobjective, expressionistic, and symbolic in contrast to the objective, impressionistic art of most adults. In the adult artist there is a conscious effort to retrieve the "naive" perspective of childhood—either in the kinesthetic "action paintings" that resemble children's scribbling or in the disregard for perspective or rejection of conventional rules for spatial orientation, exemplified in the work of Chagall, who is regarded by DiLeo as being most successful in this effort. Both the distinctions and the resemblance are illuminating in understanding child art and helpful during a visit to an avant garde museum exhibit.

Is the Trend toward Realism Born or Bred?

In his study of the collected drawings of a few children, Gardner (1980) also relates the evolution of drawing skill to successive changes in other spheres of development. The basic developmental course in drawing is familiar: from random motor marking to geometric forms to intricate patterning, which Gardner describes as establishing a "vocabulary of lines and forms." He sees the subsequent depiction process of objects, of persons (albeit in fixed patterns or schema) as characteristically rhythmic, vital, and expressive, representing an important means of expression, maybe a "summit of artistry."

We are familiar with the next steps: the elementary school child's effort to achieve photographic realism being regarded as consistent with other major drives of the period, allowing, of course, for the exception of individual children for whom depiction remains a special means of probing and expressing. Even while accepting this sequence toward realism as predominant, Gardner raises questions concerning its inevitability, bringing to bear two very different kinds of evidence: children in other cultures who do not follow this sequence[1] and, within our own culture, progressive schools where what he calls "the values of pluralism" counteract, to a degree, the predominant impulse toward literalism.

Most significant is Gardner's exposition of the linkage of the evolution of drawing as a symbolic tool at successive stages with the emergence and progression of other symbolic systems. What is clearly expounded is, on the one hand, the general parallelism in terms of increasing mastery in different areas—in forming language, in using clay, in drawing—and, on the other hand, the different specific characteristics of the path that maturing takes for each medium. Especially in the early stages there is a calendar difference in acquisition of successive stages of mastery for each medium. The two-year-old is far more advanced in dealing with experience through the medium of language than he is in representing his knowledge in the dominantly solitary and two-dimensional medium of drawing.

There is more correspondence between psychological developmental

1. I am grateful to have come upon this analysis. It has dispelled a troubling enigma of years. A framed picture on my wall, presented by Lucy Mitchell, has a notation saying that the picture was drawn by a boy in Bali, under nine years old, whose father is a fisherman. Its well-executed boy fishermen and the symbolic fish completely covering the field of the picture did not look like a 9-year-old's drawing to me, but it was all clear when I read on p. 160: "In Bali, for example, youngsters are compulsive about filling space; their charming repetitive little forms are drawn separately yet snugly across the page, as if driven by some horror of a void." I should have trusted Lucy Mitchell.

characteristics and drawing and other avenues of expression in the later preschool stage when representation in drawing is general, with the objects depicted standing for a whole class of objects, and when the child's conception of
how the whole world around functions is still organized on a general, undifferentiated level. What he draws "stands for," does not image; resemblance
bears on conceptual maturity, not visual representation.

In the stage of the child's "Reach Toward Realism" Gardner relates the
dominant trend toward objectively realistic portrayal in the arts to the growing
drive toward accuracy in the use of language as a more complex and more
adequate medium of communication and to the psychology of latency in the
emotional sphere. Still, as in other instances, Gardner, although accepting this
image of the dominant trend, asks for room to consider alternative trends,
surely for some children as well as for other societies. He asks that we "negoti-
ate" the generally accepted trend toward literalism in the middle years with a
degree of openness. We now have available a revised interpretation of the trend
toward "literalism" and "realism," which has also been considered as universal
in studies of sequence of play (Franklin, 1983). These studies illustrate once
more how much developmental theory reflects inevitably the life circumstance
(educational practice and theory as examples) provided for the maturing
process.

Stage Theory Modified

Sequential studies of drawing skills ask questions as to how far the developmental course is continuous psychologically or, by contrast, how much the changing
skills and content reflect basic psychological shifts in successive periods. The
seeds of later creative mastery appear at the intermediate stage—the five- to
six- to seven-year-old child—both in the attention and care which children give
to drawing activity and in the emerging motivation to master techniques of
representation in ways that are clear enough to communicate meaning. The
ambiguous, attractive qualities that characterize drawings produced during
such a transitory period may resemble the consciously designed products of
adult artists but it is generally agreed that there is an important difference
between the child's technical goals and the intent of the adult artist in communicating individual meaning as well as in the nature of the subjective experience. In the later stages, children may turn toward copying of various kinds as a
means of accurate representation. How much this trend becomes dominant in
any child's total drawing modality is influenced by the suggestions and pressures that are put forth by teachers and others who influence the drawing
activity and that differ widely in various school situations. The extent to which
differences in school environments such as are associated with contrasting
theoretical orientation, (modern in contrast to traditional) influence characteristics of a developmental stage has been analyzed in a study of nine-year-olds
in four different school climates (Minuchin, Biber, Shapiro, & Zimiles, 1969).
On several dimensions of that study the children of the most modern (pro-

gressive) school were seen as more openly expressive in their interpersonal relations and more likely to project individualized meanings into their creative activities.

As is true in other areas of development, the stage sequence image of increasing complexity is a useful generalized concept but it only roughly corresponds to the course of each individual's development, influenced as it is by personality and differing values of the adult environment (Shapiro & Wallace, 1981). Maturing is not a clear-cut displacement of earlier forms and skills but rather the gradual emergence of a greater variety of skills available to the mood and intended meaning of the maturing child-artist.

The Teaching Role

What, in the light of these interpretations, is the teaching role? Centrally, it means allowing the child to follow his natural sequence: accepting the rate at which he turns to representation when young as well as the way he becomes interested in portraying perspective at a later stage. It also means avoiding the error of interpreting drawings that represent stages in the acquisition of drawing skills as being emotionally expressive—a point of emphasis by both Arnheim and DiLeo though their rationale is derived from different psychological positions. In one way or another, to varying degrees, the authors decry one-sided emphasis on either personality factors or cognitive development as the key to understanding the drawing sequence. In Arnheim's words—"the educator of tomorrow should be able to view the thinking and perceiving mind in interaction with the aspirations, passions and fears of the total human being"— the ideal goal embraces the entire developmental panorama.

Reduced to simplest terms these interpretations say to teachers: Do not draw for children; let them discover the use of the medium on their own; do not ask, "What is that you are drawing?" or give the child suggestions of *what* to draw or, in other ways, push the child prematurely to communicate visual resemblance. But these simple terms do not construct an image of the complex teaching–learning reality. So it is interesting to turn to two presentations of school.

One Teacher

It is interesting to turn to two examples of school programming in art experiences which, sharing the general psychological orientation of the studies by Smith, Arnheim, DiLeo, and Gardner, take responsibility for aligning the specifics of educational practice with a theoretical substratum. In *Art Experiences for Young Children* (1973) Naomi Pile presents a rare synthesis of a body of theoretical concepts relative to the creative process, and a manual of concrete teaching procedures for a meaningful art experience in the early years. From her perspective, the young child has a natural urge to use real materials to express the inner and outer world of his experience and unique ability to draw upon and give expression to unconscious processes. It is a dynamic process; it needs understanding and support. His art products are expressions of feelings as well as ideas, so it is to be expected that the extent of control of line, space, or mass may vary; in fact, it behooves us to understand, for example, that seemingly regressive periods of messiness and formlessness may herald a period of new growth and control. (We have noted this kind of interlude in other content in the developmental course.)

She sees drawing as a kind of linear language through which the child focuses and increases comprehension, "a form of communication in which the child who draws speaks to himself, for himself and to the external world." His drawings are personal and deeply felt, extremely so in the case of one four-year-old, for example, who, having completed a drawing of his toy bear, said, "Don't hang it up with pins because I don't want Teddy to get stuck and have holes in him." She asks us to focus not on the product but on the complexity of the inner process and the ongoing interaction between the child and the experience. "It is the *act* of painting . . . which is the deepest motivation because then the child is stimulated by the feelings that working provokes and by the appearance of his work as it emerges"—an Arnheim voice in the classroom.

From this author's perspective the knowledgeable teacher carries a complex role that is stimulating as well as supportive. She expands the children's horizons, takes them on trips to see sensitively how things are, to build up rich visual memories. Stimulating the children's perceptions through questioning and observing is the teaching mode: "Which is the tallest building you can see from where we stand?"; "How many green things can you see?" At other times, it means looking intently at a special tree, or rubbing the patterns from manhole covers onto paper, or noting the varied colors in a mound of fresh fruit in a vendor's cart. The teacher's questions are intended to evoke experiential associations, to focus on the feeling level as well as the visual and the physical until the children's free associations take over and the children, themselves engaged with the subject, turn to expressing or depicting it in some self-chosen medium.

This book is unusual and exceedingly valuable in the way in which the author not only presents a practical, detailed description of the desirable working setup for art activities, but continuously makes explicit the theoretical basis for the teacher's practical decisions about paints, tools, space, easels, and other materials. The rationale for the mode of teacher response to and stimulation of the children's engagement is also made explicit and amply illustrated from observational records. One seldom finds the "why" of an educational program so clearly stated, or the "how" so specifically illustrated. I would do best to quote.

With respect to color:

Since color is so closely related to feeling, it is important to let children mix colors so that they can express the subtlety of what they feel. . . . Urging a child to adhere to realistic color presentation against his own wishes is urging him to deny his own feelings. . . . Painting an object an expressive color does not imply that the child does not know the color of reality. (Pile, 1973, p. 34)

And on a technical point:

The importance of quality paint brushes cannot be overemphasized. If a brush is too thin, it spreads when it should not, does not hold enough paint, and wiggles as the child works. This is very discouraging for a [young] child because he cannot separate his actions from the actions of the tools and will see himself as performing poorly. (Pile, 1973, p. 36)

Or in the area of affect:

A teacher must never discourage "unhappy" pictures. Her concern will be to overcome not the pictures but the causes of discontent they describe. If the causes are unknowable, it is far better to let the pictures happen than to turn them off because the work process itself can be therapeutic. (Pile, 1973, p. 104)

And Another

One does not often find books for educators that involve the reader both in empathic responsiveness to what is being read and in following a disciplined theoretical analysis of the content presented. In their book *Art: Another Language for Learning,* geared toward the elementary years, Cohen and Gainer (1976) have designed their presentation so that it, too, serves both these functions. They present findings from research studies and interpretive theoretical analyses of children's art in stimulating juxtaposition with fully written narrative accounts of children's and teachers' jointly searching experiences. The latter are wide ranging, dealing with technique, meaning, explanation, and the way in which conceptual confusion or emotional conflict may be resolved through graphic expression.

A chapter is likely to open with frank writing about the teachers' self-feelings, doubts, and hesitations, as well as pleasures, in actively guiding the children toward productive expressiveness in the arts media, inviting the reader inside the teaching–learning process. In juxtaposition there are reviews of how the scholarly literature—Arnheim, Jones, Lowenfeld, Piaget, Dewey, and others—has contributed insight to underlying processes. The reader is led to shift the mental set—first, to *get in there* with the essence of the children's experience, then, move away and think analytically about what has been happening. It is to be expected and not surprising that, when we read, subsequently, the implications and concrete suggestions for methods of stimulating children's expression and thinking through art, we find we have been offered an excellent paradigm for teaching in any field.

Following is an abbreviated illustration from the chapter on "Learning to See":

"I can't draw a tree. Do it for me," one child said. There followed a discussion about how there is no one way to draw a tree; then, a time for looking out the window and telling what each one saw as a tree; a trip outside the school for touching the trunk, reaching around it, picking up fallen leaves and branches; and later a time for painting and looking at each other's trees. From the children, looking at their products. "Wow, they sure are different!"[2]

In Sum

These highly developed conceptions of art experience from two teachers seem to express and fulfill the evolution of the Deweyan image of learning. While his earlier works concentrated on cognitive aspects of experience as the source of learning, his thinking shifted to more unifying, consummatory concepts. It was the combination of knowledge and the aesthetic aspects of experience that he saw as the source of the greatest richness. In integrated form, this image continues to represent a guiding principle for education (Cuffaro, 1982).

Symbolic productions in drawing or painting can be mined for multiple insights—developmentally and psychodynamically—if we can draw on analyses that have been made from different perspectives, from, for example, in the studies mentioned, cognitive theory, art history, or projective psychology. We can see how attainment of the ability to symbolize experience in this nonverbal medium comes as a discovery, an emergence not directly teachable. The images of key elements in the child's first concepts of some basic life experiences are there to be read, as well as the movement from holistic, generalized perception to differentiated concepts. We can see, as the child gains experience, the multiple ways in which correspondence can be achieved: through affective attributes or significant details that are parts of the wholes being depicted, or through spatial forms resembling the spatial organization of the objects, or through contour lines reproducing silhouette features. We can recognize inner emotional equilibrium or disequilibrium as projected by unusual emphases, sequences, proportions, and so on, of the figures drawn or painted. Both thinking and feeling are functionally determinant of the symbolic representation of selected elements of experience, though not always equivalently potent, in governing the content or the qualitative character of the symbolized statement. How much these insights contribute to deepening the experience of drawing for children depends once more on the art of teaching.

---

2. This method is analogous to Lopate's way of leading children to use poetic forms to express thought and feeling (see Lopate, 1975).

CHAPTER 9

Dramatic Play: Interpretation, Reorganization, and Synthesis

I can only guess what the content of Leonard's dramatic play would be if he were a child today instead of 65 years ago, when he came to play with me in the backyard of our brownstone house in Brooklyn. Today there would surely be bursting bombs or attacking monsters, but, in that relatively tranquil era, Leonard's aggressive fantasies got no further than "wild Indians." They lurked behind the two lilac bushes which grew in the back corners of the yard against the fence. The "Indians" stole out from time to time, only to be caught and conquered—shot, stabbed, mauled—with considerable wear and tear on the lilac bushes.

To his parents, in their vernacular, Leonard himself was a "wild Indian"—an uncontrollable child whom they alternately indulged, cajoled, and punished. Who can be sure whom he was shooting behind those bushes? The Indians? Himself? His parents? His mother always brought his reading book along when he came to visit in the hope that, somehow, the pleasure I had begun to find in books would be magically transferred to Leonard. Forlorn hope. Leonard stayed in the back of the yard, working on his own inner world when, with my older sister[1] as the teacher, we enacted the benign drama of playing school outside the kitchen window in the front space of the yard. The kitchen window, protected on the outside with fixed vertical bars, was the major prop for the play. The row of spaces formed on the sill between the bars provided a symbolic reference to the hidden order and contents of a teacher's desk: a "raw" material that would have met with Caroline Pratt's approval. The rest came through in words and gestures.

Those backyard hours linger as primordial experience when I reread "Play as a Growth Process," the paper condensed from a presentation at the

---

1. Charlotte B. Winsor, Teacher Education Specialist Emeritus, Bank Street College of Education.

Vassar Summer Institute. The experienced duality in childhood of the "wild Indian" fighting and the quiet play about school survived and reappeared from the perspective of the observer in the 1951 formulation: "Play serves two different growth needs in the early years, learning about the world by playing about it . . . and finding an outlet for complex and often conflicting emotions."

Play as a Growth Process (1951)

What do we have in mind when we think of play? What do children do when they play? Children's play has the quality of intense, absorbing experience, a bit of life lived richly and fully. There are zest and wonder and drama and a special kind of immediacy, without thought for the passing of time. There is nothing to be accomplished, no sense of what is right or wrong to check the flow of spontaneity, no direction to follow. Whatever is at hand can become suitable materials for play. The essence of the play experience is subjective, something within the child that may not necessarily become obvious to the one who observes the course or form of his activity.

Play as an activity may take numberless forms. It may be just physical activity, an overflow of energy, of exuberance. Besides running, skipping, hopping, children like to slide, seesaw, and swing. Although these play experiences require a degree of patterning in coordination, they belong among the natural playful uses a child makes of his body. If his play is as free as his energy is boundless, he is likely to embroider the basic patterns: he soon finds it more fun to hop on one foot, to slide down on his belly instead of his bottom, to swing standing up.

Playing may be something quite different from the lively expression of physical energies. It may take quiet, delicate forms such as playing with sounds and words. The chanting of younger children, the nonsense rhyming of the older ones are play forms.

The child is playing when, with his hands, he impresses himself on things around him. He pounds the clay and smears the paint. He creates with blocks even when he is only stacking them high or lining them up low. He makes the mud take shape. He fits things together and takes them apart. There are pleasure and satisfaction in what one's hands can make of the physical world, and the child, in his playful remaking of the world around him, lays the cornerstone of his feeling about himself in relation to that world.

Now we come to the world of play that is most challenging and enticing: dramatic play. Here the child can take flight. He need no longer be a child. He can make himself over and be a wolf or an engineer or a mother or a baby who is crying. He can re-create the world not only as he really experiences it but even in

Adapted from Play as a growth process. *Vassar Alumnae Magazine*, 1951, 37 (2), 18–20.

the strange aspects that symbolize some of his deepest wishes and fears. It is this kind of play—or rather the values that it has for growth—that I would like to consider.

What do play experiences do for child growth? If a child can have a really full, wholesome experience with play, he will be having the most wholesome kind of fun a child can have. For a child to have fun is basic to his future happiness. His early childhood play may become the basic substance out of which he lays down one of his life patterns: namely, that one not only can *have* fun but can *create* fun. Most of us as adults enjoy only a watered-down, manufactured kind of fun—going to the movies, shopping, listening to a concert, or seeing a baseball game—and do not feel secure that some of the deepest resources for happiness lie within ourselves, free of a price of admission. This is one of these securities that compose a positive attitude toward life in general.

In dramatic play, children also find a sense of confidence in their own impulses. There are no directions to follow, no rules to stick to. Whatever they do will be good and right. Wherever their impulses lead them, that is the way to follow. This is the freedom children should have in their play, an absence of boundaries and prescriptions that we cannot grant them outside their play lives.

Another important by-product of play is the feeling of strength it yields to the child, a relief from the powerlessness and helplessness that many children feel keenly as junior members of our well-ordered adult world. In play we give them an opportunity to counteract this powerlessness to a degree. It is the child's chance to lay the plans, to judge what is best, to create the sequence of events. Dramatic play is one of the basic ways in which children can try out their talents for structuring life. The fact that they deal with symbols rather than realities does not detract from the sense of mastery.

As you watch children playing, you see the ingredients of the child world spread out before you, differing in complexity and elaboration according to the level of maturity. When a two- or three-year-old plays train, he does so simply. The train goes. It makes sounds. Just a block and a child saying "Choo" may be Johnny's idea of a train, but very soon he meets up with Mary, who has been very much impressed with the odd way people sit in trains, looking at one another's backs. To another child in the group a train is not a train unless it whistles. Soon, a composite train emerges: it goes, it says "Choo," it whistles intermittently, people sit in it one behind the other. Children at all levels pool their ideas in free dramatic play, expose one another to new impressions, stimulate one another to new wondering and questioning. Can we fail to recognize this process as learning? Can we neglect to notice that here learning is going on in a social atmosphere full of pleasure and delight? In reliving and freely dramatizing his experience the child is thinking at his own pace with other children. He is learning in the best possible way.

More than that, the ways of the world are becoming delicious to him. He is tasting and retasting life in his own terms and finding it full of delight and interest. He projects his own pattern of the world into the play and, in so doing, brings the real world closer to himself. He is building the feeling that the world is his, to understand, to interpret, to puzzle about, to make over. For the future, we need citizens in whom these attitudes are deeply ingrained.

We would be seriously in error, however, were we to assume that all play of young children is clear and logical. Horses are more likely to eat lamb stew than hay, and what starts out to be a boat often ends as a kitchen stove without any obviously clear transitions. Often when play violates the line of adult logic we can see that it has a special kind of coherence all its own—perhaps the coherence of an action rather than a thinking pattern. Playing dentist may take the form of sitting on a keg and whirling one's feet around because the wonderful dentist's chair is the outstanding recall for the child. Teeth and drills may be altogether omitted while the child accentuates through his play what impressed him most. It makes sense in child terms even though it may not to the adult who is told that the children are playing dentist when what meets the eye looks like a crowd of whirling dervishes. To understand children's play we must loose our imaginations from the restrictions of adultness and the limitations of logic that is tied in within literalness and objective reality.

If free play is to yield these values in terms of children's growth needs, it requires a skilled guiding hand, especially when children are collected in groups as they are in nursery schools. There is a way of setting the stage and creating an atmosphere for spontaneous play. Most important in this atmosphere is the teacher's sensitive understanding of her own role. Sometimes the teacher needs to be ready to guide the play, especially among the fives, sixes, and sevens, into channels that are beyond the needs of the nursery years. But she must guide only in terms of the children's growth needs. Her guidance may be in terms of her choice of stories, materials, trips, experiences. It may function through discussions. Without skillful guidance, a free play program for successive years can become stultified and disturbing to children.

One of the main problems with respect to play which we are working through as teachers is: How much shall the teacher get involved in the children's play? Shall she correct, suggest, contribute, participate? I do not have the answer, but I hope teachers will continue to think about and talk about this problem. We have still to discover what the optimal points are at which the teacher can step in, offering new material or ideas to enrich the play. In our teacher-training institutes we encourage teachers to have imagination and use it, but if you teach this too well, the teachers themselves (and this goes for parents too) will be expressing themselves in the play, and before you know it they will have taken the play away from the child. This, naturally, is closely related to teacher personality. Some people intuitively know when it is best to withdraw and take a passive role, when a new idea will not be an intrusion, and when stimulation had best be indirect. It behooves us all as teachers to think: Are we stimulating and developing the children by our active teaching, or are we becoming so active that the children are overwhelmed and restricted by the flood of our bright ideas?

Day in, day out, we affect children's play by the things we provide them to play with. We choose equipment and materials with care and thought and have accepted the premise that a good share of play materials should be of the "raw" variety—things like clay, blocks, paper, mud, which the child can freely shape to his own purposes and upon which he can impress his own pattern. These are in contrast to the dolls and trains, trucks and doll dishes which come in finished form and are adapted, as established symbols, into the flow of the child's free play. One of the interesting questions in education today has to do with what balance shall be kept between raw and finished materials, recognizing that each kind serves a different function with respect to play and may meet varying needs of individual children.

To return briefly to the point that children's play cannot always be understood from the vantage point of logic and realistic accuracy: The inner coherence of play is as often based on emotion as it is on logic or action. If it seems incomprehensible, rambling, or slightly insane it is because we cannot read the deep emotional life of children, because we do not understand adequately how feeling can transform thought, at all ages.

We know that children are full of feeling—deep and good, hard and strong feelings. They get mad and glad with intensity. Their feelings are as quick, as volatile as they are deep. This vital aspect of their life experience needs outlet through play quite as much as their developing curiosities and their effervescent energies. Many of us who can accept play as a child's way of interpreting life intellectually often stop short at allowing children full freedom in expressing the feeling aspects of their lives. Or else we make the error of thinking of emotional expression of this kind in terms of negative feeling, of avoiding repression of hostility and such. This, to be sure, is an important aspect of wholesome growth. The chance to express negative feeling through play can save the child considerable anguish. The dolls he is allowed to hit leave him better able to face his real-life troubles successfully.

But there is the positive aspect of a child's emotional life, which should not be overlooked. Covering the doll lovingly with layers of blankets is as deep and important an experience as the smacking and the spanking. What we must remember through all of this is that the child does not necessarily play out what his actual experience has been. He may instead be playing out the residue of feeling which his experience has left him with—quite another dimension psychologically. It has been possible only to indicate this latter point briefly.

Summing up, we can say that play serves two different growth needs in the early years: learning about the world by playing about it (realizing reality), and finding an outlet for complex and often conflicting emotions (wherein reality and logic are secondary). We adults need to understand this process more deeply than we do and to continue to improve our techniques for providing experiences through play by means of which the child can freely express feeling and creatively master reality.

Cognitive–Affective Synthesis: The Play Experience

The Nature of the Experience

Play is the young child's way of satisfying the basic impulse to experiment and explore—to move from the known to the less known—and to rehearse—to deepen and solidify what is already mastered territory. In playing it is possible to think through, to assimilate experience in piecemeal fashion, stripped of the contextual complexity of experience-in-the-real. The thinking, judging, problem-solving is child generated; situations are created that lead to new questions and new problems to be solved, in situ, so to speak. Concurrent with the objective learning experience there is an implicit learning about oneself in terms of capacity to do, to think, to imagine, and confidence in one's powers to create a miniworld of one's own. The potential value of the experience depends, of course, on the climate provided and structured by the adults who create the school setting for play activity; on whether the children's unique level of absorption and the intense attention they give to their play configurations are recognized as positive factors.

Play is both content and process. Play is a self-initiated elaboration of some piece of mastery. Dramatic play is essentially an elaboration of mastery in the conceptual plane—namely, the capacity to symbolize, to depart from fixed connotations and to move in a universe of "as if" meanings and representations. Whatever the play, whether macrocosmic or microcosmic in Erikson's terms (1950 [1963]), the experience has obvious positive qualities for the children. It is distinct from other experiences: there are no directions to follow; the child can indulge and act out the course of his own associations—both feelings and ideas—no matter how far from reality they may be, without being corrected or censured; he is his own author and stage manager as he selects from the complex, often confusing, reality of his daily living the piece of action or meaning or feeling that he wants to relive and with what symbolic forms he wants to reproduce it and rehearse it. He may be creating his own private world or he may find interchanging his thinking and his active playing with other children fulfilling and stimulating. Even though the content of their play often symbolizes some of the sadder, frightening aspects of being young in a perplexing grown-up world, the children, almost universally, enjoy the experience deeply.

The maturing process of symbolization appears in personal form in changing self-roles, from "being" babies and dogs for the three-year-olds to "playing as though" they were jailers or captains a few years later. The shift of identity establishes a safe distance between self-identity and symbolized identity, expressed in the shift between the three-year-old's saying "I'm a dog" and the older children's "Let's pretend." There is also the transforming and maturing of object meanings: the blocks at first are cars, pushed along on the floor by the three-year-old until, within a few years, the same blocks are the substantial

In this paper I have included excerpts from three presentations I have given on the subject of play: "Play as a growth process: New directions," in *The Creative Process*, ed. C. B. Winsor (New York: Bank Street College, 1976); "Play experience as a developmental process," address to Phi Beta Kappa assembly, Barnard College, New York, April 1979; and "Theory into practice: What play is and what it isn't," address to Conference on Play, cosponsored by Hasbro Center for Child Development and Education, and Loyola University of Chicago, Washington, D.C., May 1979.

means for a complex representation of a skyscraper with an airplane landing on the roof. The symbolized figures and objects perform repetitive action patterns—go in and out, open and close, up and down, across—at first by gesture. Later the same patterns appear in the new forms of elaborate constructions of doorways, gates, elevators, and bridges. The play objects are used to simulate the change processes that alter the nature and quality of things—washing, cooking, cleaning—with increasing observance of the real way in which these processes are carried on outside the play world.

Dramatic play in school evolves usually from a one- or two-child activity to a complex interacting social process, encompassing advanced forms of verbal interchange, cooperative construction projects, preplanned as well as spontaneous action and plot sequences. In the advancing stages of socialized play we see projected a whole range of modes of interchange and possible roles.

In the children's progressing play it is a long thinking distance between the three-year-old's playing a mail carrier, dramatically laden down with a heavy bag of letters which are offered as presents to anyone who will take one, to the seven-year-old group's building of a post office with signs and chutes for geographic destinations, a spot for postmarking letters, and a window for selling stamps. The course of this thinking has qualities specific to the fact that the thinking is part of a play process. Where ideas are going to lead is undirected, and the enactment of one idea may generate new questions to be put through the symbolization process, new possibilities for roles to be taken, and a flowing "what if" thinking stance in planning new action—altogether a permanently important paradigm for the cognitive process.

It is not easy to distinguish these developmental cognitive changes that are age- and stage-connected from what seem to be personality trends—styles of behavioral response. In the interpersonal relationships that are part of the fabric of the play we see domination–submission patterns in some children's play, as well as instances of repeated patterns of mutually satisfying interchange in the play of others. Some children take the "helper" role; some are the "idea" people, while others struggle to bring the blocks into congruence with their images; some are sure it will come out right, others that "it'll never work." In the progressing elaboration of social play, we see not only young social relations and adaptive thinking but also the projection of self-feeling— maybe a passing mood of conquest or defeat. To the teacher it is significant and worrisome when for some child the pattern, the content, or the mood quality is repetitive day after day rather than being alternatively responsive to the changing course of reality experience and the stimulus to try new schemes generated within the play experience itself.

We also observe certain differences in thematic patterns, indicating either transitory or lasting individual differences in the imaginative processes. Some play episodes are almost like free association; others are time-consistent scenic places. Some move through free-flowing verbal discourse, some in clear plot sequence. Some involve a lot of object manipulation; others build on words. On the other hand, events in terms of content have recurrent themes that can be developmental-stage located, to a degree—for example, being left behind, going away and coming back, hiding and being discovered are likely to appear at younger ages than escaping, killing, dying and coming to life again.

An Elaborating Concept

The development of play as a mode of learning had its most salient expression, I dare say, in the City and Country School and later, with variations, at the Bank Street School for Children. In fact, in its early beginnings, the City and Country School was called the Play School, but there was a clear rationale between play and learning. The heart of the matter was giving the children an opportunity to selectively and independently rehearse their experience, to reproduce symbolically the physical and ideational relationships of their ongoing encounters. The play action at any stage generates inquiry; the pursuit of the questions generated leads to changed action. While recognized as a cyclical process, it was not entirely self-fed in a learning-oriented play curriculum. It became the teacher's function to extend the children's direct experience in their environment, both for finding answers to their questions autonomously and for stimulating new lines of inquiry and content for play. The choice of materials, the setting, and the teacher's role, whether responding to the children's play directly or planning some new relevant experience outside school boundaries, composed what in another milieu would have been called an instructional method. It is interesting to note the different individual emphases and contributions of the early thinkers who valued blocks as the ideal medium for play and made play the center of the learning environment for young children.

To Caroline Pratt (Winsor, 1974) it was essential that the child be offered concrete but highly adaptable materials with which to "play" his way toward understanding. She invented a unit system of plain wooden blocks as a tool for realizing ideas in concrete form. Since they have no given representative content, they offer the greatest latitude for the child's own imaginative processes to move back and forth between idea and thing. Because they are constructed in varying scaled sizes, based on a unit system, they are suited to working elaborately with dimensions of the thing universe—verticals, horizontals, balance, proportion, enclosures, exits, entrances, steps, slopes, tunnels, bridges, and so forth. In Miss Pratt's "pure" approach, supplementary objects needed for projecting action and people (doll figures, cars, and so on) were also "raw" in character, preferably fashioned by the children themselves, but always with a minimum of prestated representative meanings. What was provided for play had the quality of openness and universality; specificity of meaning was endowed by what the child projected. Any physical object could live many symbolic lives.

Lucy Mitchell (1934 [1963]) also sought the materials and context that would make it possible for the young child to play back his experience, through projection of images and symbolic enactment of relationships, as he begins to perceive them in the world around. She had especial interest in the play that reenacted "work processes," in where and how imaginative leaps in play sprang from the child's direct experience with the way work is done in his life environment, close to or far from home. With the benefit of planned trips into the extended environment, his play schemes became early learning adventures into human geography.

Harriet Johnson (1933 [1974]) added another perspective. She pointed to the child's use of blocks as an art form in which there is a developmental sequence in the mastery of techniques: repetition, bridging, enclosures, balance, patterning, decorative embellishments. From the perspective of aesthetics, constructions may have value per se and satisfaction as "designs." Or they may be used as the media for symbolic expression of experience. In either case she pointed to the basic aesthetic elements in the use of the unit blocks as material, in simple and elaborated form, that persist at later stages when building with blocks becomes the means for engaging in dramatic play—when the child, in her words, "speaks with his blocks."

At the same time that the City and Country School and the Bank Street School for Children were giving play a central position in the curriculum for the early years—the 1930s—the Play Schools Association was operating a program in several elementary public schools in New York City to supplement the regular program through afterschool and summer sessions. In searching old sources, I find Clara Lambert's pamphlet (1948), published originally in 1938, describing the theory and practice of the Play Schools Association. In a short space she successfully presented a comprehensive view (including illustrative material) not only of how to make play a learning medium but also of how children use it to express their conflicts, desires, and hopes about their place in the world.

She showed early insight into the relation between children's perceptions and emotions (the children were a low-economic-level population) and the kind of knowledge of their real-life situation that teachers needed for sensitive, competent functioning. Her small pamphlet had the special value of being both clearly stated theoretically and lavishly illustrated from observation enriched by feelings of empathy for the children and their families. She described a population aspiring to upward job mobility, and, in their play, she saw the children's introjection of their parents' rejection of their own humble occupations and stations in life. I quote: "Even worse than this attitude toward lowly jobs is the feeling of shame attached to joblessness and relief. Some children playing about with puppets one day put on a spontaneous dramatization. . . . One puppet was elegantly dressed in red satin and lace, the second was a replica of Charlie Chaplin in his tramp days, and the third was a nondescript man. The elegant lady disposed of this last character, 'Scram, you reliefer.' "

Another perspective—play as a way of resolving conflict—was introduced from outside the sphere of progressive education and was later absorbed into it, in different ways by different educators. "Reading the language of play," to use Lawrence Frank's phrase, acquired new depths when it was understood that young play, as it moves back and forth between reality and fantasy, not only *mirrors* the child's thoughts, feelings, wishes, and fears but is a means by which the child can work out and gain strength vis-à-vis emotional problems that he cannot deal with directly in the open stream of events and relationships. The symbolizing process, enacted with things, activities, identities, and relationships, provides the safety of distance, freedom to express unacceptable or frightening affect, catharsis to make up for defeats and frustrations. It was this aspect of play experience that interested students of personality most—Lois Murphy, Ruth Hartley, Lawrence Frank, Susan Isaacs, and others. Only gradually, and in some places, did it become part of educational thinking.

It was part of a period when prevention was a dominant theme in psychiatry, when there was interest at the national level in the quality of life experience for the individual that would promote positive mental health, when the potency of the early years of childhood had been accepted, and when the idea that a certain kind of education might be one road toward the mental health goal was in the air in Washington. It was in this climate that the National Institute of Mental Health supported an observational study of play in which the teacher's role in creating a setting for "educational therapy" was clearly explicated (Hartley, Frank, & Goldensen, 1952). Subsequently, there was confusion about the limits of the teacher's therapeutic educational role and argument about the merit of interpretations to children, based, as they were, on assumptions about underlying motivations.

In giving play an important position in the education design, we are thinking on two developmental fronts. *First*, we talk about play as an important thinking medium, meaning that play action not only symbolizes what is understood but also generates curiosity and new inquiry. The answers the child generates in his play to his own incipient questions bear varying and changing degrees of resemblance to reality. His play is a blend of the way things are perceived and understood as far as they can be within the limits of his experience and a flight toward what they might be when they are not understood. As he moves toward the transition years of six and seven, the play moves closer to reproducing reality and reflects the knowledge accrued through both his play and formal learning skills.

The *second* process, the feeling and emotional phases of experience, is simultaneously interwoven with the speaking, role-taking, action patterns of the total play process. The desires, the wishes, and the hopes are mirrored in the roles, the conversation, and the action patterns of the play. Under the cover of the symbols we see the wishes for strength, for power, or maybe for escape from pressure. The symbolizing provides safety for expressing otherwise unacceptable feelings of hate and anger, and it is believed that this symbolized expression decreases the toll that unexpressed hostility would otherwise take in the developing personality. Clinicians provided insight into this aspect of the positive potential of play experience before it became part of educators' perspective.

The Teacher's Role

The goal from this perspective was to develop teachers who could think broadly and deeply about possible motivations, be imaginative about how to help resolve conflicts through the action and relationship possibilities in the educational situation available to them, and, finally, keep a keen observational eye open in readiness to correct original hypotheses about motivation. For example, aggressive behavior, direct or symbolized, might indeed be the displaced outcome of anger against the indulged new baby. On the other hand, it might also be the expression of temporary imbalance among wished-for, imagined new kinds of competence for which necessary skills are not yet available. These alternative interpretations obviously dictate different teacher roles. That opens up a hard-to-resolve problem in the field of teacher education: how to develop teachers who can sustain the thinking stance of the scientist—observe, hypothesize, act; observe, rethink, act accordingly, and so forth—and at the same time sustain the quality of certainty and confidence in their actions that young children, especially, need from adults. We have been provided with a full account (Katz, in press) of the presumed subliminal associations of a teacher, related to a conflict between two children on the matter of taking turns on a tricycle. The teacher's thinking may have developmental or personality referents, for example: "Will Robin or Leslie's present pattern of behavior cause either of them trouble later on if it is left unattended now?" or "Perhaps this is the first time Leslie exhibits self-assertion and this is a sign of overcoming shyness." These are illustrations of what Katz calls "clinical" judgments, "the processes of taking into account the meaning of the behavior of each individual child."

Apart from the questions of learning and conflict resolution, it is important to see in spontaneous dramatic play the essence of experience with freedom from the restrictions of adult logic and control, with sense of strength and confidence in one's own impulses, with pleasure in re-creating the world in one's own terms—an ideal paradigm for autonomous and creative functioning and, one hopes, a psychological stance, established early, with which to withstand the pressures toward conformity and the safety of subservience waiting in the world outside. That was part of our original rationale and central to our value systems.

Regression

There came a period when play became the whipping boy to those psychologists who constructed programs in early childhood focused on correcting for presumed cognitive deficits of children from low economic populations. Play was regarded as largely expendable in the curriculum, an extra-learning appendage. The educator's responsibility was to be fulfilled by a variety of techniques for advancing cognitive facility—prescribed cognitive tasks, concept rehearsal, programmed learning, and others—representing direct teaching of cognitive processes such as differentiation and classification (Bereiter & Engelmann, 1966; Deutsch, 1967). What had happened?

The educators who for years had done yeoman service in the interest of stimulating thinking as an indigenous part of play experience never used the term *cognition*. They regarded thinking about experience, so organized as to be tool-worthy for more thinking, as the core of the teacher's function. Play was the child's way of stating knowledge and confronting new questions. The seeming overemphasis on social-emotional development as compared to intellectual growth in the educational literature came about because the social-emotional aspect of the educational process had scarcely been recognized at all. It needed to be made more explicit. One way was to point to how play also served this developmental need. Thus, the learning–thinking function of play was taken too much for granted, left too implicit in the total philosophy; consequently, because ideas have a drift of their own, it lost a certain priority in some of the exemplars within the early childhood profession itself. But play as a mode of thinking had a healthy, continuous history at Bank Street and at the City and Country School and other institutions with a similar philosophy.

When psychologists made a hurried entrance into the field, many reacted to surfaces and immediacy. The brief historical overviews which were presented as background for antipoverty projects bespeak lack of knowledge of the theory, content, and methodology of well-established play-curriculum philosophy and the extent to which thinking as much as social development was of central concern. The result has been wasteful. Much that was tried in the compensatory programs did not work out, partly because available knowledge and insight were not exploited. Criticism can be distributed both ways: those who knew a great deal spoke and wrote too little; others moved too fast on what they did not know enough about.

Recovery

That brings us, happily, to great resurgence of interest in the play of childhood (Bruner, Jolly, & Sylva, 1976).[2] By four different criteria, I think it is fair to say that the subject has achieved maturity in the psychological domain and shares the characteristics, good and bad, of other major areas in psychology. *First,* observational, inferential formulations are being supplemented by systematic hypothesis-testing studies. *Second,* there are controversial theoretical alignments about what play is and what its function encompasses. *Third,* a developmental course with reference to stages and environment has been formulated. *Fourth,* there is a changed perspective on play in relation to learning. From the wealth of material available, I want to select a few examples to illustrate these four trends in the progressing maturity of play as a field for investigation and for more refined enactment in education.

1. Assumption Testing
One study (Freyberg, 1973), employing a control-group design, found that

2. In this comprehensive volume there are 71 individual contributions which review the importance of play in the context of animal evolution and child development, its role in dealing with the world of objects and tools, and its position in evolving social roles and in the mastery of the basic symbol systems (see also Stern, 1978).

kindergarten children of lower-economic-level population responded as hypothesized to training sessions in which *story plots were played out* for them by the investigator, using props, toy figures, sounds, talk, and make-believe roles. The children were *invited to pick up the themes* and carry the play through in their own ways. "Once the idea caught on with the group, the investigator was largely excluded and the plots took all kinds of spontaneous, original, and sometimes surprising turns." This group showed *significantly greater and more lasting improvement* in imaginativeness, positive affect, and concentration than the control group, who were given jigsaw puzzles to assemble and Tinkertoy materials to play with but no stimulation on how to play. The inference is not that the children in the experimental group learned how to play in these short sessions but that the experience served as a catalyst to develop skills already within the resources of the child that remain latent under conditions of limited experiential background and cognitive stimulation. This finding parallels the experience of teachers in the early Headstart days who decided that, for children from the low economic group, they needed to take more active roles in stimulating dramatic play than they had been accustomed to doing. In a short time, these children, too, became the initiators.

In another study (Fein, Branch, & Diamond, 1975) the relation between the type of toy, age, and sex of child at the 20- to 26-month period was investigated through systematic observation, rating, and statistical procedures. In this study the term *less prototypical* is used to mean less cup-like cups, less truck-like trucks, and so forth. The investigators assumed on the basis of developmental cognitive theory, and it was borne out, that children at this stage would depend more on "high prototypical" materials and that symbolic pretend use of the "less prototypical" (less literally representative) materials would increase only gradually with age. Another investigator (Stern, 1975) reports a similar trend in a systematic observational study of children between three and five years of age, in a naturalistic school situation. In her terminology, the children as they grow older tend to use the clearly representative signifiers less and the semirepresentative signifiers more.

In a review of nonverbal representation Franklin (1973) reports findings which corroborate the sequence from use of realistic toys in the earlier stages to the kind of dramatic play by older children that involves use and construction of less realistic objects. Noting, however, that this sequence is not reported universally in other studies, she raises the broader question of other types of correspondence that may underlie symbolic meaning besides the resemblance dimension represented in "realistic" vs. "unrealistic." She draws on Werner's (1957a) psychological correspondence concept: "Early apprehension of the world is structured in terms of global, affective, action-dynamic qualities." Early symbolic constructions, formed on the basis of such properties, may show little resemblance to that which they represent. Attention to similarities that are less global, more specific and differentiated is presumed to come later.

Franklin (1983) takes exception to the view that describes the trend toward increasing "realism" in pretend play as universal without considering the extent to which many children develop an interest in fairy tales or find their own ways for inventing nonrealistic sagas. She sees the maturing process, instead, as a developmental trend toward greater "inner coherence" whether the content is reality oriented or fantastical, expressed in self-imposed standards of consistency in the way roles are enacted and aspects of scale and style projected. From this perspective pretend play interweaves realistic and fantastic elements, creating "dramas of childhood play (which) would seem to have much more in common with the myth-making, literary works, and even scientific theory-building than with conventionalized rule-governed games."

These views lead me to recall the seemingly orthodox position that Caroline Pratt took on providing "raw" materials for children's play at the City and Country School, meaning those materials which allowed greatest leeway for the child's projections. In this connection I recall Irma Black,[3] who was a teacher of two-year-olds at Bank Street in the 1930s. Free spirit that she was, Irma did not accept the orthodox theory of "raw" materials for those young children. She added materials to her toy shelves that had a closer resemblance to the objects they represented and invited us in to see how much preferred they were by most of the two-year-olds for their play. But were there also some children whose early play reflected the insights of Pratt or of Werner's theory or who were like some of the young children in Biber's study of drawing, who found less visually accurate ways for indicating resemblance from the beginning?

In Garvey's study of play (1977) we have access to a comprehensive, experimentally designed study of play processes. The study situation was a play setup, separate from the children's preschool location but similar as a surround to what we would find in a play-oriented schoolroom. Sets of three preschool children at a time were observed in the course of their free play in this room, with maximum care to relieving the strangeness of the situation for the children. Among the play themes that parallel findings from observational data, the study reports a high frequency of planned play that deals with "treating and healing" and even higher frequency for the episodes labeled *averting threat.* Some results, however, appear contrary to live school observations—for example, the finding that the children play out stereotyped roles, with restricted scope of action, in their impersonation of characters such as cowboy, fire fighter, witch, or nurse.

2. Theoretical Differences

In the past, different theories about play seemed to be able to live at peace beside one another, accepted as representing different interpretative perspectives as well as different kinds of concrete knowledge about how different children play. This is no longer true. Theories collide while the arduous task of gathering evidence is gaining headway. For example, the role of play in relation to cognition has had an irregular history. As I have mentioned, the traditional view that

3. I. S. Black occupied the position of chairman, Publications Division, Bank Street College of Education, until her retirement in 1972.

play is play and learning is learning, and not at all in the service of each other, influenced the designs for several of the antipoverty early-childhood programs. But at the same time, there was growing allegiance to the Piagetian view of play as the natural and important mode in childhood whereby new experience could be assimilated into the child's existing system of ideas and find temporary equilibrium with previous experience and individual needs. Balanced by the changes involved in the process of accommodating to reality, the developmental sequence of play experience, in this view, is regarded as an integral part of the development of intelligence.

But there was discontent with a view of the play process that failed to encompass the function of play as reflecting affect, positive and negative, and affording a means toward clarification and relief of emotional problems. A carefully recorded, continuous account (Curry, 1972) of the way children played out a traumatic experience (they saw a man fall to the ground from the bucket of a crane-like machine) documents the cognitive–affective interaction view. I quote: "The children in addition to and while mastering their anxieties through play had achieved some cognitive gains. The space play triggered by the accident increased the children's interest in and understanding of outer space, its danger as well as the scientific principles involved in its mastery (gravity, distance, etc.)." Curry leans toward Sutton-Smith's concept of the transformational nature of play: essential change in content being contributed by the child's internal dynamics.

Sutton-Smith (1971a) argues that Piaget's (1962) analysis of the role of play deals only with convergent conceptual processes—the mode of logic—and is inadequate with reference to the divergent processes of creativity, originality, and expressiveness. Sutton-Smith (1971b) sees play as a distinct phenomenon involving transformation of feelings, volitions, and thought through imaginative structures which have a character of their own. More would be understood, he claims, if play were studied as a phenomenon per se rather than as an epiphenomenon related to major cognitive or affective processes. When connoted as playfulness, it represents a transformation of feelings, volitions, and thoughts into novel combinations which are internalized as a sustained expressive system, related to creativity, originality, and imagination—the divergent rather than the convergent processes. He distinguishes playfulness from the four modes of knowing—exploration, imitation, testing, and world construction—which the child pursues and elaborates through play activity.

This view is supplemental rather than alternative to the position that play has been given with respect to cognitive development and conflict resolution. The thesis is that there are qualities involved in play activity distinct from and in addition to the ways in which it helps the child "know" his world and feel mastery in it. In part, this refers to the playing around subsequent to the phase of mastery. More importantly, it seems to refer to what empathic observers of children's play have noted previously and to what one might call the subjective aspects of the play experience or affect feedback. Sutton-Smith calls it phenomenological satisfaction, referring to the pleasure derived from the novelty of one's responses, from having been the initiator of the action, and the positive feeling that one's own way of doing things is so much fun.

In this same vein, taking a more comprehensive view of play as life experience, Singer (1973) writes: "The essential point is that if we regard make-believe play and its subsequent development as an 'as if' attitude or capacity for fantasy and daydreaming *as a skill* rather than as an outcome of some conflict, we can see this skill as being available within the personality repertory for a great variety of functions . . . [to] be put into the service of a great range of human desires." He sees dramatic play as one phase of the lifelong function of fantasy, not as a bridge which leads from young, egocentric, cognitive modes to mature, objective mastery of reality. From this view, the fantasy mechanisms of dramatic play are not lost to the progressive maturing of logical processes but remain an important cognitive skill throughout life, internalized into private symbolism, constituting the ideational material of daydreams and reverie. The basic "as if" attitude, the capacity for fantasy, the facility in divergent thinking and ideational fluency are, in total, regarded as important potential within the personality repertoire for a great variety of functions. There is increasing individual variation at later stages in the functions served by fantasy with respect, for example, to creativity, release of aggression, or internalized self-image. In this view, imaginative-play predisposition is viewed as a personality trait. There is a growing impression from the wealth of contemporary studies that the dramatic play of the preschool child is part of a lifelong developmental process, reaching back to the sensorimotor experience of infancy and forward to the internalized, symbolized fantasy of mature life.

Another comprehensive concept of the function of play comes from another field, in a book aptly called *Transformations: An Anthropology of Children's Play*. The author (Schwartzman, 1978) disputes the idea that play is a distortion of reality and that play illusions come gradually to correspond to true reality. In contrast, she argues that play creates its own reality, which is characterized, in part, by an *allusion* to, not a *distortion* of, events—*allusion* meaning a figurative or symbolic reference. The nature of the process is such that it needs investigators tolerant of disorganization, unpredictability, loose and fuzzy definition to produce theories that will *allude* to play with the quality of flexibility that characterizes the anthropologist's way of studying people in their own terms.

3. Developmental Course: Stages and Environment
How the child moves from being a sensorimotor response system to being a symbolizing mind is a field of inquiry that fascinates, challenges, and disturbs. Our knowledge in this field falls short of mastery as the dimensions of inquiry shift among investigators.

In contrast to Piaget's formulation (1962), El'Konin (1971) gives language a central role in the symbolization process that takes place in play. The relationship of speech to the objects and activities of play changes significantly in the course of the preschool years. Following Vygotsky (1978), El'Konin suggests that an early stage in which speech follows the activity with the object is replaced by the kind of play in which the naming of objects influences the course of the play: "The original relationship object-action-word is changed into a fundamentally new relationship: word-object action" in which the author sees the "emancipation of the word from the thing" on the path toward the processes of abstract thought in later stages.

Franklin (1983) also takes the position that language or, more accurately, speaking serves an important function in the play process, related to stabilizing and organizing the action and experience involved. She illustrates multiple ways in which children verbally establish a sphere of play as distinct from reality, among them, assigning unrealistic identities to objects, agreeing as to what is to be the "play space," speaking in the character of an assumed role, and preplanning the course and content of the projected play activity. But she does not adhere to the commonly accepted concept of sequence toward predominantly realistic dramatic play. Instead she illustrates persisting interest in fantastical play expressed, at times, by indulging in contradiction and paradox and, perhaps, satisfaction of unconscious wishes. In this view, advancing maturity is expressed not in a sequence from fantasy to reality but rather in new modes of dealing with ongoing reality-oriented or fantastical play, exemplified, in later stages of development, in the way roles are enacted and with respect to matters of scale and style. From this perspective, language serves not only a reflecting or communicating function in play experience but is intrinsic also to formulation and creation of meaning that is part of the imaginative re-creation of experience.

Do all children go through a stage of dramatic play, in accord with Piagetian theory? Smilansky (1968) answers in the negative: the culturally deprived Israeli children, between ages three and seven, did not spontaneously engage in dramatic play but moved toward rule-governed play forms instead. Eifermann (1971) offers contrary findings: children from a similar sociocultural group that she studied in Israel did not skip the symbolic play but came to it at a later developmental period. The question of ages and stages continues to haunt us years after some of us argued with Gesell about the errors and dangers of his normative age profiles (Gesell, Halverson, Thompson, Ilg, & Costner, 1940). Beyond the disagreement as to whether a developmental stage can be skipped or whether it is just differently placed chronologically, there is a common inference: the specific nature of the family and cultural milieu is a crucial factor in determining the pattern in which a given developmental potential is realized.

In our own country, teachers report that the play and play productions of children entering Headstart and day care centers differ in quality from those of children from middle-class populations in preschool settings. These observations and other cross-cultural studies point to the error of treating developmental trends as universal when investigations have been limited to a selected child population, as was the case in earlier studies of play, Piaget's as well as our own. Consensus on this question is in line with work in other psychological domains on the issue of invariance of developmental stages. There are developmental sequences in play, but the expression of given potentials is a function of how much these potentials are nurtured and elicited by family and cultural milieu.

There is an increasing number of studies that document the ways in which the conditions of the life environment influence the forms and sequence of play as a developmental process and appear to inhibit the appearance of symbolizing play activity. Deprivation of primary needs creates an inhibitory emotional tone not conducive to playing (Mattick, 1965). In authoritarian, hierarchical family cultures, play is likely to remain imitative, on a work-like level. Children from deprived families, whether in our urban slums or the uprooted Israeli families, are more likely to play in the testing and contesting modes related to survival in threatening environments, though they respond to stimulation on how to play symbolically when the opportunity is offered. Obviously, study in the future will need to be designed in the context of interactional processes between the developing human organism and the specific influencing factors of given environments.

4. The Changed Perspective

When we consider the learning functions served by play, we are on familiar ground, but here, too, there are new developments as well as conflicting views. Where play is regarded positively as an energizer and organizer of cognitive learning, the educational position leans toward providing variation and widened scope of play opportunity. This runs counter to purposes and methods that are based on direct training in cognitive skills and where learning and play are seen as antitheses of one another.

New methods of coding observational data have been worked out to permit more differentiated analysis (Stern, Bragdon, & Gordon, 1976). Quantification makes it possible to pursue hypothetical formulations concerning, for example, the relation between play in early childhood and later academic proficiency or personality development, or between the nature of child's play and the expression of aggression in real situations (Singer, 1973). The utilization of more systematic methods of study—techniques for coding observations, quantitative analysis of data, experimental studies, and formulation of hypothetical, sequential, and causal relations—represents an increasingly disciplined approach to understanding play in early childhood (Weisler & McCall, 1976).

Perception of play as learning has gained new dimensions as the result of Piaget's (1962) analysis of the function of play. The work of Piaget and of Almy (1968), among others, has contributed significant theoretical foundation for the previously perceived linkage between play and cognitive processes and, ipso facto, for the importance of play in relation to learning. From Piaget's view, symbolic play is part of the assimilation process: that phase of cognitive dynamics by which a child absorbs and integrates experience in terms of his own repertoire of wishes, previous habits, concepts, and so on. He blends reality to fit what he "knows." Adjustment to objective reality is deemphasized. Through play, new abilities—physical and conceptual—are retained and remain available as precursors for further development and the ability to cope with the symbol systems essential to competent functioning in reality.

Similarly, the concept of dramatic play as a central process in the emotional life of the child has acquired changed meanings. When play was perceived primarily as a process of catharsis, it appeared as a medium for fulfilling wishes and resolving conflicts which could not be managed in reality. Both pleasure and mastery were involved. In the more recent ego psychology of Hartmann and Erikson, play has a place as an autonomous ego function, including a drive toward mastery of reality through experimenting and planning maneuvers in play activity, independent of the need for conflict resolution. Psychoanalytic theory, once predominantly in the service of clinical material, has been applied as the conceptual base for understanding play observations of normal children made by teachers and assistant teachers (Gould, 1972).

Psychodynamic views on the value of play in meeting the need to master anxiety by displacement and to work through normal developmental conflicts through symbolic projection were somewhat lost in the wave of interest in cognitive capacity. The psychodynamic view is currently gaining renewed interest as there is growing recognition of the interdependence of cognitive and affective factors. An elaborate play scheme about a sinking boat can scarcely be understood, motivationally or conceptually, without recognizing the simultaneity of cognitive–affective play elements.

The value of play experience in the socialization process has long been recognized: the lessening egocentrism, the extended empathic sensitivity, and the adaptive modes for making a going play scheme that meets one's own and another's perceptions and wishes. In some places, at present, this function of play is brought into focus and lends a certain direction to the teacher's role. From one perspective, we can see an analogy here between the course of socialization in play and what is posited for the developmental relations of play and cognition. A tentative equation suggests itself: the positive give-and-take and the working acceptance of another's view in early play experience may be to mature social development what the symbolizing play process is claimed to be to the more mature ability to deal with abstractions.

The Teacher's Role—Once More

This brings us back to the teacher's role in providing the kind of stimulation, attitude, and insight that will support the emergence of this human potential. It is now expected that the teacher's way of guiding the play experiences—how to facilitate, listen, perceive, and set the stage—will be based on a theoretical understanding of the course of development in the early years and how play experience can be emotionally supportive and intellectually generative at the same time. It is expected that the materials and experiences provided to stimulate play and the climate of aware, interested, but nondirective teacher contact with the playing, as it goes on, will be sensitively matched to the cognitive frontiers and the affective concerns of the children—both as individuals and as members of a developmental stage. It is clearer now that there can be no fixed rules as to when to intervene—as protector or stimulator, as the case may be— exactly because of the importance of applying general precepts to the particularities of the situation. In a sense, the teacher is asked to analyze and nourish the play simultaneously and try to achieve the best possible match.

The increased awareness of differences in the way children from different subcultural and sociocultural settings play is a second factor indicating the importance of a variable role for the teacher. The teacher's way of leading children toward the symbolization experience and toward facility in elaborating it dramatically has to be adjusted to the stress conditions of children's lives, to the meanings of objects, the precepts, the idea systems of the subculture, as well as to family attitudes toward the value of playing, and certainly toward its place in school—the institution for learning.

Gain and Loss over the Years

The progress made in moving the play experience to a more integral place in the national educational scheme is modest; by contrast, understanding of its function in development has progressed among educators and takes a major place in psychological research activity. Though only on a small scale in terms of national programs, there is increasing understanding of the play process by teachers as an integral developmental process. Some of the advance is represented in the nature of the questions being considered individually by teachers as well as in formal educational meetings. I have referred to some of these questions already: how to judge when, as a teacher, to offer supplementary stimulation to the children's play enactments, when to judge fantasy as potentially traumatic and in need of control; how to move a child out of a fixed role, how to take a cue from the play content as to what next reality experience will be stimulating to thinking and different playing, and, in general, how to support without intruding.

Play's loss of place in the curriculum must be acknowledged whether we can meet it or not. Some of the deficit represents problems we can engage modestly on our own in our working settings, namely, how to communicate to parents and teachers our views on the importance of the play experience as a developmental and learning experience—especially to groups in the population which see skills proficiency as the road to survival and play as a luxury they cannot afford. Some of the loss is of a larger dimension, locked in with the regressive back-to-basics momentum on a national level and the associated relegation of play to the plane of amusement, when it is provided for at all. A more serious inroad on the educational process comes from the extended experience with television in all social classes and the increasing prominence of unreal characters in dramatic play who act out themes of power and conquest. Inevitably there is an associated loss of the experience of play as a medium for projecting and understanding reality and for dealing with the limitless range of feelings and ideas that are the given substance of childhood. The increasing negative influence of television on the nature of meaningful play in school is a problem to program planning in schools like Bank Street. As a result there is a tendency toward restricting the extent of TV play within the school program and toward increasing direct stimulation of experiential play by the teacher than was formerly considered desirable.[4]

If we take all of this into account, it is encouraging to note the esteemed place that play now holds in educational and psychological circles compared to its status fifty years ago, when it was viewed as a somewhat maverick concept in the minds of a few frontier educators.

4. This material is from an interview with Lia Gelb, associate dean for programs in education, Bank Street College of Education, New York, N.Y.

CHAPTER 10

Is There a Unitary Dimension Underlying Creative Activity?

Interest in understanding the creative process in ways that would support its fulfillment in the early years of schooling led me back to my file of records of preschool children in the 1930s and 1940s. How did these young children manage the mysteries? By what creative reorganization of the known elements of their experience did they find satisfactory ways of settling the unknown. It was highly stimulating subsequently to become acquainted with Chukovsky's penetrating interpretations of young children's verbal exchange which he had observed in the Soviet Union, with all its autonomy, poesy, and creative errors (1925[1963]).

Recently I found it interesting to pair selections from Chukovsky's and my own records of observations which illustrate the universality of emergent creative thinking and the basic human wish to understand beneath the surface. (A refers to the American, R to the Russian quotations.)

Existence

> *(R) Say, mother, when I was born, how did you find out that I was Yurochka?*

> *(A) Janet: "Once I was a wee, wee baby." Then she turned to Carolyn—"Once you were a wee, wee baby," and went around the table saying the same to each child. Each one was pleased. When she got to me (the teacher) she stopped and I said, "Once I was a wee, wee baby, too." She grinned. "Were you really?" I assured her and added, "And your mommy and daddy once were babies, too."*

> *At this she smiled, nodded, then hesitated and said, perplexedly, "But who wheeled me then?"*

(R) Alik thought of a good way to postpone the death of his mother: "Mommie, now I know everything. You'll eat yogurt both in the morning and in the evening, and I'll not eat it at all. That way we'll both die at the same time.

The World

(A) "What is behind the sky?" Teacher: "Air, Caroline, just like the air that is all around us." Caroline: "But how does the air get through the sky?" Teacher: "Well, you see the sky isn't hard, it really is all air." Caroline: "But why can't we see through it?" Teacher: "Because it is so very high and far away." Caroline: "But how did the sky get there?" Teacher: "It just happened." Caroline: "When did it happen?" David: "When there were no people." Teacher: "Yes, long ago, before there were people." John: "All the people were inside their mothers." Caroline: "No, all the people were in their houses with the door shut. They were asleep and the sky just happened. Now I know how the sky came."

(R) The mother was getting ready to bake some pies. The five-year-old daughter was sitting on the window sill. It was twilight. She asked: "Where do the stars come from?" The mother was a little slow in answering—she was busy with the dough. The girl followed her mother's motions and within a few minutes announced: "I know how stars are made! They make them from what is left over from the moon." This spontaneous thought was suggested to her by the process of preparing the dough for the crusts of the pies. She noticed how her mother . . . cut away from the large stretched piece the "leftover" bits and shaped from them the crusts for another dozen or so small pies.

(A) Riding on a bus on a trip passing a reservoir, Bobby said, "But I want to know where the water comes from." Sally: "It rains and snows and the snow melts." Bobby: "Well, where does that come from"—he answers himself—"from the clouds. Their stomachs get full and then they bust."

The reading stimulates a question: How much of these young ways of creating images of reality is sustained in later years toward the experience of continuously re-creating it?

Premature Structuring as a Deterrent to Creativity (1959)

From a variety of sources it is possible to derive a concept of creative teaching that can be related meaningfully, first, to the psychological problem of loss of individuality under the impact of socializing pressures in child rearing and education and, second, to the realities of teaching children in a classroom.*

I do not want to take the easy way of crossing the bridge between psychology of personality and teaching practice and say that the matter is simply whether or not the teacher herself is a creative personality. Not that one may safely or wisely deny the importance of this factor. Indeed, one might say that the teacher's personality is a necessary but not sufficient condition for the stimulation and support of creativity in children. The teacher, as an individual, may be one of those free spirits whose painting of a human figure can say "tired" without leaning over in a literally dejected posture, or whose note of consolation to a friend would not bear the slightest resemblance to a Western Union form. Her image of Abraham Lincoln may retain at its core the inner feeling of individual integrity and independence while its content is drawn factually from such contrasting sources as Carl Sandburg's weighty volumes and a fourth-grade reader's capsule on the Great Emancipator. In such a teacher, we may be guaranteed sensitivity to upsurges of spontaneous thinking and feeling in the children, but this is not yet the model of the creative teacher. In addition, she needs specific skills and techniques before we can assume that as a teacher she is contributing, not in a passive and diffuse manner, but directly, first, to the freedom of thought and feeling of the children, and second, to the disciplined mastery of form and technique. Through these techniques, fresh feeling and thought must be processed before spontaneity can be transformed into productive creativity.

Despite the critics of teacher education who talk so forcibly these days, qualified teachers, thus defined, do not arise, like Venus, from the waves of liberal arts colleges. If much of teacher education is faulty, and I tend to believe that it is, the answer is not: away with it, but rather: more and different.

In this paper I should like to take the position that the teacher's opportunity to support the creative potential of children is not entirely a function of her own creativeness, that it is not located preferentially in one subject matter as against another, and that it is not to be realized in any deification of easily perceived originality of art products or verbal forms. On the positive side, it is important to be aware of how much creativity in childhood might be nourished through known educational practices although ordinarily these may not be classified by educators as "creative" or perceived as such by philosophical and psychological students of the creative process.

The particular proposition I mean to develop is indicated in the title of this paper, namely, that education traditionally has imposed a structure of didactic instruction, right–wrong criteria, dominance of the logical-objective over the intuitive-subjective on the learning child so early in the course of emergent awareness of his world and of himself that, except for unusual individuals,

*Adapted from Premature structuring as a deterrent to creativity. *American Journal of Orthopsychiatry*, 1959, 24 (2), 280–90.

creative potential is inhibited or, at the least, diminished. The problem is not whether education is responsible for supplying children with tools, techniques, knowledge of their culture's present and past, and essential modes of social control and communication. There is no doubt that it is, and that to sustain a desirable degree of social-cultural continuity, it must fulfill this responsibility. The problem is how skillfully teachers can place these offerings within the developmental sequence that stretches between the phase of exposure and that of mastery, and how relaxed, imaginative, and generous they can be in nourishing and guiding the exposure phase. By an exposure phase I mean two things: (1) the early years of childhood when the child is exposed to the world's wealth of sensations and relations and only expected to be able to exert minimal degrees of control and reason, and (2) the repeated initiation of each of us at all stages to new raw materials of sensation, expanded awareness of unorganized facts, and the unresolved contradictions inherent in the physical and the human universes.

This general proposition can be illustrated with respect to three aspects of the educational process. Expressed in question form, they are: (1) how to enrich the experience that intervenes between question and answer, or, in other words, how to give the question a life of its own; (2) how to extend the scope of relevance acceptable in school; and (3) how to allow for the individual idiom in children's realistic and fantasy reconstructions of experience.

Before proceeding to the analysis and illustration of each of these teaching functions, let us turn back to the implied promise of the opening sentence and make explicit a concept of creativity that can serve as a foundation for criticizing old practices or embracing new ones.

Erik Erikson, in discussing sublimation of pregenital libido and the diversion from sexual drives to nonsexual, culturally channeled goals, puts us on the track of our problem at its very source. Agreeing with Freud's position that society is too autocratic in demanding impossible feats of sublimation from its children, he says, "By all means, render unto society that which is society's but first render unto the child that libidinal vitality which makes worthwhile sublimations possible" (1950 [1963]). Augusta Alpert expresses the view of many of her analytical colleagues in her criticism of the kind of rearing and schooling that succeeds in releasing an abundance of creative energy but fails, for certain children, in channeling this energy into creative productivity and allows it instead to continue to feed instinctual gratifications. It follows that she considers the primary problem of education to be the steering of a child's development "between the Scylla of repressive discipline and the Charybdis of too permissive discipline" (1949). In Gardner Murphy's writing on this subject the frame of reference is somewhat different. We are no longer swimming midstream between two modes of discipline; instead we are immersed in the processes and relationships of stimulating sensitivity, encouraging discovery, and deepening the capacity to wonder.

Murphy describes a pattern of successive stages in the evolution of creativeness and the role of adults in stimulating or repressing it. First, there is a period of open sensitiveness in which the "first huge responsibility of the teacher is to encourage, to give freedom, to swing wide the gates to whatever a child's or adolescent's mind wants to explore, to make contact, to know, to grasp, to assimilate the new to the self" (1956). The second period is one of incubation, patterning, and ordering of knowledge and experience which accumulates into vast systems preconsciously; out of this come the creative bursts, the insights, and illuminations that constitute Murphy's third stage. The fourth stage is the inescapable one, if creativeness is to be productive, "of 'hammering-out,' the sifting and testing, the critical evaluating and perfecting of work done" (1956). The educator's role is to support this process, not only during the first sensing and exploring period, but subsequently by allowing the child freedom to incubate and providing experiences to be incubated, to help sustain a mood of searching, to tolerate a degree of chaos and irrelevance and freedom from social regimentation, and, finally, to represent the evaluative judgment of the adult world.

From a physiologist and from a philosopher come parallel warnings against shortcutting the periods and processes of initiation, wonder, and search. Ralph Gerard emphasizes the importance, in the life of science, of the imaginative processes that feed and prosper in the free atmosphere of the unconscious, yielding, in turn, the premises and questions which become the vital substance for the reasoning and checking procedures of scientific method. He is not naively optimistic that imagination in science can be taught, but he is quite passionate in his concern that it should not be stifled by overemphasis on validating techniques at the expense of the generative stirrings of the mind. In his words: "To teach rigor while preserving imagination is an unsolved challenge to education" (1946).

Finally, the philosopher Alfred North Whitehead has said, and who would be so presumptuous as to paraphrase his exquisite language:

> In training a child to activity of thought, above all things we must be aware of what I will call "inert ideas"—that is to say, ideas that are merely received into the mind without being utilized, or tested, or thrown into fresh combinations. . . . [In the rhythmical cycle of education] the stage of romance is the stage of first apprehension . . . knowledge is not dominated by a systematic procedure. We are in the presence of immediate cognizance of fact. . . . Education must be essentially a setting in order of a ferment already stirring in the mind: you cannot educate mind in vacuo. We are concerned with the *ferment*, with the acquirement of precision, and with the subsequent fruition. . . . The stage of precision . . . is the sole stage of learning in the traditional scheme of education. . . . You had to learn your subject, and there was nothing more to be said on the topic of education. The result of such an undue extension of a most necessary period of development (the period of precision) was the production of a plentiful array of dunces, and of a few scholars whose natural interest had survived the car of Juggernaut. (1929)

By borrowing from all these fine minds I hope I have strengthened the proposition stated above, namely, that education has been identified traditionally with the structuring process, an umbrella-like term for Murphy's "hammering-out," Gerard's "conscious reason," and Whitehead's "precision." To the extent that education continues to make this part of the learning process its predominant function, it sacrifices the generative potential of the creative drive. It prematurely imposes a mold instead of providing a developmental sequence from exposure to mastery and thus ultimately to creative productivity.

I would like to think that this formulation might be useful in thinking about and evaluating concrete teaching practices. It might also be useful in systematic studies of teacher personality by less concentration on the teacher in general personality terms and greater focus on the characteristics of personality that could support the sequence of a prolonged, exploratory, subjectively expressive phase followed by the technically mastered and logically organized phase of the learning process.

The kind of creative teaching I have in mind is no figment of my imagination. It exists; it can be observed; it has its own techniques and troubles; it is hard to do. Far from letting the children follow wherever their impulses lead them, it takes responsibility for stimulating, guiding, channeling, presenting, and explaining; it cannot be accomplished by a passive teacher; it does not create Whitehead's bête noire, the inert mind.

Let us turn to teacher, children, and classroom and illustrate the first of the three formulations presented earlier: how to enrich the experience that intervenes between question and answer. As a matter of fact, this is happening all around us in our schools today. It happens every time schoolchildren stand watching the thick hot tar pouring onto a new street, or the seals making slithery dives into the tank below them; or go back to a pathetic tree in the school yard to see whether the buds have opened; or try to see whether a turtle will come when you sing to him; or put together a report for the class on why Brooklyn would not be a good location for a wheat farm—or any one of many instances of wondering more deeply and thinking harder on one's own steam. From the creative mind of Lucy Sprague Mitchell have come the most systematized contributions to the specific techniques for sensitizing children to their world and stimulating them to discover relationships independently through guided search and exploration.

Perhaps the clearest illustration of such a technique is the replacement of the recitation by the discussion period. When successful, this technique symbolizes the process of encouraging children to be able to sustain a question, to play with it, toss it back and forth to one another, refine it, basically to accept the questioning mood without need to engage in anxious, prompt closure by means of ready-made, encapsulated answers delivered by the teacher. What follows is taken from a discussion in a fourth-grade class where the children have been studying and reading books, individually and as a group, on the westward movement in the United States. One of the books contains a fictional family named Burd:

T: What were the reasons the Burd family moved to Ohio?

Sally: Because of the Indians?

Children: What? Indians? What did you say?

T: You mean the danger of Indians is their reason for going West? Do you think a family would move West for the reason that there were Indians?

Sally: No.

Roger (raising his hand): The land was cheaper. There were too many taxes in the East.

Carl: It was too expensive to live.

T: That's what Roger meant. . . . What are taxes?

Marjorie: You pay them to live.

T: How? (Children seem puzzled.) What kind of taxes are there in New York?

Lillian: It's like apartment building taxes—you pay them to live there. You pay to use the telephone.

T: Is that what taxes are? (No one answers.) That's rent, not taxes. What's the difference between rent and taxes?

Carl: You pay to build a house. It's very hard to explain.

T: Do you pay a tax to build? Not exactly. You pay money for the property. When do you pay the tax, Carl?

Carl: There are taxes after you live there. You pay money to the government.

Tommy: When you buy in a store, you pay a city tax. Tax goes through the people in the "front" of the business.

Sandy: Everyone pays taxes. When you buy candy. . . .

Children (interrupting): Not always, no, not for everything.

T: What kind of candy don't you pay taxes for?

. . .

Sandy: If you make over $600 you pay taxes.

T: Yes. That's called an income tax. You pay the government so many dollars for all the money you earn over $600 a year.

Mary: Who is Uncle Sam?

T: Do you know what a cartoon is?

Children all say yes and nod their heads. All begin talking at once about Uncle Sam, his clothes, what he looks like, the colors in his clothes.

One boy calls out: Where did he come from?

Another: Why was he called Uncle Sam?

Mary: He's like the mystical [sic] uncle in our story.

T: What is a mythical uncle?

Caroline: It's one you've never seen, only heard about—you know, like letters and talking.

As the content of discussion moves from child to child and from children to teacher and back again, ideas are tried out, checked, extended, and differentiated in the process intrinsic to any thoughtful discussion. The teacher was carrying her responsibility for informing: what taxes are for, to whom they are paid, what part they may have had in the settlement migrations in American history. Of particular interest, in the context of this paper, are certain qualitative aspects of this teaching method, namely, the learning atmosphere which makes positive use of personal references when young children are trying to think in impersonal, general terms; the concreteness of the children's imagery expressed in the idea that the "tax goes through the people in the 'front' of the business"; and the opportunity for all the children, through one child's uninhibited articulation, to come face-to-face with an idea far more complex than the idea of taxes per se. It is one level of conceptual maturity to realize that Uncle Sam is only a symbol for government, in his mystical-mythical way; but when the last child's comment connects the symbolism inherent in the Uncle Sam figure with the intrinsic symbolism of spoken and written language, we are in the presence of creative insight.

Unfortunately, every good idea or technique is likely to appear, sooner or later, in distorted form. The following example stands in marked contrast to the one we have just discussed. The "show and tell" period is a device that was based on recognition of the importance of intercommunication among children. Each child has a turn to tell or show something to the class while one child is in charge. There is no ideational integration or teacher guidance in the following record of one teacher's review of show and tell rules:

T: What were we saying about Show and Tell?

Janet: Make it as short as possible! And give somebody else a chance!

T: What should you leave out?

Edna: Tell the main points.

T: What else should you do before you speak?

Edna: Plan?

T: Good! The first thing to do is plan.

Frances: Get to the point.

John: You have to talk clearly.

T: Whom do you look at?

John: The class.

Charles: Talk slowly.

T: Who remembers another important point?

Edna: Well, uh, it's like, uh, you have to pick out what people would like.

What spontaneous thought or half-formed idea would stand a chance in this "discussion"? And if it does not have a chance, the question is, will it not, in most instances, atrophy?

The second question to be considered—how to extend the scope of relevance acceptable in school—moves us up to the foremost frontiers in educational thinking. There are no ready-made techniques with which to complete this rhetorical question; instead it requires a courageous effort, on a conceptual level, to integrate psychoanalytic theory of the dynamic unity of unconscious and conscious productions with the social-cultural critique of our society's submission to logic and objectivity as the royal and even the exclusive road to truth.

Lawrence Kubie speaks against the tendency to fragment symbolic thinking and feeling into conscious and unconscious systems. He claims, and is interested in testing the assertion, that if education could find techniques for limiting the dissociative processes that exclude preconscious formations from a seat at the table of learning, creative power would be so vastly released as to affect the way children learn the three Rs as well as the kind of pictures they paint or the poetry of their written or spoken language (1957).

All around us, from such disparate sources as the revolutionary thinking of present-day physicists, the paperbound edition of Suzuki's *Zen Buddhism*, Riessman's sociological anxiety about externalization in the form of "groupism," Rollo May's plea that we restore man to his place as subject rather than object, we sense a growing momentum to make the man of reason, in his nineteenth-century robes, move over and share the throne with the inner man.

On a humbler level, the writer has been whittling away at this problem in the job of teaching child development to student-teachers at the graduate level by emphasizing a few guiding principles for receiving and responding to children's expression: there are more kinds of sense than logical sense; in children we have an opportunity to realize the sense that lies beneath the superficially strange interplay of symbolized ideas and feelings; it is a crime against creativity to push the child's mode of responding to life too hard and too fast into adult forms of classification and reality testing, to make him feel that fantasy is foolish or that all experience can best be ordered in a right–wrong continuum.

True, there may be no ready-made techniques for this aspect of the learning process, but there is an attitude that can run through teaching pervasively and be acted out concretely, as I have tried to indicate in the second formulation presented above: how to extend the scope of relevance acceptable in school. One example is the general acceptance of the idea that we should hold off asking a child *what* he is drawing, or pointing out how preposterously large the man is alongside the house he lives in. But this attitude should not be confined to the crayon box. I have seen it, happily, in other modes and places, as illustrated in the three following instances:

> A group of six-year-olds were getting ready to play circus in a building of Madison Square Garden they had busily constructed. There was the usual six-year-old preoccupation with the tickets, understandable enough when you stop to think what a ticket is, the rather serious matter of being in or out—with one of the boys conscientiously counting and preparing them. Suddenly this same boy lost interest in the tickets, sat down on the floor near the building and began to pat and hug a big soft floppy tiger, evidently slated to be one of the characters in the show. No one ridiculed him or chided him; no one minded that his young self was still living alongside his more mature one. The young self was once one of the "irrelevants" in school.

> Five-year-olds were having frankfurters for lunch when one of them got an inspired thought and burst out with: "You know what, frankfurters come from frankfurter seeds." The teacher waited. "No," said another child, "they come from a pig," and another: "They come

from a machine that makes a big shape like a circle and puts it all in." A few more bites of lunch, and the question of questions from another: "Where does Mary come from?" and the reply from the child next to him: "From her mother's stomach, of course." *Come from* makes a lovely string for all kinds of ideas and feelings at five. The teacher was in it, too. "Where did the potato come from?" and before she was through, her teacher self was explaining that those little specks in the potato are called "eyes." That did it. That was about the funniest joke they had ever heard, and the teacher did not shush them. No one told the first child it was wrong to think by analogy or that babies can't be talked about in the same breath with frankfurters and potatoes or that it isn't funny that people have to share the word "eyes" with potatoes.

A fifth-grade class in an underprivileged neighborhood was studying South America. The teacher was working to get the children to use language for meaning rather than for echo. One of the boys wrote:

"The Condor is a very huge bird. It's eyes and nose is more sharper than ours. If it is flying through the air and smells a dead animal it circles down, down and down. The Condor's feet are pulled up like the wheels of an aeroplane. On the way down it uses it's sharp eyes. As soon as it spies it's pray it glides. You can imagine how it's wings go. one wing goes down while the other goes up. Then the other goes down while the other goes up. As he is landing his feet are stuck out and he land. When he starts eating imagine a farmer coming, the Black Condor grabs his pray and soars into the air. It goes to it's nest and the Condor family have a feast."

The teacher will correct the grammar and the spelling, but how much might be gained if first she could appreciate, in her own mind, the truth of the imagery, the child's feeling for the freedom and mechanism of flight, the projected necessity to flee and the waiting nest in outer space.

And now the third and final question: how to allow for the individual idiom in children's realistic and fantasy reconstructions of experience. There is a prerequisite to this question which I will state without elaboration: It is the assumption that the children are being seen and accepted as the people they are, not in terms of class or race stereotypes or character trait labels.

What we have in mind here as the individual idiom is described by Lawrence Frank when he says: "As the child learns to perceive the world as defined for him by tradition, he creates that world" (1946). For each child there exists a private world, not apart from reality, but shaped by him through the particular needs, sensitivities, and capacities that are peculiarly his. In Frank's view, this represents the essence of the creative process of maturing which, if protected in its early stages from adult sanctions, corrections, and restrictions, can yield healthy individuality.

Concurrent interrelated processes take place at every successive stage of development: the child creates and re-creates the world around himself, building a pattern of coherence for his impressions, concepts, roles, and relations; at the same time he creates and re-creates his sense of himself, through selective identifications, until in Erikson's formulation, at maturity he achieves an identity that is distilled out of all that has gone before without disconnecting with any of it.

Can this process be perceived? supported? Where does it fit into classroom life? The answer is circular, to a degree. In a classroom planned for variation rather than homogeneity this individuation process is open to anyone with eyes that see, but only the teacher who is sensitive to and cares about individuality can plan and carry through variation of program and relation with any degree of subtlety. This does not altogether depend upon the teacher's sensitivity and values, however. The changes in school curriculum have moved gradually to replace concert methods of teaching and strictly normative standards of achievement. Elementary school people will quickly call to mind, for example, the use of committees with varied assignments, the restructuring of the unit classroom into areas of interest, the assortment of books to replace the single reader series, and the increased leeway for contributing special interests to the group as a whole.

There are encouraging signs that good education is not considered synonymous with the efficiency of the teacher in casting each child's free flow of feeling and thought into the mold of adult-structured coherence. Important among these signs is the expanding provision being made for spontaneous dramatic play in the nursery and primary years. It is revealed in the creation of original plays in the elementary years to replace the formalized acting out of a ready-made story or play; roles are no longer assigned according to stage-casting criteria of appearance and elocution or used as barter for good behavior.

As you all know, in their undirected dramatic play or dramatization, children weave an amazing whole out of the conjoint complexities of their cognitive and affective experience (Biber, 1951). Reality is reproduced, fragmented, transformed, misunderstood, and corrected through the same fabric of ideas and interplay of characters onto which inner feelings of love and pain and joy and sorrow and fantasies of one's lowliest and most magnificent self are projected. Dramatic play as a means of constructive wondering and symbolic resolving was invented by children (Levinger, 1956). The role of the teacher in giving it house room in school is a subtle and delicate one, and unfortunately this delicate use is rarely seen even in the classrooms where it is offered as an activity. Here is a teaching technique to be learned and studied in the context of appreciation for the value of this nondirected, nonstructured process in the basic creativity of the maturing personality.

The following illustration of a free-flowing play scheme comes from a first-grade class:

Small automobiles chug noisily down the chalked streets bearing food from Jane's grocery store to the cluster of houses and apartments where Helen, Nancy and Iris are cooking, feeding and putting to bed an assortment of dolls.

Three children are chugging autos up the sloping ramp of long triangular blocks across the bridge to New Jersey. Rena, having determined her route, starts across the Queensboro bridge at the other side in order to patronize David's gas station on Long Island. Tony calls out to her from the bridge: "Sorry, you'll have to find another way. I'm fixing it."

Rena, intent on getting gas for her truck, continues to move across the bridge. Tony calls out: "Can't you see that I'm repairing? I put a red light out there so no one would go, and now someone took it away and put a green one up!?"

Rena starts to back carefully. Tony stops his repairing long enough to look up, cries with consternation in his voice, "You're going right down the middle of the train track! I'm still fixing and your car is too big for this bridge." Rena says crossly, "There ought to be more bridges." Then hesitatingly, "Shall I go back across the water or what?" Tony, with impatience, "Yes, and sink yourself."

In summary, I am aware that, in the interest of illustrating how the teacher can nourish the emergent exploratory processes, I have not tried to deal with the question of structured mastery of experience; of how to provide form, skill, organization; how to tighten up what is open and loose; how to pattern what is unformed; how to guide the merging of the self with the social design of the environment and yet sustain the individual idiom. There is much to be said and learned of how much the creativity of personality depends also on the quality of the structuring experience itself. But here I have tried to make only one point. For the sake of creativity, conceived as part of personality and potentially realizable in everyone, to some degree, education needs to develop and teach the methodology for being receptive and responsive to all the points of beginning in the child.

Changing Concepts of the Creative Process

Looking back on the paper I wrote on creativity in 1959, I am impressed by its innocence. I took for granted that one could talk about creativity without defining it. That was because I moved in a world of children and learning and teaching, where it was implicitly understood and valued. If questioned, there would have been multiple answers: new combinations of ideas or words or motions or colors that bring forth what had had no previous existence, or ways of moving from one medium of expression into another that refreshed and embellished old meanings, or projecting in some external, communicable form an experience in the realm of feeling, or discovering a new route toward the solution of a problem.

Without stopping for a definition beyond a quick reference to "freedom of thought and feeling," I assumed a potential for creative functioning in childhood and tried to illustrate with specific instances how the choice of learning experiences, the climate for learning, and the teacher's role in our program were related to the general purpose of bringing that potential to the greatest possible fulfillment. Further, it seemed important to find a few superordinate concepts about the educational mode sufficiently general to be applicable beyond the particularity of our own school milieu and chosen methods—useful for teachers with children in very different settings. Obviously, the three teaching approaches I presented were correctives for the major errors of the traditional school: its narrow curriculum, its focus on end product, the almost exclusive value placed on the logical functions, and its pressure toward uniformity.

In the decade of the 1950s the question of creativity—what it is and what educators could or should do about it—gained prominence as an educational issue and status as an area of investigation. This is explained by some as a response to the acceleration of change in this century, to the challenge posed by the revolutions in technology and social organization. There was declining confidence that the old ways would yield solutions to the major problems of increasing tensions for individuals, recurrent international crises, and abuse of the earth's resources (Taylor, 1975). To one investigator (Barron, 1963) the increase in research on creativity that followed Guilford's presidential address on the subject to the American Psychological Association in 1950 marked a change within the discipline itself. Guilford saw a "coming of age" in which psychology, having weaned itself from its origins in philosophy, was ready to approach complex problems of meanings and values, such as the feelings of "solitariness of self" and its mitigation by stimulation of creative imagination.

As a Psychological Function

It is interesting to go beyond the message to the teacher on how to "nourish the emergent exploratory processes" in the opening years of childhood, how to deepen sensitivity and the expressive modes as fruitful ways of ingesting and remaking encountered experience. Moving away from childhood, there has arisen an ever-increasing interest in understanding creativity as a kind of human functioning that seems to represent something distinct both in the way experience is processed and in the small number of individuals for whom this psychological mode is sustained. Attempts to understand the creative process reflect, naturally, the variety of perspectives with which we are familiar in all our efforts to penetrate the particular mechanisms of psychological functioning. In which psychological areas will we find significant understanding of creativity?

It is possible and useful, I think, to organize the amazing wealth of theoretical and applied work in the area of creative functioning so as to recognize substantially different approaches. There is, first, the work that focuses primarily on how creative functioning is psychodynamically related to basic drives and unconscious processes. There is a second perspective which, while still giving some homage to the unconscious as an influencing factor, is oriented toward understanding creative functioning from the perspective of its various forms of observable expression and seeking insight by projecting it theoretically within a variety of systems of psychological functions. Though there are varying images and emphases in this group of theoretical interpretations, there appears to be a common view that creative functioning has qualities that distinguish it as a psychological process and/or experience. There is a more current view in which creative functioning can be understood as a great leap within the known course of maturing psychological functioning, expressed in extraordinary utilization of the various known forms of functioning, which include, for example, factors of style and values along with abilities.

From Psychoanalytic Theory

In my reading of the psychoanalytic perspective in relation to creative activity I find a contemporary rejection of the traditional view of art as derivative, as a defense against neurosis by the mechanism of sublimation. The earlier view is seen as having neglected analysis of the distinguishing characteristics of art—form, style, structure, imagery—by which neurotic conflicts are transformed into what is aesthetically positive (Slochower, 1974). Replacing sublimation, the concept of symbolism is seen as nuclear in psychoanalytic theory and symbolic transformation as crucial for the creative process in art and culture.

Interpretations from a psychoanalytic view vary in their conception of how creative functioning is related to unconscious, preconscious, and conscious functioning and interaction among these processes. In one view the creative process is conceived positively, as an exchange between the conscious and preconscious realms, movement between the restriction of logical, rational thought and the freer processes of daydream and fantasy. This view is well known as "regression in service of the ego" (Kris, 1967). In another view (Kubie, 1967), creativity depends on the free flow of symbolic imagery associated primarily with preconscious functioning, which is regarded as the wellspring of creative thought, related to healthy and adaptive functioning. In this view, unconscious processes, related to fear and guilt, could diminish the creativity potential. A more radical view (Jung, 1946) distinguishes two fundamentally different creative processes: the "psychological," dealing with human consciousness and experience; and the "visionary," based on the unconscious, having reference not only to the sphere of the individual but also to the collective unconscious of mankind, comprising racial memories from the distant past. In this view there appears a certain skepticism about ever explaining creativity beyond recognizing its source in the interaction of conscious and unconscious processes. There are other formulations which give primary position to unconscious process; that of Arieti (1976), for example, who describes creativity as a "magic synthesis" in which deep, underlying structures, inaccessible to direct observation, become involved with the higher level structures of consciousness to create a "tertiary" process, providing a new level of psychological functioning.

Experiential Perspectives

A second perspective moves toward understanding creativity in terms of various familiar systems of psychological functioning, drawing more, though not exclusively, on experiential material than on making hypothetical induction from unconscious or preconscious processes. From the perspective of the Gestalt psychologist Wertheimer (1959), creative thinking is a productive kind of thinking in which stresses and tensions in a problem lead successfully to changing perceptions and restructuring until a solution emerges, "a better Gestalt is found." Expressed differently, steps in creative thinking comprise a consistent line of thinking in which whole perceptions are divided into subwholes and reconstructed into new configurations, a process by which "to go on from a nuclear, inadequate relation to a clear, transparent confrontation." Creative activity is thus conceived within the scope of problem-solving activity.

Schachtel's view focuses on creativity as a process of perceptual openness in relating to the world around from varied perspectives repeatedly, with intense interest, unhampered by the constraints that characterize conventional thought processes (1959). This image of "openness to the world" as characterizing the creative process is obviously contradictory to Kris's image of regression to preconscious levels as sources for creativity. In retrospect, it is the image of "openness to the world" that seems analogous to what I thought of as a corrective for "premature structuring."

Maslow's related, more comprehensive view of the creative process (1972), identified as the "humanist" view, moves beyond the concepts of Gestalt organization of experience or special receptivity designated as "openness" to a holistic view of creative functioning. Built on a basic drive to realize full potential and the assumption of capacity for creativity as potentially universal, creative functioning is identified as the complex, multifaceted "self-actualization" of individuals within the range of "normal" apart from "special talent creativeness." A few illustrations of the characteristics ascribed to a group of self-actualized creative people by Maslow may illustrate the holistic nature of the concept. The descriptive qualities include a special kind of perceptiveness: seeing the fresh, the raw, the concrete in contrast to the abstract and categorized; more spontaneous expressiveness and less self-criticism; freedom from stereotype and cliché; attraction to what is unknown, mysterious, and puzzling; ease in dealing with what may be uncertain or anarchic; and even the tendency to find certain kinds of commonality in dichotomous entities. These qualities and others such as deeper self-acceptance, less dependence on approval from and less hostility toward others, are taken as indicating greater resolution between "the forces of the inner depths and the forces of defense and control."

This interchange among psychological domains is also expressed in the capacity to move between taking a childlike perspective and then reconsidering it with the rational, critical eye of the grown-up. Maslow clearly distinguishes the image of universal potential creativeness in which he was especially interested from the creativity involved in producing great works of art, for which he outlines familiar successive stages involved in production. Thinking of Wertheimer, Schachtel, and Maslow, one sees a view of imaginativeness and creativity, not as a defensive outcome of conflict, but as a freshly directed, exploratory drive and a basic positiveness and receptivity to the world around.

From Different Realms

It is not surprising to find that some psychologists, also interested in understanding creativity within the orbit of conscious psychological functioning, were not as ready to separate it from the role of the unconscious as were those who took a humanist position. For Adler (in Taylor, 1975) interest in creative functioning held a central position, going well beyond interest in the creative process or product as such. It was conceived as a force for shaping and enriching all experience with an image of "fulfillment" in view. Bridging the decades, this position can be seen as that of a psychologist-activist who was interested not only in building a generalized "creative power of the self" for the individual but also in extending this perception toward serving society more usefully. We see psychology as responding to a particular social era. From the viewpoint of dynamic processes, in terms of unconscious functioning, this uplifting image was conceived as derived from a need to compensate for underlying feelings of inferiority, fitting with the orthodox image of a primitive negative to be overcome.

Among certain personality theorists, such as Henry Murray (1968), we find basic acceptance of Freudian concepts of unconscious determinants of behavior. But for Murray this acceptance is modified by special interest in understanding and supporting the positive aspects of human behavior, especially the fundamental role of creativity—in concept and in function. Murray's broad concept of creativity as an aspect of human functioning is expressed in his inclusion of "creativeness" in his taxonomy of needs formulation, in his concept that some degree of creativity is required generally for adaptation to new situations as they arise, and in his inclusion of growth toward self-actualization and creativity as one of the successive eras and stages in life.

In the analysis of a research project carried through by Rothenberg (1971), a psychiatrist with both clinical and research experience, we find another image of the essence of creativity. It is seen as distinct from other psychological processes in the capacity to utilize two or more contradictory ideas, concepts, images simultaneously. Although in this view creativity is essentially a conscious process, the capacity to unearth unconscious material simultaneously is the basis for calling it "Janusian" thinking, using the term metaphorically with reference to the Roman god with two faces who "looked and apprehended in opposite directions simultaneously." The creative process involves simultaneity of opposition, a concept which the author applies, interestingly, to the inner structure of Eugene O'Neill's creativity as expressed in his dramatic productions. Applied to the study of the creative process, this dualism calls for recognizing that, in part, creativity can be understood in terms familiar to us, but that there is a uniqueness psychologically which we may recognize but which we are not in a position to explain causally.

It is interesting to note, briefly, the thinking of the novelist and biographer Koestler (1964), whose view resembles Rothenberg's. In both theories, the creative process is conceived as the unusual coming together of two frames of reference which are habitually incompatible, though the process is conceived by Koestler as combination, not as a dynamic juxtaposition of antithetical components, as Rothenberg proposes. When Koestler turns to the question of sources he sees creative art as involving several levels of consciousness, with "underground" levels playing a decisive part in truly creative art in a way that is reminiscent of Kris's thinking.

These brief expositions of the views of Adler, a clinician; Murray, a personality theorist; Rothenberg, a research-minded psychiatrist; and Koestler, a man of letters, remind us of the complexity of this psychological domain and the universal interest in understanding the special forces that motivate and ultimately produce what is uncommon and wonderful. To state it simply, all these varied interpretations have a common thread: special kinds of psychological factors and processes operate in creative functioning, characterized by a distinct and more than usual "free" quality—a tendency to cross over and incorporate ordinarily disparate orbits of experience.

Creativity: Extraordinary But Not Different

It is time to recognize dissenting voices in which the concept of creative functioning as qualitatively and functionally distinct from other psychological functions is replaced by new views of how creativity can be understood as extraordinary utilization of known familiar functions. In his defense of this position, Perkins (1981) proceeds systematically to illustrate how former assumptions about creative functioning cannot be substantiated. For example, he disputes the concept that insight is related to extended unconscious thinking and takes the position that "many mental leaps are explained by ordinary mental processes of recognizing and realizing," processes that do, however, accomplish quickly what one might attempt more consciously and deliberately over a somewhat longer period. Besides making a similar systematic analysis of other functions, Perkins takes a critical view of well-known theories of creativity which deal with particular domains, such as Koestler's bi-sociation theory, and more recent theories, such as the attribution of intuitive, visual, artistic, divergent functions to the right brain. By contrast, he looks positively on interpretations that relate creativity to multiple personality characteristics, among them, seeing things in unusual ways, accepting unconventional thoughts, exhibiting independence of judgment, being highly observant, tolerant of ambiguities, and appreciative of complexity. Though studies of members of different professions—student artists, writers, architects, scientists—show differences and some contradictions in the ways these personality characteristics are expressed, Perkins concludes that "the efforts to relate creativity to personality have been more successful than the efforts to relate it to abilities." In the end, he presents a multifaceted image of creativity as it is expressed with reference to abilities, style, values, beliefs, and tactics and recapitulates his point of view: "Abilities involved in extraordinary creating are not different in kind. They can be understood as exceptional versions of familiar mental operations such as remembering, understanding, and recognizing."

With both acceptance and revision of Piagetian theory as a base, we have been given another exposition of the creative process that also places it within the known, understandable range of psychological functioning. Feldman (1980) points out how the subjective experience of surprise and elation in moving from one stage to another in the Piagetian sequence in childhood is similar to moments of sensing creative accomplishment at any level, while recognizing that such moments are high points in ongoing processes in both the cognitive and the creative realms. The commonness of the experience for an "infant" and an "astronomer" has been given an appealing title: "The Having of Wonderful Ideas" (Duckworth, 1972). Besides the element of surprise common to major creative leaps and to the child's insight into one of the universal Piagetian concepts, the author points to a subjective sense that the "new" level is really obvious, superior, and irreversible.

In Feldman's analysis adults' feelings about creative accomplishment parallel children's insight experience: a solution once achieved seems obvious; there is a gradual process of "pulling" toward a solution and a sense of the irreversibility of the solution once it is achieved. The course of the experience has certain similarities for child and adult. There are steps in sequence that lead to solution, and the solution, not to be learned directly, will have been constructed in response to a perceived problem. But the child's creative experience has only personal subjective meaning in contrast to the adult's search for insight in areas of knowledge and expression beyond what is already universally known and understood. The search may be exhaustive, involving successive efforts with varied known concepts and techniques until the "practitioner has reached the limits of his discipline." This may generate a new level of search—"new combinations," "divergent domains," "different realms of experience"—beyond the familiar and the known.

In building up to his preferred "process" in contrast to the "trait" view of creative functioning, Feldman reviews critically the well-known research findings. With reference to studies in which creativity is treated as a distinct trait, he reviews the restricted relation to IQ, the doubtful predictability of measures of creativity in nonacademic domains, as well as the limited predictability of test scores into the years after college.

While recognizing a positive contribution from studies which have related creativity to a broader concept of varied personality characteristics—that is,

Barron (1955, 1968) and MacKinnon (1965)—Feldman remains critical. Primarily, he rejects concepts in which the source of creativity is located deep within the individual and turns alternatively to what he has called the "process" view. Thus, creativity is a stage in an ongoing psychological process; a qualitative advance, when it occurs, which is similar in both intellectual development and creative works. From a similar perspective Steinzor (1976) describes the successive changes in the way a child "plays horse." The play moves from a general playing out of the activity element—trotting around on a broom while chanting "giddy up"—to a next stage when he centers on specific characteristics of the horse—the shape of the head, a few special sounds; later, a name and a bridle are needed to fulfill the symbolization. The reintegration of newly perceived relations that takes place in such successive creative play activities is seen as being parallel to the way intelligence develops.

As noted above, this developmental concept of creativity brings together the insight experience of the child and the creative heights of the artist.

Not only does Feldman place creativity within the course of recognized developmental sequence, he presents a fresh image, with principle and illustration of the kind of educational experience that is needed to stimulate and support creative potentiality. Not surprisingly, he aligns his image with the British model of an open, free school and uses the term *The Child as Craftsman* to symbolize the goals and design of an educational experience in which the learning experience engages multiple available energies, plans for extended experiential involvement, and is one from which children derive deep satisfaction and built-in motivation. The basic congruence of this image and principle with Bank Street educational philosophy and practice over the years is gratifying. The experience is conceived as a course expressed subjectively: "Sustained commitment, satisfaction and joy in accomplishment will naturally lead to occasions that require one to go beyond the limits of one's craft . . . to reach the limit and find yet another problem to be solved, . . . an idea to be expressed. . . . these are the conditions which favor creativity" (Feldman, 1980).

Through a Lifetime

From his study of Darwin and subsequent studies, Gruber (1974, 1980b) has developed a distinctive approach to the study of creativity. His method concentrates on analyzing the processes and works of a clearly recognized creative individual: how methods, purposes, and images change over a period of time and how this evolutionary process is perceived both by the creative individual in search of insight and by the scholar searching for understanding of the psychological process. For the latter this requires thorough immersion in the detailed recording of the years of experience, action, and reflection in a creative lifetime. In this view, to encompass the complexity of creative process functioning as well as the motivation that sustains long years of study for an individual, there is no alternative to "whole person" thinking and analysis, in detail and in depth, accessible only through an individual life story.

From this perspective there is little to be gained from studies of the creative process that have moved from trying to identify specific traits to a broader view of talents on to a still more comprehensive concept of personality attributes as the distinguishing factor. Both the methods of analysis and the qualifications of judges of the creative process are questioned. The sources for data themselves are in question: "There is no powerful reason for believing that any child can function creatively in a typical classroom."

The functioning of the creative process is perceived as a complex system in which the "organization of knowledge, purpose and affect are all brought to bear on the work." Each of these domains is fully described in terms of psychological processes. A few selected illustrations may communicate the complexity of the conception and its analysis.

From the perspective of organization of knowledge, creative individual thought is seen as a process of "continuous, multifaceted" struggle, as ongoing connection and interconnection of ideas, proceeding epigenetically, in particular and uncommon ways that lead to the "uniqueness of the outcome." Considering creativity as "purposeful work" calls back the familiar issue of how to place the influence of unconscious processes. As in Perkins and Feldman, this question is regarded as subordinate in this analysis. Without dismissing the reality of unconscious functioning, Gruber moves creative processes out of that realm; creative work, in his view, is built on the transformation of such motives into a "unique and effective system of conscious purposes." Gruber sees "purposeful work" as a way of living: continuous engaging in exploratory "enterprises" beyond specific tasks accomplished or problems solved. Autonomous selection of activities, cross-referencing of insights from disparate areas, and choice by values are coordinated in a self-determined "network of enterprises" that distinguishes the life patterns of creative individuals, in which horizons are expanded at the same time that selected boundaries are established.

Another dimension, organization of affect in relation to creative functioning, is seen as being minimally understood, reflecting almost exclusive interest in negative emotions—"anxiety, anger, fear"—and failure to recognize motivation in terms of positives—"visions, hopes . . . and sensuous pleasure in the creative area itself."

From a different perspective we have returned to the concept of creative functioning as a psychologically distinct process. In distinguishing his position on creative functioning from that which places it within the usual developmental sequence, Gruber (1980a) reviews basic characteristics: creativity is purposeful work in an extended span of life experience; creative processes involve resolution of a complex web of relationships; the creative person is one who develops an unusual life perspective which involves seeing and feeling the world as others do but also continually constructing and reconstructing radically new kinds of perceptions and perspectives that lead to creative productivity as the fruit of the "deep tensions intrinsic to a creative life."

The Creative Experience in Stages

We enter another universe of thinking when we turn from the differing views on how to place creative thinking within the broader spectrum of psychological processes to a more focused view, looking into the nature of the creative experience itself. Contemporary thinking is well past being satisfied with a "Eureka!" or an "Aha!" image of creative insight. Instead we have analytical studies of an out-of-the-ordinary psychological process that can be understood as a recognizable sequence of different kinds of experience from which the outcome—the creative product—is achieved by relatively few people. It is interesting that the general sequence of an elaborating process in successive stages has been described in basically similar terms though the complex nature of the experience is projected through different perspectives of psychological functioning. I have in mind one formulation in general psychological terms (Taylor, 1975), a psychological study in depth of several great scientists (Gruber, 1981), and an analysis of the experience by a scholar of the arts (Doyle, 1976).

For a commonly accepted analysis of the successive stages, we can turn to a summary (in briefest form) as described by Taylor (1975). There is an initial phase, "exposure," of high receptivity to sensory data, open acceptance of information, avoidance of premature closure, followed by a "pre-divergent" phase of assimilation and reformulation involving both induction and unconscious incubation. The "Eureka!" phase which follows is described as the sudden moment of reformulation when the familiar becomes unfamiliar, when psychological processes using reversals, opposites, analogies, and metaphors stimulate new perceptions, and the "reorganization of the environment is congruent with personal perception." That is a beginning, not an end. The stages that follow involve, first, reformulation and development of insights and, then, expression and communication requiring painstaking work as well as experience of criticism or censorship in a mood of psychological tension.

In his study of three creative scientists, Gruber (1981) analyzes in detail the substantive experience of these creative minds, presenting the evidence for how sudden moments of insight are embedded in a complex thinking process over a period of time. From his study of Poincaré's self-study of the stages by which he achieved insight into an abstract mathematical problem in the context of sleepless nights and a foot-on-the-step-of-the-bus illumination, Gruber finds verification of his own concept of creativity as a blend of purposeful work and spontaneity. He would add the importance of an extended series of episodes as the source of changing successive insights. I appreciate Gruber's more developed image of a scientist thinking creatively as someone engaging in a flexible, shifting, problem-solving process, a constant reorganization of ideas, either remembered or worked out. The "thinking process goes over the same ground many times . . . focuses on the particular aspect, now on that . . . looks at it from varying points of view . . . diagrams it . . . formulates equations, constructs visual images of the whole problem or of troublesome parts . . . with a perspective that makes it possible for something to be at once old and new." And then there is the question of whether and in what ways this analysis, focusing on the creative scientist, can be generalized. Can such analysis of the creativity of the scientist illuminate the creative experience of the artist?

In reading Charlotte Doyle's paper on the creative process from the perspective of the creative artist (1976), I find that her analysis has common ground with Gruber's in the image of defined successive stages, the recognition of a complex, ongoing process that takes time and may be engaged in through a lifetime, and for which there is a sense of direction from the beginning. The distinction of this analysis rests on the image of the subjective experience as it is projected in the work of the creative artist. The artist thinks through the medium, Doyle writes, "the painter in form and color, the poet in images and words." By contrast, one recalls the medium for the scientist: abstraction and search for indisputable evidence. The artist finds original ways to express the complexity of experience, particularly the simultaneity of the modes of understanding and feeling. The medium of expression is described as a kind of reality principle, a chance to become aware of what we think and do not know or understand. In Doyle's words, it "puts the clouds in our heads out in the world." There is no single moment of discovery, but there is a decisive period, termed the *period of total concentration*—an experience of complete absorption in the work, when the resources and developed skills find expression. In this author's conception of the experience we read about "periods of incredible joy . . . [when] interaction with the work becomes smooth and flowing as a dance . . . [and] all the patterns of the mind are potentially active." I quote the following summation:

> The creative process involves freedom and spontaneity . . . demands discipline and concentration, a commitment to work. It involves the primitive and the emotional, intelligence and thought . . . calls upon fantasy and inventiveness, a willingness to deviate from what is; demands honesty and commitment to truth. It is an expression of self and it cannot take place without forgetting the self; it is a joy and a terror, it is its own reward; it requires encouragement and understanding from others. (1976)

In this brief review of sequence in creative experience, we get some small insight into where the creative processes of scientist and artist move together, especially in the conception of recurring insight experience as a phase of an ongoing process. But the difference in the content and the nature of these two modes of experiencing calls for further analysis of questions dealing with choice of these alternative modes for creative expression and for consideration of educational programs for children.

The question of whether creative functioning is related to intelligence and, if so, in what way has been much researched and argued. Recognition that intelligence tests as constructed were inadequate and irrelevant as a base for understanding creative processes led to new methods of measuring and studying "divergent" thinking, which was designated as most relevant to understanding creativity (Guilford, 1967). Briefly, the category *divergent thinking* referred to an easy flow from one idea to another, with a much wider range of unusual associations than ordinarily expected and less defined solutions to problems. When studied through newly developed procedures, it was characterized as yielding a variety of responses distinguished by fluency, flexibility, originality, and readiness to search for new information via new paths.

This identification of creative processes with divergent thinking processes, an accepted interpretation for a considerable period, has been opened up for reconsideration. Divergent thinking processes, developed as a construct describing creative behavior in general, has come to have less universal relevance. Particularly with reference to goals and methods in the sciences, the concept of open-ended pursuit in search of depth of insight has been judged inapplicable. For the scientist, the search is for understanding changing processes which, while still open to fresh and free associations, need to be more focused on the specific content of the problem of the search and predominantly involve convergent modes of integrating experience. Perhaps it begins to be clear that the convergent–divergent dichotomy in relation to creative processes, in which science has been identified with convergent processes and the arts and literature with divergent processes, needs to be modified beyond an either–or concept.

I find Hudson's study (1966) of English schoolboys a useful source for integrating the changing conceptions of the phenomenon. The drift toward either converger or diverger patterns (organized vs. open, in the most general terms), as expressed in preferences in courses of study as well as life-style and attitudes, is seen as a first step in adolescence—a movement toward one or another major identity. The direction any individual takes is the product of basic tendencies, family, and social realities. The complex of these factors will lead some toward art or literature, where the search engages divergent processes; some toward the sciences, where convergent thinking is dominant. But we are advised to pause over the word *dominant* and make room for shifting cross-perspectives between diverging and converging thought processes related to changing mood and new insights over the years. Basically, these are alternate modalities, blends of personality dominance and ideational maneuver for searching and understanding beneath the surface of events within which extraordinary insights we call creative may or may not appear. Are we ready to look for what is shared and what is different in the searches toward creative insight between those that are art- or science-grounded?

The Educator's Way

For the educator's approach, I draw on Bank Street staff writing and projects as a prototype for what is to be found, in somewhat similar forms, in other experimental schools. Stimulation of creative processes is not allocated to the position of a subject area within a curriculum. It is an indigenous factor in all areas—in social studies and in science, as well as in painting and language and dramatic representation with techniques appropriate to the content. Creativity is a long-standing fundamental criterion for judging the quality of children's learning and a teacher's teaching (Lewis, 1979).

A clear example of how to stimulate and guide without invading or dominating the creative process appears in a working paper prepared for a program designed to reorient teaching methods (Lord & Smith, 1971). Here the content was painting, and two general suggestions were made in the beginning: (1) Do not set a topic but ask questions, and (2) make comments on the process involved without making value judgments on the product. The suggested interaction between teacher and child is presented with full examples through seven stages of development: from the early stages of discovery of the medium and control of line, color, shape, to later stages, up to seven or eight years of age, where the child is working with combinations of symbols and discovery, on a broader basis, of concepts of environment, society, and art.

There is a clear rationale for the teacher's role which is not, in any sense, a laissez-faire invitation to be "expressive." The communication is both personal outreaching and technical, but never directive. Contemporary studies not only have advanced general understanding of how thinking processes are interrelated with expressive activity but have also illustrated how this insight can influence the teaching role and perspective. "By reviewing the work [of the children] for evidence of personal involvement, exploration and sense of competence, a teacher can guide a class successfully from week to week in the creation of meaning" (Smith, 1983).

The commitment to composing the kind of school life that brings the creative potential of children to greatest possible fulfillment has been deep and continuous in Bank Street history. It was the heart of the matter when Lucy Sprague Mitchell was identified with the educational ferment of Caroline Pratt's Play School in MacDougall Alley (Pratt & Deming, 1973) in the early years of the century and remains central in the programs for children and teachers that have been developed by Bank Street College since then. I have before me a report of a three-year Bank Street project located in a New York City public school in the 1970s, entitled "The Arts and the School: A Program for Integrating the Arts in an Elementary School" (1971; see also Biber, 1972). In this program the *arts* had a broad meaning, including dance, drama, expressive language, and crafts, in addition to the visual-tactile forms. *Integrating* meant bringing new content areas and new expressive forms into classroom life in ways that vitalized the learning experience in social studies, reading skills, and sciences.

Phillip Lopate (1975), a poet and member of the Teachers and Writers Collaborative, worked with the teachers and children in a New York City public school. His book is a deeply human account in which he tells openly of his doubts about how to make poetry, or any creative writing, important to these city children and to their teachers. He wanted to find activities that would bring their deep-running passions and latent feelings, their unusual capacity for sensing the under surfaces of passing experience, to open, communicable expression. In his view there is no such thing as a "creativity curriculum" divorced from personalities and social context. His rapport with the children— trust, friendship, understanding, shared pleasures, troubles, and excitement— grew gradually as he established a writing club, engaged them in acting out soliloquies, writing scripts, tape-recording radio plays, and, finally and gloriously, helped them put on a heroic performance of "West Side Story." He integrated writing experience with the performing arts and opened the world of satisfaction that comes from communicating and exchanging feeling and thought with others.

One of Lopate's lessons is called "walking around." He takes the children out walking on the street and asks them "to note down in word paragraphs" anyone or anything that catches their eye. "No generalizations, just the facts," in order to retrieve some of the freshness that has been worn threadbare by daily, indifferent passing by.

Lopate would have enjoyed going along with Lucy Mitchell and the Bank Street student teachers of the 1930s as they walked the streets of Greenwich Village, carrying out the first of what Mitchell called "five-finger exercises" (1935). They were asked to stand for fifteen minutes on some road (street, harbor, rail, or airway) and record all they could see that was connected with the road. No interpretations, just recorded observations. It was the beginning of sharpening the observing eye of the beholder. Lucy Mitchell (1935) would have been ready to value increased sensitivity that serves creativity as much as mastery of primary social-studies knowledge. Some kindred spirits never meet. For me, something is validated when I bring them together in my reading and recollections.

At least two others of my acquaintance belong in this assemblage of those who have confronted the meaning of the creative process in terms of their own subjective experience with creating. Ben Shahn (1957) is speaking:

> It is not a spoken idea alone, nor a legend, nor a simple use or intention that forms what I have called the biography of a painting. It is rather the wholeness of thinking and feeling within an individual; it is partly his time and place; it is partly his childhood or even his adult fears and pleasures; and it is very greatly his thinking what he wants to think.

And I turn to David Hawkins (1967):

> The essential construction of sciences is a personal way of being related to the universe . . . primarily a way of knowing, and the knower is always the artisan of his personal knowledge. . . . The tight formulation and logical sequencing must be learned, but they cannot be learned first. . . . What comes first is absorption in subject matter. No one learns by being led blind along a path he cannot begin very soon to see for himself.

For the political leader who turns to poetry to make his appeal, we have to cross a big sea to another society:

> I have long aspired to reach for the clouds,
> Again I came from afar
> To climb Chingkang Shore, our old haunts.
> We can clasp the moon in the ninth heavens

And seize turtles deep down in the five seas.
We'll return amid triumphant song and laughter.
Nothing is hard in this world
If you dare to scale the heights.

This is a poem published in a Chinese newspaper on January 1, 1976. It was written by Chairman Mao to remind the Chinese people of his early triumphs and published at a time when the policies of the Cultural Revolution seemed to be endangered.

PART 4

Integrating Theory and Practice

CHAPTER 11

The Widening Circle

It is more than fifty years since I first met Lucy Mitchell. In the forty years of our work together, I found a way of converting the ideals of my younger years into a lifelong confidence that the school in our society could be a great vitalizing force for children and for the shape of the world they would eventually create. Those years have a life and a history of their own, full of how we, with others, met practical problems, forged a method, clarified a theory, and established a small institution that took a respected forefront position in education. But, apart from all that, there is the distinct quality, the personality that an institution develops as it grows. For Bank Street, the core of its basic style, its modes of personal interchange, and its commitment to selected values are rooted in the years when Lucy Mitchell was an inspired guide and an indefatigable co-worker. When we recall her talents, there is a full count: brilliant writer, geographer, teacher, craftsman, artist, as well as practical planner. When we think of the qualities of the person, other words come freely—disciplined intellect, clearheaded critic, original and playful spirit, humanist, enthusiastic believer, unembarrassed dreamer.

In view of our contemporary interest in finding the connectives between the years of youth and maturity, it is not surprising that we are interested in looking back on the childhood experiences of a pioneer. Where were her roots? What was her childhood? Where did her extraordinary strength and commitment come from? Without being so reckless as to make direct logical or psychological inferences between her childhood and her mature life pattern, I have found it interesting to review and reflect on her beginnings, as she did herself at various times in her life. Here, then, are a few vignettes, interesting as images of the externally constricted and rich inner life of a privileged child in the early years of our century, foretelling the autonomous spirit of a pioneer educator dedicated to providing questioning, searching, and embellishing experience as the right of childhood.

In her autobiographical writings, we read:

I had a little book in which my Puritan father insisted that, at the end of each day, I should record my sins by pasting in a gold star for complete virtue, a silver star for a small sin, and a red star for a big sin. . . . This moral discipline . . . soon developed in me a sense of guilt—as it was intended to do. . . . My father also thought . . . any attempt at an art expression was a waste of time. . . . But I had a strong native love of color and of design and an impulse to experiment with them as art media, first in objects, later in words. When I first began to record my sins, I chose red stars because I loved red! Also, I tried to make a pleasing pattern of stars on the page (a week's record) and simply licked on a gold star when I thought it would improve the design! (1955)

.   .   .

I admired and feared my handsome Father who was always right and made me feel I was the "wrong" kind of person. . . . my art indulgences were secretly practiced—hidden bits of red yarn tied onto my underwear, wild impossible stories told to younger children, notebooks filled with dreams and hopes and child philosophy, all hidden guiltily from any eye. It may be that Father, unwittingly, turned me into a writer (1953).

And, in her later years, she wrote:

Now, I find a dominant desire to "reflect"—a kind of reflection that combines thinking, which I have always tried to do, and meditation, the germ of which was early twisted by guilt and in middle life was crowded by doing. . . . I feel a renewed urge to write just for my own satisfaction—sometimes to clarify a thought, sometimes just to experiment with the lovely sound and rhythm of words. I recognize these impulses as an essential part of the child "me" that never died and are now reasserting themselves without the cramping early guilt (1955).

What makes nonconformists? It is tempting to ask an old-fashioned question: Are they born or bred? I draw on two far-apart childhoods that explain me to myself and the road I took. Young Lucy Mitchell, the child of a wealthy Chicago family, created a secretly independent life for herself: She recorded red stars in the little book of moral behavior that she had to keep for her father even though red was the color designated for recording sins, and secretly tied wisps of bright red yarn on her petticoats when it was denied her in her outer clothing because she loved the color red!

In almost the same decade of the nineteenth century, another small

*girl walked bravely on a Saturday to the outskirts of Warsaw, where she
lived with her poor, orthodox Jewish family. In her hand she carried a
handkerchief. She was testing the tenet of her upbringing: to carry any
object on the Sabbath symbolized working and insomuch a denial of the
consecration of the day to prayer and meditation. There would be a
punishment from God for breaking the faith. The child walked and waited
but there was no sign from God. She was lost to orthodoxy forever. She was
my mother.*

The Developmental-Interaction Approach: Bank Street College of Education (1977)

Theoretical Rationale

The rationale for this philosophy of education has evolved from diverse sources
over the years. From the beginning, the philosophy has been an amalgam of
issues of social change, focus on the nature of childhood, and radically changed
teaching–learning strategies. In its early leaders it reflected the revolt against
the conformist, anti-individualistic Victorianism of the day. John Dewey, as
educator more than as philosopher, was the major source for creating a fresh
educational design that recognized the worth of individuality, gave priority to
skillful thinking and problem-solving, highlighted learning through direct contact and interaction with the environment, and organized the internal school
world as a cooperative social system.

Because these educators were thinkers at least as much as practitioners,
there was an edifice of educational theory in the making as they observed,
generalized, hypothesized, and made new trials, using the natural situation of
the classroom as their "laboratory." Lucy Mitchell (1950) and Harriet Johnson
(1928 [1972]) were the seminal minds who laid the groundwork for the Bank
Street philosophy, concurrent with the work of Caroline Pratt (1948) in the City
and Country School.

By 1959 it seemed fruitful to examine critically the rationale—the basic
assumptions about learning—that was the foundation for the educational practices presumed to attain the stated values and goals. Knowledge of the growing
field of child development and psychology of learning had indeed influenced
these assumptions, but they had been primarily derived from the direct experience of observing and teaching children in school. The ultimate validity of these
assumptions would rest on the difficult task of evaluating success with the
goals. But an intermediate criterion was proposed. To what extent would formulations and viewpoints in the field of psychology, arrived at independently of

Adapted from A developmental-interaction approach: Bank Street College of Education. In M. C.
Day & R. K. Parker (Eds.), *Preschool in action: Exploring early childhood programs* (2d ed.).
Boston: Allyn & Bacon, 1977.

the field of education, corroborate these assumptions and thus provide a firmer theoretical base for the practices? On an exploratory basis, it became clear that this educational system's assumptions about what would "enhance learning" were congruent with two lines of psychological thought (in fact, both were needed to support the totality): the psychodynamic theory of personality and cognitive theories of learning (Biber, 1959a).

A few years later, when the Headstart program was being inaugurated, a more highly developed psychological rationale for preschool education was formulated. It refined the previous concepts and distinguished more clearly between those concepts and the implications for the teacher's role, always keeping in mind that educational goals influence the use the teacher makes of psychological concepts. The rationale was drawn from psychodynamic theory, especially as it affects the understanding of motivation and autonomous ego processes (Sigmund Freud, Anna Freud, Erikson, Sullivan, and Hartmann), and from the work of Gestalt and developmental theorists (Wertheimer, Lewin, Piaget, and Werner).

Developmental Concepts

Six theoretical formulations were presented as fundamental to educational planning.

> 1. *The autonomous ego processes of the growing organism synchronize with increasingly strong motivation to engage actively with the environment, to make direct impact upon it, and to fulfill curiosity about it.*[1]

The term *autonomous* in this connection refers to the position that ego processes are propelled by motivations independent of instinctual drives. The course of development of ego processes depends, in important measure, upon the qualities of support, restraint, and stimulation that characterize the environment.

During the preschool years, action is both a way of life and a mode of learning. The child becomes increasingly skillful in using his total body as a coordinated instrument at the same time that he perfects the more specialized manipulative skills. In exercising these skills he engages in an endless variety of contacts with the reality of the physical world. These contacts (including the experience of making an impact by transforming objects—changing forms, bulk, consistency) yield him direct knowledge of the physical world. Gradually, through various forms of nonverbal representation and with growing mastery of language, he begins to deal symbolically with his experience, as he becomes capable of increasing mastery in the world of ideas and empowered with new modes for creating order and coherence out of the stream of experience.

Motivation to activity—sensorimotor, representational-symbolic, idea-

---

1. This statement and the five other italicized statements that follow are quoted from Biber and Franklin (1967).

tional-conceptual—is intrinsic; it is regenerated through the pleasure and power of mastery and the fulfillment of curiosity. Fundamental patterns of approach, exploration, problem-solving, and conceptualization take shape in early childhood and condition the course of future learning.

2. *The course of development, characterized by qualitative changes or shifts in the individual's means of organizing experience and coping with the environment, may be viewed overall in terms of increasing differentiation and hierarchic integration. This general line of development can be discerned within different stages and with regard to the pattern of growth in various spheres (for example, motor activity, emotional development, perceptual-cognitive functioning).*

The developmental-stage concept is a theoretical tool for marking the nature of the qualitative changes that take place from stage to stage and for highlighting the salient psychological processes that characterize successive stages, contributing a consistency of pattern within diverse behavior elements. Although there are modal age correlations for the succession of developmental stages, they are influenced by cultural and experiential variables.

In general terms, the preschool years are characterized by a shift from conceptualization in terms of holistic, global properties to increasing differentiation in which the various aspects of objects and situations are clearly articulated, related to one another, and reorganized in terms of principles of subsumption, causality, or means–ends relationships. More specifically, this is a period when the child can perceive and use his perceptions of differences between self and nonself, things and symbols, person and function, inner and outer reality, real and make-believe, behavior and motivation. The integration into higher order concepts takes place through the self-generated processes of play and the formal and informal transactions among child, older children, and adults.

3. *Progress from earlier to later levels of functioning in any domain (emotional, intellectual, or social) is characterized by moments of equilibrium in which the individual's schemata are adequate for the task at hand, and by moments of instability in which currently operative structures are breaking down but new ones are not sufficiently developed to take over completely.*

Development is not a smooth course. Regressive behavior in any domain may indicate a troubled gap between existing schemata and the satisfactions they have previously afforded, on the one hand, and, on the other hand, the forward projection of new ways of performing with the means to implement them. In the later preschool period, the child's dissatisfaction with his own representative products may be the precursor of the impulse to depict more realistically (a characteristic of the next stage of development). Similarly, at this stage, resistance to rules and regulations may be signs of the wish and readiness to participate more in rule-making.

Periods of disequilibrium that are expressed in what seems to be regressive behavior may in fact be cues to developmental changes. An awareness of this will influence the steps taken to carry children through disturbing periods and guide them to new stages of stable functioning. This developmental principle can act as an important supplement—often, a corrective—to the interpretation of regressive behavior as originating solely in emotional stress.

4. An individual does not operate at a "fixed" developmental level, but manifests in his behavior a range of genetically different operations. Earlier or more "primitive" modes of organization are not eradicated, but become integrated into the more advanced modes of organization.

The stage theory is a way of ordering functional patterns in terms of an earlier-to-later, primitive-to-advanced sequence. While this sequence holds in general, an individual child does not function exclusively in terms of the operations characteristic of a certain level of development. He is capable of employing a variety of operations, drawing simultaneously or alternatively on more primitive and more advanced forms. It has been suggested that the mature person, and possibly the more creative one, is one who sustains a genetically varied repertoire of possible structuring.

For the preschool child, a "mixed" level of functioning is perhaps more characteristic than a "fixed" level. This can be seen in rapid shifts from free-wheeling fantasy to logically demanding reality in a given play sequence or in diverse explanations of natural phenomena, some in egocentric terms and others with understanding of objective elements and relations.

5. The self is both image and instrument. It emerges as the result of a maturing process in which differentiation of objects and other people becomes progressively more refined and self-knowledge is built up from repeated awareness and assessment of the powers of the self in the course of mastering the environment. The shape and quality of the self reflect the images of important people in the growing child's life.

During the first two or three years of life, the child establishes the distinctness of self as a physical organism and a psychological entity, referring to himself and his belongings as "I," "me," and "mine." Thereafter, the preschool child's advancing conceptual organization of experience proceeds outward from the central nucleus of the self. A potent integrating process takes place during this period as the more remote, impersonal elements of experience gain meaning by being bridged to self-related content.

Construction of the self-image is recognized by theorists of all persuasions as a crucial developmental task. The nature of the self-image reflects the assessing stance of the adult as well as what the child means, as a person, to the significant adults in his life. It reflects also the child's internalized feelings about, and evaluation of, his own skills, performance, and coping patterns (insofar as he has had opportunity to know what these are).

6. *Growth and maturing involve conflict. The inner life of the growing child is a play of forces between urgent drives and impulses, contradictory impulses within the self and demanding reality outside the self. The resolution of these conflicts bears the imprint of the quality of interaction with the salient life figures and the demands of the culture.*

The way conflicts (inevitable in the course of growth) are resolved is a major factor in the formation of basic attitudinal patterns and modes of interacting. The preschool child is still resolving certain elemental processes that are part of the later stages of infancy. In addition to his emotional dependence and highly charged feelings, his cognitive immaturity makes coping with separation, sharing, and frustration distressful and potentially traumatic. He is at a disadvantage in being cognitively bound to immediacy of time and space, not yet able to see things from another's vantage point or to sustain constancy of feeling under changing circumstances.

Other conflicts of this period are part of the leap ahead: the drive for independence associated with increased competence when there is not yet sufficient ability to manage without adult control and assistance and the ambivalence of wanting to move toward the grown-up child status while loitering in the pleasures and protection of being the little child. The dependence–independence conflict in its early stages is an active process at this period.

Program Activities for the Preschool

Illustrations of the learning experiences provided for the preschool child are organized in this section within the framework of the developmental-educational goals but particularized for the preschool child. The advantage in relating specific learning experiences to specific goals is that it clarifies rationale at the implementation level. From another point of view there is a disadvantage. It conceals the complexity of what is involved: the goals are interdependent, and the techniques have multiple effects. The choice and evaluation of any technique should not be based only on its effectiveness for a particular goal. The material presented in a later section will illustrate how the teacher guides a complex activity to serve multiple goals.

Learning Experiences Related to Goals[2]

1. *To serve the child's need to make an impact on the environment through direct physical contact and maneuver:*
    Exploring the physical world: e.g., equipment, space, and physical protection.
Children engage in a wide variety of physical maneuvers—climbing, stacking, riding and steering, sliding, swinging, balancing, heaving—requiring

2. The following italicized statements are reprinted by permission from Biber, Shapiro, and Wickens (1977).

coordinated use of the whole body as the means for exploring the physical world in the large.

Through these self-initiated activities and the variations the children invent they develop rudimentary knowledge of the world and how it works, gaining basic experience with space and direction.

> Constructive, manipulative activities with things (presymbolic): e.g.,
> variety of materials—blocks, clay, sand, and wood.

Through these constructive-manipulative activities (experiences in transforming objects—changing bulk, form, consistency, and pattern) the "things" of the environment become better known. At the same time, the children develop facilities with the kind of action responses that are the basis for later symbolic reorganization of experience.

The new skills are accompanied by knowledge of oneself as capable of these many ways of using and changing the physical world.

> 2. To promote the potential for ordering experience through cognitive strategies.
>
> Extending receptiveness and responsiveness: e.g., variety of sensory-motor-perceptual experiences, focus on observation and discrimination.

The teacher heightens the observing, discriminating proclivities of the children by marking passing experience with special accents, by changing figure–ground formulations so that certain elements stand out from the contextual mass. The child has an opportunity to discriminate when he or she stands quietly beside a fish tank to watch the fascinating way the fish swish past one another without "bumping" or listens to the sound of water swirling down the drain. Keen, discriminating observation is not only a way of gaining immediate knowledge; it is also the basis for constructing a conceptual network. A child's awareness of what is happening around him is one way of his feeling connected and belonging.

> Extending modes of symbolizing: e.g., gestural representation; two-dimensional representation with pencil, crayons, paints; and three-dimensional representation with clay, blocks, and wood.

The materials and schedule offer a full opportunity for representing and rehearsing experience symbolically: a music or rhythms period to move like a kangaroo or the way a lame man walks or the wind rushes by; time and a setting in which to use crayons or paint to create images of a man or a house or a tree on a two-dimensional surface and to use blocks or boards to make three-dimensional constructions that are reminders of boats or planes or farms or jails.

These activities are important learning experiences in that they represent the shift from dominance of the sensorimotor mode to symbolic reference as the instrument for integrating experience. To be able to take the "as if" stance (this picture is not a real ship but it is as if it were a ship)—to be able to deal with the symbols in place of the real things—is the precursor for later stages when letters, numbers, and sounds will stand, at a more abstract level, for objects, facts, and ideas.

> *Developing facility with language: e.g., word meanings and usage, scope of vocabulary, mastery of syntax; playful and communicative verbal expression.*

The teacher stimulates the use of verbal symbols as referents for all kinds of experience: to give a name to a physical action, to label objects as they are used or encountered, to translate desires or needs into words. Similarly, the function of written language is demonstrated in numerous contexts.

In addition to direct attention on language usage, there is an atmosphere of "language all around." Conversation between children and between adults and children is encouraged in one-to-one form and in group discussion. It is valued as a means for expressing personal feelings and sudden insights and for playfully inventing new forms, as well as for serving practical needs and pursuing further inquiry.

> *Stimulating verbal-conceptual organization of experience and information: e.g., verbal formulation; integration of present and nonpresent; accent on classification, ordering, relationship, and transformation concepts in varied experiential contexts.*

In this approach there is high-priority interest, both in theory and in practice, on stimulating the conceptual organization of experience. The questions put to the children and the comments made by the teacher as she observes and partakes in what they are doing reflect the purpose of establishing a thinking stance about experience as it transpires. There is a pervasive aura of "let's think about what is happening here and think ahead to what may happen." The children are stimulated to "if-then" thinking in social situations, in their play activities, and in their orientation in the school building. Questions are put to them that stimulate perceptual and conceptual search maneuvers. The teacher does not wish to elicit an answer at the moment of inquiry or confusion. She prefers to hold the question open and initiate children into ways to find answers.

The second intent—to stimulate differentiating and ordering the content of experience in the immediate present—is expressed in the organization of the setting, in the use the teacher makes of events that arise spontaneously, and in the experiences planned with a specific conceptual target in mind.

Comparative thinking is a much-used paradigm in the course of talking about events as they occur. From ongoing experience, concepts such as *same*, *different*, and *belong together* are extrapolated repeatedly, wherever opportune in the course of events.

Other teaching strategies are focused on *conceptualizing experience along a time line.* The primary ordering of events into a before-and-after scheme is encouraged by regularizing the sequence of activities and events in the daily program, reviewing the sequence with the children, and noting such changes of sequence as must surely occur in a flexible program. Awareness of sequence of events over a short time span elaborates to awareness of periodicity over longer spans—birthdays, seasons, school time, and vacations—and the children's reactions offer the teacher clues to how much stimulation to think beyond the boundaries of the immediate present is suitable.

The sense of oneself growing and changing is, of course, the core of the concept; it is a deeply personal insight to be shared with a trusted teacher. A five-year-old, looking over to the next area where the three-year-olds are playing, asks the teacher beside him, "Do you know what I looked like then?"

The techniques represented in these illustrations are a small sampling of the teacher's repertoire. They are suggestive of how teachers aim to help children master a great deal of confusion and complexity. When the child is successful, events, especially those in his personal experience, are related to an ordered movement of time. The changing character of the object world, animate and inanimate, becomes less magical in the context of the child's emerging understanding of the phenomenon of growth and aging. (Biber & Franklin, 1967)

> 3. *To advance the child's functioning knowledge of his environment.*
>   *Observation of functions within school: e.g., heating system, water pipes, kitchen, and elevator.*

The children learn, at first, the geography of a larger situation: the need to go *up* to the music room and *down* to go home, the way to get to a friend's room, the way to the kitchen, the two ways to get to the playground. They learn the essential functions performed by the people around them (the nurse, the helpers in the kitchen, the secretary in the office, the maintenance workers) through seeing them and talking to them where they are at work. They go to see how the building works; the world becomes known, spatially and functionally, through direct observation and contact. There is pleasure in curiosity fulfilled and power through knowing.

> *Story-reading: e.g., stories about nature, work processes, people's roles and functions.*

Reading stories to the children, an important part of the program, serves several ends. It may stimulate new curiosity, be pleasing in patterned or rhythmic verbal form, amuse as comedy does, offer the pleasures of fantasy, or touch deeper emotional levels. Books—stories—the printed word—are windows through which to know a bigger world. Being read to is a step on the way to wanting to be able to read. Story-reading time is a period of questioning and commenting by teacher and children, sometimes for inquiring, sometimes for making connections between the story characters and events and personal experience: The teacher elicits active participation, not uninterrupted passive attention.

> *Observation of functioning environment outside the school: e.g., to observe work processes, natural processes—building construction, traffic regulation; to visit police, fire fighters, farm and dairy.*

The learning experiences through which children acquire organized knowledge about the world beyond the school are developed to suit their expanding interests and cognitive facility: their ability to deal with the phenomenon of space symbolically (think geographically) and to comprehend complex chains of transformation in nature (biological or agricultural) or in the inanimate world (the work processes). The overall curriculum design contains a roster of such learning experiences regarded as suitable to, and desirable for, children at different age levels, taking into account variation in prior learning experience.

A suitable geography experience for three-year-olds may be to walk around the block and take note of what there is on the four streets: where the park ends and the stores begin, where there are only houses, and so forth. For five-year-olds, a trip to look out on the surroundings from the top of the neighboring church tower yields content for more elaborate thinking: the streets that command the movement of vehicles, the changed perspective from top to down and from near to far, and so on. The three-year-olds' interest in food may lead to the local supermarket; the older children's would take them to a wholesale market and, eventually, to a farm or an apple orchard.

Frequently, a trip is planned to supply needed information or clear up problems related to the children's dramatic play: to the railroad station to see how the train comes out of the tunnel; to the river's edge to talk to the person who ties up the boats; or to a building site to see the open elevator shaft. Back in the classroom, the trip experience reverberates in what the teacher initiates—recording the children's recall, displaying pictures taken on the trip or relevant newspaper articles, reviewing the new words encountered—and in the children's rehearsal and reexpression in drawings, block buildings, or dramatic play.

> *Discussion of contemporary events which children hear about: e.g., war, demonstrations, strikes, space activities, street violence, explorations, and earthquakes.*

The discussion period is a socializing activity in the sharing of recall, management of disagreement, floating of hypothetical explanations, and adaptation to a group form of communication. The teacher guides the thinking toward more advanced organization (by introducing beginning–end, cause–effect formulations) but accepts a wide scope of relevance when the children depend on offering personal material as the way of being part of the discourse. When the material the children offer from what they hear around them is benign though complicated—excitement about Skylab or men walking in space—the teacher will be responsive but will keep the information seeking and information giving on the broad general terms suited to the children's level of comprehension. Even demonstrations, strikes, and the like can be understandable to children if dealt with in broad strokes.

4. To support the play mode of incorporating experience.

*Nourishing and setting the stage for dramatic play activity: e.g.,
experiences, materials, and props.*

The most elaborate form of symbolizing experience in childhood is seen
in the self-initiated dramatic play through which children relive the most meaningful aspects of their experience. The playing is an active process by which the
children assimilate experience, selecting salient components of their impression
of the real world of how things work and what people do and recomposing them
into new configurations.

Since this kind of play is regarded as fundamental in the whole course of
representational thinking and as a natural way for young children to gain
cognitive mastery through reliving experience symbolically, it is given an
important place in the curriculum. Only by being attentive to the content and
movement of the children's play can the teacher perform her role, namely, to
offer additional materials or more content that will move the play toward a
more challenging or satisfying level and to be able to accept having her suggestion refused when the play has found its own inner-directed course. Furthermore, it is from the interests, quandaries, and misperceptions that come to the
surface in spontaneous play that the teacher finds many significant cues for
planning the more organized and directed learning experiences of the curriculum.

*Freedom to go beyond the restraints of reality in rehearsing and
representing experience.*

Self-initiated play serves another developmental purpose. It is a means of
expressing and dealing with emotion, of fusing subjective and objective without
embarrassment since, at this stage, the child's sense of adequacy is not yet
invested in strict adherence to rules of logic or literally faithful representation.
The freedom to allow affect to govern certain symbolic formations rather than
adhering consistently to objective reality makes it possible for children's dramatic play both to deepen positively toned emotions and to be catharsis for
negative experiences of defeat, frustration, and pain. It requires, as well, a
teacher who understands the developmental "sense" the children's dramatic
play involves as a vehicle both for firming up knowledge of the way the world is
and for fantasizing a world that works for one's inner needs.

5. *To help the child internalize impulse control.*
   *Communicating a clear set of nonthreatening controls: e.g., limits,
   rules, and regulations.*

The emphasis is on helping the young child to gradually accept the restraints on his impulsive behavior by helping him to understand the need for
rules and regulations, to enjoy the pursuits and the relationships that control
makes possible, and to take into account the direct feedback from his aggressions
against other children. There are specific restraints on individual behavior (e.g.,
do not break apart another child's block building) that children can come to
recognize as self-protective, in reverse. Clear communication about the "what"

and "why" of rules and regulations is an important aspect of establishing a rational authority system to which the children are invited. Rejecting threat and punishment, teachers bring more potent motivational forces into play to check and channel impulses originating in the basic energies, drives, and conflicts of young, growing children.

> *Creating a functional adult authority role: e.g., understandable restraints, alternative behavior patterns, and nonpunitive sanctions.*

The teacher's communication needs to come close to what the children are experiencing. Often, she helps the children penetrate the components of the situation, at times when they are in control and at times when they are not. For example, three children are waiting impatiently for a turn on the much-prized tricycles. The teacher articulates the children's feelings: "It is hard for John to wait; it is hard for Susie to wait." This approach encourages cognitive processes of differentiation in a social dilemma, which is a base for establishing a rational rather than an arbitrary authority code.

At times, the teacher helps the child find acceptable alternatives for disruptive behavior. When she stops children from fighting, she says. "You could fix it with words," offering the verbal alternative in the idiom of childhood. The implicit message is: These impulses are understandable, not evil, but they have a negative impact that is unacceptable; there are alternative behavioral patterns by which to manage them. In the last analysis, these techniques are dependent on the extent to which the teacher establishes simultaneously a supporting, ego-strengthening relation that motivates the child positively.

> 6. *To meet the child's need to cope with conflicts intrinsic to this stage of development.*
>
> *Dealing with conflict over possession displaced from the family scene: e.g., fostering special relation of child to single adult, guidance in learning to share things as well as people.*

In the school situation the young child encounters familiar problems with new characters—the teacher's interest, attention, and care must be shared with other children. The teacher, recognizing each child's need not to be lost among the others, finds ways to particularize the relationship: She listens to each child with the same investment and communicates with him in terms of his particular preferences, his sense of humor, or his particular trouble spots. Gradually, the child, though still dependent, can stop being possessive; he is able to feel closely related to the teacher while knowing she is similarly related to others.

To the young child with strong primitive affect, the "things" he wants and loves are very much a part of the self; giving away can be felt as a deep violation or a great loss. From this perspective, the teacher expects "sharing" to be learned slowly and does not make arbitrary demands. Instead, she helps to diminish the emotional charge by putting possession on a functional basis ("When he is through using it, you will have it").

> *Alleviating conflict over separation related to loss of familiar context*

of place and people; e.g., visits from home people to school, in-
terchange of home and school objects, and school trips to home
neighborhoods.

For many children, the problems associated with leaving home behind
and taking part in school life are compounded by the fact that they cannot yet
keep constancy between experiences separated in time—they cannot belong
both to home and to school simultaneously. This is, of course, further complicated when the total gestalt of the school situation is markedly different from
that of the home, requiring the child to adapt alternately to contrasting life
environments.

There are a variety of ways of helping children resolve this conflict. On a
long-term basis the curriculum can be developed so as to maximize the continuity of school experiences with the children's out-of-school lives.

Accepting ambivalence about dependence and independence: e.g.,
selection of areas of curriculum most suited to independent explora-
tion and acceptance of regressive dependent behavior under stress.

Toward the end of the preschool period, increasing physical strength and
general competence bolster the child's drive to become free of adult direction
and control. But this wish runs counter to the opposite wish, to enjoy the secure
position of the protected child. Headstrong resistant behavior may alternate
with weeping appeals for help in the face of trouble. Basically, the teacher's role
is to provide experiences in the school curriculum that allow for more independent exploration and problem-solving and to offer the child realistic feedback
knowledge of his powers and limitations.

7. To facilitate the development of an image of self as a unique and
competent person.
    Increasing knowledge of self: e.g., identity, family and ethnic mem-
    bership, and awareness of skills.

The teacher's role in helping the child be clear about his identity and
sphere of belonging is implicit in aspects of the teacher's function that have been
referred to previously: in the specificity of her response to his needs, inclinations, and performance; in bringing together his family and school worlds; in
helping him become aware of his skills as she joins in the pleasure of his
accomplishments.

Clarifying sense of self: e.g., as initiator, learner, and autonomous
individual

The teaching strategies, the organization of classroom life, the functional
authority role of the teacher, and the learning experiences given priority in the
curriculum are designed to give the child increasing competence and a feeling of
worth as a person.

The teacher contributes to this process by gauging suitable levels of
challenge for tasks to be undertaken, by encouraging trials, by helping the child
to analyze failure, and by encouraging new trials until the child begins to

perceive learning as an ongoing process that he ultimately accomplishes for himself. While the teacher guides and helps, the child is the major actor in this learning environment, actively selecting instead of passively accepting, initiating instead of responding. He questions, he explores, he perceives, and he solves problems. Presumably, he will internalize these modes as part of his image of himself.

> Advancing integration of self: e.g., self-realization through reexpression in symbolic play, latitude for individual mix of fantasy with knowledge of objective reality.

The value of free dramatic play as a natural medium, at this stage of development, for reassembling objective impressions and for symbolizing affect has been noted in the earlier section on dramatic play. In this kind of play the children themselves determine content, sequence, timing, and juxtaposition, projecting the mix of fantasy and reality that represents the cross-currents of their thoughts and feelings.

> 8. To help the child establish mutually supporting patterns of interaction.
> Building informal communication channels, verbal and nonverbal: e.g., adult–child, child–child.

Conversation is encouraged among children and in small groups with an adult. When children are in conflict, the teacher opens up an interchange between them, helping them to see the components of the situation from one another's perspective.

The teacher protects the communication of meaning. She accepts and values expression of feeling; she herself communicates expressively, not only verbally. She helps the child communicate meanings and intents even when his language is inadequate, listens to the thinking behind his verbal expression, and does not correct verbal usage if doing so will deflect or inhibit communication. She stimulates communication among the children, sometimes by making collective observations of what different children have done, sometimes by directing a line of questioning back into the child group: "You could ask Mary, that's something she knows about."

> Cooperative and collective child-group relations: e.g., discussion periods, joint work projects.

How this goal is furthered has been indicated incidentally in the descriptions of program activities; the children's adaptations to one another's flow of thought and action in their spontaneous play schemes that occasionally need teacher guidance; and the teaming up for job responsibilities such as watering plants or setting tables.

Story reading and discussion periods are used as opportunities for building a community of interests and for developing skills in collective thinking processes, whether by pooling, countering, or incorporating. The trips into the environment acquire a great in-group charge, heightened by realization that strange, busy adults are willing to answer the children's group-originated questions. Cooperative activities among young children cannot be expected to run a smooth course. The teacher helps the children develop group mores—helping one another with problems, comforting in times of distress, enjoying working together—that support the processes of learning and socialization.

> *Creating supportive adult roles: e.g., source of comfort, troubleshooter, solver of unknowns, investor in child's learning.*

The teacher's investment in the child's learning is the foundation for the effectiveness of teaching strategies. Among these, it is perhaps useful to point again to the teacher's availability to give help, clarify ideas, and suggest new materials; bring a child's semiformed intent or idea to a productive condition; and respond to a child's work in terms of its particularity, understanding the child's investment in the process. On another level, it is equally important that the teacher be a resource who can resolve trouble and who can give wholehearted support without relinquishing responsibility for controlling what it is hard for children to manage.

> *Establishing models of human interchange which value individuality: e.g., teacher–teacher and supervisor–teacher relationships.*

The teacher's potential for creating a sound learning environment is closely related to the way other people in the school setting enact their roles: the administrators, the ancillary personnel (psychologists, nurses, and social workers), the community leaders, and the parents.

A Multiple-Goal Activity

The material in this section, a record of the sequence of a cooking episode, illustrates how the teacher's commitment to multiple developmental goals is expressed in her planning and guiding of a program activity.[3]

Part 1: Preparation. This episode is an account of a sequence of planned activities culminating in a cooking experience for four-year-old children. Part 1 details the preparation in the classroom for the purchase of the food and the group's trip to a local store.

The fresh pears at lunch evoked the excited comment "apples" from Spanish-speaking Fernando.

"Well, this is a fruit," said Miss Gordon encouragingly, "but it has another name. Do you remember the apples we had last week?" "They were hard to bite," said Joey.

"And we made applesauce," said Rosina.

"This fruit is called a pear, Fernando; let's taste this pear now. We'll have apples again."

---

3. This section is reprinted by permission from Biber, Shapiro, and Wickens (1977). Part 2, describing the return to the classroom and the cooking operation, is omitted here.

The teacher responds to what is correct in the child's response, valuing his category association. First, she wants to support communication and willingness to experiment with language; later she gives the correct name. The children strengthen the experience by relating it to previous experience in which they were active.

"Mine's soft," said Joey.

"Can we make applesauce again?" begged Rosina.

The teacher replied, "Perhaps we could do what Janice wanted to do. Remember? To take some home to her family?"

"To my mommy, and my grandma, and Danny."

"Not to my baby," said Rosina. "He's too little. Him only drink milk."

"Tomorrow we'll buy lots of apples," said Miss Gordon.

The teacher is building a sense of continuity by recalling earlier intentions that had been expressed by the children.

She rarely corrects use of pronouns in four-year-olds. She knows the child will learn through greater social maturity and hearing language.

After rest, Miss Gordon asked the children how they could take home their applesauce. "What can we put it in?"

Rosina ran to the house corner and returned with two baby food jars. "I bringed lots," she said. Miss Gordon remembered that Rosina had come to school lugging a bag full of baby-food jars, many of which she had put away. "A good idea! And your mommy said she would keep more for us. Let's write a note to tell her we need them tomorrow."

Rosina dictated a note: "I got to bring bunches of jars to school. We are going to make applesauce. I love you, Mommy." And painted her name with a red marker.

The teacher helps children to think ahead to steps in a process.

The use of a tense form, though incorrect, represents learning for the child. The teacher does not correct at this moment, when she is responding to the child's pleasure in solving the practical problem that had been posed. She is strengthening the connection between home and school.

The teacher helps the children learn that writing is a recording of meaning and a way of communicating.

The next day was jar-washing and arranging time. Each of the children put his jars on a tray on which there was a large card with the child's name.

Janice sets out one jar for her mother, one for her grandmother, one for her brother, and, after a pause, one for herself.

Rosina changed her mind. "My baby can have a little bit," she said. So she needed a jar for her father, her mother, her baby, and herself.

Joey and the teacher figured out that he needed six, and that Fernando needed nine!

The children are actively involved in the steps preparatory to the planned activity—an experience in organization which has personal meaning.

The teacher's plan calls for recognition of one's own name and one-to-one counting of family members.

The teacher turned their attention to a chart near the cooking corner. She had made a recipe chart, pasting colored magazine pictures next to the names of the items they would need to make the applesauce, and had taped a stick of cinnamon to the chart.

Miss Gordon said, "Let's look at the recipe chart. I have a list so we can remember to buy everything."

The children said, "Apples."

Miss Gordon checked her list.

Then, "Sugar."

The children were silent as they looked at the stick of cinnamon taped to the chart.

Miss Gordon suggested, "Smell it. Have we had it before?"

Joey remembered: "Toast! What we put on toast!"

"Yes," said Miss Gordon, and then gave the word, "cinnamon."

The children are having a dual experience—pictorial representation and formal symbol usage.

The teacher supplies the word after the children have revived their direct experience with the phenomenon.

Now they were ready to start.

Outside the building, the children pointed out a large truck loading lumber across the street. This was an often observed activity which the boys wanted to watch.

Then Miss Gordon asked if they remembered the way to the fruit stands, and they went on pointing out familiar places: where the buses turn, where Joey's uncle used to live when there were houses there, the place they saw the snails in front of the fish store.

The children remembered to hold hands among the crowds at the fruit store.

The lumber yard is a known landmark and serves as a point of departure and return. Young children are reassured by having small, understandable pieces in a confusing city environment, and the teacher helps them by encouraging them to begin to perceive familiar objects as guideposts.

Mr. Gus greeted them.

"We want apples. We want lots of apples," said the children.

"Sure, sure," answered Mr. Gus. "What kind?"

The children looked at all the apples so beautifully arranged. Varieties of red apples were displayed alongside other fruit. Next to the McIntoshes were yellow apples.

Miss Gordon took down one for the children to feel and to look at.

Mr. Gus supplied the name, "Golden Delicious."

These words delighted the children and they decided to buy some red McIntoshes and some yellow "golden" apples.

"Then we can taste two different kinds of applesauce," said Miss Gordon.

Mr. Gus divided the fruit purchased into four bags, two with yellow apples, two with red.

The colorful array of fruit is a visual display of classification. The children use color as the criterion for selection. The teacher exploits this incidental experience with classification and uses it in connection with the plan to make applesauce.

The children helped the teacher count the three dollars needed for the purchase.

At another store, they looked into and sniffed the spice racks, choosing one type of cinnamon.

The salesman said, "Twenty-five cents"; as the children watched, the teacher gave him a dollar.

"It's only twenty-five cents," protested Janice. "I'll get change," replied the teacher reassuringly.

These children have more than usual experience in handling money in store situations.

On the way back, they passed "their" fruit store. At the next one, Fernando smiled and said, "My Mommy goes here."

The others chimed in about their mothers' purchases and the stores they went to. Some knew the names of the stores.

Miss Gordon pointed in the direction of other shopping areas.

Across the street from the school block, the teacher stopped the group. "Where are we?"

"I see the wood place!"

"Oh, school is right down there. I go this way every day with my brother."

By this time, the teacher was holding a few bags of apples, and the street crossing was managed with coatsleeve holds and careful walking.

The teacher welcomes the children's blending their intimate personal recalls with the knowledge-focused trip.

In this paper an effort has been made to describe briefly a comprehensive preschool program that has been evolving over six decades. We take the position that the basic principles and practices are applicable from one educational social milieu to another, recognizing, at the same time, that successful implementation in a change-process situation requires sensitivity and imaginative adaptation.

The Developmental-Interaction Approach Applied

I have been reading three books that speak of the maturing of the developmental-interaction position. The theoretical constructs and value premises of that position appear and are expounded as the foundation for three different kinds of educational purpose. Each is continuous with, but a long way beyond, the vision of the private experimental schools for middle-class children of the early and mid-century, when the progressive philosophy was generated and took root.

In *Threes and Fours Go to School* (1974), Sylvia Krown reports a comparative compensatory program for deprived and middle-class children in Israel whose goals, methods, and criteria of progress are explicitly derived from this position. In *The Learning Child* (1972), Dorothy Cohen addresses parents, assuming that they will be interested in the basic elements and theoretical rationale for the program, methods, and activities and will appreciate specific and fully developed illustrative material on how it all happens in classrooms. In *The Middle Years of Childhood* (1977) by Patricia Minuchin, the developmental-interaction position, briefly summarized, is placed in the context of a comprehensive review of the literature of developmental psychology, especially useful to psychology students. A brief description of a design for an elementary school is presented as one model for application of that orientation in psychology to education.[4]

In all three books, the developmental-interaction viewpoint provides the orientation for analysis. Because these three books differ from one another in the focus of the content—preschool and middle years, educational practice, and research findings—it is interesting to trace how the common point of view of the authors penetrates and influences their educational preferences and research critique.

The Life Circumstance of the Non-European Children

Sylvia Krown's book is the report of a two-year research study based in Jerusalem. It was designed to study the effects of a preschool program on the behavior of three- and four-year-old children from Middle Eastern and North African families when compared to children of better educated and more skillfully employed parents of Western European origin. There were three groups of disadvantaged and advantaged children together; one group of the disadvantaged alone.[5] While following the basic principles of a psychoeducational program, practices were systematically adapted to the needs of the disadvantaged children, as hypothesized. Systematic, assiduous record-taking provided data for assessment of initial deficit, and documentation of the changing, progressing behavior of the two different groupings of children in response to the human-relations climate and program stimulation. These data were the basis for a comparative analysis of developmental gains at the end of the program.

One of the significant contributions of the study is the dynamic in-

4. Both Dorothy Cohen and Sylvia Krown were graduate students in my class in child development at Bank Street College in 1936 and 1942, respectively. Patricia Minuchin was my associate in the Research Division between the years of 1950 and 1965. I value greatly my association with each of them and am especially gratified by their dissemination of this orientation into the field where psychology and education cross.

5. In this study, the term *disadvantaged* has major cultural significance. The privileged children came from families of European heritage; the disadvantaged children came from families recently arrived in Israel from North African and Middle Eastern countries; in addition, those families represented low socioeconomic status and minimal education.

terpretation of the specific kind of deprivation that the non-European children suffered in the nature of the mother–child relationship. The mothers loved their children and provided for their physical needs, demonstrated affection when the children were "good," and punished them for unacceptable behavior. But the continuity of being accepted and understood, good or bad, was absent. The large size of the families contributed to minimizing the sense of self for the individual.

The mothers had a limited concept of their role. Though not oppressed by great poverty, they were discouraged by the burden of large families and the dictates of a strong code for keeping the home clean, which they managed partly by keeping the children out of the house.

For the children this inadequate mothering role meant premature independence for which they were not emotionally ready, involving conflict between the unfulfilled strong needs for dependency, consistent love, and protection and the daily demands of adjusting to the real, relatively noncaring world they lived in. It is to this constellation of negative emotional factors that the author attributes the characteristics of the children as they entered the school situation: suspicious of people, wary of close relationships, showing signs of feelings of inadequacy, inferiority, and confused self-identity. Their impulsive behavior and low frustration tolerance were attributed to their having missed the establishment of basic trust in the parents.

Similarly restricted in the area of intellectual development, the mothers did not see themselves as the "bridge or translator of the outside world to the world of the child." There was limited language communication. The children's expression of natural curiosity was looked upon usually as a nuisance; the major parental goal was teaching the child to obey and conform to the rules of the home.

It was this relatively unfocused, nonverbalized, and nonexplicated lifestyle in the home that seemed to explain to the author and her colleagues the initial deficiencies of many of the deprived children's ways of responding to the school situation, namely, their inability to perceive and delineate things clearly, their reluctance to explore and ask questions, their lack of a sense of order or expected sequence, and their difficulties in entering the world of cause-and-effect thinking.[6]

Emotional Expression and the Play Curriculum

In this school setting, the complex role of the teacher in emotional development is clearly formulated. At one level it is recognized that the program itself offers

---

6. To an unusual degree, this book presents the rationale providing the connections between developmental theory and educational practice. This is done throughout the various sections, and in a way that makes it quite different from the usual pattern of presenting theory first, followed by illustrations of practice. And the rationale is the more convincing because of the rich evidence presented from the teachers' diaries, which record not only observations of child behavior but also reflections, doubts, and self-criticism on the part of the teacher-recorders.

natural outlets for feelings and fantasies, and the teacher's involvement may appear to be inactive, in a literal sense, even while she is actively engaged in observing, thinking about the significance of what is being projected, storing away the insight, and planning how to move the child to greater differentiation of reality.

A more active therapeutic role is also often assigned to the teacher—to encourage expressions of fears and conflicts and to help the children to resolve them by open verbal expression and communication, as well as in their dramatic play and other creative activities. It is important to note that the technique of release through expression is always followed by guidance toward resolution through reality involvement.

> Reuben was a bright, constructive, and cooperative child, but he was frightened of animals. He screamed and was fearful every time he saw goats in the nearby field. The teacher encouraged him to talk about his fears and led a group discussion with the children about their fear of animals. She told them she too had been afraid of dogs when she was little and the children told about their private fears. . . . In the nursery, the children had turns holding the hamster on their laps each day as his cage was cleaned. They would pat it and talk about its behavior. Reuben was revolted at first but after a while brought himself to touch it gingerly. At a later stage, he fought for the privilege of holding it every day and finally he was allowed to take it home for the holidays. (Krown, 1974, p. 49)

At another level, the teacher accepts and verbalizes the feelings of the child that are at the base of hostile, destructive, or self-destructive behavior, but, at the same time, provides sanctions against primitive retribution. "I know how angry you are that he threw your block building down; it would make anybody angry, but you may not hurt him." (Krown, 1974, p. 46) The interpretive comment may generate the expectation of a relation to the teacher which could interfere with her primary teaching role. Also, the interpretation may not hit the mark, and if it does not, it creates so much more psychological noise in an already oversaturated situation. The teacher is aware of these possibilities: "Of course, the teacher must be very careful and sparing in her interpretations and may express them only when she has reason to be sure of her ground" (Krown, 1974, p. 51). A child's aggressive acts are understood as a step in the direction of making contact—the essence of becoming socialized. The teacher's role is the slow task of leading the child toward replacing aggressive acts with positive social maneuvers.

The author's analysis of free play as part of the developmental goal reviews the successive stages by which the children move from vague, generalized symbolization—to carry a wheel and "be" a car—to complex cooperative projects representing "our neighborhood," which includes apartment houses, stores, roads, and electricity, or vehicles of transportation. At each stage, the teacher supported and fed the intellectual process by introducing more awareness of concrete details, stimulating incorporations of children's own observations on neighborhood trips in their play projects, and helping them find solutions to the problems generated in the play as their projects become more complex and elaborated.

At the same time that the teacher appreciates and encourages this progress toward gaining cognitive power and storing up information on the functioning environment, she remains aware that these young children will also be utilizing the play opportunity for the expression of fears and wishes and the projection of hostility. The fantasied wild animals, the prisoners and jailers, the cowboys and "bad men" still have a place, along with the play schemes of pilots and passengers climbing the ramp to enter the planes that fly to the desert. The teacher respects the shifts back and forth from the real world to the fantasy world that may occur in any play episode.

The "Trip" as an Example of Areas of Study

Because a play curriculum is so often misunderstood as being cognitively casual, I appreciate the authors' conscientious effort to present specifically the learning goals which were the foundation for the selected curriculum areas. The activities for each area chosen for study—the trips, the discussions, the didactic games, the expressive activities—were built around these goals and adapted to the children's potential and motivated interests.

For example, a trip to a railroad station was undertaken following a spontaneous discussion about trains stimulated by a child's report to the group about a trip he had taken with his mother. At the station, the children's experience was partly spontaneous—watching people buying tickets, listening to announcements from the loudspeakers, inspecting the mailbags assigned to the freight cars. Some of the experience was more directed and probably prearranged—a guided tour by the stationmaster to see the trains, the tracks, and the signals, and "a special treat," a little ride for them on the train.

In the days after the trip, their experience was relived in play, developing gradually from blocks placed on chalk-drawn "tracks" to more elaborate components—signal lights, railroad workers' hats, and a ticket puncher. The rehearsal of the experience appears in another context in the group discussions with the teacher in which the children talked about their experience—what the tracks looked like, differences between trains and other means of transportation, the feeling of riding on a train. This sequence is familiar to teachers who use play experience as a learning mode.

Other areas of the curriculum followed similar principles of learning for the young child: building on children's spontaneous, experience-derived interests; providing direct observational experience with the functioning reality of the environment; establishing a play mode in the classroom that facilitates the children's absorption and sorting out of experience through their own ways of reenacting and rethinking; and, finally, extending and consolidating conceptual mastery through teacher-led group discussions.

Stimulation of Verbal Expression

While the spontaneous play and the associated program activities were the experiential base for language competency and environment, the teachers took an active role in stimulating the expression of the children's experiences into an articulate verbal-conceptual modality. The world of *doing* was also a rich world of talking, listening, questioning, and answering between and among the children and the adults. In addition to the stimulation of language usage, in the form of question-raising, descriptive and denotative comments, that the teachers fed into the situation at any appropriate moment in the course of ongoing program activities (which they call unstructured language learning), they engaged in numerous "structured" language activities. Many of these were in game form, specifically aimed to sharpen perception, stimulate classification and differentiation, and find fun and pleasure in language usage and creative verbal byplay.

For the disadvantaged children who were so much inclined to be silent, there had to be slow, sensitive steps to lead them to verbal interchange. First, there was a basic sense of common good feeling requiring great patience in order to establish contact, nonverbal as well as verbal, with an unresponsive child. Then, the teacher introduced use of simple language, speaking even though not getting response, translating actions and gestures into words; group singing, finger games, an exaggerated operatic kind of language, rhythmic chanting, and, all through, communication of acceptance and the adult's willingness to wait for the child's readiness to relate to her with words. Not all the non-European children were equivalently deprived of stimulation and equally retarded in the use of language symbolically or in communication. Responsive, interacting teachers were trying to realize the children's varied individual potentialities, some three years after infancy.

Analysis of Change

The assessment of the changes in the non-European population from the time of entry to the close of the two-year program is summarized and described qualitatively from study of the records. The extent to which these children reached or did not reach the level of the privileged children during the same period is documented in the analysis of the observations. In brief, they report the change in the deprived child population during the experimental period and the areas in which differences have and have not been eliminated:

Physical Appearance: From a tight, defensive posture; troubled, suspicious, angry expressions; depressed manner and rare smiling; undirected haphazard activity *to* alive, alert smiling or passionate crying; heads up and eyes no longer averted; bodies used with ease; louder, more assertive voices. *Deprived and privileged children almost indistinguishable.*

Activity–Passivity: From passive, uninterested mood; disinterest in toys and inability to play; aimless wandering and haphazard activity *to* purposeful activities and enthusiastic use of materials; readiness to try new experiences, initiate and carry through goals; taking exploratory steps and asking questions. *Similar to privileged children* though subjects of play differed from those of privileged children.

Relations to People: From general suspiciousness and defensiveness; fear of and shrinking away from teachers; tendency to withdraw; "loner" in play *to* naturalness and open expression of appeal or feeling; trust in teachers; mutual acceptance and joint play. *Similar to privileged children* except that some continued to interact with only two or three others and some (who came from extreme home pathology) continued to present markedly disturbed behavior throughout.

Impulsivity vs. Ability to Tolerate Frustration and Delayed Gratification: From impulsive darting about, destruction of products; running away *to* controlled, directed behavior; predictable emotional reactions; more restrained, verbally expressed aggression; toleration of frustration without temper and acceptance of limitations and delayed gratification (a slower process). *Similar to privileged children* except some still had temper tantrums.[7]

Mode of Thinking: From early "fog" and confused sense of time, place, and order *to* awareness of self, people, and things; more oriented, sense-activated, clear observation; to perceptual elaboration expressed in play and art; to pleasure in regularizing and classifying; interested, curious, and imaginative with materials and language *but* only some engaged in searching, how-and-why questioning, and self-motivated exploration; many still needed priming from the teachers to pursue their line of questioning; found it hard to assimilate cause–effect thinking; showed remnants of passive acceptance and dependence on teacher for stimulation.

Self-Concept and Self-Esteem. Within a pattern of general progress for the deprived children toward more sensitivity and awareness of themselves and others as individuals, differences on this dimension appear between the homogeneously grouped deprived children and the heterogeneously grouped child groups. In the *homogeneous* group, the deprived children made the most deep-seated gains—self-confidence; readiness to perform; goal-directed play; expressions of self-worth, pride in work and mastery (having internalized, seemingly, feelings of being accepted and valued); positive leadership. In the *heterogeneous* groups: marked improvement in self-confidence, initiative, and sense of purpose generally, but more ill at ease and diffident; imitating what privileged children were playing and troubled by not understanding; pervasive, unjustified feelings of inferiority; taking roles of followers though in reality they could have reached leadership positions; an overall "slightly sad and shadowy quality."

Language. The deprived children gained in richness of vocabulary, sen-

---

7. Here there is a note by the author suggesting that perhaps "we" lacked understanding of their cultural values, which expresses once more the unusual and admirable self-analytical posture of the staff.

tence construction, clarity of pronunciation; in communicative verbal facility—talking, rhyming, use of similes, connective and relative terms; in listening and concentrating and taking part in group discussions *but,* in comparison to the privileged children, they had a less easy flow of words, used incorrect grammar, used full sentences only in response to teacher request, had a more limited vocabulary and body of available information, especially in areas not developed in the school program. In all, vocabulary and information level were still inadequate for the age level, and the gap in information and language usage between deprived and privileged had widened in the two years.[8]

This program has the unusual advantage of being administered by a questioning and self-questioning staff whose reflections were recorded in their report:

> It was not easy to determine the proper balance in programming for each child. When and how much did he need opportunities for his own exploration and play and when was it preferable to give him more drill in perception and verbal expression? (Krown, 1974, p. 67),

which went on to similar questions involving decisions on procedure. For example:

> when to step in and when to give the children time to solve the block-building problems themselves. . . . It was not the same for all the children and thus there was no absolute rule for the teachers. (Krown, 1974, p. 114)

and the self-questioning: "The children are not always pleased at our readiness to help them when they build. Perhaps we don't always sense the correct moment."

.   .   .

What Sylvia Krown did in relating the postulates of developmental-interaction theory to the particulars of educational practice in the preschool years, Dorothy Cohen did for the primary and elementary years. There is an advantage to the reader (parent, student, teacher) in the active way in which she takes the position of both critic of the old and advocate of the new—moving back and forth from analysis of what has been and is wrong with traditional educational practices to the practices and values of the nontraditional inheritors of the progressive school philosophy.

Her critique is focused on (1) failure to understand and adjust to concepts of developmental sequence, (2) the restricted, outdated view of the learning process and curriculum content, and (3) insensitivity to how the mounting

8. This brings us back to a question we have met up with earlier: Would these findings have been different if the programs had been developed for the developmental period of infancy prior to the three-year-old level?

problems and rapid changes in the larger society affect the world of childhood. I can only recount briefly a few examples of how she justifies her criticism, sometimes on the basis of developmental stage misalignment and neglect of motivational factors, other times because of antisocial value premises, and sometimes both.

> American children in the primary grades learn about the voyage of the Nina, the Pinta, and the Santa Maria; or the first long, hard winter of the Puritans. What possible meaning can these experiences have for them in terms of human suffering, aspiration, tragedy, or triumph, or in terms of their historical significance? How can historical events mean anything to children who do not yet understand time in its fullest sense, even if they can rattle off names and dates? (Cohen, 1972, p. 150)

The Developmental Error

Unless there are connections in a child's mind, at this developmental level, with his own culture and within the scope of his geographical concepts, such facts are merely sterile information. What is more, the learning experience is likely "to be a bore." It follows that Cohen decries those educational schema in which children are offered "fact-laden packets mechanically attached to a meager, basic structure of skills."

In her analysis of the problems of the skill subjects, we find a mixture of pointing to the methods and assumptions that need to be corrected, a plea for more study to gain insight into this complex area of human growth, empathy for troubled parents, and anger at the distorted social pressures that make so much trouble for parents and children, not to mention teachers. This really sums up the moods—positive and negative, but seldom neutral—that generate the spirit of liveliness and intensity that characterizes this book.

To illustrate: Cohen reviews in detail the successive, slowly developing psychological insights that are essential before a child should be expected to master the mystery of being able to read, and the individual differences in traversing this course. She argues against the rigid timetable for rate and age of reading competence of the traditional school, which denies these developmental realities and results in praise or humiliation of children—both responses irrelevant from a theoretical point of view. Besides, it does considerable damage to the internalization of self-image for those who do not progress at a fast rate. "Denying the differences in readiness among primary-grade children is a way to build feelings of inadequacy . . . brand some children as failures." Further, "the excessive pressure to achieve, the hysteria about reading, the skewed priority given to reading in the primary grades, and the accompanying competitiveness add up to potential disaster" (p. 186).

In a similar vein, Cohen decries the premature emphasis on correct form in writing, the misplaced priority of the mechanical over the conceptual, and the accent on the mechanics (when children are just tasting the world of writing) that takes priority over the essential element of what there is to communicate about through this newly acquired mode. Not that form never matters. Rather, "the conflict is one of timing and consideration for the most teachable moment. Obviously, form strengthens content, yet form without content is hollow and meaningless" (p. 191). When this approach is applied to arithmetic, the third of the skill subjects, a consistent principle emerges, namely, the necessity to guard "the recognition of concepts during the period when the mechanical aspects are being painstakingly learned" and, put more generally as a basic learning principle: "Only as they [children] recognize the meaningfulness of the skill will the chore aspects take on the relation of necessary parts to an understood whole."

The use of developmental-stage characteristics as criteria for content and organization of curriculum is fully documented and illustrated in the exposition of learning in the intermediate grades. The criteria for choice of content and method should be the stage-associated level of intellectual grasp (not an IQ measure), the child's need to be competent and independent, and awareness of the associated conflicts—the pull to the peer world, the growth toward internalized morality, the maturing of social-sex identification, and the riverbed of deep feeling that is intrinsic to this stage of development.

Curriculum as Knowledge and Method

If it is kept in mind, for example, that children eight and nine years old are still in a transition stage between the concreteness of the earlier period and the emerging capacity to deal with abstractions, the choice for study of another culture would fall on peoples such as the Eskimos, Aztecs, Bedouins, or Indians, in preference to Greeks, Florentines, or Romans. As Cohen says, these are all remote and foreign cultures but the life styles of the first groups have reasonably uncomplicated physical reality that is readily observable to this age group of children, while the social and aesthetic implications of the latter cultures are too subtle for them (Cohen, 1972, p. 247).

Similarly, in each of the substantive areas of the curriculum, the author describes developmentally based curriculum choices and teaching methods. And, as is true throughout the book, she takes on the doubting Thomases. She is well aware that breaking with the traditional curriculum and selecting the content that holds greatest meaning in child terms will lead to anxious inquiries about what is being left out—important dates, places, events. In rebuttal, she points to the massive forgetting of superficially acquired facts, to which any traditionally educated adult can testify, and the long-run gains, by contrast, of deeply understood, feeling-invested, conceptually disciplined knowledge.

Not only content but method needs to be altered radically. In the science area, a general concept such as the interdependence of living organisms can be mastered at this stage if the methods follow the mandates of Lucy Mitchell's "direct experience," geared to the children's concrete thinking style. For foundation, there is direct observation of woods, streams, swamps, backyards, and parks, reading man's history in the banks of rivers and lakes and the layers of rock formations. The sequence is observation, questioning, and analysis, leading to pursuit of complex questions such as how a river is formed and what changes its flow, or how important is the relationship of one animal or plant to another.

Social Sensitivity

No matter how well adapted to the children's natural interests, modes, and rates of learning the curriculum may be, it would be shallow and incomplete if the study of history, for example, did not help children to "see" the people and their feelings as part of every social enterprise. Cohen writes: "The continuity of human endeavor and feeling must be consciously extended into the study of man and his social experiences as children grow beyond the action-oriented learning style of their younger years." There is a dimension to human experience, past or present, that is not to be missed if the children's maturing perspective and initiation into the adult decision-making society are to be socially and personally constructive and satisfying. It needs to be built up during the learning years. It is important to ask, for example:

> What were Rosa Parks' feelings the day she refused to sit in the back of a bus in Montgomery, Alabama? How did the men who conquered Peru feel about taking the belongings of a strange people and keeping them? How did the Indians feel when the skills by which they had always lived could no longer be applied to the living conditions imposed upon them by the white conquerors? (Cohen, 1972, p. 276)

Obviously, from this viewpoint, learning and understanding must take more than the cognitive route, find more than verbal-ideational patterns with which to give deeper insights and convey meanings. The curriculum therefore gives high priority to expression in symbolic form (nonverbal and verbal)—the arts, dramatization, creative language—as another essential mode for grounding and integrating personal experience, as well as a means of extending sensitivity to the vast panorama of human endeavor. "With thought and feeling both at work, children must re-create their experiences symbolically in order to recognize the patterns inherent in them."

Corrosive Influences of Our Times

I cannot close this brief account of Dorothy Cohen's book without referring to another important theme that runs throughout. From her own professional experience and the studies of others, she gives a highly disturbing account of negative changes in children in all social classes today as compared with previous decades—changes attributable to definable social problems and faults in our contemporary society. The picture she draws of child life and the world around is grim, with little relief. She is concerned about evidence of boredom, indifference, and low enthusiasm; resistance to recognizing the feelings of

others and the use of cold logic to evade morality; the change in hero figures—
for example, from Paul Bunyan, whose talents were rooted in human abilities,
albeit larger than lifesize, to contemporary figures whose strengths come
through magic and the help of the supernatural; and the cynical acceptance of
and experience with overt and covert value systems in the larger society which
contradict those of the school.

None of this is mysterious in her view. The correlates of these changes
can be found in the social scene: planned obsolescence and rapid replacement of
play materials designed for continuous, creative, imaginative use; the loss
of opportunity for the kinds of self-directed play activity that are rooted in
traditions of childhood as a result of the changeover from natural to urban
environments; mechanization that cuts back the opportunities for children to
partake in the important real-life activities of keeping a family going; the
prevalence of modern mass media as an influence on switching values to posses-
sions and position from qualities of character as ideals for living. In sum,
"children are being seduced into a consumer instead of a producer outlook on
life far too early . . . becoming cogs in the wheels of social efficiency and big
business operation . . . being manipulated to satisfy skewed priorities" by
which powerful advertising of school materials and curricula takes the place of
thoughtful appraisal by professionals. These are shocking truths. One hopes,
with the author, that a nontraditional school curriculum in a humanistic school
environment could be one form of constructive defense against corrosive social
influences and misdirected educational influences.

.   .   .

In Patricia Minuchin's book we come to a shift of focus: the center of
attention is a review of available knowledge of developmental facts and processes in "the middle years of childhood," the title of her work. The implications for education, approximately from the years six to twelve, reflect the
author's alignment with the developmental-interaction position. Instead of
focusing on a design of educational practice and mustering the appropriate
theory in support of it, as Krown and Cohen have done, Minuchin undertakes a
cumulative process by which her review and analysis of research findings lead
her to favor a particular educational orientation. Like Krown and Cohen, she
has a basic reference point for her preferred educational design: a value perspective, a clearly expressed image of what she considers the optimal course of
development in childhood generally, and in the middle years in particular. It is
the anchorage of these three authors in a common value system, as well as their
allegiance to developmental theory, that accounts for the extent of congruence
in the three books despite their differences in purposes and thinking styles and
in the potential reader audiences to which they have addressed themselves.

In the research-review sections, Cognitive Development, Social Development, and Individual Development preceding a chapter on the school, Minuchin follows a consistent pattern. Each chapter opens with a factual survey of

the research literature, covering what has been learned about the child in the middle years and reviewing current advances in understanding the nature of the developmental processes involved. But this is a book for thinking and probing, not only for factual review. So the author moves consistently toward a reflective mood, in which problems that have been disciplined in order to fit into experimental designs are projected onto the larger canvas of complex, daily living reality, particularly with respect to functioning in school. Minuchin warns against applying the findings of the restricted conditions of the laboratory too literally to the "natural life" situations of home, street, or school. Thus the route proceeds from facts to wider implications beyond experimental situations to guidelines and projections as to what school could be for the elementary school child. To some of the questions she raises, Minuchin thinks there are acceptable answers in known educational procedures for those who wish to choose them; to others, she sees a wider area of unknowns calling for more study.

Research has to be bounded, but thinking about it does not. Minuchin's comments following her reviews of findings are an exhilarating example of how much can be gained by criticizing and reflecting after the data have been processed.

Cognitive Development: Trends and Individual Variation

After reviewing the accepted central trends, age located, in cognitive development, Minuchin calls attention to a study in which children of a common age showed wide variation not only in cognitive style but also in emotional response, expressed in fruitless repetition, abandonment, anger, and self-criticism.

> The use of the mind to think, to learn, to ask questions, and to handle preferences is part of the whole functioning personality. The way children approach such tasks is defined in part by their stage of development and their intellectual style, but it is also defined by their individual ways of handling complexity and frustration, both in cognitive and emotional terms. (Minuchin, 1977, pp. 26–27).

She is not content to leave the review, in terms of central tendencies, alone. The group-dynamics literature (techniques and findings) is fully reviewed, expounding the teacher's responsibility for establishing the "climate" of the classroom, for recognizing potential leadership within the group, for understanding subgroup relationships within the classroom structure, and for developing techniques for opening communication and creating change. While on the whole this approach is accepted as moving in a positive direction, Minuchin raises salient critical questions, many of them dealing with the failure to give sufficient consideration to developmental characteristics at different stages as they might affect group functioning. She asks, for example,

> If we know that many six-year-olds are preoperational in their thinking, unable to grasp the interrelationships of a logical system, how consistently can they [be expected to] handle their own plans or be guided by their own norms? (p. 116)

As children grow older, in the middle years, they shift the basis for categorizing objects from simple proximity, from perceptual and functional similarities, to more categorical groupings that represent more organized thinking operations, showing a grasp of logical relationship. But, Minuchin remembers,

> classification is not always a matter of logic, even for adults. . . . we often sort people, objects, and experiences . . . on the basis of affect or interests. . . . we do not expect or wish such personally valid forms of categorizing to drop out of the child's repertoire as he or she grows older. (p. 18)

In one study of children, six to ten years of age, it was found that the youngest children could solve the problems presented by simple trial and error, the oldest could work out appropriate strategies for solution, but the eight- and nine-year-olds showed the poorest ability to solve the problems. Minuchin uses this finding to remind us that periods of disequilibrium and reorganization are to be expected in the growth process. She writes:

> If we look at underlying processes, when the child is confused or makes errors, often it will be clear that he or she is not lazy or indifferent, but is actively growing toward a new level of mastery, exploring new mechanisms, and developing new schema for logical thought. (p. 24)

It is this level of understanding that teachers need over and above knowledge of central trends and developmental sequence.

The summing up of findings in the studies of training in verbal mediation in the transition period between five and eight is somewhat equivocal, but, in general, Minuchin concludes that adult encouragement of children's verbalization is probably growth supporting in most instances, and explains why. Here, too, we find the important qualification to the general finding:

> It is probably ill-advised to highlight verbal mediation at the expense of direct experience or to ignore the value of non-verbal forms of consolidation and mastery. As in other aspects of adult intervention in children's development, timing and balance are crucial. (p. 30)

Social Development: In the Context of a Social Ethic

Research studies on the development of prosocial behavior reflect, as they must, the contradictory state of affairs in our society. The gradually maturing capacity for empathic and helpful behavior runs counter to the society's dominant values of independent behavior and competitive achievement, internalized by the middle-years child. In Minuchin's words, "We live in a complex culture that presents the child with mixed messages. The culture values helpful behavior, yet it values other things that are not easily compatible with such behavior" (p. 53). Thus, research often has indicated that there is a decrease in cooperation with age over a span from about age four to age eleven. Minuchin points to the salience of the dominant society's value, whatever it is, in influencing child behavior, whether the society be large or small. Thus, the kibbutz children in Israeli society were found to be aligned with cooperative behavior and identified with group goals into the middle years.

There are differing concepts of what constitutes optimal moral development and differing opinions on what factors determine its quality and its course of development. Minuchin reviews the studies stemming from a relatively restricted position that focuses on behavior and contrasts them to studies based on broader, more complex views that deal with the conceptual superstructure: "a rational view of authority and a social ethic that includes responsibility and consideration for others" (p. 66). In the latter framework, we read about Piaget, Kohlberg, and Hoffman, each of whom is inclined toward a specific kind of learning experience that is presumed to build toward a fundamental humanistic conscience. Minuchin calls attention to Dewey's view of the school as a total coherent environment, a natural workshop with intrinsic potential for building social responsibility. It is on this comprehensive approach and less obvious techniques that she elaborates, indicating how nonauthoritarianism is internalized as an intrinsic part of the learning experience in the kinds of school that are characterized by

> willingness of adult authorities to admit error . . . [in which] children are allowed to participate in decision-making . . . [and] teaching allows for the discussion of ideas, encourages questions, and organizes the learning curriculum so that fact, interpretation, and opinion can be evaluated. (p. 68)

It is this kind of experience that affects the child's "internalized images of how to function as a person in authority or as a member of a group."

Individual Development: Competence and Creativity

The image of the author's template for an optimal learning environment gradually takes clearer shape as one reads along. In quite a few instances, Minuchin moves from commentary that elaborates on developmental implications of research findings to more specific educational programmatic suggestions. When she describes Suchman's problem-solving program (1961) and Allender's inquiry program (1972), for example, she grants that they may create some change in the short run, "but it seems unlikely they can sufficiently affect intellectual development if they are interjected into the curriculum of schools in which traditional forms of subject mastery are emphasized."

Or, in another instance, she deals with motivation of the middle-years child to incorporate new standards of competence into his creative efforts in order to yield them a position of being shared and recognizable by others. Here Minuchin describes the different ways in which this new motivation and potential are dealt with. She contrasts formal, skill-focused lessons as the presumed path toward competence with methods that provide experience with a variety of media, to be freely explored, while being supplemented with such technical guidance as the child may need to produce the effect he has in mind. Where awareness of developmental processes underlies the program, the child is offered a wide spectrum of creative exploration and communication, ranging from ceramics to original playmaking—all in the interest of "building a repertoire for the skillful expression of creative image" (Minuchin, 1977, p. 38).

The Relevant School Image

In summing up the differences between the behavioral and the developmental approaches, Minuchin writes: "From the viewpoint of child development, therefore, the appeal of such an efficient approach to learning [the behavioral, which she describes] must be weighed against its drawbacks and weaknesses" (p. 103). The alternate, developmental-interaction viewpoint is expounded in terms of its basic principles and developmental goals, its preferred teaching and learning processes, educational philosophy, curriculum choices, and teacher role. In illustration a study of the evolution of the Monarch butterfly from beginning to end in a second-grade classroom brings underlying principles and program procedures into sharp and convincing focus. In general, this brief section seems to pull together the author's commentaries in the chapters reviewing research—her preference for taking a comprehensive developmental perspective and using it as a guide toward educational practice—as well as amplifying her initial general statement on preferred human values. From her review of comparative evaluative studies, Minuchin moves toward advocating a certain openness in educational design: "A developmentally oriented setting must be flexible." A learning environment can be expected to have certain common effects consistent with its purposes and practices, but there must be room for expecting and adapting to differences in the way individual children respond to its mores and opportunities in terms of their individual structures and styles.

At the close, I find myself admiring the internal architecture of this book—the gradual summoning of evidence and reflection toward building an image of educational design to match advanced knowledge of the maturing process and fulfill the author's selected criteria of optimal development and preferred human values.

In the last few pages, Minuchin opens up a fundamental issue, reminding us that "there is no *proof* that either a behavioral or developmental orientation is 'better.'" It is essential, however, to recognize that these divergent positions represent alternatives. Preference for one or the other position deserves serious consideration since the choice has far-reaching differential effects on individual development and the changing nature of society itself. In this presentation, Minuchin has mustered the evidence supporting the developmental-interaction view with which she is aligned.

.   .   .

The developmental-interaction position appears to have taken wing.

CHAPTER 12

A Value Base for Selection of Theory

It is interesting to try to account for one's consistent affinity to certain kinds of thought systems over a lifetime despite changes in life circumstance, intellectual exposure, and personal affiliations. I can trace the roots of my allegiance to the developmental psychologist view to my graduate student days at the University of Chicago in the late 1920s. It was a time of ferment among the zoologists that was felt in the old "Psych" building on Ellis Avenue, on the edge of the main campus. The unpretentious physical housing was symbolic—psychology as a discipline was separating itself from philosophy and building its identity as a discipline.

Occasionally, a zoologist came across Ellis Avenue to help establish the linkage of psychology to the biological sciences. I remember a talk to the graduate students in psychology by Ralph Gerard, who crossed my horizon again many years later when, in 1955, he addressed a Bank Street College conference on "Imagination in Science." "Science," he said, "is an attitude, and a method and the results thereof. Science attacks and solves problems by applying imagination to sensory experience but, in Coleridge's lovely phrase, 'curbed and ruddered by reason.' . . . It is not a body of facts and their relations, not a set of dogmas; it is a way of life. . . . Science is a certain approach, a dedication, attitude, way of operating, and it need not be limited to professional scientists." Yeasty ideas such as these were in the air on the Chicago campus back in the 1920s. They led me to cross Ellis Avenue in the other direction to get a small taste of what was going on among the zoologists.

I asked for and was granted admission to the course in "ecology" taught to students majoring in zoology by Dr. C. Ward Allee. The mind-stretch of what the zoologists were saying appealed to me. In the groping mood of the student, I was wary of skeletonizing and oversimplifying intellectual complexities; to take on the struggle to comprehend complexity

275

*seemed to me the nobler and more interesting path. After an interview, Dr.
Allee agreed to let me try it, although I did not have the formal
prerequisites. I don't remember what I said but in a way that is clear to me
only now, my own commitment to a "better world" and my young faith in
mankind's basic goodwill and potential must have come through and struck
a responsive chord.*

*In the fall of 1925 or 1926 our ecology class went on a field trip to
Turkey Run, Indiana, to collect specimens from the rocky streams and raise
questions for later pursuit in class and laboratory. It was cold at night in the
open cabin alongside the stream which, if I recall correctly, was at the
bottom of a small canyon. The sleeping quarters were primitive, and
blankets offered scant protection from the cold. In the early morning, when
it was barely light, I awoke to the sounds of a fire being laid and cans being
readied to brew the coffee. It was Dr. Allee himself, and it seemed natural to
offer my assistance while the others were still asleep. It was an experience of
pure pleasure: the stark feeling of the woods in early light, the warmth
from the fire, the companionship with an inspiring teacher.*

*Any contact with the Chicago zoologists in the 1920s led to C. Judson
Herrick (1932), whose theory building was actively in process and much in
the air at the time. His major argument was with those who held a
narrowly mechanistic view of human behavior and, like John B. Watson,
dismissed the phenomenon of consciousness—part of their need, as Herrick
saw it, to react against traditional forms of mysticism. His work was clearly
the forerunner of the "organismic" view as recently expounded by the
increasing number of developmental psychologists. He conceptualized the
human mind, "the thinking machine," as an active, creative agent.
"Mind," he wrote, "is not the product of the activity of some particular
piece of the body working in isolation and independently of other processes.
Its organs are not insulated from their surroundings like an ice machine in a
tropical city." Or in another place:*

> *If I use my legs to go to the brook to get a drink or to the library to
> get a book, the physiological function of walking is defined not merely
> in relation with the "inner economy" of the body, but also in relation
> with the "correspondence" of that body with the environing things
> which motivate the act.*

*There is a terrible temptation to assign certain events in one's life
history to destiny rather than happenstance. How did it happen that in 1931
Harriet Johnson asked me to accompany her and our first Bank Street
students to Ashley Montagu's lectures at the New School for Social
Research, and that the course I later developed on child development took
root as a sequel to attending the lecture? I did not know then that Montagu
was to become a lifelong opponent of the conception of nature in which
animals are seen as necessarily in a constant state of warfare with one
another—"a grossly one-sided and false perspective." To the contrary, "a*

principle of mutualism, of cooperation, is the fundamental principle which appears to have governed the relations of organisms from the very start." Only recently did I happen to find the paper in which Montagu refers to Allee's work as substantiation for his position (Allee, 1938 [1951]).

Psychological Perspectives and Early Childhood Education: Some Relations between Theory and Practice (1977) with Margery B. Franklin

The aim of this paper is to delineate some of the central issues that confront us, as psychologists and educators, in this period of accelerated application of psychological theory and research to early childhood education.

In the past decade we have seen a rapid growth of programs in early childhood education. Many have arisen as part of an awakened sense of social responsibility, especially the recognition of the urgent need to deal with the plight of children from poor and minority group populations. Some have arisen in response to the demands of middle-class families, especially those where mothers work, for increased care and/or tutelage for their preschool children. Others have developed to serve primarily as "laboratories" for the study of the initial stages of development. Though differing in purpose and pattern, these programs have in common the conviction that the child's experience during the early years has important and enduring effects on his subsequent development, in fact, on all his transactions in the world of people and ideas.

The sources of underlying conceptualizations are many and diverse, but it is clear that a significant proportion reflect the direct impact of interest and effort on the part of curriculum developers, who draw heavily on aspects of theory and/or research in child development. Whereas some programs are eclectic, drawing on an assortment of theoretical precepts, others are based, more or less rigorously, on theory-specific concepts about the nature of psychological development and related appropriate methods of education. Some programs are comprehensive in nature, encompassing the totality of experience and relationships that are planned and provided. Others are circumscribed components inserted into the matrix of a general program. In almost all corners, however, we see a more and more widespread effort to bring the concepts and findings from the academic discipline of child psychology to bear on the education of young children.

The complexities of interrelations between psychological theories and educational ideologies, between the findings of research and the implementation of specific goals in practice are indeed awesome. A number of recent books and articles (Fein & Clarke-Stewart, 1973; Sigel, 1972) reflect an intensified effort to come to grips with the intricacies of these complex interrelationships.

Adapted from Psychological perspectives and early childhood education: Some relations between theory and practice. In L. G. Katz (Ed.), *Current topics in early childhood education* (vol. 1). Norwood, N.J.: Ablex, 1977 (coauthored with Margery B. Franklin).

There is, for example, increasing recognition of the question of values inherent in the establishment of any educational program, as well as greater awareness of the sociopolitical implications of intervention programs, originally designed to provide "compensatory" education for children of so-called disadvantaged backgrounds. This heightened awareness, expressed in the self-critical reflection evident in the current writings of psychologists and educators, stems no doubt, in part, from the fact that many of the innovative programs in education failed to achieve their stated goals in the time allotted. But another factor, with more positive implications for the future, is the increased interchange between psychologist program developers and educational practitioners that necessarily occurred as more psychologists moved into the heretofore unfamiliar territory of the school and more educators consciously sought psychological-theory bases for curricular planning.

On the contemporary scene we see a diversity of programs reflecting the influence of differing psychological viewpoints. We have seen, also, in the past five or six years, a changing attitude toward the evaluation of outcomes of differing educational programs, a growing tendency to reexamine the earlier assumptions and techniques underlying evaluative procedures. The programs included in the Planned Variation Experiment for Headstart and in Project Follow Through provide an extraordinary opportunity to observe the linkage of underlying values, theoretical suppositions, educational goals, and methods of implementation that characterize widely divergent programs in early childhood education.

In this paper we shall focus on three central currents in the field, undertaking to clarify the differing assumptions on which they are based, the differing ways in which they draw on and utilize psychological concepts, and on the ways in which they therefore involve young children in qualitatively different encounters with people, problems, and ideas in the school setting. We begin by looking at two approaches to early childhood programming which are based quite explicitly on two divergent psychological perspectives: the behavioristic-learning-theory perspective and the Piagetian cognitive-developmental perspective. For our third case we examine in somewhat greater detail a long-established program design recently designated as the developmental-interaction approach (see chap. 11). From the perspective of psychological theory this approach represents an integration of cognitive-developmental stage concepts and ego psychology formulations. In the case of the developmental-interaction approach, theory has an important place as a basic rationale for practice, but essential elements of this educational design have roots in the progressive education ideology of the John Dewey period.

The final section of the paper is concerned with a summary statement of the issues arising in our discussion of these three central approaches to early childhood education, including a consideration of some of the problems that must be confronted in the task of evaluating effects of differing modes of education.

At the outset we may say that we do not claim to approach our task here as neutrals, as impartial observers, or as disinterested bystanders who are simply reporting on the current scene. We speak from the perspective of developmental-interactionists but we have attempted to present alternative views in their own terms.

The Behavioristic-Learning Theory Approach

A growing number of programs in early childhood education reflect the direct impact of contemporary behavioristic psychology. These approaches share in common the idea that many basic concepts of other psychologies—concepts such as *cognitive structure* and *underlying motivation*—are not only vague but superfluous, and may be counterproductive in the context of education, where presumably one wants to change behavior in an efficient manner. At the core of all behavioristic psychologies lie the precepts that (a) observable behavior or performance constitutes the primary datum for the scientific investigation of the learning process and for approaches to behavior change, and (b) the basic principles of learning are the laws of classical and operant conditioning. In the behavior modification movement, which appears to be the strongest among behavioristically oriented approaches to educational programming, emphasis has fallen on the use of operant conditioning techniques as developed in Skinner's work (1953).

In the view of behavior modifiers oriented toward educational programming, any attempt to change or modify behavior in the classroom (which encompasses not only the eradication of "problems" but the process of education in toto) requires: (a) analysis of the present situation in behavioristic terms, (b) specification of the desired behavior changes, and (c) specification of the techniques appropriate to their realization. In line with their conviction that any program must be based on empirically demonstrated "facts" concerning the efficacy of given techniques, psychologists who advocate the use of behavior modification techniques in the classroom have done a considerable amount of research to validate their claim that the principles of learning derived from Skinnerian studies of pigeons and rats in laboratory settings are applicable to the analysis and modification of classroom behavior.

Among programs resting on behavioristic precepts are those of Bereiter and Engelmann (1966) and Bushell (1973). While not rigorously following a specific behavioristic paradigm, Bereiter and Engelmann drew heavily upon the precepts of behaviorism in developing specific teaching techniques for their "academic preschool."

Bushell's behavior analysis program (another of the Follow Through models) represents a systematic attempt to apply contemporary behavior modification methods to classroom programming and management. Like all behavioristically based programs, Bushell's program involves the systematic, regulated administration of reinforcement as the principal means for teaching children the behaviors considered requisite for success in school. The behaviors at issue encompass a wide range: from appropriate social behavior in the classroom to the acquisition of specific academic skills. As in other such programs, positive reinforcers include candy or other snacks, access to favorite toys, access to favorite activities such as art, recess, and/or listening to stories. And when there is adequate basis for considering it a positive reinforcer, the teacher's attention, or more specifically the teacher's expression of praise, is utilized as a means of controlling behavior (i.e., teacher's praise is a social reinforcer, its delivery contingent on the child's producing an appropriate behavior). Withholding of such reinforcers is the primary means of reducing and ultimately eradicating those behaviors designated as undesirable. For example, the withholding of praise is used as a controlling technique when the teacher, noticing that one child is being inattentive, gives emphatic praise to another child who *is* paying attention.

Considering the principles of behavioristic psychology as a basis for educational programming involves coming to grips with several related questions. One question, raised by behaviorists themselves, concerns the efficacy of specific procedures for achieving a circumscribed end result (a given behavior or set of behaviors). As we have said, the argument for the efficacy of behavior modification techniques in classroom settings is buttressed by reference to studies designed to demonstrate that the regulation of reinforcement (i.e., the establishment of reinforcement contingencies) is effective in bringing about observable and measurable behavior change. And, indeed, many of the studies cited in the context of such an argument provide strong evidence that aspects of observable behavior can be regulated through such procedures. However, behavioristically inclined educators show increasing concern with (a) the extent to which a given learned behavior generalizes to situations other than the one in which original training occurred, and (b) whether continuing production of the desired behavior is contingent upon the continued administration of a given reinforcer. This ties into the question of "durability" of behavior change, and to the possibility of "fading out" reinforcers such as candy and toys in preference to self-administered reinforcers (e.g., "Gee, I'm a good kid for doing that!"). On these issues—generalization or transfer, durability, and the substitution of less tangible for more tangible rewards—evidence is not so conclusive. In other words, it is not clear that behavior modification techniques produce behavior changes which transfer readily to new situations and which can be maintained without the regular administration of tangible rewards. Most behavior-modifier educationalists see these as technical problems to be overcome through improvements in training methods.

When we survey current programs in early education which draw on behavioristic psychology, and which generally make use of behavior-modification techniques (including the extension into setting up a token economy), we find that in fact these programs typically reflect adherence to highly traditional conceptions of the goals of education and of appropriate modes of conduct in the classroom, leading to an emphasis—at the preschool level—on circumscribed academic content and socially conforming behavior. The influential programs of Bereiter and Engelmann (1966) and Bushell (1973) stand as prime examples here. In our view, children in such classrooms are not only learning the specific skills and modes of conduct which are the "target behaviors" of the program, but are inevitably picking up other messages, learning other things, as well. For example: that learning itself consists primarily in the acquisition of specific items of information or highly specific procedures to be applied to given materials; that questions have specific answers which are right *or* wrong, and that knowledge of the correct answers (or, more explicitly, giving the correct response) is the path to success; that the path to success (and presumably to feelings of competence or self-worth) involves a straight line to the teacher or other authority who holds the key as to what is right or wrong and dispenses the goodies when correct answers are forthcoming. If the teacher is not excessively authoritarian, he or she can be perceived as a harmless and pleasant game-player, a source of gratification to the child who makes *discernible* progress in mastering academic skills or controlling his or her socially unacceptable behavior. It seems that the child who is having difficulties is likely to learn that teachers are people who sometimes dispense punishment and very often leave one in a praiseless limbo to cope alone, people who cannot be counted on in times of need but only when one is "good." One works or behaves properly in order to achieve external rewards, at first tangible rewards like candy and/or the privilege of playing with a favorite toy or engaging in a preferred activity, and perhaps subsequently (if training is successful) to receive praise from some momentarily benevolent authority figure.

It seems to us that this kind of system must inevitably promote a dichotomy between work and play, or—more broadly—between doing something because one *has* to and doing something because one *wants* to. The hidden assumption of the program developers seems to be that academic work or acceptable social conduct is not pleasurable in itself (except for the exceptional preschooler who can administer self-reinforcement); the system of dispensing rewards on a contingency basis serves—albeit unintentionally—to communicate this assumption to the children. Of course, there is substantial evidence that certain kinds of academic tasks and social behaviors are indeed difficult and even distasteful to many children. In our view, this should lead to fundamental questions about the appropriateness and value of various learning–teaching situations for children of different ages, rather than to an emphasis on improving methods of shaping behavior. The underlying model for the token economy is the marketplace, where bartering—the buying and selling of goods and services—is the fundamental mode of transaction. We believe that children being educated in classrooms based on this model must be learning that the ethics and modes of human conduct appropriate to the marketplace are appropriate modes for interpersonal interaction in the classroom, and perhaps in the world at large.

While denying that the technology of behavior modification is inherently bound to an underlying educational ideology, some behaviorists have recently stressed that the task of defining educational goals and values is indeed a serious one, demanding critical consideration. In a recent review, Winett and Winkler

(1972) deplore the fact that most current behavior modification programs reflect in their choice of target behaviors adherence to a highly traditional form of education. Krasner and Krasner (1973) attempt to show that there is no conflict whatever between the use of behavior modification techniques (as used in a token economy) and the open classroom approach. We suggest, however, that the prevalent pattern is not merely fortuitous: The behavioristic method of technology requires analysis of input and output in discrete units, observable and measurable. (This is, in fact, its strength, particularly in assessing the effects of a given training procedure.) This necessarily leads to a selection of "target behaviors" that can be handled in such terms; it promotes an emphasis on product rather than process; on isolated responses or behaviors rather than on whole patterns within and across time periods; on forms of learning that are readily susceptible to quantitative measurement. Notions like "change in cognitive structure" or "increased self-awareness" must be translated into behavioral terms and are severely distorted, even obliterated, in the process. This is no loss to the behaviorists, whose epistemological framework does not require, or indeed allow, such concepts. And, as we suggested above, the circumscribed focus on predetermined "target behaviors"—also stemming from the technological emphasis—is conducive to a neglect of "side effects," that is, the other learning processes that occur in the total context and that may be equally or more significant in the long run. In any event, behavior modification is by its own claim a technology; as such, it provides a method of teaching and sets limits on the kinds of behavior that can be taken as objectives in the educational process, but it provides no positive guidelines or implications with regard to broader objectives or goals. We have argued that the technology itself has value implications and that the sometimes hidden ideology of behavioristically based programs is closely tied to the view of human nature, learning, and development that is inherent in behavioristic psychology.

The Piagetian Cognitive-Developmental Approach

The impact of Piagetian theory on the field of early childhood education has been one of the most striking developments of the past decade. Twenty years ago, Piaget was virtually ignored by mainstream American psychologists, and only a small group of educational theorists was concerned with the implications of Piagetian thinking for educational practice. In the past fifteen years or so, profound changes have occurred in the American psychological establishment. While behaviorism is still a strong force, few would deny that its all-powerful position has been weakened as cognitive developmentalism has achieved greater prominence. Stemming in part from these changes within the academy, there has been an upsurge of interest in explicating the implications of Piaget's thinking for educational programming (Schwebel & Raph, 1973) and the establishment of total preschool programs that view themselves as based on Piagetian thinking. The influence of Piagetian formulations is also manifest in program planning within the British Infant School movement and some of the open classroom programs here and abroad that have evolved since the publication of the Plowden Report.

It is clear that Piaget's work has strong implications for education, but the task of translating Piagetian thinking into educational practice involves considerable interpretation and decision-making. The differences among currently extant "Piaget-derived" curricula reflect the crucial role that curriculum developers play in bridging the gap between psychological theory and the specifics of educational practice (Piaget, 1970).

An active organism view lies at the base of Piaget's approach. In this view the organism is seen as the source of acts rather than as a pawn pushed and pulled by the operation of external forces. The understanding and explanation of human behavior cannot be reduced to analysis of external conditions as causative, either in terms of a prior sequence of environmental events or in terms of present situation variables. Instead, one must focus on what the organism brings to the situation and how this enters into or governs performance. Most important, what the organism brings to the situation is conceptualized in terms of underlying mental structures rather than in terms of biologically defined proclivities (as in instinct theory), collections of stimulus–response connections, or propensities to emit a given response under given conditions (as in behaviorism). Behavioral data are thus viewed as a basis for making inferences about the nature or status of underlying cognitive structures, not as the primary object or end of analysis. As physiological structures determine the types and range of stimulation to which an organism at any phylogenetic level is sensitive and thus its "effective environment," so psychological structures constitute the equipment through which the human organism "knows" the world, and govern his modes of transaction with the social and physical environment in which he lives. It is not necessary to posit any condition of need or deprivation, or of specific external stimulation as such, to account for the activation of structures. The functioning of structures is inherent to organic life; this is at the nexus of the "active organism" viewpoint. As already implied, the tent of constructivism is intertwined with the active organism assumption. Basically, constructivism is the view that human beings create their knowledge, that knowledge results from the transformation of material that occurs as psychological structures are brought to bear vis-à-vis the "materials" of the world.

Since learning is an active process and knowledge is constructed rather than "acquired," the child must be provided with an environment which furthers his own natural tendency to act on and with objects, to explore, manipulate, and experiment. He must be allowed, indeed encouraged, to take initiative, to pose problems, and to generate solutions for himself, even when the problems may seem trivial to an adult and/or the solutions may be wrong from an adult point of view. In infancy, in the sensorimotor period, direct action on objects is in fact important, for the child's schemas or psychological structures are organizations of action patterns which become differentiated, and further coordinated or integrated in the process of motoric activity, as he discovers the properties of objects and achieves some understanding of relationships through active manipulation of various materials. Such direct exploration and handling of objects are also important at the preschool level during the preoperational period, when the child can see the effects of his actions as he handles and arranges materials in varying ways, and thus gains "physical knowledge" from observing the ways in which objects respond to various manipulations (e.g., dropping a crayon and seeing it break; dropping a metal rod and finding that it does not break), and "logico-mathematical knowledge," which is abstracted from the coordinations of actions themselves. However, at the preschool age, the child is already beginning to engage in mental activity where actual overt action may, at least in some cases, be abbreviated or nonobservable as the child carries out internal rather than external actions—a development related to the advent of representational thought.

The traditional approach—so evident in many behavioristically oriented classrooms—of presenting circumscribed content to preschoolers, predetermining right and wrong answers, and reinforcing those which have been designated as "correct" by the teacher or program developer is not only fruitless but may be detrimental because it stifles the tendency of the child to move out into the world, to take initiative, to explore and discover for himself, and so may hinder rather than facilitate genuine cognitive advance by making the child relatively passive in relation to the outer world. That such methods work at all would, in Piaget's view, have much more to do with the inherent propensity of the child toward psychological activity, his tendency to create meaning or order out of chaos, than with the specific methods employed.

In speaking of the teacher's role vis-à-vis the child's learning, Lavatelli (1970) has drawn the following implications for preschool education from the Piagetian framework: "The teacher's role is to stimulate and to guide, not to teach specific responses, not to tell the child the right answer, nor even to tell him when he is wrong. The teacher must have confidence in the child's ability to learn on his own. When he is wrong, she may ask questions or call attention to cues that he has missed so that he has more data to assimilate, but giving him the right answer will not convince the child. He must be convinced by his own actions" (p. 49).

Perhaps the best known (or, shall we say, the most widely assimilated) aspect of Piaget's theory is that which has to do with the four major stages of cognitive development: the sensorimotor, the intuitive or preoperational, the concrete operational, and the formal operational. We shall confine ourselves to a few general comments, and subsequently discuss how Piagetian stage theory has been used in the Lavatelli and Kamii programs.[1]

Essentially, development is defined in this view as a series of sequential, ordered changes in the cognitive structures that constitute the human organism's learning apparatus. As we have already said, these changes occur as a

1. A third program is discussed in the original article (see Weikart, Rogers, Adcock, & McClelland, 1971).

result of organism–environment interaction. A stage may be characterized as an internally organized or integrated group of cognitive structures. Each stage is built upon the previous one and in this sense may be said to derive from it; thus, it is not possible to skip a stage in development. At the same time, each generic mode of thought or stage involves a fundamentally new organization into which previous modes are hierarchically integrated, and therefore change is not merely quantitative (as in the behavioristic view) but qualitative. New structures cannot be reduced to (or fully explained by) earlier ones; they exhibit emergent properties.

With regard to education, the broad and yet profound implication of this view is that modes of thought are qualitatively different at various periods in the child's life, that children at different stages of development will therefore interpret and respond to external situations in qualitatively distinct ways, and that relative consolidation of earlier modes of functioning provides the basis for developmentally more advanced modes. It follows that curricula should be "stage appropriate," that is, that various components of the program should be designed with as full an awareness as is possible of the child's modes of functioning. The fact that the generic forms of cognitive structures and the sequence of stages are rooted in biologically based proclivities (although not explained by them, as we have said before) means that there is some rough correspondence between age and stage. One can expect, for example, that preschool children are using and developing cognitive structures that are profoundly different from those used by seven- and eight-year-olds. Since there is, however, no reason to expect a one-to-one correspondence between age and stage, or indeed that any individual child will show uniform cognitive functioning, teachers must have ways of assessing each child's modes of functioning in order to provide him with an optimal learning environment.

We have said that if one takes seriously the idea that the child is the agent of his own learning (i.e., accepts the active-organism-constructivist premise), then one of the central objectives of preschool education is to help the child become as active a learner as possible, to provide conditions in which his natural powers can be exercised to full advantage. Both programs referred to are very much concerned with this broad objective. In this connection, they have given careful attention to the types of materials to be included in preschool classrooms, to the kinds of activities that are likely to promote the child's taking an active stance vis-à-vis the environment, and to the role of the teacher as guide and stimulator rather than as transmitter of information.

Accepting the active organism tenet involves rejection of traditional methods of teaching in which the child is treated as a passive recipient of "knowledge." But acceptance of this tenet does not provide specification of what constitutes the optimal degree of structure and direct instruction in the learning environment, the appropriate balance between relying on the child's self-initiated action and directly stimulating or leading him to engage in given activities. In this regard there are marked differences among Piaget-based programs, with Lavatelli's program emphasizing structured training sessions on classification, seriation, and number concepts as a supplement to less structured classroom activity, and Kamii (1973) arguing that genuine learning must occur within a context and so should not be programmed as training sessions at the preschool level.

Lavatelli and Kamii not only adhere to the general implications of cognitive stage theory but also draw systematically on Piaget's study of thinking during the preoperational period as a base for curriculum planning. Both programs emphasize the importance of play as an area of activity where the preoperational child spontaneously utilizes and so further develops his myriad, stage-characteristic cognitive capacities. These programs also reflect careful attention to the sequential developments within the specific areas of classification, seriation, number, and space concepts—as Piaget has described them. Lavatelli's program includes as an important component structured training sessions (modeled on the tasks Piaget designed to investigate the development of logical thought), many of them apparently designed to teach concrete operations to the presumably preoperational child. According to Kamii (1973), this represents a misapplication of Piagetian theory: (a) preoperational children should not be prematurely pushed, through training, toward the concrete operational stage; (b) logical thinking should not be artificially separated from the development of physical knowledge, as occurs when such focused training sessions are established; and (c) classification, seriation, and other elements cannot be thought of, and should not be taught, as separate skills, or indeed as skills in any sense of the term.

We see, then, that the programs which draw on Piaget differ in the specific use of this theory as a rationale for preschool education but share adherence to general implications of the cognitive-developmental perspective and a focus on promoting cognitive growth in the preschool years. These programs reflect similar values in their explicit effort—on the level of implementation—to foster the child's sense of himself as an autonomous learner, a questioner, an explorer, a problem-solver; his sense of the teacher as a guide, helper, and source of useful information rather than an authoritarian figure dispensing praise and blame for right and wrong answers; his sense of school as a democratic social system in which exchange with peers is as highly valued as any other endeavor. In our view the dramatic contrast with the "hidden message" of behavioristically oriented programs is evident, and we see this as stemming from fundamentally different educational ideologies which, in turn, are linked to the different views of human nature and functioning underlying the two psychological theories at issue.

In significant ways, the value orientation and therefore the particular learning environments established for children in these Piaget-based programs are similar to those of the "child-centered" programs, which owe a great deal, in terms of their origins, to the work of John Dewey as well as to the influence of psychodynamic theory (cf. next section). Furthermore, among those who turn to Piagetian theory as a basis for preschool planning, there seems to be increased emphasis on considering the "whole child" rather than on focusing, in a narrower way, on cognitive development. Writing on Piaget's theory in relation to education, Overton (1972) has said that "the development of thought is not viewed as a process isolated from the total development of the child, but rather as a process integrated throughout with the child's interests and values, moral feelings, interpersonal emotions, and most generally his personality" (p. 95). In successive formulations of long-range and short-term objectives, Kamii has increasingly stressed the importance of "socioemotional" functioning and development in relationship to cognitive growth. However, the fact remains that Piaget's theory deals to a very large extent with the evolution of *cognitive* structures and provides relatively little of a substantive nature concerning other related aspects of development. One might say that in developing programs which are geared toward the child's total development, Piagetian program planners have gone outside or beyond Piagetian theory, formulating objectives and related modes of implementation which are *consonant* with the Piagetian perspective but not based on Piagetian theory as such.

The Developmental-Interaction Approach

There is a large measure of common ground between the programs based on this approach and those that adhere more exclusively to cognitive theories of development. But the difference between them is crucial to the planning of learning experiences, the teaching strategies, and the nature of the teacher–child relationships. Essentially, proponents of this approach take the position that, while cognitive-developmental theory is a valuable component for the construction of an educational design, it is not, by itself, sufficiently comprehensive to serve as the foundation for the totality of the educative process.

The developmental-interaction approach utilizes two major stage formulations of the developmental sequence: the cognitive-developmental, drawing on Werner (1940 [1957a]) as much as Piaget, and the framework developed within ego psychology, most specifically by Erikson (1950 [1963], 1959). From the perspective of cognitive development the maturation of the child is seen as a series of changing ways of gaining and organizing his knowledge of the universe of things, people, and ideas. In general terms the world he first knows through his senses and his physical-motor maneuvers is fundamentally altered when he can deal symbolically, through verbal and nonverbal modes, with his experience. During the next period, the preschool years and first primary years, he becomes a primitive conceptualizer, ordering the complexity of his experience by comparing, grouping, classifying, numbering, and postulating causality. However, the elements of these processes are still much influenced by perceptual factors, coexistence in time and space, and more importantly by a lingering egocentricism in which self-feelings and wishes influence the contours of the child's image of the world. Not until the middle years of childhood does his conceptualizing become more objective, adhering to logical rules so that he can think in categorical terms independent of perceptual attributes, master concepts by delineating constancies in the object world, and deal with multiple classifications as he becomes aware of relativity of class membership of a given item.

In the second formulation, successive stages of development are characterized as generalized affective-social patterns, comprising the whole complex of self-feeling and self-image, of attitudes and images toward others, and of the style of individual functioning in relation to the opportunities and expectations of a given society. In this perspective, these phases of psychosocial development are closely related to phases of psychosexual epigenesis and reflect the basic conflictual nature of the maturing process—both the conflicting impulses within the self and the struggle between self-generated impulses and the demands of reality outside the self. The stages are defined as polarities—alternative resolutions of the basic conflicts. The relative health of these resolutions is determined by the quality of interaction with the salient figures in the child's life and compatibility with cultural ideals. Thus, with primary emphasis on functional outcomes rather than the particular organically based conflicts or developmental tasks to be solved in successive stages, the stepping stones to healthy personality development spanning the preschool years have been defined as: a sense of trustfulness in others and trustworthiness in one's self; a sense of autonomy through making choices and exercising control; a sense of initiative expressed in a variety of making, doing, and playing activities in cooperation with others and in an imagined projection of the adult sex role.

Both these developmental theories assume basic organismic functions which are operative across the life span, and an invariant sequence of stages in development; in this respect they are maturational theories, rooted in metaphors of biological growth. But at the core, both are interactionist theories, claiming that the development of stage-specific structures and functions, as well as movement from one stage to the next—that is, development itself—occurs as a function of organism–environment interaction, the reciprocal interplay between the organism's propensities and activities and that which impinges on him from outside, the environment. It is a premise of the developmental-interaction view under discussion that the separation of these major developmental sequences—the cognitive-intellectual and the affective-social—has important heuristic value but that, in utilizing these formulations in connection with educational planning, it is essential to be continuously cognizant of their interdependence in the way children and people actually function. Cognitive-intellectual and affective-social processes are sometimes seen as constituting parallel and partly overlapping systems. Actually, the loading of curriculum designs is influenced directly or indirectly by the position taken with respect to these theoretical alternatives: the primacy of one system rather than the other or—the third alternative—a genuinely integrative interactionist view (cf. Mayer, 1971).

Integrative formulations appear in other psychological domains. Creativity has been conceived as a synthesis of various modes of intellectual functioning including divergent thinking, transformation processes, sensing of ambiguity, perceiving of patterns, and "playing" with ideas as well as logical thinking. From this viewpoint, creativity depends also on closeness to experiences of the inner life that underlie motivation and the affective-social patterns of the personality.

The developmental-interaction approach, as it has evolved at the Bank Street College of Education over half a century, had its roots in the progressive education movement. In that era, as in our own, it was expected that innovation in education could correct basic faults in our democratic society. What was needed was a totally different life of learning for children, one that would correct for the conformisms and authoritarianism that characterized the zeitgeist and was reflected in the school. In contrast to "compensatory" programs (which also aim to correct for basic faults through educational innovation) the goals of the earlier experiments embraced educational programs as total ideologies and the children as "whole" individuals.

A radically altered learning environment and new instructional strategies and curricula were developed by educators in accord with Dewey's theories of experiential learning. They sought to implement his major tenets: the child learns through his own active involvement and through interaction with the phenomena of things, people, and ideas in his environment; there is a continuous process of "collateral" learning, the formation of attitudes that are both emotional and intellectual and govern the development of basic systems of preference and aversion. In Dewey's words (Dewey & Dewey, 1915): "The greatest of all pedagogical fallacies is the notion that a person learns only the particular thing he is studying at the time."

This basic educational ideology was developed and refined over a period of six decades. Changes evolved through informal and formal modes of experimentation and revision, based on the observations and insights of the educators working directly with the children. Outstanding thinkers in this group were Mitchell, Johnson, and Pratt. Among their special curriculum contributions can be mentioned the development of an intentionally comprehensive educational design for the years following infancy, the use of spontaneous play as a tool for learning suited to the idiom of early childhood, and a method for the study of environment in which a cognitive search for relationships is the basis for formulating general principles.

Historically, there is a complex relation between what was happening in those years on the educational front and the advances in the knowledge of human functioning represented in the work of developmental psychologists, in psychodynamic formulations, and in the principles of preventive mental health. From one perspective, the contribution of these psychological schools of thought can be looked at as a validation of principles derived from an experiential base by educators who observed and theorized as part of their professional function. A more dynamic interpretation is probably closer to the truth. The educators, committed to building educational practice on a rationale of child development research and theory, sought and found in the contributions of these psychologists not only a congruent view but also refreshment and stimulation for further change in practice. The evolution of the developmental-interaction view represents the progressive integration of both these streams of thought and experience.

In the developmental-interaction approach the inseparability of cognitive–affective processes governs the suitability of teaching methods. The possible merit of a technique is weighed in terms of multiple possible effects. Thus, learning experiences designed to further cognitive facility are weighed in terms of the simultaneous learning that is going on with respect to self-image, attitudes toward others, work patterns, and general behavioral modes. Practically, this calls for paying close attention to side effects as well as target success in any intentional teaching strategy and, finally, screening both orders of outcome on the basis of preestablished values.

Side effects sometimes supply a positive increment. Thus, in a given story, the teacher may find material for a target in the cognitive domain— mastery of concepts of multiple roles, for example. If she takes time and makes room for one of the children to enlighten the others from his own experience (his father is a fire fighter), she is simultaneously serving a goal in the noncognitive sphere, namely, to help children establish mutually supporting roles and see one another, as well as the teacher, as sources of information. Alternatively, restricted attention to a target goal may have negative outcomes. The teacher who responds to a preschool child's drawing by pointing out a disparity in size relations and who pressures the child to adhere more closely to external reality is violating one of the essential processes by which children achieve a strong sense of self: to have their creative products accepted and recognized as the end of an integrative process in which they, as individuals, find symbolic ways of dealing with both the logical and alogical aspects of their experience.

The curriculum design for this approach incorporates the educationally relevant precepts of cognitive-developmental and ego psychology theory. It takes the view that children are basically curious and impelled to make an impact on their environment; that they are equipped with autonomous ego functioning independent of instinctual drives. Learning takes place through action—concrete and conceptual—and interaction with the objects, people, and ideas of the environment. Knowledge is gained and adaptive patterns are established through exploration, manipulation, and investigation. Productive, creative use of knowledge is maximized when there is opportunity for representational reinterpretation of experience. The definition and quality of the interpersonal relations—teacher-to-child and child-to-child—affect and are affected by affective-social patterns. Matching curriculum designs and the learning atmosphere to successive developmental stages takes into account both level of cognitive functioning and stage-specific psychosocial characteristics, drives, and conflicts. Motivation to learn is regenerated by satisfied curiosity, the pleasures and intrinsic rewards of mastery, identification with teacher figures, and the internalizations of the trusted adults' confidence in the child's competence.

These general precepts about the course and the process of development influence the teacher's perception of the child as an individual. The child is not expected to function consistently at a given developmental level. Earlier forms of thinking, expression, and adaptation continue to appear even when his pre-dominant response patterns have become more advanced. From the viewpoint of creativity, having a varied repertoire, being able to continue to use the more primitive forms is seen as an advantage. It is expected that periods of instability are likely to alternate with other periods in which skills, feelings, and action patterns support one another and yield a highly integrated behavioral outcome. It is important, therefore, that the teacher can perceive periods of "regression" or "disturbance" when they occur as being, possibly, part of the complex phenomenon of development and not necessarily an expression of emotional disorganization.

The purview of a child's individuality includes, in addition to the behav-ioral picture, awareness of the inner processes through which self-image evolves. This requires that the teacher differentiate the elements in the learning environment in terms of how they may influence the child's own assessment of his skills, the clarity of his social sex role, his sense of himself as a learner, and his store of courage and know-how for coping with difficulty. The teacher knows and communicates with the child as a particular person. She is aware of his strengths, difficulties, and desires and these are brought into the open. This is made more possible to the extent to which the teacher has absorbed the precepts of the interaction of cognitive-intellectual and affective-social processes.

Ideally, in these classrooms, as in cognitive-oriented programs, children are actively engaged in exploring their environment and sharing their experi-ences in an atmosphere where questioning, searching, and problem-solving are encouraged (and there is no embarrassment about not knowing, among children or between children and teachers). The aim is to provide an abundance of experience and encounter, a variety of situations to which the children need to adapt, plenty of alternatives from which to make choices, and an appropriate setup for self-initiated exploratory play. Direct contact with phenomena and people takes priority over the vicarious; the salient situations for learning exist outside the classroom as well as inside.

Here, in contrast to the emphasis on structured lessons that are promi-nent in most programs in which cognition is the primary focus, the instruc-tional method is weighted toward making maximal use of the children's varied, ongoing experience, as it transpires, as the prime material for stimulating cognitive processes. When it is successful, this method produces a pervasive climate of why, wherefore, and wherefrom kind of thinking. The teacher uses every appropriate opportunity to stimulate differentiated observation and com-parison, to encourage the search for causes and origins, and to bring the orderly passing of time, the contour of spatial reality, and the transformations of growth to awareness. This occurs in innumerable contexts: in recognizing the separate series of landmarks that distinguish different routes to the play roof; in recording the successive weights of the growing gerbil; in using the known sequence of the schedule of activities to predict what is coming; in exploring the building to find where the heat in the radiators comes from.

The teacher uses various ways of stimulating thinking at appropriate moments. She helps elaborate a child's experience through verbal expression, she rephrases a child's expressed thought or action in a way that lifts the level from particularized performance to a more generalized concept; she offers material for analogous thinking; she puts questions that stimulate perceptual and conceptual search maneuvers. In the course of story reading, she opens up questions for later pursuit that are a little ahead of the children's thinking level. In instances of social dilemma, she unravels the elements of difficulty and helps the child compose a possible solution to the problem. She stimulates anticipatory thinking by posing if-then formulations.

As part of the program design the teacher takes initiative from time to time in introducing certain preplanned learning episodes focused on clarifying specific concepts—similarity, difference, size, part–whole, and so forth—using objects and events that are experientially familiar to the children. Also, the classroom is so organized—spatially and functionally—that cognitive functions such as sorting, classification, and recognition of written symbols are practiced incidentally to daily classroom functioning. Structured learning episodes in the realm of cognition during the early years of childhood are only supplementary to the context-embedded methods for stimulating conceptual organization.

In line with the importance attached to cognitive–affective interaction, the program is designed to nurture the intuitive processes, the capacity for feeling and emotion, for reflective as well as goal-directed thinking in order to bring the totality of imaginative, productive functioning to its highest power. One of the established goals, "to increase the range and depth of children's sensitivity to the world around them" has aesthetic components as well.

This view insists on the importance of giving expressive activities a significant place in the curriculum. The children are provided with ample opportunity, equipment, and encouragement for many forms of symbolic expression, verbal and nonverbal, for reliving experience by representing it in personally meaningful terms, for fantasizing as well as reasoning, for synthesizing the subjective and objective aspects of experience. Their activities in this domain are free from any restraints of imposed standards for duplicating reality or adhering consistently to the relations implicit in logical organization.

The method used for stimulating and enriching spontaneous dramatic play of young children has been highly developed in this program. The teacher observes, provides materials or a few extensions of ideas, and perhaps takes a passing role in the play temporarily, but she does not teach how to play. This kind of spontaneous play, originating in the self-determined conceptualization and enactment of the children, individually or in small groups, serves a dual function. It is recognized as an essential learning mode for this stage of development: a medium for externalizing thought in which the child gains new cognitive mastery over nascent conceptual content. It is equally valuable as an experience in which the wondering, problem-solving, and conceptualizing of the groping child mind fuses with the wishes, fears, longings for strength, pleasures, and pains of the burgeoning inner self—in other words, a self-initiated creative process in which the child integrates his understanding of objective reality with his personal meanings and feelings.

Still other techniques are involved in supporting the children's interactions with one another and helping them to function as a group. In the way the children's joint play and activities are organized, in the issues considered crucial in settling disputes, in the guidance for how and when to listen and be heard in a group discussion, the teacher establishes mores of social interchange: ones that maximize the children's learning from one another and offer guidelines for the socializing experience of cooperating, helping, consoling, and coping with disagreement and conflict of interest. In this setting, the child finds himself in a learning environment in which he is a major actor, so organized that he can gain a sense of his own competence through the experience of autonomy—selecting, planning, initiating, decision-making. His ways of transforming and reconstructing experiences are valued for aesthetic qualities and expression of feeling as well as for evidence of cognitive mastery. There is a wide latitude for varied personal interaction on many levels since the social climate is not rigidly stratified between stronger and weaker, knowing and not knowing, adult and child. The teacher is looked to not only as a guide for penetrating the how and why of the external surround but also as a willing, dependable resource for dealing with fear, loss of direction, anger, or loneliness when there is hurt and with a sense of justice when there is controversy. When this is successful, the child finds strength and pleasures in creating order through his expanding thought processes, from sharing depth of feeling with teachers and children, and from recreating symbolically the meanings (real and fantasied) that are of the greatest moment to him.

As has been indicated earlier, the teacher carries a complex role in the implementation of this ideology. Her interactions with the children cannot be standardized; she has to be sensitive and adaptive to the simultaneity of thinking and feeling processes. As in the cognitive-oriented programs, she needs to be able to assess the level and the pattern of the child's cognitive functioning; here, she needs, equally, to be aware of how stage-specific, social-emotional drives and conflicts are being worked through by the individual child. The teacher seeks to understand and respond to the child's meanings and feelings in whatever way they are communicated. The lack of standardization, like the requirements for awareness and responsivity, makes the teacher's role challenging but often very difficult. Perhaps more than in other programs, successful realization of educational goals depends upon the teacher's ability to take genuine initiative in translating basic precepts into a productive learning environment. The unusually complex requirements of the teacher's role constitute a challenge to teacher education not readily met within the framework of most teacher education programs.

Final Considerations

Here we may focus on the question: To what extent does adherence to a given psychological theory as the basis of an educational design restrict the comprehensiveness of the program?

Of the three approaches, behavioristic learning theory appears to be the most limiting when applied to education, generating a technology geared to behavioral change in circumscribed areas. The mechanisms involved turn out to be—though presumably without intention—matched to the philosophy and limited goals of traditional education. Specifically, the role of the child to adult, of learner to teacher, inherent in the teaching techniques derived from behavioristic learning theory matches the quality of these relationships inherent in traditional educational philosophy.

By contrast, the psychological territory of cognitive-developmental theory is far more extensive. The explanatory concepts in this theory contribute to a complex, internally consistent image of learning and growth, not in terms of behavioral change per se, but with reference to an active organism constructing knowledge of the world through interaction. In its application to education this theory mandates responsibility for a comprehensive program with specific criteria for suitable environmental input and for the nature of the interaction between child and adult. Nevertheless, as we have argued, the focus on cognitive processes is a limiting perspective: the sphere of affective-social patterns is not a fully developed aspect of this theory. Even though there has recently been recognition by some curriculum planners of this school that cognitive processes cannot be supported and stimulated without consideration of concomitant social emotional processes, the cognitive-developmental theory itself does not provide guidelines for the design of this aspect of the learning environment.

The developmental-interaction approach is a whole child approach. Educationally, its goals comprise affective-social as well as cognitive aspects of development. The question of which stands at the center and which at the periphery is irrelevant since the primary thesis is that both these domains of psychological functioning are continuously interactive. This view prescribes the most comprehensive program planning of a learning environment with specific guidelines as to the variation of learning experience and the consideration of teacher–child interactions both in general overall terms and in the choice of focus in the particular moment-by-moment exchanges between teacher and child.

As has already been indicated, no one developmental theory stands as adequate rationale for this approach. Both cognitive and affective-social theories are a requisite foundation for the enactment of the educational philosophy which shares certain basic values with the cognitive-developmental approach but includes concepts of healthy personality derived from psychodynamic theories.

The reference to two lines of theorizing as a foundation for an educational program brings a question—or issue—to the fore that is especially pertinent to the general implementation of theory in programming. The attempt to draw on multiple theoretical sources sometimes leads to a patchwork—matching parts of educational practice to this or that theory; this, in fact, characterizes many programs which have not been dealt with in this presentation. By contrast, in the developmental-interaction approach, an integrative theoretical view has been developed which governs overall decision-making as well as the continuous interactional modes. It is in this connection that the important issue of target and side effects has been raised in the previous discussion. The position has been taken that target-focused techniques inevitably have side effects and that limited theoretical foundations, most extreme from the behaviorist point of view, lead to neglect of the totality of input, and, consequently, lack of awareness of the complexity of what is internalized by the child. With all too brief illustrations we have attempted to indicate the implicit decision-making going on in a teacher's mind as she shapes her interactions with the children. At this point perhaps it should be reiterated that excellence in enacting this educational role is not readily come by and involves a special kind of teacher preparation.

Toward Theoretical Integration

In the paper "Psychological Perspectives and Early Childhood Education" (1977) Margery Franklin and I dealt comparatively with three theory-based approaches to educational programming for the preschool years. Our discussion of the three models—behavioristic, Piagetian cognitive-developmental, and developmental-interactionist—emphasizes the basic conflict between behavioristic and cognitive-developmental orientations and reflects the concern with cognitive functioning that was dominant at the time. Looking back, I see that we made only passing reference to programs that represent another psychological perspective—psychoanalytic theory—which was not in the forefront of educational considerations during that period. Since so many of the fundamental concepts of psychoanalysis have become basic in contemporary thought, in and beyond the fields of psychology and education, it would be a strange omission to pay no attention to the forms that early childhood education has taken, at various times, in response to that revolutionary contribution to the understanding of human behavior.

Psychoanalytic Theory Applied: The Walden School

The Walden School founders[2] and teachers, like other progressive school adherents, were dedicated not only to vitalizing the experience of education in its day-to-day reality but also to educating for competence and commitment to social progress. But the Walden School position differed from others in the course to be followed. The founders held that effective socialization depends not only on inducing active, knowledgeable involvement in the wider world of ideas, problems, and social purposes (the Deweyan view) but also on a prior resolution of the largely unconscious problems intrinsic to the maturing of the individual. This called for recognition of the importance of the inner life of

2. They were Margaret Naumberg, Claire H. Raphael, and later Margaret Pollitzer and Elizabeth Goldsmith.

feeling, for sensitivity to the child's need for help in resolving conflicts intrinsic to psychosexual development, as they had been illuminated by Freudian theory. It called for an educational environment that would allow, in mood and program, for some release of unconscious emotional needs through positive and personal forms of expression. If there was to be hope for improved social functioning in the large, it must begin in the free realization of individuality through conflict resolution and in the expression of feeling in relation to action and self-knowledge.

Perhaps the key difference between the Walden School and other progressive schools such as the City and Country School and the Bank Street School for Children in the 1930s lay in the teacher's role. Whereas the teachers at City and Country and Bank Street became increasingly sensitive to children's feelings and beneath-the-surface needs, they were primarily committed to offering a wide and open opportunity for expression and mastery through sympathetic communication and motivated activity in a positive, supporting social environment. The teachers at Walden, in addition, were involved in fulfilling the growth needs of the children through adjusting not only the curriculum but also their interpersonal relations to the children according to their insights into unconscious mechanisms and how these could best be dealt with in the school situation and through teacher–child relationships.

The Role of Psychoanalytic Theory: Susan Isaacs

In this same period the two volumes by Susan Isaacs became available to the American and English reading public (1930, 1933). Isaacs had the rare gift of moving easily between sensitive observations of children's thought and behavior and incisive theoretical analysis of the processes involved. She herself was as much teacher as psychoanalyst—imaginative, penetrating, and systematically questioning in both roles.

How did her psychoanalytic insight affect her image and practice of early childhood education? In her words the Malting House School "was not a 'psychoanalytic school,' as was sometimes said by other people. I do not know what a 'psychoanalytic school' might be, nor, I imagine, did those who so spoke of it" (1933 [1972]). She goes on to say that she was a trained teacher of young children and a student of Dewey's educational theories long before she knew anything about Freud. Psychoanalytic insight did not alter her educational perspective; it supported and deepened it. "Educational reform," she wrote, "has not had to wait for psychoanalytic knowledge, although the latter had undoubtedly influenced educational thinkers . . . by its emphasis upon the significance of the child's feelings, whatever these be, and of the imaginative life, whatever form this takes."[3] Nor, perhaps I should add, has it had to wait for

---

3. The application of psychoanalytic theory to childhood education and teacher training has had continuous vitality, as can be seen in the programs and the writings of Selma Fraiberg, Anna Freud, Lili Peller, Maria Piers, and others.

the contribution of Piaget's epistemology, though because of that knowledge it has moved toward greater insight into the evolutionary course and intrinsic modes of cognitive processes. Neglect of history can be costly. Has a mistake been made in using Piagetian theory as the central structure for educational design? And was a mistake made in an earlier period in the undifferentiated application of the new, stimulating Freudian theory in some progressive schools?

In addition to building an extensive body of recorded evidence of children's intellectual and social experience in the school, Isaacs undertook a second task: to compare the processes of psychoanalysis and education and to define the optimal role of the teacher. In brief, her position was as follows: Whereas it is the analyst's role to uncover, accept, and follow up not only the love of the child, but also his hate and to tolerate its expression, it is the teacher's role to attract mainly the forces of love, to be the good but regulating parent, to give opportunity to express aggression but in modified form, and not to attract to herself the negative, explosive reactions of hatred and oppression. Whereas it is the analyst's role to probe beneath apparent equilibrium and get at the anxiety underlying surface peacefulness, it is the teacher's role to make use of the child's wish to achieve and create without penetrating what it may cover. This does not negate the value of the teacher's interest and understanding of deep symbolism, but it is her role to make use of unconscious trends only as they are available in conscious life. Whereas the analyst may take on any aspect of a child's conflict, it is the educator's role to act stably as a wise parent—mild, tolerant, friendly (see Bernard, 1967).

Isaacs spells out the task of the educator that she considers consistent with deeper knowledge of the maturing process and the unconscious problems the child needs to work through to achieve social adaptation and creative functioning. The school environment should supply some outlet for unconscious wishes and fantasies. Opportunity for free, unhindered imaginative play should be seen not only as a means to discover the world but also as a way to reach psychic equilibrium, in working through wishes, fears, and fantasies "so as to integrate them into a living personality." There should be opportunities for sublimation through creative art activities and ready companionship for engaging in cooperative expression of fantasy in dramatic play.

I read the Susan Isaacs volumes as they appeared. They deepened and extended my understanding of the educational philosophy that was the foundation for Harriet Johnson's design for early childhood education and was at the core of my own teaching of child development.

The four schools I have mentioned that were experimenting with a new style of learning and teaching for the preschool years—the Malting House School in England, and the Walden School, the City and Country School, and the Bank Street School for Children in the United States—were clearly aligned with the Deweyan theory of education. They had a common commitment: to create an experiential mode of learning, to give breathing space to individuality, and to relate the new education to images of a changed social order. There were some differences and disagreements among them as to implementation. Over the years, ongoing adaptation of practice to theory and testing of theory against practice in these schools were reflected in many ways: for example, in changing attitudes toward permissiveness, variation in the extent of teacher participation in or interpretation of the children's spontaneous imaginative productions, and shifts in the quality of interaction between family and school.

Establishing and Revising the Theoretical Base

Obviously, theories of development and learning have implications for the strategies and content of education. Psychologists have often served—some actively, some passively—as guides or critics of varieties of educational practice on the basis of theoretical formulations. Theory has, in turn, been affected by the accumulating data not only from controlled study and experimentation but also from clinical and naturalistic observation of child behavior. For some, the questions raised are predominantly "applied" in nature—how to use existent theories in interaction with existent practice—and there is no simple, straight-away answer.

I have found it interesting to look briefly into the ways in which several psychologists, with an orientation toward psychoanalytic theory have contributed varying insights on the course of development and associated implications for child-rearing, educational practice, and research method.

Within the conspectus of psychoanalytic theory Erikson's developmental schema (1950 [1963])—the eight stages of man—has been a useful tool for understanding the origin of alternative personality components—the way particular kinds of child-rearing or educational practice can influence the outcome of the conflicts that characterize successive stages. A stage theory deals with the dynamic constellations that are dominant in an invariant succession of developmental periods—no mere inventory of behavior norms. Erikson illuminated this complex conceptualization of the stage-by-stage maturing process by schematizing the alternative influence of contrasting child-rearing practices at successive stages.

In the very earliest stage of dependency and helplessness in infancy, the quality of adult–child relation, primarily the extent to which the child can rely on another person, becomes the foundation for lifelong attitudes of basic trust or mistrust. At a later stage, the development of autonomy as a personality characteristic is related to the period when the child's skilled use of body musculature and locomotion are ascending skills. Cultural, subcultural, and family perspectives about the value of self-determination influence the way the child's autonomous attempts at independent locomotion and related feats are treated (encouraged or discouraged) and have lasting influence on his style of life long after the early years of childhood. Denial of the expression of autonomous impulses at this early stage may become the foundation for feelings of shame and self-doubt. Each stage for each child represents a constellation of alternate possibilities.

Which conflicts of successive stages are resolved positively, which personality qualities and attitudes become dominant, depend upon the insight and values of the adult figures—parents, relatives, teachers—and the nature of the adult–child relationship from the earliest stages into emerging maturity.

A clear and thoroughly analyzed description of the revision of theory to take account of new knowledge was contributed by Robert White (1963) in his discussion of independent ego energies. He found it necessary to depart from orthodox Freudian theory in order to include the growth processes manifested in exploration, manipulation, language, practicing of motor skills, growth of cognition, intentional actions, and emergence of higher thought processes—all constituting the adaptive processes by which the individual relates to his environment. In his view these ego processes have intrinsic energies and are directly motivated without being derived by transformation from the energies associated with instinctual drives. Reality is not passively received; learning about the world is slowly constructed through active, varied, and persistent exploration. Neutral energies of the nervous system, alongside but not derived from instinctual energies, are motive forces for exploring the environment. Interactions lead to knowledge of what can and cannot be done, called "competence" by White, and to the subjective residue of these interactions, called "sense of competence." The incorporation of the work of developmental psychologists such as Piaget and Werner into psychoanalytic theory led White to this revised theoretical system. It is predominantly an action system which serves as support for that school of educational practice whose central postulate is the importance of active, self-initiated, experiential learning.

At about the same time, Stone and Church (1968) tried to come to terms with the problem of comprehensive theory. They recognized the efforts of psychologists to integrate psychoanalytic theory, especially as it illuminates the areas of motivation and emotion, with maturational developmental theories, especially those that are concerned with cognition. But they found these efforts unsatisfactory on the basis that neither psychoanalytic nor maturational theories make sufficient provision for learning and the role of context in behavior. Stone and Church resorted to what they called "synthetic eclecticism," claiming exemption from opprobrium for doing so by noting that such respectable scholars as Gardner Murphy and Gordon Allport had taken the same path. The very title of Allport's paper on this question, "The Fruits of Eclecticism—Bitter or Sweet?," has the sound of a soul struggle among psychologists. Allport (1964) expounds the position that reactive, particularistic theories (e.g., behaviorism, stimulus–response, and empty organism) must be supplemented with proactive theories (ego psychology, aspiration level, self-actualization, and so on) in order to comprehend the "planful, inventive, aspiring, hopeful behavior of man." To quote:

> For all the subtlety of "reinforcement schedules," the characters in Professor Skinner's *Walden Two* remain as reactive as an array of patellar knee jerks. In real life a *challenge* is something more than a *stimulus*.

Thinking creatively with symbols is something beyond responding to signals.

In a later formulation Stone and Church, recognizing more organized efforts toward synthesis of compatible views, described a changing orientation toward a "new and coherent eclecticism."

In her systematic, observational study of early development, Escalona (1968) describes behavioral change as a continuous developmental process in which given propensities for activity and perceptual sensitivity interact with what the infant encounters in every specific aspect of his life environment. She illustrates how the developmental process takes place as part of the interchange of complex variables. The nature of maternal response to an infant varies; its differential impact needs observation and analysis.

In identifying the sequential stages associated with separation between self and environment, development of a relation to another human being, and emergence of volitional behavior, Escalona deals with an enlarged sphere of influences. Recognizing the complexity of concurrent influencing factors, she is concerned not with a general description of child-rearing technique but with the specific means of implementation adapted to recognition of individual differences in the maturing patterns of children as these interact with variable patterns of parental care-giving. The analysis of the developmental process is built on consideration of coexisting influences, a complex matrix of "experience patterns." The neglect of coexisting variables may explain the failure to find relationships.

From the educational perspective, we too have resisted single variable approaches in maintaining that not cognition alone but at least the cognition–affect complex should be at the base of educational design. If this premise, that it is essential to study the organism as a whole in the context of relevant field conditions, can be the foundation of the study of the more complex interactional processes of later developmental stages, we may find new dimensions for verifiable continuity of life-style in successive stages.

From Dewey and Piaget: Lawrence Kohlberg

The question of the role of education in relation to moral development has had major attention in recent years, advanced theoretically and experimentally, by the work of Kohlberg and his associates. Besides drawing on Piaget's cognitive theory and Dewey's philosophy and practice of progressivism, this movement has an original philosophical orientation. The endpoint for individual development is justice, defined as reciprocity between the individual and others in the social environment. The ultimate image is a *free and powerful character*, a phrase used by McLellan and Dewey in 1889. In contrast to a mere statement of psychological principles, this view is an ideology which embodies a series of successive stages, constituting a path toward the final stage: autonomy and internalization of a code of justice.

There are two ways in which this philosophical position has been expressed: (1) in a general image of what constitutes a desirable learning environment (Kohlberg, 1968), and (2) in newly devised educational programming which stimulates organized thinking with reference to moral development as a distinct area. In the interest of stimulating cognitive development, schools need to be designed as active experiential programs where knowledge is structured through action, not didactically presented through verbal materials, and thinking is not identified with correct rule application. The goal is the development of fundamental cognitive operations, not of specific discrimination and labeling skills. The positive image is a school where cognitive goals are defined developmentally and mediated through relatively active and self-selected stimulation, available in the play and in the constructive, aesthetic social activities of a progressive school. In this image there is primary interest in the movement of thought that takes place in play, conversation, and emerging conceptions of life, death, reality, sexual identity, and good and evil, in contrast to programs narrowly focused on cognitive stimulation.

This image of school is identified as representing a cognitive-developmental viewpoint in which knowledge is derived through experiential problem-solving and a communion of thinking with others. There are skills to be learned—reading, for example—but these are seen as tools, means toward engaging in significant successive stages of maturing cognitive processes as well as social and ethical codes of behavior. Developmentally, cognitive development is seen as a continuous course of "greater differentiation, integration and adaptation," in accord with the principles of sequence in Piagetian theory: an ordered, invariant sequence of conceptual development, in hierarchical order of chronologically successive stages (Kohlberg & Mayer, 1972).

Education, conceived developmentally, has the responsibility for stimulating the reasoning processes, encouraging understanding of rational ethical principles, and leading toward internal standards of adequacy. These concepts as applied favor educational principles that are process- rather than product-oriented, where what is particular is conceived in relation to the surrounding whole. Also, from this point of view, goals of education that are concerned with aspects of functioning such as curiosity, spontaneity, and independence of judgment are considered too narrowly relevant to a given cultural ethos, often internally contradictory, and therefore not suitable as movement toward the concept of justice as the universally relevant goal.

To some educators (Feldman, 1980), this is a restricted view, overly concentrated on the ideological progression toward a concept of justice and the self-regulating mechanisms within the child. Kohlberg's application of Piagetian theory has been questioned by some who also favor a stage-developmental view and the image of a guiding, not a directing, teacher figure. But they do not see this general formulation as adequate for defining objectives and methods for a curriculum, for the choices to be made from among the possible activities, bodies of knowledge, and role images in relation to successive levels of development as well as values and ultimate goals. In addition, there is the goal of individualizing instruction and helping each child "to integrate experience from conceptually distinct domains."

Kohlberg's emphasis on advancing cognitive-moral reasoning as the primary means toward the goal of justice also leads to dismissing the place of psychodynamic theory and mental health concepts as relevant to the same goal. Actually, psychodynamic theory calls for reeducation of impulses, parallel to the reeducation of thought processes in cognitive psychology. In an enlarged view there is a significant developmental process in the growth toward emotional maturity and the interaction of cognitive and affective processes. In this dimension successive stages represent movement from fulfillment as an individual self in the early stages to functioning as an extended self—a sequence which is essential to becoming capable of and motivated toward reciprocity (and justice) in human relations. What Kohlberg dismisses as a "bag of virtues"— namely, self-realization, self-actualization, self-confidence—can be seen as steps in a developmental process which, like cognition, reflects the interaction of given propensity and environmental influences.

Allowing cognitive theory to serve as the major criterion for educational programming, Kohlberg finds a wide range of fundamentally different designs acceptable. For example, a Montessori program appears acceptable even though it offers minimal opportunity for invention through fantasy organization of experience and takes little interest in working on how best to meet the child's need to cope with emotional conflicts. It is not surprising to find that a more comprehensive theoretical base for educational planning leads to more selectivity in the endorsement of programs (Shapiro & Biber, 1972).

It is in the area of the responsibility of education for moral development that Kohlberg (1981) has made a significant contribution. From a philosophical-ethical base, moral development is conceived in terms of universal concepts of ethics and defense of rights—one's own and others' in a democratic society— and these are presented as significant goals of the maturing process. From extensive study of varied populations, he has formulated a theory of successive stages in moral development that are aligned with the course of cognitive development as explicated by Piagetian formulations. Maturing means "greater differentiation, integration and adaptation" in successive stages of irreversible change during which the child constructs his own logical and ethical principles. Changing concepts of justice are aligned with successive developmental eras. For example, for the preschool child at stage 2 "right is serving one's own or others' needs and making fair deals in terms of concrete exchange"; for the mature adult (and not all adults achieve maturity) stage 6 "assumes guidance by universal ethical principles that all humanity should follow."

During the past decade there has been an extensive program of moral education in a selected number of schools, well researched and employing a variety of methods to test the effects of different approaches to stimulating moral reasoning, among them adaptation of the Socratic dialogue for child–teacher interchange, separate from other classroom activities. In a review of studies it was found that direct discussion of moral dilemmas produces significant advance (a half-stage of reasoning). But the gains have been smaller than had been expected and have not always been maintained. The programs did not lead to a radical reorganization of thinking about moral issues.

As a result, Kohlberg and his colleagues developed a more comprehensive approach in which moral education becomes an integrated component of a school's functioning (Kohlberg, 1980). In this approach there is special attention "to realistic issues that arise in school, the nature of moral behavior as well as moral thought and an active role for teachers as moral advocates" (Minuchin & Shapiro, 1983). This shift to a democratically organized classroom as the base for encouraging moral development has the promise of relating this aspect of development to other psychological functions and sociological influences.

This change has theoretical significance inasmuch as it moves stimulation of moral thinking from a verbal-theoretical plane to the issues and conflicts of learning and living together in the social situation of the classroom and the school. This approach is preferred by those who have been critical of method that separates thought and action in this sphere. Sullivan (1977) believes that "thought directs action and action directs thought and so on and so on. . . . all of us mere human beings must act in ambiguity in many situations and in the process of acting we really begin to clarify how we think." A more active role for the teacher and the location of moral thinking within the classroom are in line with the Deweyan image of learning in a democratic society.

From Gilligan's perspective (1982), we find questioning about the applicability of the moral stages sequence, as formulated, to women. The assignment of women to a lower stage of reasoning than men may be the outcome of, first, the failure of the analytic system and, second, insensitivity on the part of those who conduct the interviews to the qualitatively different priorities in women's value systems. For women, for whom the caring function is central, the conception of morality centers on the understanding of responsibility and relationships. For men, the conception of morality is based on fairness, linking moral development to the understanding of rights and rules.

These recent revisions broaden both the procedures and concepts of moral development, making this a less narrowly cognition-centered approach.

Theory as Resource and Problems of Integration

There is another question to raise about the relation of theory to practice: Is it spurious or at least premature to posit a body of theory or theories sufficiently comprehensive to be the foundation for the multitudinous aspects of an educational design? Those who question the sequence from theory to practice take the position that the starting place should be a value statement of what children "ought to be and become." Although it is important to have a general theoretical viewpoint as a basis for selected goals and practices, it is considered questionable to attempt to align the number and variety of decisions and choices that comprise an educational program with particular theoretical constructs.

Developmental theory and areas of knowledge and human endeavor should be drawn on as resources in developing curriculum, not as sources (Spodek, 1970).

The present mood of both psychologists and educators points in two directions: first, theory should not be insulated from application, nor should practice be allowed to escape responsibility for articulating theoretical foundations since cross-fertilization is essential to sound progress in both spheres. (I heard Kurt Lewin express this view to a meeting of educators many years ago.) Second, existing theories, differing in substantive ways but with a common ideological basis, need to be combined and integrated in the direction of developing more comprehensive super theory.

On this second point, Murphy (1973) documents the contributions of both psychoanalytic and child development studies to specific areas of functioning, such as separation and deprivation, aggression, mutual influences of ego and id, and integrative capacity. While she is appreciative of the increasing communication between psychoanalysts and child developmentalists in recent years, she does not think there has been sufficient concentration on individual differences in the course of development in either body of studies. Longitudinal, naturalistic, observational studies are essential if we are to understand variability in adaptation involving basic biosocial factors—body change, self-image, changed environmental demands. She is interested in "the contributions that a serious consideration of individuality could make to both these disciplines and to their influence on each other." In a broader view, she says, "we need collaborative thinking to extend the range of concepts available for understanding the complexity of personality development."

The lack of articulation between dimensions of individual variation and developmental stage theory is discussed by Shapiro and Wallace (1981). They review briefly the precepts of developmental stage theory that are common to both Freudian and Piagetian thinking. These include the distinctness of each successive developmental stage, the applicability of this theory to all human beings, and a concept of a "desired end state" in maturity. Application of these basic principles leaves unanswered questions. For example, consideration of the variation in environments in different world areas leads us to question the assumption that developmental stage theory is universally applicable. Other questions have to be raised in the domain of the school. Shall the dominant changes that characterize shifts in stage sequence be allowed to obscure the extent of continuity between stages? Has sequential analysis established a concept of forward progress that leads to characterizing behavior at any given stage in terms of what it has not yet become? How do we take into consideration the persistence of underlying issues in an individual's growth, though changed in form at different stages? Or, more generally, has the abstract level of developmental stage thinking lost the individual?

Turning from theory to application, Shapiro and Wallace decry the too-literal application of developmental stage theory to educational practice. Teachers should use theory (rather, theories) as guides for understanding but not as directions for practice. Not only can teachers benefit from acquaintance with theory but, far more than has been recognized, theorists need interchange with teachers as a source for greater understanding of how individual children function, from year to year, within the educational sequence. Expressed more generally, this may "signal a new approach to theory-building in which the struggle is to retain rather than to efface the individual."

It is time to ask not only how existing theories can be used in interaction with existing practice but also who shall be involved in crossing the two terrains. Zigler made a clear, strong statement on this question at the hearings of a National Commission (1976). In his view, researchers are a national resource who should not limit their activities to gathering new knowledge; they should become activists in the task of solving real-life problems. He makes the further point that the theoretical structure of a field is enriched when workers turn some of their attention to applied issues. The combined effort of researcher and educator was Lucy Mitchell's image for Bank Street from the beginning, although the loading was on the side of the educational program (see Antler, 1982).

In his analysis of theoretical issues in developmental psychology, Zigler, like Murphy, and Shapiro and Wallace, is concerned about the inadequacy of theoretical systems to deal with individual differences. "Nothing in Piaget," he writes (using Piaget as one among other "grand designs"), "allows one to assess the effects of either the state of the organism or differences in the environment that give rise to individual differences in development. . . . For all the talk concerning the importance of the individual, the environment, and the interaction between the two, both the individual and the environment are treated as constant" (Zigler, 1973b). In the interest of advancing toward a theoretical structure for developmental psychology, he looks toward another kind of collaboration. Where Murphy sees gain in integrating psychoanalytic and child development thinking, Zigler argues in favor of collaboration between child developmentalists and learning theorists.

As we have seen, during the decade of the 1970s, interest in delineating a psychological theory base adequate to serve as a foundation for educational practice came into sharper focus. The issue was raised in different forms, but much of the discussion centered on two related questions: If there is not a single theory, is there a combination of theories that can serve as a base for educational practice? Is there an important distinction to be made between "integrative" as contrasted with "eclectic" combinations? (see Werner, 1978)

The influential concept of a "family of theories" reflects the idea that theories can be grouped according to shared assumptions, with members of a given family differing in certain respects but sharing a set of views that is clearly distinct from—and typically opposed to—the shared assumptions of other "families." The idea of a "family of theories," articulated by Reese and Overton (1970) and others, rests on Bernard Kaplan's (1967; n.d.) formulation. Drawing on Pepper's (1942) concepts of root metaphor and world hypotheses and Abrams's (1953) discussion of critical theory, Kaplan delineated two major "families" of developmental theories: the mechanistic-passive organism view, and the organismic-active organism view. The organismic model is anchored philosophically in the views of Leibniz, Kant, Hegel, and Cassirer. It is represented in the biological theorizing of von Bertalanffy. At the center of this view is the concept of a spontaneously active organism in which the whole constitutes the condition of the meaning of the parts and knowledge is seen as growing from the activity of the organism on its environment: knowledge is constructed rather than "found." In this perspective, change is accepted as given; development is conceptualized in terms of levels of organization (or stages); process is more significant than product; active engagement and experience are more significant for development than is specific, circumscribed training.

Within this basic world view, and its corollary organismic theory, Kaplan (and Reese and Overton) include three major developmental perspectives that may thus be said to comprise a "family of theories" sharing a conceptual base; at the same time, each articulates specific concepts to accord with the particular aims and contents of different spheres of interest. Thus, Werner's (1957a, 1957b) and Piaget's contributions deal with organismic functioning and development primarily in terms of cognition, broadly construed, and Erikson's work emphasizes psychosocial aspects of development. The grouping of these theoretical perspectives in one "family," and the sharp division drawn between this family on the one hand and behavioristic approaches comprising another "family," brings to the foreground the irreducible differences between organismic and behavioristic world views and strongly supports the idea that in drawing implications from developmental theory to educational practice, we must attend closely to the underlying presuppositions of different theories. Unfortunately, at times, differences in practice are dismissed as vague personal preferences or inclinations without awareness of the underlying relations to a body of theory. Reese and Overton argue for a distinction between "good eclecticism," where ideas from different theoretical structures are drawn into a whole structure, and "random eclecticism," where strands from different theories are combined without sufficient attention to questions of compatibility.

In an analysis of conceptual foundations for psychological theories Franklin (1981) distinguishes psychologies of mind, organism, person, and situation and presents positions in which more than one of these perspectives has been incorporated, as previously described with respect to the "family of theories" position. From this perspective she sees the developmental-interaction position both as psychology of mind—incorporating psychodynamic and developmental concepts as theoretical base—and as psychology of the person in its interest in the wholeness of thinking and feeling as well as the uniqueness of individual processes in reality functioning. The "whole child" image represents a needed combination of theoretical concepts to avoid oversimplification of multiple, complex processes. This level of theory combination is described as being in the service of "deepening" theoretical perspective insomuch as it is concerned with several levels of interpretation and leads to more differentiated, integrated analyses of complementary viewpoints.

Having spent a good deal of time attempting to synthesize streams from

Piaget, Werner, and psychodynamic theorists (Biber, 1972, 1981), I find it both interesting and somehow reassuring to discover that psychologists working on the level of metatheory, rather than on developing a theoretical base for educational practice, should come to a similar grouping. This is not accidental. Clearly, my own theoretical interests and preferences were formed if not explicitly articulated in terms of the kinds of deep, underlying compatibilities and values that make for integrative rather than eclectic theoretical structures.

Afterword

In bringing this book to conclusion, I want to say a few words about the broader issues in early childhood education that concerned me over the 50-year period from the early 1930s to the present.

It is only occasionally recalled now that progressive education had its origins in a movement whose goal was the fundamental reconstruction of our social system. The extent to which a changed educational system can provide a successful means toward such a goal raises more questions in our own era than it did in the 1930s, but the image survives and the attempt to realize it is reenacted periodically. When John Dewey turned to revolutionizing educational experience as a channel toward reconstructing society, he provided for many of us who were young in those early decades of the century a means of transforming general ideals for social change into the reality of revolutionizing a potent social instrument—the school system. If we were to free the child's intellectual capacity, we had to make learning an active, self-generating, searching experience; if we were to be responsive to the goal of educating the whole child, we had not only to stimulate independent thinking and reasoning processes but to open avenues toward creative reorganization of experience as intrinsic to the learning process; if education was ultimately to effect social change, we had to bring the reality of how the world functions into the classroom curriculum; if we expected children to become awakened to the advantages of a democratic society, we had to provide the experience of living democratically in the social setting of the schoolroom, of being part of a cooperative structure characterized by egalitarian interpersonal relations.

The decades of the fifties and sixties offered a theoretical challenge. The time had come to integrate methods and concepts of the learning process into a new paradigm. Education was still the medium of the socialization process, but new insights into basic psychological growth in childhood influenced method and deepened understanding. Developmental and psychodynamic theory became stimulants for changing practice and, at the same time, supported pre-

309

viously accepted modes that were derivations from the Deweyan democratic philosophy.

The decade of the sixties was also a challenge from an applied perspective. Early childhood education came to be seen as a social ameliorative for the damages of poverty and prejudice during the first years of life. Government support stimulated an era of experimentation; psychologists became actively involved in establishing experimental preschool programs designed to compensate for what many considered the core of difficulty in advancing educationally: inadequate development of cognitive functioning. There was disagreement among us, both as psychologists and as educators, on the validity of isolating cognitive processes from other processes that also reflect the pervasive effect of total life circumstances and that exist in dynamic interaction with the cognitive side of the child's functioning.

By the seventies our thinking was directed toward clarifying the developmental-interaction point of view: the implications for education of perceiving identifiable successive patterns of growth as a function of chronological age, of placing emphasis on the child's interaction with the social and physical environment within the context of preferred values, and, finally, of recognizing the interaction between cognitive and affective spheres of experience.

We are living in an era of ferment, of astonishingly rapid change. Those of us who have been in this field for a while are always interested in new developments, encouraged to see the energy, resourcefulness, and social concern of those involved in developing new programs and elaborating their rationale. It is too early to say what will happen in the face of the eighties—in education and in the wider world. But as I look forward, I hold to my lifelong confidence in the positive motivation and creative spirit of those who are young now, and in their ability to forge solutions to the problems of this era.

References

Abrams, M. *The mirror and the lamp.* New York: Norton, 1953.

Alberty, B., Neujahr, J., & Weber, L. *Use and setting: Development in a teachers' center.* North Dakota Study Group on Evaluation, Grand Forks: University of North Dakota, November 1981.

Allee, W. C. *Cooperation among animals.* New York: Henry Schumann, 1938 (rev. 1951).

Allender, D., & Allender, J. *I am the Mayor: Inquiry materials for the study of city government.* Philadelphia, Pa.: Center for the Study of Federalism, Temple University, 1972.

Allport, G. W. The fruits of eclecticism—bitter or sweet? *Psychologia,* 1964, *7,* 1–14.

Almy, M. (Ed.). *Early childhood play.* New York: Selected Academic Readings, 1968.

Alpert, A. Sublimation and sexualization. *The Psychoanalytic Study of the Child* (Vols. 3, 4). New York: International Universities Press, 1949.

Andrus, R., Nash, H., & Stanton, J. *The education of children under six in public schools: programs and standards.* Chicago: National Association for Nursery Education, n.d.

Antler, J. Progressive education and the scientific study of the child: An analysis of the Bureau of Educational Experiments. *Teachers College Record,* 1982, *83*(4), 559–91.

Arieti, S. *Creativity: The magic synthesis.* New York: Basic Books, 1976.

Arnheim, R. *Art and visual perception.* Berkeley: University of California Press, 1974.

The arts and the school: A program for integrating the arts in an elementary school. New York: Bank Street College of Education Project Report, 1971.

Baratz, J. C. Teaching reading in an urban Negro school system. In F. Williams (Ed.), *Language and poverty.* Chicago: Markham, 1970.

Baratz, S. S., & Baratz, J. C. Early childhood interventions: The social science basis of institutional racism. *Harvard Educational Review*, 1970, *40* (1), 29–50.

Barron, F. The disposition toward originality. *Journal of Personality and Social Psychology*, 1955, *51*, 478–584.

Barron, F. *Creativity and personal freedom* (rev. ed.). Princeton, N.J.: Van Nostrand, 1963.

Barron, F. The dream of art and poetry. *Psychology Today*, 1968, *2*, 19–23.

Bereiter, C., & Engelmann, S. *Teaching the culturally disadvantaged child in the preschool.* Englewood Cliffs, N.J.: Prentice-Hall, 1966.

Bernard, V. S. *Teacher education in mental health: From the point of view of the psychiatrist.* New York: Bank Street College of Education, 1967.

Bernstein, B. Language and social class. *British Journal of Sociology*, 1960, *11*, 271–76.

Bernstein, B. A critique of the concept of compensatory education. In C. B. Cazden, V. P. John, & D. Hymes (Eds.), *Functions of language in the classroom.* New York: Teachers College Press, 1972.

Bettelheim, B. *The children of the dream.* New York: Macmillan, 1969.

Bettelheim, B. *The uses of enchantment.* New York: Random House, 1976.

Biber, B. A nursery school puts psychology to work. *69 Bank Street*, 1934, *1* (3), 1–11.

Biber, B. Play as a growth process. *Vassar Alumnae Magazine*, 1951, *37* (2), 18–20. [See chap. 9, this volume.]

Biber, B. The implications for public education of research in learning. *Proceedings of the California Association of School Psychologists and Psychometrists*, March 1959a.

Biber, B. Premature structuring as a deterrent to creativity. *American Journal of Orthopsychiatry*, 1959b, *29* (2), 280–90. [See chap. 10, this volume.]

Biber, B. Preschool education. In R. Ulich (Ed.), *Education and the idea of mankind.* New York: Harcourt, Brace & World, 1964.

Biber, B. The "whole child," individuality and values in education. In J. R. Squire (Ed.), *A new look at progressive education.* Washington, D.C.: Association for Supervision and Curriculum Development, 1972.

Biber, B. The child development associate: A professional role for developmental day care. *Theory into Practice*, 1973, *12* (2), 89–96.

Biber, B. Evolution of the developmental-interaction point of view. In E. K. Shapiro and E. Weber (Eds.), *Cognitive and affective growth.* Hillsdale, N.J.: Erlbaum, 1981.

Biber, B., & Franklin, M. The relevance of developmental and psychodynamic concepts to the education of the preschool child. *Journal of the American Academy of Child Psychiatry*, 1967, *6* (1), 5–24.

Biber, B., Shapiro, E., & Wickens, D. *Promoting cognitive growth: A developmental interaction point of view* (2d ed.). Washington D.C.: National Association for the Education of Young Children, 1977. [See chap. 4, this volume.]

Birns, B., & Golden, M. The implications of Piaget's theories for contemporary infancy research and education. In M. Schwebel & J. Raph (Eds.), *Piaget in the classroom*. New York: Basic Books, 1973.

Blank, M. Some philosophical influences underlying preschool intervention for disadvantaged children. In F. Williams (Ed.), *Language and poverty*. Chicago: Markham, 1970.

Blank, M., Rose, S. A., & Berlin, L. J. *The language of learning: The preschool years*. New York: Grune & Stratton, 1976.

Bloom, B. S. *Stability and change in human characteristics*. New York: Wiley, 1964.

Boas, F. *The mind of primitive man*. New York: Macmillan, 1911.

Bock, G., Stebbins, L. B., & Proper, E. C. *Education as experimentation: A planned variation model: Volume IV-B. Effects of Follow Through models*. Cambridge, Mass.: Abt Associates, 1977.

Bowlby, J. *Attachment and loss: Volume 1. Attachment*. New York: Basic Books, 1969.

Bowman, B., & Kemble, E. Should the public schools control child care services? In J. D. Andrews (Ed.), *Early childhood education*. Washington, D.C.: National Association for the Education of Young Children, 1976.

Bowman, G. W., & Mayer, R. S. *BRACE* (Behavior Ratings and Analysis of Communication in Education). New York: Bank Street College of Education, 1974.

Bronfenbrenner, U. *Two worlds of childhood: U.S. & U.S.S.R.* New York: Russell Sage Foundation, 1970.

Bronfenbrenner, U. *The experimental ecology of human development*. Cambridge, Mass.: Harvard University Press, 1979.

Bruner, J. S. State of the child. *New York Review*, October 27, 1983.

Bruner, J. S., Jolly, A., & Sylva, K. (Eds.). *Play: Its role in development and evolution*. New York: Basic Books, 1976.

Bushell, D. The behavior analysis classroom. In B. Spodek (Ed.), *Early childhood education*. Englewood Cliffs, N.J.: Prentice-Hall, 1973.

Bussis, A. M., Chittenden, E. A., & Amarel, M. Alternative ways in educational evaluation. In V. Perrone, M. D. Cohen, & L. P. Martin (Eds.), *Testing and evaluation: New views*. Washington, D.C.: Association for Childhood Education International, 1975.

Caldwell, B. M., & Freyer, M. Day care and early education. In B. Spodek (Ed.), *Handbook of research on early childhood education*. New York: Free Press, 1982.

Carini, P. F. Observation and description: An alternative methodology for the investigation of human phenomena. Grand Forks: North Dakota Study Group on Evaluation, University of North Dakota, 1975a.

Carini, P. F. The Prospect School: Taking account of process. In V. Perrone, M. D. Cohen, & L. P. Martin (Eds.), *Testing and evaluation: New views*. Washington, D.C.: Association for Childhood Education International, 1975b.

Cazden, C. B. *Child language and education.* New York: Holt, Rinehart & Winston, 1972.

Cazden, C. B., Baratz, J. C., Labov, W., & Palmer, F. H. Language development in day care programs. In E. Grotberg (Ed.), *Day Care: Resources for decisions.* Washington, D.C.: Office of Economic Opportunity, 1971.

Chan, I. Early education in China and its implications in the United States. Paper presented at the Asian American Bilingual Center, Berkeley, Calif., April 1977.

Chauncey, H. (Ed.). *Soviet preschool education: Volume 1. Program of instruction.* New York: Holt, Rinehart, & Winston, 1969.

Chukovsky, K. *From two to five.* Berkeley and Los Angeles: University of California Press, 1963 (First published in 1925).

Cohen, D. H. *The Learning Child.* New York: Pantheon, Random House, 1972.

Cohen, D. H. Television and the child under 6. In B. Logan & K. Moody (Eds.), *Television awareness training.* New York: Media Action Research Center, 1979.

Cohen, D. H., Lerner, M., & Weissbourd, B. *A look at children in China.* Urbana, Ill.: ERIC Clearinghouse on Early Childhood Education, 1976.

Cohen, E. P., & Gainer, R. S. *Art: Another language for learning.* New York: Citation Press, 1976.

Cohn, W. On the language of lower-class children. *School Review,* 1959, *67,* 435–40.

Cole, M., & Bruner, J. S. Preliminaries to a theory of cultural differences. In I. J. Gordon (Ed.), *Early childhood education.* The Seventy-First Yearbook of the National Society for the Study of Education, Part II. Chicago: University of Chicago Press, 1972.

Cole, M., Gay, J., Glick, J., & Sharp, D. *The cultural context of learning and thinking.* New York: Basic Books, 1971.

Cordes, C. Child advocates push for policy on infant leave. *American Psychological Association Monitor,* August 1983.

Cremin, L. A. *The transformation of the school.* New York: Vintage Books, 1964.

Cuffaro, H. K. Unfolding and connecting Dewey's thought from a teacher's perspective. Ph.D. Thesis, Teachers College of Columbia University, 1982.

Culkin, J. M. A schoolman's guide to Marshall McLuhan. *Saturday Review,* March 1967.

Curry, N. E. Current issues in play: Theoretical and practical considerations for its use as a curricular tool in the preschool. Unpublished thesis, University of Pittsburgh, 1972.

Darlington, R. B., Royce, J. M., Snipper, A. S., Murray, H. W., & Lazar, I. Preschool programs and later school competence of children from low income families. *Science,* April 11, 1980, *208,* 202–04.

Deutsch, M. *The disadvantaged child.* New York: Basic Books, 1967.

Dewey, J. *Democracy and education.* New York: Macmillan Free Press, 1944 (originally published 1916).

Dewey, J. *The school and society* (rev. ed.). Chicago: University of Chicago Press, 1945 (Originally published 1899).

Dewey, J., & Dewey, E. *Schools of tomorrow.* New York: Dutton, 1915.

DiLeo, J. H. *Young children and their drawings.* New York: Brunner/Mazel, 1970.

DiLeo, J. H. *Child development: analysis and synthesis.* New York: Brunner/Mazel, 1977.

Doyle, C. L. The creative process: A study in paradox. In C. B. Winsor (Ed.), *The creative process.* New York: Bank Street College of Education, 1976.

Drucker, J., & Shapiro, C. B. First scribbles: The emergence of an ego function. *Journal of the American Academy of Child Psychiatry,* 1979, *18* (4), 628–46.

Duckworth, E. The having of wonderful ideas. *Harvard Educational Review,* 1972, *42,* 217–31.

Eifermann, R. R. Social play in childhood. In R. E. Herron & B. Sutton-Smith (Eds.), *Child's play.* New York: Wiley, 1971.

Eisner, E. W. On the uses of educational connoisseurship and criticism for evaluating classroom life. *Teachers College Record,* 1977, *76,* (3), 345–48.

El'Konin, D. Symbolics and its functions in the play of children. In R. E. Herron & B. Sutton-Smith (Eds.), *Child's play.* New York: Wiley, 1971.

Ellison, R. What these children are like. Paper presented at Seminar in Education for Culturally Different Youth at Dedham, Massachusetts. New York: Bank Street College of Education, 1963.

Engelmann, S. and associates. *Distar Instructional System.* University of Oregon, Palo Alto, Calif., 1972.

Erikson, E. H. *Childhood and society.* New York: Norton, 1950 [1963].

Erikson, E. H. Identity and the life cycle. *Psychological Issues,* 1959, *1* (1) (Whole issue).

Escalona, S. K. *The roots of individuality.* Chicago: Aldine, 1968.

Featherstone, J. The primary school revolution in Britain. Parts 1, 2, 3. *New Republic,* August 10, September 2, September 9, 1967.

Fein, G. G., Branch, A. R., & Diamond, E. Cognitive and social dimensions of pretending in two-year-olds. Manuscript, Yale University, 1975.

Fein, G. G., & Clarke-Stewart, A. *Day care in context.* New York: Wiley, 1973.

Feldman, D. H. *Beyond universals in cognitive development.* Norwood, N.J.: Ablex Publishing, 1980.

The first week in a Pennsylvania school. *Progressive Education,* 1942, *19* (1).

Foster, J. C., & Mattson, M. L. *Nursery school education.* New York/London: Appleton-Century, 1939.

Fowler, W. On the value of both play and structure in early education. *Young Children,* 1971, *27,* 24–36.

Fraiberg, S. H. *Every child's birthright: In defense of mothering.* New York: Basic Books, 1977.

Frank, L. K. The fundamental needs of the child. *Mental Hygiene,* 1938, *22* (3).

Frank, L. K. Creativity: An inquiry. *Western Arts Association Bulletin,* 1946, *40* (4), 5–17.

Franklin, M. B. Nonverbal representation in young children: A cognitive perspective. *Young Children,* November 1973, *29,* 33–53.

Franklin, M. B. Perspectives on theory: Another look at the developmental-interaction point of view. In E. Shapiro and E. Weber (Eds.), *Cognitive and affective growth: Developmental interaction.* Hillsdale, N.J.: Erlbaum, 1981.

Franklin, M. B. Play as the creation of imaginary situations. In B. Kaplan & S. Wapner (Eds.), *Toward a holistic developmental psychology.* Hillsdale, N.J.: Erlbaum, 1983.

Freyberg, J. T. Increasing the imaginative play of urban disadvantaged kindergarten children through systematic training. In J. O. Singer (Ed.), *The child's world of make-believe.* New York: Academic Press, 1973.

Gardner, H. *Artful scribbles.* New York: Basic Books, 1980.

Garvey, C. *Play.* Cambridge, Mass.: Harvard University Press, 1977.

Gerard, R. W. The biological basis of the imagination. In B. Ghiselin (Ed.), *The creative process.* New York: New American Library Mentor Book, 1952 (Reprinted from *Scientific Monthly,* June 1946).

Gesell, A., Halverson, H. M., Thompson, H., Ilg, F. L., & Costner, C. S. *The first five years of life: Guide to the study of the preschool child.* New York: Harper, 1940.

Gilligan, C. *In a different voice.* Cambridge, Mass.: Harvard University Press, 1982.

Ginsburg, A., & Knitzer, J. The contributions of developmental psychology. *Newsletter,* Division of Developmental Psychology, American Psychological Association, February 1976.

Ginsburg, H. *The myth of the deprived child.* Englewood Cliffs, N.J.: Prentice-Hall, 1972.

Ginsburg, H., & Knitzer, J. On helping children. *Newsletter,* Division of Developmental Psychology, American Psychological Association, February 1976.

Golden, M., and Rosenbluth, L. *The New York City infant day care study.* New York: Medical and Health Research Association, 1978.

Goldman, I. Boas on the Kwakiutl: The ethnographic tradition. In S. Diamond (Ed.), *Theory and practice.* The Hague: Mouton, 1980.

Goldsmith, C. *Better day care for the young child.* Washington, D.C.: National Association for the Education of Young Children, 1972.

Gould, R. *Child studies through fantasy.* New York: Quadrangle Books, 1972.

Greenspan, S. I. *Intelligence and adaptation: An integration of psychoanalytic and Piagetian developmental psychology.* New York: International Universities Press, 1979.

Gross, D. W. Some observations on the group care of infants. In M. Cohen (Ed.), *Developing programs for infants and toddlers*. Washington, D.C.: Association for Childhood Education International, 1977.

Gruber, H. E. *Darwin on man: A psychological study of scientific creativity*. New York: Dutton, 1974.

Gruber, H. E. Afterword. In D. H. Feldman, *Beyond universals in cognitive development*. Norwood, N.J.: Ablex Publishing, 1980a.

Gruber, H. E. The evolving systems approach to creativity. In S. Modgil & C. Modgil (Eds.), *Toward a theory of psychological development*. Windsor, England: N.F.E.R., 1980b.

Gruber, H. E. On the relation between "Aha" experiences and the construction of ideas. *History of Science*, March 1981, *19*, pt. 1 (43), 41–59.

Gruber, H. E., & Voneche, J. J. (Eds.). *The essential Piaget*. New York: Basic Books, 1977.

Guilford, J. P. *The nature of human intelligence*. New York: McGraw-Hill, 1967.

Guttentag, M. Evaluation and society. *Personality and Social Psychology Bulletin*, 1977, *3* (1), 31–40.

Hapgood, H. *The spirit of the ghetto*. New York: Funk & Wagnall, 1902.

Hartley, R. E., Frank, L. K., & Goldensen, R. M. *Understanding children's play*. New York: Columbia University Press, 1952.

Hartmann, H. *Ego psychology and the problem of adaptation* (D. Rapaport, Ed.). New York: International Universities Press, 1958.

Hawkins, D. The informed vision. In J. Kagan (Ed.), *Creativity and learning*. Boston: Houghton Mifflin, 1967.

Headstart in the 1980's, review and recommendations, report to the President. Washington, D.C.: Administration for Children, Youth, and Families, Headstart Bureau, September 1980.

Hein, G. E. An open education perspective on education. Grand Forks, N.D.: North Dakota Study Group on Evaluation, University of North Dakota, 1975.

Hein, G. E. The science of watching and wondering. *Urban Review*, 1976, *9* (4), 242–48.

Herrick, C. J. *The thinking machine* (2d ed.). Chicago: University of Chicago Press, 1932.

Hess, R. D., & Bear, R. M. (Eds.). *Early education: Current theory, research and action*. Chicago: Aldine, 1968.

House, E. R. *Evaluating with validity*. Beverly Hills, Calif.: Sage Publications, 1980.

House, E. R., Glass, G. V., McLean, L. D., & Walker, D. F. No simple answer: Critique of the Follow Through evaluation. *Harvard Educational Review*, 1978, *48*, 128–60.

House, E. R., & Mayer, R. A critique of "The educational imagination in evaluation," by E. W. Eisner. *Journal of Aesthetic Education*, 1981, *15*, 117–20.

Howe, I. *World of our fathers*. New York: Harcourt Brace Jovanovich, 1976.

Hudson, L. *Contrary imaginations*. Harmondsworth, Middlesex, England: Penguin Books, 1966.

Hymes, D. Introduction. In C. B. Cazden, V. P. John, & D. Hymes (Eds.), *Foundations of language in the classroom*. New York: Teachers College Press, 1972.

Isaacs, S. *Intellectual growth in young children*. London: Routledge, 1930 (1948).

Isaacs, S. *Social development in young children*. London: Routledge, 1933 (Reissued: New York: Schocken Books, 1972).

Jahoda, M. *Freud and the dilemmas of psychology*. Lincoln: University of Nebraska Press, 1977.

Janis, M. J. *A two-year-old goes to nursery school*. London: Tavistock, 1964.

Jensen, A. R. How much can we boost I.Q. and scholastic achievement? *Harvard Educational Review*, 1969, *39* (1), 1–123.

John, V. P. The intellectual development of slum children: Some preliminary findings. *American Journal of Orthopsychiatry*, 1963, *33*, 313–22.

Johnson, H. M. *Children in the nursery school*. New York: John Day, 1928 (Reissued, New York: Agathon Press, 1972).

Johnson, H. M. *The art of block-building*. New York: Bank Street Publications, 1933 (Reprinted in E. S. Hirsch [Ed.], *The Block Book*. Washington, D.C.: National Association for the Education of Young Children, 1974).

Joint Commission on the Mental Health of Children. Report to the Congress of the United States of America. June 30, 1969.

Jung, C. G. *Psychological types*. New York: Harcourt Brace, 1946.

Kagan, J. Cross-cultural perspectives in early development. Paper presented at the Annual Meeting of the American Association for the Advancement of Science, Washington, D.C., 1972.

Kagan, J. Late starts are not lost starts. *Learning*, 1973, *2*, 82–85.

Kagan, J., Kearsley, R. B., & Zelazo, P. R. The effects of infant day care on psychological development. In J. Kagan (Ed.), *The growth of the child: Reflections on human development*. New York: Norton, 1978.

Kagan, J., & Klein, R. E. Cross-cultural perspectives in early development. *American Psychologist*, 1973, *28* (11), 947–61.

Kamii, C. Piaget's interactionism and the process of teaching young children. In M. Schwebel & J. Raph (Eds.), *Piaget in the classroom*. New York: Basic Books, 1973.

Kaplan, B. Lectures on developmental psychology. Unpublished manuscript. Worcester, Mass.: Clark University, n.d.

Kaplan, B. Meditations on genesis. *Human Development*, 1967, *10*, 65–87.

Katz, L. G. Four questions on early childhood education. *Child Study Journal*, 1970/71, *1* (2), 43–51.

Katz, L. G. The professional preschool teacher. *Young Children*, in press.

Keniston, K., and the Carnegie Council on Children. *All our children: The*

American family under pressure (1st ed.). New York: Harcourt Brace Jovanovich, 1977.

Kessen, W. (Ed.). *Childhood in China.* New Haven: Yale University Press, 1975.

Klein, J. W. *Headstart basic educational skills project.* Washington, D.C.: Headstart Bureau, 1978.

Klein, J. W., & Lombardi, J. The CDA program. *Children Today,* 1982, *11* (6), 2–6.

Koestler, A. *The act of creation.* New York: Macmillan, 1964.

Kohlberg, L. Early education: A cognitive-developmental view. *Child Development,* 1968, *39* (4), 1013–62.

Kohlberg, L. High school democracy and educating for a just society. In *Moral education: A first generation of research and development.* New York: Praeger, 1980.

Kohlberg, L. *The philosophy of moral development* (vol. 1). San Francisco: Harper & Row, 1981.

Kohlberg, L., & Mayer, R. Development as the aim of education. *Harvard Educational Review,* 1972, *42* (4), 449–96.

Kohnstamm, G. A. Experiments on teaching Piagetian thought operations. Paper presented at the Conference on Guided Learning of the Educational Research Council of Greater Cleveland, 1966.

Krasner, L., & Krasner, M. Token economies and other planned environments. In C. E. Thoresen (Ed.), *Behavior modification in education.* The seventy-second yearbook of the National Society for the Study of Education, part I. Chicago: University of Chicago Press, 1973.

Kris, E. Psychoanalysis and study of imagination. In *Selected papers of Ernst Kris.* New Haven: Yale University Press, 1967.

Krown, S. (In collaboration with M. Many). *Threes and fours go to school.* Englewood Cliffs, N.J.: Prentice-Hall, 1974.

Kubie, L. S. Education and the process of maturation. In *Today's children are tomorrow's world.* New York: Bank Street College of Education, 1957.

Kubie, L. S. Blocks to creativity. In R. L. Mooney & T. A. Razek (Eds.), *Explorations in creativity.* New York: Harper, 1967.

Labov, W. The logic of non-standard English. In F. Williams (Ed.), *Language and poverty.* Chicago: Markham, 1970.

Labov, W. The logic of non-standard English. In J. L. Frost (Ed.), *Revisiting early childhood education.* New York: Holt, Rinehart & Winston, 1973.

Lambert, C. *Play: A yardstick of growth.* New York: Play Schools Association, 1948 (First published in 1938).

Lavatelli, C. S. *Piaget's theory applied to an early childhood curriculum.* Boston: American Science and Engineering, 1970.

Lawton, J., and Cooper, F. Piagetian theory and early childhood education: A critical analysis. In L. Siegel & C. Brainerd (Eds.), *Alternatives to Piaget: Critical essays on the theory.* New York: Academic Press, 1978.

Lehmann-Haupt, C. Review of Ravitch, D. *The troubled crusade: American education 1945–1980*. New York: Basic Books, 1983. *The New York Times*, September 7, 1983.

Lerner, E., Murphy, L. B., Stone, L. J., et al. Methods for the study of personality in young children. *Monographs of the Society for Research in Child Development*, 1941, 6 (4, serial no. 3).

Levine, J. A. *Day care and the public schools*. Newton, Mass.: Education Development Center, 1978.

Levinger, L. Dramatic play: An intellectual and creative process. In *Imagination in education*. New York: Bank Street College of Education, 1956.

Lewis, C. *A big bite of the world: Children's creative writing*. Englewood Cliffs, N.J.: Prentice-Hall, 1979.

Lopate, P. *Being with children*. New York: Doubleday, 1975.

Lord, L., & Smith, N. R. *Painting*. A Working Paper in Project Follow Through. New York: Bank Street College of Education, 1971.

Lustman, S. L. Impulse control, structure and the synthetic function. In R. M. Lowenstein (Ed.), *Psychoanalysis—a general psychology: Essays in honor of Heinz Hartmann*. New York: International Universities Press, 1966.

MacDonald, J. B. Perspective on open education: A speculative essay. In B. Spodek & H. J. Walberg (Eds.), *Studies in open education*. New York: Agathon, 1975.

MacKinnon, D. Personality and the realization of creative potential. *American Psychologist*, 1965, 20, 273–81.

Maddi, S. R. The strenuousness of the creative life. In I. A. Taylor & J. W. Getzels (Eds.), *Perspectives in creativity*. Chicago: Aldine, 1975.

Mao Zedong. Poem quoted in the *New York Times*, January 2, 1976.

Maslow, A. H. A holistic approach to creativity. In C. W. Taylor (Ed.), *Climate for creativity*. New York: Pergamon Press, 1972.

Mattick, I. Adaptations of nursery school techniques to deprived children. *Journal of the American Academy of Child Psychiatry*, 1965, 4, 670–700.

Mayer, R. S. A comparative analysis of preschool curriculum models. In R. H. Anderson & H. G. Shane (Eds.), *As the twig is bent: Readings in early childhood education*. New York: Houghton Mifflin, 1971.

McLellan, J. A., & Dewey, J. *Applied psychology: An introduction to the principles and practices of education*. Boston: Educational Publishing, 1889.

Minuchin, P. Processes of curiosity and exploration in preschool disadvantaged children. Final report of study supported by Office of Economic Opportunity contract OEO-2403, June 1968.

Minuchin, P. Correlates of curiosity and exploratory behavior in preschool disadvantaged children. *Child Development*, 1971, 42, 939–50.

Minuchin, P. Evaluating preschool programmes: Issues and problems. In F.

Miller (Ed.), *The young child in focus.* Melbourne, Australia: Australian Preschool Association, 1976.

Minuchin, P. *The middle years of childhood.* Monterey, Calif.: Brooks/Cole, 1977.

Minuchin, P., & Biber, B. A child-development approach to language in the preschool disadvantaged child. In M. A. Brottman (Ed.), *Language remediation for the disadvantaged child. Monographs of the Society for Research in Child Development,* 1968, *33* (serial no. 124), 10–18. [See chap. 6, this volume.]

Minuchin, P., Biber, B., Shapiro, E., & Zimiles, H. *The psychological impact of school experience.* New York: Basic Books, 1969.

Minuchin, P., & Shapiro, E. The school as a context for social development. In P. Mussen (Ed.), *Handbook of child psychology* (4th ed.), vol. 4: *Socialization, personality, and social development,* E. M. Hetherington (Ed.). New York: Wiley, 1983.

Minuchin, S., Montalvo, B., Guerney, B., Rosman, B., & Schumer, F. *Families of the slums.* New York: Basic Books, 1967.

Mitchell, L. S. *Young geographers: How they explore the world and how they map the world.* New York: John Day, 1934 (Reprinted by Basic Books in 1963).

Mitchell, L. S. Social studies for future teachers. *Social Studies,* May 1935, *26,* 289–98.

Mitchell, L. S. *Our children and our schools.* New York: Simon & Schuster, 1950.

Mitchell, L. S. *Two lives: The story of Wesley Clair Mitchell and myself.* New York: Simon & Schuster, 1953.

Mitchell, L. S. Becoming "more so." *Children Here and Now,* New York, Bank Street College of Education, 1955, *3,* 2–5.

Mittelmann, B. Mobility in infants, children, and adults: Patterning and psychodynamics. In *The psychoanalytic study of the child,* (vol. 9). New York: International Universities Press, 1954.

Morton, L. *Freud and Dewey on the nature of man.* New York: Philosophical Library, 1960.

Murphy, G. The process of creative thinking. *Educational Leadership,* October 1956, *14,* 11–15.

Murphy, G. *Human potentialities.* New York: Basic Books, 1958.

Murphy, L. B. Some mutual contributions of psychoanalysis and child development. In B. B. Rubinstein (Ed.), *Psychoanalysis and contemporary science* (vol. 2). New York: Macmillan, 1973.

Murray, H. A. Components of an evolving personological system. In D. L. Sillis (Ed.), *International encyclopedia of the social sciences* (vol. 12). New York: Macmillan and Free Press, 1968, 5–13.

Mushkin, S. J. *Evaluations: use with caution.* Evaluation, 1973, *1* (2), 31–35.

National Institute of Health. *Perspectives on human deprivation: Biological, psychological, and sociological.* Washington, D.C.: U.S. Department of Health, Education, and Welfare, 1968.

Novikova, L. I. The development of personality in the collective. *Soviet Pedagogy,* 1967, *40* (3), 98–117.

Overton, W. F. Piaget's theory of intellectual development and progressive education. In J. R. Squire (Ed.), *A new look at progressive education A.S.C.D. Yearbook.* Washington, D.C.: Association for Supervision and Curriculum Development, 1972.

Palmer, F. H. Has compensatory education failed? In *Up-date: The first ten years of life.* Gainesville, Fla.: Division of Continuing Education, University of Florida, 1976.

Palmer, F. H., & Andersen, L. W. Long term gains from early intervention: Findings from longitudinal studies. In E. Zigler & J. Valentine (Eds.), *Project Headstart.* New York: Free Press, 1979.

Patton, M. Q. *Qualitative evaluative methods.* Beverly Hills, Calif.: Sage Publications, 1980.

Pavenstedt, E. *The drifters.* Toronto: Little, Brown, 1967.

Pemberton, P. Group day care, part I. An overview. In B. D. Boegehold et al. (Eds.), *Education before five.* New York: Bank Street College of Education, 1977.

Pepper, S. *World hypotheses.* Berkeley, Calif.: University of California Press, 1942.

Perkins, D. N. *The mind's best work.* Cambridge, Mass.: Harvard University Press, 1981.

Piaget, J. *The psychology of intelligence.* London: Routledge and Kegan Paul, 1950.

Piaget, J. *Play, dreams, and imitation in childhood.* New York: Norton, 1962.

Piaget, J. *The science of education and the psychology of the child.* New York: Orion Press, 1970.

Pile, N. F. *Art experiences for young children.* New York: Macmillan, 1973.

Pratt, C. *I learn from children.* New York: Simon & Schuster, 1948.

Pratt, C., & Deming, L. The play school. In C. B. Winsor (Ed.), *Experimental schools re-visited.* New York: Agathon Press, 1973.

Pratt, C., & Wright, L. *Experimental practice in the City and Country School.* New York: Dutton, 1924.

Project Developmental Continuity, a Headstart demonstration project linking Headstart parents and the public school. Washington, D.C.: Office of Child Development, 1977.

Provence, S. A program of group day care for young children. In P. Neubauer (Ed.), *Early child day care.* New York: Jason Aronson, 1974.

Raph, J. B. Language development in socially disadvantaged children. *Review of Educational Research,* 1965, *35,* 389–400.

Ravitch, D. *The troubled crusade: American education 1945–1980.* New York: Basic Books, 1983.

Reese, H. W., & Overton, W. R. Models of development and theories of development. In L. R. Goulet & P. B. Baltes (Eds.), *Life span developmental psychology: Research and theory.* New York: Academic Press, 1970.

Rhine, W. R. The role of psychologists in the national Follow Through Project. *American Psychologist,* 1983, *38* (3), 288–98.

Riessman, F. *The culturally deprived child.* New York: Harper, 1962.

Rivlin, A. M., & Timpane, P. M. (Eds.). *Planned variation in education: Should we give up or try harder?* Washington, D.C.: Brookings Institution, 1975.

Rosen, J. Matching teachers with children. *School Review,* 1972, *80* (3), 409–31.

Rothenberg, A. The process of Janusian thinking in creativity. *Archives of General Psychiatry,* 1971, *24,* 195–205.

Schachtel, E. G. *Metamorphosis.* New York: Basic Books, 1959.

Schoellkopf, J. An assessment of twenty years of practice and experiment. Paper presented at Conference on Nursery Education, Sarah Lawrence College, Bronxville, N.Y., April 25, 1959.

Schwartzman, H. B. *Transformations: The anthropology of children's play.* New York: Plenum Press, 1978.

Schwebel, M., & Raph, J. (Eds.). *Piaget in the classroom.* New York: Basic Books, 1973.

Scriven, M. Common fallacies in program evaluation: An evaluator talks back. Paper presented at the California Association for the Education of Young Children, Annual Convention, Sacramento, Calif., 1976.

Senn, M. J. E. Insights on the child development movement in the United States. *Monographs of the Society for Research in Child Development,* 1975.

Shahn, B. *The shape of content.* Cambridge, Mass.: Harvard University Press, 1957.

Shapiro, E. Educational evaluation: Rethinking the criteria of competence. *School Review,* 1973, *81* (4), 523–49.

Shapiro, E. Toward a developmental perspective on the creative process. *Journal of Aesthetic Education,* 1975, *9* (4), 69–80.

Shapiro, E. Education and evaluation: Cutting through the rhetoric. In B. Spodek & H. Walberg (Eds.), *Early childhood education.* Berkeley, Calif.: McCutchan, 1977.

Shapiro, E., & Biber, B. The education of young children: A developmental-interaction approach. *Teachers College Record,* 1972, *74,* 55–79.

Shapiro, E., & Wallace, D. Developmental stage theory and the individual. In E. Shapiro & F. Weber (Eds.), *Cognitive and affective growth: Developmental interaction.* Hillsdale, N.J.: Erlbaum, 1981.

Sigel, I. E. Contribution of anthropology to a psychology of reasoning. Unpublished M.A. thesis, University of Chicago, 1948.

Sigel, I. E. Developmental theory and preschool education: issues, problems, and implications. In I. J. Gordon (Ed.), *Early childhood education.* The seventy-first yearbook of the National Society for the Study of Education, part II. Chicago: University of Chicago Press, 1972.

Sigel, I. E. Contributions of psycho-educational programs in understanding of preschool children. Paper presented for Burg Wartenstein Symposium no. 57, Werner-Gren Foundation for Anthropological Research, Vienna, Austria, 1973.

Sigel, I. E., Saunders, R. A., & Moore, C. E. On becoming a thinker. Paper presented at the Learning Resource Center Workshop, Hightstown, N.J., April 1977.

Sigel, I. E., Secrist, A., & Forman, G. Psycho-educational intervention beginning at age two: Reflections and outcomes. In J. S. Stanley (Ed.), *Compensatory education for children, ages 2 to 8*. Baltimore: Johns Hopkins University Press, 1973.

Silverstein, B., & Krate, R. *Children of the dark ghetto: A developmental psychology*. New York: Praeger, 1975.

Singer, J. L. *The child's world of make-believe*. New York: Academic Press, 1973.

Singer, J. L., & Singer, D. G. *Television, imagination and aggression: A study of preschoolers*. Hillsdale, N.J.: Erlbaum, 1981.

Skinner, B. F. *Science and human behavior*. New York: Macmillan, 1953.

Slaughter, D. N. What is the future of Headstart? *Young Children*, 1982, *37* (3), 3–9.

Slochower, H. The psychoanalytic approach: Psychoanalysis and creativity. In S. Rosen & L. E. Abt (Eds.), *Essays in creativity*. Croton-on-Hudson, N.Y.: North River Press, 1974.

Smilansky, S. Promotion of preschool "culturally deprived" children through "dramatic play." *American Journal of Orthopsychiatry*, 1965, *35*, 201–02.

Smilansky, S. *The effects of sociodramatic play on disadvantaged preschool children*. New York: Wiley, 1968.

Smith, M. Brewster. Perspectives on selfhood. *American Psychologist*, 1978, *33* (12), 1053–63.

Smith, N. R. The developmental origins of graphic symbolization. Unpublished doctoral dissertation, Harvard University, 1972.

Smith, N. R. *Experience and art: Teaching children to paint*. New York: Teachers College Press, 1983.

Solley, C. M., & Murphy, G. *Development of the perceptual world*. New York: Basic Books, 1960.

Spodek, B. What are the sources of early childhood curriculum? *Young Children*, 1970, *26* (1), 48–59.

Spodek, B., & Walberg, H. J. *Studies in open education*. New York: Agathon Press, 1975.

Stanton, J. What is education for the child before he is six? *Progressive Education*, April 1939, *16*, 227–33.

Steinzor, L. Piaget on cooperation, creativity and cognitive process. In C. B.

Winsor (Ed.), *The creative process.* New York: Bank Street College of Education, 1976.

Stern, V. The school environment inventory. New York: Research Division, Bank Street College of Education, 1974. Mimeo.

Stern, V. Symbolization in play: Developmental trends and unresolved issues. Paper presented at Wheelock College Symposium, "Symbolization and the Young Child," Boston, 1975.

Stern, V. Review of "Play—its role in development and evolution," Eds. J. S. Bruner, A. Jolly, and K. Sylva [New York: Basic Books, 1976]. *Young Children,* 1978, *33* (4), 80–81.

Stern, V., Bragdon, N., & Gordon, A. *Cognitive aspects of young children's play.* Final Report. New York: Research Division, Bank Street College of Education, 1976. Mimeo.

Stevenson, H. W., Lee, Shin-Yun, & Stigler, J. The reemergence of child development in the People's Republic of China. *Society for Research in Child Development Newsletter,* Summer 1981.

Stone, J. G., & Janis, J. G. *Project Headstart Daily Program I.* Washington, D.C.: Bureau of Child Development Services, 1974.

Stone, L. J., & Church, J. *Childhood and adolescence: A psychology of the growing person.* New York: Random House, 1957; 2d ed., 1968; 3d ed., 1973; 4th ed., 1979.

Suchman, J. R. Inquiry training: Building skills for autonomous discovery. *Merrill-Palmer Quarterly,* 1961, *7,* 147–69.

Sullivan, E. V. Piagetian theory in the educational milieu: A critical appraisal. *Canadian Journal of Behavioral Science (Rev. Canad. Sci. Comp.),* 1969, *1* (3), 129–55.

Sullivan, E. V. Study of Kohlberg's structural theory of moral development: A critique of liberal social science ideology. *Human Development,* 1977, *20,* 352–76.

Sutton-Smith, B. Piaget on play: A critique. In R. E. Herron & B. Sutton-Smith (Eds.), *Child's play.* New York: Wiley, 1971a.

Sutton-Smith, B. The playful modes of knowing. In *Play: The child strives toward self-realization.* Washington, D.C.: National Association for the Education of Young Children, 1971b.

Taylor, I. A. An emerging view of creative actions. In I. A. Taylor & J. W. Getzels (Eds.), *Perspectives in creativity.* Chicago: Aldine, 1975.

Television and behavior: Ten years of scientific progress and implications for the eighties. Volume 1. Summary report. Rockville, Md.: U.S. Dept. of Health and Human Services, NIMH, 1982.

Ulich, R. (Ed.). *Education and the idea of mankind.* New York: Harcourt, Brace and World, 1964.

Victor, B. Questions about Piagetian theory and application. Unpublished paper, 1978.

Vygotsky, L. S. *Thought and language* (E. Hanfmann & G. Vokar, Eds. & Trans.). Cambridge, Mass.: MIT Press, 1962.

Vygotsky, L. S. *Mind in society: The development of higher psychological processes* (M. Cole, V. John-Steiner, S. Scribner, & E. Souberman, Eds.). Cambridge, Mass.: Harvard University Press, 1978.

Wadsworth, B. J. *Piaget for the classroom teacher.* New York: Longman, 1978.

Wallace, D. Project Headstart. In B. Boegehold et al. (Eds.), *Education before five.* New York: Bank Street College of Education, 1977.

Weber, E. *Early childhood education: perspectives on change.* Worthington, Ohio: Chas. A. Jones Publishing, 1970.

Weber, L. Moral issues for teachers. *Proceedings of the World Congress in Education,* Université du Quebec à Trois-Rivières, July 1981.

Weikart, D., Rogers, L., Adcock, C., & McClelland, D. *The cognitively oriented curriculum.* Washington, D. C.: National Association for the Education of Young Children, 1971.

Weisler, A., & McCall, R. B. Exploration and play: Resume and redirection. *American Psychologist,* 1976, *31,* 492–508.

Werner, H. *Comparative psychology of mental development.* New York: International Universities Press, 1957a (First published in English in 1940).

Werner, H. The concept of development from a comparative and organismic point of view. In D. B. Harris (Ed.), *The concept of development: An issue in the study of human behavior.* Minneapolis: University of Minnesota Press, 1957b.

Werner, H. *Developmental processes: Selected writings of Heinz Werner* (S. S. Barten & M. B. Franklin, Eds.). New York: International Universities Press, 1978.

Wertheimer, M. *Productive thinking.* New York: Harper, 1959.

Westinghouse Learning Corporation and Ohio University. *The Impact of Head Start: An evaluation of the effects of Head Start experience on children's cognitive and affective development.* Washington, D.C.: Government Printing Office, 1969.

White, R. W. Ego and reality in psychoanalytic theory. *Psychological Issues,* 1963, *3,* (3).

Whitehead, A. N. *The aims of education.* New York: Macmillan, 1929.

Winett, R. A., & Winkler, R. C. Current behaviour modification in the classroom: Be still, be quiet, be docile. *Journal of Applied Behaviour Analysis,* 1972, *5,* 499–504.

Winsor, C. B. *Experimental schools revisited.* New York: Agathon Press, 1973.

Winsor, C. B. Blocks as a material for learning through play—the contribution of Caroline Pratt. In E. S. Hirsch (Ed.), *The Block Book.* Washington, D.C.: National Association for the Education of Young Children, 1974.

Zachry, C. B. *Emotion and conduct in adolescence.* New York: Appleton-Century, 1940.

Zigler, E. F. Project Head Start: Success or Failure? *Children Today,* November–December 1973a.

Zigler, E. F. Metatheoretical issues in developmental psychology. In M. H. Marx (Ed.), *Theories in contemporary psychology.* New York: Macmillan, 1973b.

Zigler, E. F. Testimony to hearings of the National Commission on protection of children who participate in research. In *Newsletter,* Division of Developmental Psychology, American Psychological Association, May 1976.

Zigler, E., and Berman, W. Discerning the future of early childhood intervention. *American Psychologist,* 1983, *38* (8), 894–906.

Zigler, E. F., & Muenchow, S. Infant day care and infant care leaves. *American Psychologist,* 1983, *38* (1), 91–94.

Zigler, E. F., & Trickett, P. K. I.Q., social competence, and evaluation of early childhood intervention programs. *American Psychologist,* September 1978.

Zigler, E. F., & Valentine, J. (Eds.). *Project Headstart.* New York: Free Press, 1979.

Zimiles, H. Problems of assessment of academic intellectual variables. Revised version of a paper presented at the meetings of the American Educational Research Association, Chicago, February 1968a.

Zimiles, H. An analysis of current issues in the evaluation of educational programs. In J. Hellmuth (Ed.), *Disadvantaged child: Volume 2. Head Start and early intervention.* New York: Brunner/Mazel, 1968b.

Zimiles, H. A radical and regressive solution to the problem of evaluation. In L. G. Katz (Ed.), *Current topics in early childhood education, Volume 1.* Norwood, N.J.: Ablex Publishing, 1977.

Zimiles, H., & Mayer, R. *Bringing child-centered education to the public schools: A study of school intervention.* New York: Bank Street College of Education, 1980.

Index